Education, Poverty and International Development Series
Series Editor
Madeleine Arnot
Faculty of Education, University of Cambridge, UK

This series of research-based monographs and edited collections which was set up in collaboration with the late Professor Christopher Colclough contributes to global debates about how to achieve education for all. A major set of questions faced by national governments and education providers concerns how the contributions made by education to reducing global poverty, encouraging greater social stability and equity, and ensuring the development of individual capability and wellbeing can be strengthened. Focusing on the contributions that research can make to these global agendas, this series aims to provide new knowledge and new perspectives on the relationships between education, poverty and international development. It offers alternative theoretical and methodological frameworks for the study of developing-country education systems, in the context of national cultures and ambitious global agendas. It aims to identify the key policy challenges associated with addressing social inequalities, uneven social and economic development, and the opportunities to promote democratic and effective educational change in the name of social justice.

The series brings together researchers from the fields of anthropology, economics, development studies, educational studies, politics, international relations and sociology. It includes work by some of the most distinguished writers in the fields of education and development, along with new authors working on important empirical projects. The series contributes significant insights on the linkages between education, the economy, communities, and society, based on interdisciplinary, international and national studies.

Selected volumes include critical syntheses of existing research and policy, work using innovative research methodologies, and in-depth evaluations of major policy developments. Some studies will address topics relevant to poverty alleviation, national and international policy-making and aid, while others will be anthropological or sociological investigations of how education functions within local communities, for households living in poverty or for particular socially marginalised groups. The authors explore a diverse range of themes from the challenges associated with providing quality teacher, professional and entrepreneurial education, to those associated with promoting gender equality, reducing gender violence, understanding the impact of poverty on constructions of childhood, or assessing the impact of learner-centred school pedagogies. They offer sharp, critical studies that are intended to have a strategic influence on the thinking of academics, researchers and policy-makers.

Decolonising Education in Islamic West Africa

This book uses perceptions and experiences of Qur'anic schools in West Afri to outline a much-needed postsecular approach, reconsidering the pla of Islamic education within African decolonial debates about educatio pluralism, and the contributions of religious perspectives in academic a international development spaces.

Decolonial theory is used to overcome the challenges of problema Eurocentric and colonialist stereotypes about religious actors and fait based schools which persist within international education scholarship a global policy agendas. Through fine-grained ethnography, chapters disc how parents and young people today engage with classical Qur'anic schoo Islamic schools and French-medium secular education in Senegal, there exposing inequalities around gender, descent-based or caste identities a socioeconomic status, as well as their influence on young people's pursuit knowledge. These findings are valuable for scholars exploring the developme education-religion nexus and promoting Education for All in communit characterised by other-than-secular worldviews.

The book will be of interest to academics, researchers and postgradu students working in the sociology of education, international educati anthropology and religious education. Practitioners involved in postcolon and decolonial debates will also benefit from recommendations regardi educational reform in plural educational contexts.

Anneke Newman is an anthropologist of development and Senior Postdocto Research Fellow at the Department of Conflict and Development Studi University of Ghent, Belgium.

Published Titles

Education Outcomes and Poverty
A Reassessment
Edited by Christopher Colclough

Teacher Education and the Challenge of Development
A Global Analysis
Edited by Bob Moon

Education Quality and Social Justice in the Global South
Challenges for Policy, Practice and Research
Edited by Leon Tikly and Angeline M. Barrett

Learner-centred Education in International Perspective
Whose Pedagogy for Whose Development?
Michele Schweisfurth

Professional Education, Capabilities and the Public Good
The Role of Universities in Promoting Human Development
Melanie Walker and Monica McLean

Livelihoods and Learning
Education For All and the Marginalisation of Mobile Pastoralists
Caroline Dyer

Gender Violence in Poverty Contexts
The Educational Challenge
Edited by Jenny Parkes

The 'Poor Child'
The Cultural Politics of Education, Development and Childhood
Edited by Lucy Hopkins and Arathi Sriprakash

Educating Entrepreneurial Citizens
Neoliberalism and Youth Livelihoods in Tanzania
Joan DeJaeghere

Education, Poverty and Global Goals for Gender Equality
How People Make Policy Happen
Elaine Unterhalter and Amy North

Reforming Education and Challenging Inequalities in Southern Contexts
Research and Policy in International Development
Edited by Pauline Rose, Madeleine Arnot, Roger Jeffery, Nidhi Singal

Mothers and Schooling
Poverty, Gender and Educational Decision-making in Rural Kenya
Fibian Lukalo

The Politics of English Language Education and Social Inequality
Global Pressures, National Priorities and Schooling in India
Maya Kalyanpur, Padmini Bhuyan Boruah, Sarina Chugani Molina and Sunaina Shenoy

Decolonising Education in Islamic West Africa
Secular Erasure, School Preference and Social Inequality
Anneke Newman

Related Titles

Educational Research Practice in Southern Contexts
Recentring, Reframing and Reimagining Methodological Canons
Edited by Sharlene Swartz, Nidhi Singal and Madeleine Arnot

For more information on the series, please visit https://www.routledge.com/Education-Poverty-and-International-Development/book-series/EPID

Decolonising Education in Islamic West Africa

Secular Erasure, School Preference and Social Inequality

Anneke Newman

Routledge
Taylor & Francis Group
LONDON AND NEW YORK

First published 2025
by Routledge
4 Park Square, Milton Park, Abingdon, Oxon OX14 4RN

and by Routledge
605 Third Avenue, New York, NY 10158

Routledge is an imprint of the Taylor & Francis Group, an informa business

British Library Cataloguing-in-Publication Data
A catalogue record for this book is available from the British Library

Library of Congress Cataloging-in-Publication Data
Names: Newman, Anneke, author.
Title: Decolonising education in West Africa : secular erasure, school preference and social inequality / Anneke Newman.
Other titles: Education, poverty, and international development series.
Description: New York : Routledge, 2025. | Series: Education, poverty and international development series | Includes bibliographical references and index.
Identifiers: LCCN 2024036736 (print) | LCCN 2024036737 (ebook) | ISBN 9781032000442 (hardback) | ISBN 9781032000466 (paperback) | ISBN 9781003172475 (ebook)
Subjects: LCSH: Islamic education—Senegal.
Classification: LCC LC911.S38 N46 2025 (print) | LCC LC911.S38 (ebook) | DDC 371.07709663—dc23/eng/20240812
LC record available at https://lccn.loc.gov/2024036736
LC ebook record available at https://lccn.loc.gov/2024036737

ISBN: 978-1-032-00044-2 (hbk)
ISBN: 978-1-032-00046-6 (pbk)
ISBN: 978-1-003-17247-5 (ebk)

DOI: 10.4324/9781003172475

Typeset in Galliard
by Apex CoVantage, LLC

In fond memory of my dear mentor Philip Stewart (1939–2022)

Contents

About the author

Anneke Newman is an anthropologist of development employed as Senior Postdoctoral Research Fellow in the Department of Conflict and Development Studies at the University of Ghent, Belgium. She previously held research and teaching positions at the Université Libre de Bruxelles, the University of Antwerp and the University of Sussex where she completed her doctorate. She served as the secretary of the British Association for International and Comparative Education and is an active member of UGent's Learning Network on Decolonisation.

Abbreviations

ACALAN	African Academy of Languages
AOF	Afrique Occidentale Française (French West Africa)
CIE	Comparative and International Education
CRT	Critical Race Theory
DER nexus	Development-education-religion nexus
DHS	Demographic and Health Survey
EFA	Education for All
EID	Education and International Development
FBO	Faith-based organisation
FNAECS	National Federation of Qur'anic Teachers' Associations
GAD	Gender and development
GEM Report	Global Education Monitoring Report
HCT	Human capital theory
ILSA	International large-scale assessment
INGO	International Non-Governmental Organisation
LOI	Language of instruction
MCD programme	Modernity/coloniality/decoloniality programme
MDG	Millennium Development Goal
NGO	Non-Governmental Organisation
NLS	New Literacy Studies
RCT	Rational choice theory
SAP	Structural adjustment programme
SDG	Sustainable Development Goal
UN	United Nations
UNESCO	United Nations Educational, Scientific and Cultural Organization
UNICEF	United Nations Children's Fund
UPE	Universal primary education
UK	United Kingdom
US	United States
USAID	United States Agency for International Development
WCARO	West and Central Africa Regional Office

Figures and tables

Figures

Tables

Acknowledgments

This book is the product of fifteen years of (un)learning, exchange and reflection. My first thanks go to everyone in Senegal who shared their lives with me. The most important I cannot name, but hopefully you know who you are. I also thank members of Cheikh Djibril's Sarr's *jamma* in Pikine, my Pulaar teacher Oumoul Soh, Abderahmane N'Gaïde and Penda Mbow for their insights and advice, and Yumiko Yokozeki for hosting me in Dakar.

As this book started with my doctorate at the University of Sussex, I owe an immense debt of gratitude to my supervisors Elizabeth Harrison and Filippo Osella for their dedication, insight and good humour. I also thank my examiners James Fairhead and Masooda Bano for their insightful feedback. I can't name everyone who supported me during my doctoral journey but I am especially grateful to: Ana Porroche-Escudero, Lefteris Zenerian and Heba Youssef for their friendship; Hannah Hoechner, Emilie Roy, Clothilde Hugon, Mame Fatou Sene, Dorte Thorsen, Marloes Janson, Hamidou Dia and Abdoulaye Sounaye for their insights into Islam and education in West Africa; and Lotte Pelckmans, Benedetta Rossi, Marie-Eve Humery, Jean Schmitz and Bruce Hall for their knowledge of descent-based hierarchies in the Sahel. Many members of the British Association of International and Comparative Education (BAICE) have also inspired and supported me in this project, particularly Rosemary Preston, Leon Tikly and Farah Ahmed.

My doctorate wouldn't have been possible without generous funding from the UK Economic and Social Research Council (grant number ES/1019677/1) which financed my tuition and living expenses under a Quota Award, my study of Pulaar at the ACI Baobab Center in Dakar through a Language Learning Grant, my participation at the European Conferences on African Studies in Lisbon and Paris, and my fellowship at SciencesPo Bordeaux through an Overseas Institutional Visit grant.

Developing and writing this book felt like doing a second thesis, and I am extremely grateful to many colleagues in Belgium who have aided me intellectually and emotionally over the last seven years. They include: Isabelle Renneson for her beautiful maps; Nadia Fadil, An Van Raemdonck and Mieke Groeninck for their discussions about Islam; Iman Lechkar and the community around her book group on Decolonial Approaches to Muslim Studies and Islamophobia; colleagues at the Laboratoire d'Anthropologie des Mondes Contemporains (ULB), particularly Joël Noret on questions of religion and class in Africa; members of the Conflict and Development Studies department at the University of Ghent and the team at the UGent Learning Network on Decolonisation. My thinking has also been greatly enriched by conversations with: Loes Oudenhuijsen, Annelien Bouland, Joseph Hill and Mayke Kaag on Islam and gender relations in West Africa; Ali Meghji on decolonial theory; and Sarah O'Neill, Friederike Lüpke and Fallou Ngom regarding maps and *Ajami*.

The writing of this book was also funded by postdoctoral fellowships from the Fonds National de la Recherche Scientifique (FNRS) and the Fonds Wetenschappelijk Onderzoek (FWO, grant number 1286023N) in Belgium. I am also very grateful to the International Research Network for the Study of Science and Belief in Society (INSBS) which awarded me an International Early Career Mentoring Grant, kindly mentored by Professor Vivian Dzokoto at Virginia Commonwealth University. This grant enabled me to draft sections of Chapters 4 and 5 on the economic skills conferred by Qur'anic schools in Senegal and the limitations of theoretical frameworks for understanding educational decision-making.

My sincere thanks also go to: my friends Ailleann O'Rourke, Carmen Himmelstine, Lara Gill, Hannan Ahmed and Sarata Sall for their emotional support; my family members Steph, Olly, James, David, Ophelia and parents Lesley and Martin for their encouragement, babysitting and great cooking over the years; my daughter Madina for her love and kind nature; and my husband Seydina who opened my eyes to a different way of seeing the world.

Finally, this book would never have been possible without the help of two very special people. The first is Olivia Barnett-Naghshineh who first introduced me to decolonial theory during her fantastic course on Decolonising Anthropology at Goldsmiths, University of London and who generously gave critical feedback on first drafts of the introductory chapters. The second is Madeleine Arnot at the University of Cambridge who is the Editor of the Routledge Education, Poverty and International Development series. She saw promise in this book's concept a long time before it was really deserved, patiently put up with my multiple requests for deadline extensions and gave the most meticulous feedback on manuscript drafts that any author could ever hope for. If this book speaks to anyone else's truth it is by the blessing of Allah; its shortcomings are mine alone.

1 Rethinking development, education and religion: A challenging nexus

This book grows out of the sense of dissonance that I experienced upon visiting Senegal for the first time in 2010 as part of a doctorate in anthropology at the University of Sussex. From this moment onwards – and particularly since 2012, when I converted[1] to Islam myself – I have been confronted with a jarring juxtaposition. Located in West Africa, 97% of Senegal's population of 18 million is Muslim (CIA, 2024). On the one hand, I have observed and personally experienced the rich and complex ways in which Muslims' everyday lives, including their educational strategies, are shaped by Islamic worldviews and moral values. For a sizeable proportion of Senegalese, their preference is for Islamic schools over state-run 'secular' schools with limited religious content. Islamic schools include classical Qur'anic schools whose basic form dates from at least the tenth century and which remain devoted to teaching memorisation of the Qur'an and moral education.

Yet, despite the popularity of Qur'anic schools in West Africa, policy discourses and academic scholarship in two fields, that of Comparative and International Education (CIE) and Education and International Development (EID), both routinely repeat tropes about their poor educational quality compared to secular state schools, as well as derogatory stereotypes about parents who opt for them (e.g. Gandolfi, 2003; MEN, 2009; Human Rights Watch, 2010). These assumptions lack a solid empirical foundation because they ignore the diversity of Qur'anic schools, the failings of 'secular' state schools, the fortunes of students exposed to either type of education and the nuances of parents' decision-making strategies (Thorsen, 2012). In contrast, scholars in African studies have, over the last two decades, produced a number of sensitive accounts of the Qur'anic schools' functioning which challenge these assumptions. The persistence of these stereotypes inspired me to explain and defend these schools, on the basis of their own logics and objectives, before an audience in comparative/international education and development studies.

However, this book is not just about preference for Qur'anic schools, as the influence of Islam on educational engagement goes far beyond this visible phenomenon. In fact, Islamic cosmology is just as relevant to Muslims' engagement with 'secular' schools. But although scholars in comparative education show an interest in values, there is a persistent lack of appreciation in

DOI: 10.4324/9781003172475-1

the field of EID – whether among practitioners, policy-makers or academics – of the influence that religious worldviews have on educational engagement more broadly. Yet, the influence of Islamic cosmology on Muslims' everyday lives is as far-reaching as a spring of water forming the earth and stone – and nourishing the plants and creatures – in an oasis garden. To only study the influence of religion on people's educational strategies when they involve preference for faith-based schools is analogous to studying the water from the bubbling spring only where it is apparent to the naked eye, rather than exploring its hidden influence in sustaining the garden ecosystem as a whole.

In short, as a result of having studied in Senegal and having lived as a Muslim for a decade myself, I noticed that three flaws reoccur within CIE/EID discussions about education in contexts where the majority of the population adheres to a religious faith. The first of these flaws relates to simplistic *stereotypes* about religious people and societies, the second concerns the *silences* which render invisible the importance of religious phenomena in shaping everyday life, and the third involves the *secular biases* in policy and social scientific theories of religious behaviour, including preference for faith-based schools. Furthermore, I have personally experienced how Euro-North American academia and development spaces are structured by secularism which makes it difficult, if not impossible, for people of other-than-secular worldviews to articulate the value of their perspectives – let alone theorise on the basis of these experiences.

This book therefore speaks to growing calls to 'decolonise' CIE and EID, although this task is slightly different in each case. A starting point is to analyse critically the colonialist underpinnings of these fields and their tendencies to devalue non-Western knowledges and their producers (Hickling Hudson, 2004; Takayama et al., 2016; Takayama, Sriprakash and Connell, 2017; Spratt and Coxon, 2020; Unterhalter and Kadiwal, 2022; Maluleka, 2023). While a few comparative/international education scholars have convincingly demonstrated the value of engaging with the philosophies of classical and contemporary Muslim thinkers (Connell, 2007; Ahmed, 2012, 2018, 2021; Maniam, 2016), this approach has rarely been applied to the two fields simultaneously and relates more to education provision than attempts at understanding trends in engagement. Finally, I propose that such a 'decolonising project' in CIE/EID is obstructed by the exclusionary dominance of secular perspectives in elite sites of knowledge production. The result is that "any intellectuality and creativity Islamic scholars may generate is unlikely to be recognized or accepted by the Western paradigm" (Ahmed, 2018, p. 792). I refer to this process as *secular erasure* and, in critiquing it, this book seeks to open up more space for decolonial potential in CIE/EID theory and praxis.

This first chapter starts off by unpacking the stereotypes, silences and secular biases in academic and policy literature on education in Muslim contexts and Islamic West Africa specifically, before situating these dynamics within the broader international education agenda and disciplines of comparative/international education and development studies. Through this exercise,

I demonstrate the urgent need to develop a counter-narrative about families' preferences for Qur'anic schools and, in doing so, offer an alternative decolonial approach to knowledge production about what I call the *development-education-religion* (DER) *nexus*. I hope that this strategy will ultimately enhance our understanding of educational engagement but that it can also inform the development of more inclusive education provision in religious-majority contexts, particularly Islamic West Africa.

Stereotypes, silences and secular bias in policy and academic scholarship

The first flaw within policy and academic literature on the DER nexus is a tendency to resort to stereotypes about religious schools and the people who opt for them. Explanations for preference for faith-based schools are usually reduced to parents' limited access to 'quality' secular schools, wilful neglect of their children or stubborn conservatism (Thorsen, 2012). Another trope that recurs in debates on parental preference for 'strong' Islamic schools, such as Qur'anic schools in Nigeria or *madrasas* in Pakistan, is that they are breeding grounds for terrorists. This stereotype has been debunked for reflecting a tiny minority of Islamic schools, yet it persists in academic, media and policy discourse (Deneulin and Bano, 2009; Bano, 2012; Hoechner, 2018). For example, one quantitative analysis attempted to correlate *madrasa* preference in Pakistan with 'radical religiosity' based on whether or not parents named their child 'Osama', assumed to signal support for Osama Bin Laden. The Islamophobia associated with the 'war on terror' discourse is reflected in the authors' assumptions that "we postulate that households that named (at least) one child 'Osama' . . . are more likely to favor a radical brand of Islam" (Andrabi et al., 2006, p. 466).

The second flaw in the literature on EID involves the silences regarding the significance of religion in people's everyday lives. Yet, in a recent study involving 25,000 interviews in more than 60 languages in 19 countries of Sub-Saharan Africa, the Pew Research Center found that 90% of people stated that religion was "very important" in their lives (2010, p. 3). In contrast, scholarly interest in the DER nexus tends to be restricted to the study of religious *institutions* and *actors* – typically schools, churches or mosques and their representatives (Stambach, 2020). With the exception of researchers using an 'Indigenous knowledges' paradigm, CIE and development studies literature often neglects to unpack how other-than-secular cosmologies and conceptions of knowledge influence educational dynamics. This tendency reflects the assumption that a 'religious sphere' exists that is separate to – and can be bracketed off from – the 'secular sphere'. As a result, attention is paid to worldviews in contexts where the influence of religious institutions is more obvious, as in contexts with high levels of preference for private faith-based schools; otherwise these worldviews are largely ignored.

In contrast to CIE scholarship, anthropologists have paid more attention to the influence of cosmologies on education, including the relevance of 'religious' worldviews in people's engagement with 'secular' schools. For instance, in an ethnographic study of the Islamic context of Zanzibar, anthropologist Julie Sommer von Würden (2015) observed how spirits or *jinn* made their presence known by disrupting or possessing students in both 'secular' state and Islamic schools. Personnel in both types of school had, therefore, developed strategies to manage them as part of the informal curriculum. Yet, such sensitivity to the relationships between cosmology and education, especially when the schools in question are 'secular', is rare in CIE/EID literature.

The third flaw in EID scholarship and practice involves secular biases, which are also evident in education policy. Although donors and policy-makers have increasingly turned towards Islamic schools to deliver Education for All (EFA) from the mid-2000s (Marshall, 2010; UNICEF, 2012), they have tended to judge such schools according to secular and Euro-North American centric educational objectives, norms of school content and pedagogy (Ware, 2014). Indeed, as we shall see, negative or inaccurate stereotypes about Qur'anic schools abound in the literature on engaging Islamic schools to meet EFA (e.g. Gandolfi, 2003; Marshall, 2010; UNESCO, 2021, p. 85). These policies involve supporting Islamic schools that already resemble 'secular' schools on a Euro-North American model or pushing schools operating according to different logics to adapt in conformity with these norms. Hence, this agenda often represents a drive to modernise and instrumentalise Islamic schools to achieve objectives, such as satisfying donor demands to increase enrolment rates, defined by outsiders who see the world through secular lenses (Deneulin and Bano, 2009; Bano, 2012). These policies usually fail to appreciate the positive contributions that Qur'anic schools *in their current form* already make to youth's futures and are at odds with popular appreciation for them. Indeed, when populations value educating children in Qur'anic rather than state schools, development agencies are reluctant to respect their preferences and instead try to coax them towards something more 'secular'. The right to a religious education is framed as subordinate to children's right to a 'quality education', inevitably framed as 'secular' or 'weakly faith-based', namely teaching religion as one topic among many within a secular framework (Deneulin and Bano, 2009).

Finally, secular biases also permeate the social scientific theories used by scholars in CIE and development studies to explain educational engagement (Newman, 2022a). Much of the research into preference for faith-based schools is conducted by economists using positivist approaches. They tend to define 'religiosity' and Islamic school enrolment as bounded variables, often taking for granted the assumption that 'faith' is a barrier to 'economic' returns and aiming to identify materialist explanations for preference (Bano, 2012). They therefore fail to do justice to the multi-faceted moral, affective and cognitive influences that religious worldviews have on people's behaviour.

In this book, I delve into the colonialist logics that underpin these stereotypes, silences and secular theoretical biases. In doing so, my intention is to offer novel ways for understanding the influence of religious worldviews, understandings of knowledge and moral values on educational engagement and school preference, illustrated using the case of Senegal in Islamic West Africa. My approach also has practical and decolonial implications and is postsecular. While secularism is usually understood as a political form of governance involving the separation of religious institutions and government, which evolved in Western Christian Europe in the early modern period, it is much more than this. Secularism is also a theory about the nature of reality in which only the immanent and material realm of existence is recognised and valued. Despite its particular historical and cultural origins, because it was wed to the Euro-North American modernist project from the Enlightenment onwards, secularism has become dominant across the globe as both a political project and a worldview informing scientific discourse (Asad, 2003).

In contrast, a 'postsecular' approach (Crockett, 2018) involves challenging the dominance of assumptions grounded in a secular worldview within scientific theorising and policy-making. Decolonial philosopher of religion Rafael Vizcaíno (2021) has referred to this hegemony as the 'coloniality of secularity', a neglected but profoundly influential constituent principle of Western modernity. An approach to educational engagement informed by postsecular and decolonial principles is, therefore, one that critiques manifestations of coloniality of secularity. This includes what I call *secular erasure* or the tendency for academic scholarship and policy and public discourse to render invisible the central relevance of other-than-secular worldviews in people's everyday lives, the contributions of these worldviews and associated knowledge systems in the construction of social hierarchies, but also their potential to inspire people's struggles – including against colonialist injustices. Second, a postsecular approach which supports decolonial projects is one which appreciates the constructions of knowledge and theorising of people on the receiving end of coloniality of secularity. Before presenting this approach in the following chapter, I start by exposing how the stereotypes, silences and secular biases relating to Qur'anic schools are the product of much deeper logics. It is these assumptions – which shape policy, practice and research on the DER nexus – to which I now turn.

Coloniality and the development-education-religion nexus

Coloniality in debates on the development-education-religion (DER) nexus takes many different forms. Here I focus on three under-researched aspects: secularity as an ideal; understandings of race and religion and their connections to development; and assumptions regarding the relationship between gender inequality and religion. These three aspects of coloniality all construct Islamic cultures as 'Other' and largely adverse to development.

Coloniality and secularity

The interpretation of Qur'anic schools and Islam by Western observers has been shaped throughout most of the twentieth century by the secularisation thesis. Inspired by the work of classical sociologists, this theory posited that 'religion' would inevitably decline in favour of scientific rationality as societies modernised (Stark and Finke, 2000; Furseth and Repstad, 2006). In turn, the secularisation thesis informed modernisation theory as development economists tended to ignore 'religion' entirely. Alternatively, they followed the assumptions of Max Weber (1904) that 'Protestant values' were especially conducive to economic growth. Meanwhile, other religious worldviews were assumed to be 'traditional', 'primitive' or 'irrational' and were framed as an obstacle to technological and social progress (Nkurunziza, 2007; Deneulin and Bano, 2009; Deneulin and Rakodi, 2011).

Scholars in the field of 'religions and development' – which is a loose subfield of development studies which seeks to theorise how development theory and practice engages with religion (Deneulin and Rakodi, 2011) – have shown that the secularisation thesis has exerted considerable influence over education debates. From the 1950s to the 1980s, both economists and philosophers of education subscribed to the assumption that secular education constituted the driving force of progressive social change. It was, therefore, promoted as a key tool to support more extensive secularisation and modernisation in society (Stambach, 2010, 2011).

By the 1990s, human capital theory (HCT) had become the dominant paradigm which informed international education policy. It grew out of the same colonialist logics as modernisation theory in its assumption that religion was incompatible with 'modern' norms. Hence, 'education' – which was defined as secular schooling on the Euro-North American model – was presumed to confer objectively measurable and universally applicable utilitarian returns in the form of economic and non-monetary social benefits. At the same time, 'strong' religious education was assumed not to confer economic skills (Stambach, 2006). In parallel, the Euro-North American liberal philosophical tradition assumed that strong religious schools encouraged social conditioning or indoctrination, promoted intolerance towards other faiths and inhibited a 'rational' or 'scientific' worldview. Even though these assumptions have been challenged through empirical evidence, they still exert powerful influence over education policy (Deneulin and Bano, 2009; Ahmed, 2012).

Subsequently, the 1990s onwards saw a 'religious turn' in development whereby donors and organisations shifted from what Matthew Clarke (2007) has described as "estrangement to engagement" with religion. The aim of this new approach was to engage religious actors to meet development objectives (Deneulin and Rakodi, 2011; Jones and Petersen, 2011; Wilkinson, 2022). From the 2000s onwards – and in the current context of the global EFA movement – it is noteworthy that development actors have turned towards faith-based schools to increase school enrolment (Marshall, 2010; UNICEF, 2012; UNESCO, 2021). Yet, their definitions of 'schooling' and 'quality education' are based on secular schools, while faith-based schools are considered acceptable just as long as they are 'weak' or 'moderate' (Carr, 1998). In 'weak' or 'moderate' faith-based schools, religion is taught in an objectified manner as one belief system among many. In effect, it is compartmentalised so that other subjects are taught within a rationalist conception of the world whereby events are explained in materialistic terms according to positivist scientific principles (Deneulin and Bano, 2009). Schools can teach religious or moral education as long as they do not compromise on the 'core curriculum' of official language(s), maths, social and natural sciences, arts and physical education (Anderson-Levitt, 2003). This model of 'quality education' disapproves of 'strong' faith-based schools which focus on religious instruction, encourage a strong religious identity and teach from within a religious worldview. Therefore, if organisations support faith-based schools to meet EFA goals, they tend to cherry-pick those whose work is compatible with secular agendas (Deneulin and Bano, 2009).

Moreover, the dominant theoretical model used for explaining educational decision-making within development studies and comparative/international education is rational choice theory (RCT) (Ball, 2007; Nkurunziza, 2007). According to classical RCT, people are rational actors who prefer the most utility-maximising option available, with utility defined in narrowly materialistic terms. Economists using RCT also tend to subscribe to the human capital thesis. Their logic appears to be that since formal, secular schooling confers economic benefits and since people are utility-maximising, parents will prefer this option. When parents' school preferences do not match the predictions of this combination of rational choice and human capital theory (HCT), economists have been found to blame direct and indirect poverty, equity barriers or the fact that schools are poor 'quality' (Hunt, 2008).

Outside of this frame is the possibility of unobservable differences in preference for valid alternatives, including those grounded in non-Western cultural and religious traditions or histories of anti-colonial resistance. Hence, proponents of RCT face a dilemma when trying to explain why parents would choose strong faith-based schools over secular schools for their children, when the latter are accessible and affordable. Masooda Bano explains in her book *The Rational Believer: Choices and Decisions in the Madrasas of Pakistan* (2012) that, in order to understand such situations, rational choice theorists have drawn upon classical sociology of religion which was, in turn, also shaped by the secularisation thesis. They often posit that choosing religious education is an 'irrational' anomaly, reflecting socialisation patterns within families or communities. This framework suggests that children are passively socialised into religious belief and later make decisions reflecting this internalised logic even if it does not benefit them materially.

Alternatively, some economists using RCT reject the assumption of irrationality by, instead, attributing religious belief and behaviour to the pursuit of 'religious rewards' sought out for materialist reasons. This is based on deprivation theory in sociology which proposes that people pursue religious rewards – like hope, reassurance or explanations for uncertainty – because of difficult circumstances like material or social poverty or psychological insecurity. Its origins lie in Karl Marx's assumption that religion is the "opium of the people" (1844) or compensatory comfort to those at the bottom of the social hierarchy. Hence, the popularity of strong religious education is attributed to social or material deficiencies which downplays the intrinsic benefits and moral appeal of other-than-secular worldviews (Bano, 2012, pp. 6–9).

In contrast, critical theorists in the field of religions and development often repeat that it is essential that we allow people to define 'the good life' from their own perspective, even if their definitions run counter to those of mainstream development (Deneulin and Bano, 2009). However, when religion is discussed within international education, it is typically in relation to a 'problem' as defined by development discourse, like low enrolment in 'formal', namely government-accredited, schools (Stambach, 2020). In reality, even the more critical scholars who study the DER nexus struggle to step fully outside of this framing, thereby neglecting to engage in wider research agendas that are less obviously useful to development agencies (Jones and Petersen, 2011). Such a tendency means that there is little research exploring the links between religion and education beyond the institutional settings of strong religious schools, which inadvertently obscures the interpenetration of other-than-secular worldviews and understandings of knowledge in 'secular' or informal educational spaces (Stambach, 2020).

These biases within EID theory and practice reflect a much broader context of global knowledge production. In sum, despite its claiming benevolent neutrality, the development industry comprises a set of colonialist regimes for the production of power/knowledge grounded in Western modernity (Escobar, 1995). Development reflects a 'geopolitics of knowledge' (Hountondji, 1997; Mignolo, 2002) whereby the post-colonial[2] peripheries or global South tend to provide *data*, while scholars based in Euro-North American academic institutions produce *concepts* and *models* which often reflect their experiences, norms and values and which are applied, usually with poor fit, to Southern contexts (Mignolo, 2002; Grosfoguel, 2007). Academic departments of development studies, especially when dominated by classical development economics, have been integral to this process (Escobar, 1995). The phenomena of coloniality of secularity and secular erasure are, therefore, the products of entrenched structural relations and systems. They are problematic because they both reflect and conceal the hegemonic yet unmarked secular-colonialist framework dominant in academia (Todd, 2016; Yountae, 2020). The first step, then, towards a postsecular analysis of educational engagement is to simply pay attention to – and create space for – other-than-secular worldviews.

Race, religion and development

The second theme that characterises scholarship on the DER nexus relates to the connections between coloniality of secularity and other manifestations of coloniality such as race and gender. In the early 2000s, development studies started to grapple with the implications of racial inequalities in the development industry and its own disciplinary canon (Kothari, 2006a; Wilson, 2012).

However, CIE and EID have barely engaged with this legacy at all (Rudolph, Sriprakash and Gerrard, 2018; Sriprakash, Tikly and Walker, 2020). These fields' "silence on race both masks and marks its centrality to the development project" (White, 2002, p. 408) as the global system of advantage and disadvantage is patterned by racial inequalities, from the framework of global geography down to individual encounters within development and aid work.

Racial categories shape EID in more subtle ways today than during the colonial period and tend to only become visible through their operationalisation in paradigms, concepts and practical approaches (Kothari, 2006a). For instance, the absence of mentions of constructions of race, otherwise known as 'racial erasure' (Sriprakash, Tikly and Walker, 2020), within international development organisations in debates about poverty, education or human capital, reproduces and masks their complicity in racialised structures of inequality and exclusion (Kothari, 2006b; Tikly, 2014; Rudolph, Sriprakash and Gerrard, 2018). Similarly, debates about 'school effectiveness' (Tikly, 2001), 'education quality' and the 'learning crisis' (Sriprakash, Tikly and Walker, 2020) lay the blame for school failure at local level, rather than in racialised global capitalism and the institutions which reinforce it. Development studies and CIE have also been found to reproduce the authoritative power of Whiteness (Kothari, 2006b) by enabling White academics to become 'experts' of countries of the global South, often without language proficiency or long-term presence there, while the reverse would never be possible (White, 2002; Sriprakash, Tikly and Walker, 2020).

These valuable insights notwithstanding, scholars of religions and development have engaged little with the 'race and development' literature, thereby neglecting how concepts used for theorising 'religion' are rooted in White supremacy (Tayob, 2020). Meanwhile, scholars of 'race and development' are arguably guilty of secular erasure because they downplay how European racial classification systems have been intimately intertwined with religion. In contrast, philosopher Anya Topolski (2018) points out how, in the sixteenth century, 'religion' was the dominant means used by European intellectuals to classify peoples. Gradually, over the course of three centuries, a more biological understanding based on phenotype came to dominate in the construction of 'race-categories', although the broad lines of delineation between peoples continued to be largely reproduced (2018, p. 60). Topolski refers to this process as the 'race-religion constellation' or "connection or co-constitution of the categories of race and 'religion'" (ibid., p. 88). She argues that it is because of the secularisation thesis that the intertwined histories of race and religion in the European context have been "conveniently suppressed" within current debates (ibid., p. 59). She also points out that the refusal among many European politicians – and even academics – to characterise anti-Semitism or Islamophobia as forms of racism is cultivated by the masking of this race-religion constellation (ibid., pp. 60, 72–75).

The concept of a race-religion constellation is useful, in my view, when trying to understand both the educational dynamics in Senegal and the problematic tendencies in their theorisation. To clarify, French colonial classification schemes were based on both religion and race as they considered that "race, religion and culture were all inextricably linked" and that "only Arabs could be fully Muslim" (Ware, 2004, pp. 250–251). In the words of Paul Marty, an influential French colonial administrator in the early nineteenth century, "as Islam distances itself from its cradle . . . it becomes increasingly deformed" (ibid., p. 250). The presence of Muslims in Sub-Saharan Africa therefore posed French administrators with a conundrum when they were considering how best to manage the populations under their control. Marty dealt with this challenge by creating the binary constructs of *islam noir* (Black Islam) and *islam blanc* (White Islam). *Islam blanc,* as practiced by the Arabs, was assumed to be the orthodox – and more authentic – version of the religion. Yet, these Muslims were suspected of being violent and a threat to European colonial projects. In contrast, *islam noir* was framed as a 'syncretic' and unorthodox form of Islam on the assumption that "sub-Saharan Islam was a recent import, that West Africans could not fully understand its tenets" (Bryant, 2020, p. 5). In short, Black Africans were not considered to be 'authentically Muslim' because of their race. However, given the prevailing stereotypes of Africans as unintelligent and lazy but largely peaceful, *islam noir* was seen as less of a menace to the colonial project, whose leaders could be productively co-opted (Launay and Soares, 1999; Ware, 2014).

The construct of *islam noir* played a pivotal role in shaping French policy in the colony of *Afrique Occidentale Française* (AOF), including towards Qur'anic schools. Its assumptions are empirically flawed because Islam reached West Africa in the ninth century, and it is no more shaped by pre-Islamic cultural influences than anywhere else (Launay and Soares, 1999). Yet, the assumptions of *islam noir* live on in academic scholarship. It explains the neglect of Sub-Saharan African societies within Islamic studies – despite one-sixth of the world's Muslim's living south of the Sahara, compared to one-tenth in North Africa and only one-twenty-fifth in Arabia (Ware, 2014, p. 18) (see Figure 1.1). The idea that Islam in Africa is inherently 'syncretic' also reoccurs within recent CIE literature. For example, the book *Troubling Muslim Youth Identities: Nation, Religion, Gender,* asserts that Senegalese youth "legitimated their local, African forms of Islam, including syncretic versions that were interwoven with ethnic customs and beliefs" (Dunne et al., 2017, p. 8).

European race-religion constellations have continued to evolve following their introduction on the African continent. Decolonial theorist Sabelo Ndlovu-Gatsheni (2015) has pointed out that some African intellectuals have reproduced the European classification frameworks which associated Black Africans with 'paganism' and Arabs with Islam, with the difference being that they assigned positive values to the former. This logic has led to a framing common among some Afrocentric African intellectuals that Islam and Muslims, even Black Muslims, are not 'authentically African' because of their religion. They also juxtapose African Traditional Religions – which are portrayed

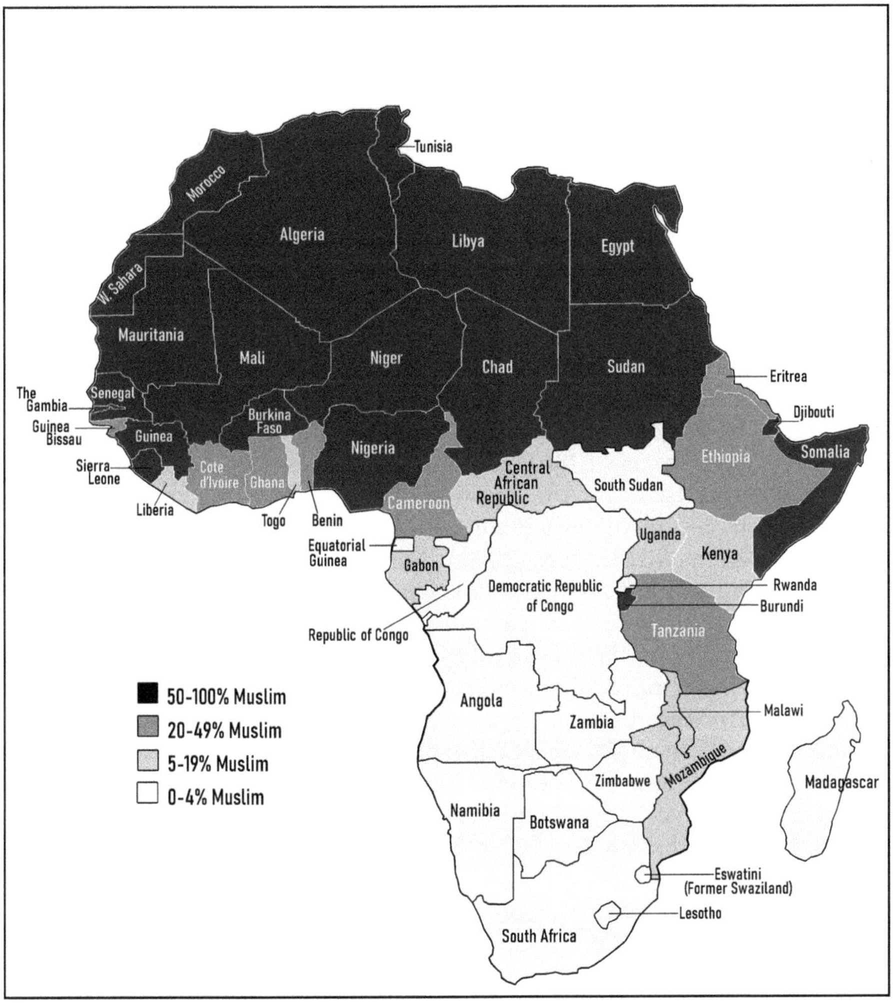

Figure 1.1 **Muslim populations in Africa, 2023**. Countries are shaded if they meet 5%, 20% or 50% thresholds according to the CIA World Factbook for 2023. Updated from Ware (2014, p. 18).

Credit: Anneke Newman and Isabelle Renneson.

as 'Indigenous', empowering and egalitarian – with the supposedly oppressive 'foreign' monotheistic religions of Islam and Christianity. Such tropes, which I refer to as *Afrocentric race-religion constellations*, have enjoyed strong influence in African cultural debates since their endorsement by Nigerian Nobel laureate Wole Soyinka in the 1970s (Ndlovu-Gatsheni, 2015; Edwin, 2016, pp. 53–55). This 'nativist' discourse has been critiqued by postcolonial political theorist Achille Mbembé (2002) because, in his words, "boundaries are demarcated between the native and the nonnative Other; and on the basis of these boundaries, distinctions can then be made between the authentic and the inauthentic" (see Mbembé, 2002, p. 245).

It is concerning that such Afrocentric race-religion constellations crop up in contemporary CIE/EID scholarship. For instance, most of the literature which pays attention to the relevance of other-than-secular worldviews in Sub-Saharan African contexts uses an 'African Indigenous Knowledge(s)' (AIK) framework which reproduces this constellation. For example, throughout the *Palgrave Handbook of African Education and Indigenous Knowledge* (Abidogun and Falola, 2020), the editors and several authors portray "Indigenous knowledge" as more authentic to Sub-Saharan Africa than "Islamic" and "Western" knowledges, which are both described as having been "imported or imposed" (Abidogun, 2020, p. xvii). Such statements ignore how millions of Black Africans have shaped – and been shaped by – Islamic worldviews, understandings of knowledge and values for a millennium. African Muslim thinkers like Kenyan Ali Mazrui (1986) and Senegalese Ousmane Kane (2016) have long shown that Islam in Africa exhibits its own internal hierarchies but is also part of the continent's rich intellectual heritage, including its anti-colonial struggles (Wright, 2013; Ware, 2014). For this reason, I prefer to avoid an AIK(s) framing and use decolonial concepts instead, whose architects encourage us to critique hierarchies grounded in colonialist logics whatever their manifestations.

Two final forms of racialisation are relevant to my analysis of educational engagements in West Africa. First, Bruce Hall, in his book *A History of Race in Muslim West Africa, 1600–1960* (2011), argued that "there are African histories of race that do not obey colonial logics" because they are instead embedded in the Islamic intellectual traditions of the Middle East and North Africa. He explains that (ibid., p. 2):

> Along the Sahel in West Africa, a long history of racial language is evident in the writings of Muslim intellectuals well before the arrival of Europeans. Sahelian writers made a fundamental distinction between "whites" . . . for those who claimed Arab pedigrees, and "blacks". . . . In these texts, "blackness" worked as a marker of inferiority that created significant legal disability for people who could be labeled in this way.

Hall goes on to clarify that European classifications of race were layered upon these Islamic constructions during the colonial era (ibid., p. 2):

> When the Sahel was colonized by France beginning in the late nineteenth century, the colonial administration used these existing local conceptions of racial difference in the organization of its rule, in part because they corresponded to European denigrations of people defined as black.

Furthermore, populations in West Africa and the southern edge of the Sahara also subscribe to descent-based hierarchies similar to a 'caste' system which often intersect with Islamic racial hierarchies. Such systems date from at least the twelfth century and significantly pre-date sustained European contact (Tamari, 1991).

Hall argues that academic understanding of such processes of categorisation in Africa are undermined by "scholarship that insists on race being understood as an exclusively European-American ideology" (2011, p. 1). To move beyond this impasse, I follow sociologists of race such as Tariq Modood and Thomas Sealy (2022) who propose that we can understand racialisation as "a process of a dominant group 'othering' a subordinate group, whether that be based on alleged biological or cultural features, or both" which, in turn, structures distribution of power and resources (2022, p. 434). In their understanding, racism involves "the operation of perceived or attributed descent" and while phenotype can be used to infer descent, this is not always the case (ibid., p. 435). In contrast to many critical race theorists who assert that constructions of 'race' are a uniquely Euro-North American phenomenon, Modood and Sealy argue that racialisation processes are plural and have originated outside of Euro-North American logics. Indeed, as I argue in later chapters, patterns of educational engagement in Senegal reflect the intersections of Islamic, European and West African forms of racialisation. Yet, the influence of these hierarchies on people's engagement with education, including 'secular' and Qur'anic schools, continues to be ignored by CIE and EID scholars (Newman, 2020b, 2021) as well as academics interested in race and development.

Gender inequality and religious traditions

Finally, in comparison to race, the study of gender has received far more attention within development studies and international/comparative education, yet here too there is persistent coloniality when thinking about non-Western societies. Hence, although research on the DER nexus does recognise the importance of having a gender perspective, coloniality of gender, race and secularity nonetheless persist within such scholarship. Indeed, the preference for secularism among gender and development (GAD) practitioners is "no secret" (Tomalin, 2015, p. 62). This reflects the generally negative portrayal of religion within White Euro-North American feminist thought (Istratii, 2021). This framing ignores how "gender inequality in religious traditions is produced by the same structures that maintain it anywhere" including within 'secular' communities (Khalaf-Elledge, 2021, p. 12). For decades, postcolonial feminists have criticised the many White Euro-North American feminists who have ignored the diverse meanings attributed to gender relations in different contexts. On the one hand, they have tended to frame 'Western' women as secular and hence liberated and, on the other hand, described 'Third World Women', especially Muslims, as oppressed by their religions and cultures (Mohanty, 1984; Abu-Lughod, 2002).

Despite the many critiques, the field of gender, education and development remains dominated by racialised stereotypes (Newman, 2023) and perspectives from the global North (Fennell and Arnot, 2008; Chilisa and Ntseane, 2010). Secular education is, therefore, overwhelmingly presented in policy and academic discourse as the solution to all the problems faced by women in the global South – and for Muslim girls in particular (Khoja-Moolji, 2018; Newman, 2020a). Yet, as we shall see in later chapters, young women's exclusion from formal Islamic education in northern Senegal meant that they lacked the religious knowledge and authority to challenge patriarchal norms that constrained their autonomy. High rates of female enrolment in 'secular' state schools did little to change this situation, contrary to assumptions within development discourse.

An underlying explanation for such secular biases in the field of gender, education and development is that practitioners and feminist theorists often employ and impose a single model of gender, rooted in the social constructivism of Judith Butler (1990), both as an analytical construct and a path for liberation. Decolonial development studies scholar Romina Istratii has argued that this framing relies on the position that gender is a total social construct with no biological basis and that all gender distinctions entail hierarchy and patriarchal domination. According to Istratii, alternative models of gender, including those which entail some version of gender essentialism grounded in biological difference, are branded as a barrier to gender equality. Yet, equality under the Butlerian framing can only be imagined through erasure of gendered difference (2021, pp. 6–11).

In contrast to Butler's model, relevant to Islamic West African contexts are alternative movements such as Islamic feminisms (Khalaf-Elledge, 2021, pp. 18–19) and African feminisms/womanisms (Edwin, 2016). They are based on the premise of genders being distinct and grounded in biological difference but ultimately complementary. Multiple postcolonial feminists and gender scholars have argued that Euro-North American models of gender are neither universal nor perceived as desirable everywhere. Nonetheless, Istratii (2021, pp. 11–14) convincingly argues that GAD scholars and practitioners have imposed a rigid interpretation of Butler's understanding of gender on to other cultural contexts. This hegemony closes off the possibility that people can advocate for improvements to their social circumstances, including by challenging patriarchal and heteronormative structures, from within their own faith traditions (Edwin, 2016; Istratii, 2021; Khalaf-Elledge, 2021).

Unfortunately, even gender and education scholars using postcolonial theory can be guilty of secular biases. For instance, 'religion' is often reduced to religious institutions, which are studied through the dominant discourses of (frequently androcentric) elites, rather than in terms of complex, fluid and shifting worldviews and understandings of knowledge (Khalaf-Elledge, 2021, pp. 57–62). Hence, within CIE/EID scholarship, 'religion', particularly Islam, is still framed in terms of the obstacles that it presents to women's 'empowerment' (Khoja-Moolji, 2018). This fails to adequately appreciate faith traditions as dynamic forces which can be constraining – but which also provide a framework from within which women exert agency (Bano and Kalmbach, 2012). In contrast, empirical research shows that Muslim women in Muslim-majority settings can perceive that strong Islamic education confers more personal, social and spiritual advantages in their context than secular schooling (Bano, 2012, pp. 143–147). I argue that silencing this reality – and denying women's right to exercise this preference – is a form of secular erasure.

Meanwhile, even postcolonial feminist literature is not immune to Orientalist tendencies. As we will see in Chapter 7, scholarship by African feminists/womanists can also reflect Afrocentric race-religion constellations which demonise Abrahamic religions as oppressive, compared to African Traditional Religions or secular worldviews which, in contrast, are assumed to be egalitarian and empowering. As a result, such scholars can easily fall prey to Islamophobic tropes when theorising the agency of African Muslim women (Edwin, 2016, p. 18).

Critical religions and development scholars like Nora Khalaf-Elledge have argued that "a decolonial GAD approach would recognize that feminist movements do not only exist in the West and political religion is not unique to the Global South" (2021, p. 3). Istratii (2021) goes further by proposing that decolonising GAD – and, I would argue, literature on the DER nexus – is only possible if gender and sexual minorities are able to theorise and struggle from within their own religious worldviews. This remains impossible unless coloniality, including the intersecting facets of race, gender and secularity, are confronted head-on in the development industry and academy.

About us without us: Studying the 'religious Other'

In addition to these themes of coloniality of secularity, race and gender, it is impossible to ignore another major limitation of scholarship on the DER nexus. This shortcoming relates to the persistent methodological orientation which fails to acknowledge and hence confront the secular positioning of its own theorists, the lack of space within the Euro-North American social sciences for people with other-than-secular worldviews to speak – or theorise – from their own perspectives, and the direct effects that this has on (re)producing the secularist theoretical paradigms critiqued earlier.

To illustrate, my doctoral training was in an anthropology department in the UK, and although anthropologists take pains to present the other-than-secular worlds of others as they live them (Kapferer, 2001), my experience of this academic culture pushed me to self-censor my conversion to Islam and thus foreclosed the possibility that I theorise from this perspective. When conducting my thesis on dynamics within a Muslim community, my supervisors expected me to reflect upon my sociological positioning, especially gender, class and, to some extent, race. I was not expected to interrogate the influence of my worldview which was assumed to be secular. It, therefore, remained invisible and outside of the frame. More problematic still, I hesitated to divulge my position after witnessing discrimination not only against

Muslim students but also religious students more generally. One colleague, who was conducting an auto-ethnography of their own religious community, was repeatedly interrogated by a professor about the possible biases they could bring to their study. This individual seemed singled out for a degree of criticism about their potential bias that was not levelled against others, including White students like myself proposing to do fieldwork in countries of the global South that they had never been to previously and where they spoke no local languages. I also witnessed doctoral students (including students of colour) across a range of disciplines contributing to this hostile climate by ridiculing people adhering to other-than-secular worldviews behind their backs or committing micro-aggressions, for instance by demanding of me at a party, "So how long is this 'not drinking alcohol' thing going to last, then?"

Moreover, a small number of anthropologists have made arguments that suggest that my experience is common within the discipline. Despite the fact that anthropologists pioneered the study of religion using social constructivist and interpretivist paradigms as early as the 1940s, the discipline operates within secular premises of logic and empiricism (Stewart, 2001; Barnes, 2020). As anthropologist of religion Charles Stewart has argued, the weight of secular biases and constructions of knowledge are evident as "the apparent goal of the anthropology of religion is to explain religious phenomena in social, political, historical or any other terms rather than concede any facticity to transcendent mysteries" (2001, p. 327).

Despite the enormous quantity of anthropological research on people who see the world through the lenses of religious cosmologies, the number of ethnographies in which Northern anthropologists question the limits of a secular worldview – and theorise explicitly from other-than-secular worldviews – is quite small (e.g. Evans-Pritchard, 1937; Favret-Saada, 1977; McCarthy Brown, 1991; Van Binsbergen, 1991; Stoller and Olkes, 2013; Barnes, 2020). To stray too far from the premises of a secular perspective risks negative judgements, from accusations of 'naivety' (Barnes, 2020, p. 9) to 'going native'. The latter is a profoundly racist discourse through which (largely White, Euro-North American) anthropologists police the boundaries of 'legitimate' knowledge. They often expel proponents of other-than-secular cosmologies (who are often Indigenous people or people of colour) from the discipline, while appropriating their knowledge for their own intellectual projects (Todd, 2016). Anthropologists who subscribe to other-than-secular worldviews must therefore make compromises and sacrifices, including self-censorship, to succeed in the discipline's mainstream Euro-North American form (Stewart, 2001; Barnes, 2020). Alternatively, secular social scientists often downplay the spiritual aspects of work produced from a 'religious' perspective (Ahmed, 2018, pp. 791–792) thereby reproducing the "'safe' secularity of disciplinary scholarship" (Vizcaíno, 2021, pp. 73–74).

It is therefore no coincidence that scholarship which applies concepts and methodological insights from anthropology of religion to the field of religions and development (Bradley, 2009; Hefferan, 2015) often reproduces this secular methodological orientation. Some theorists in this field have critiqued the dominance of positivist approaches and advocate, instead, for interpretivist methodologies which entail "studying the meanings that people give to their social practices and religious adherence" (Deneulin and Rakodi, 2011, p. 51; Hefferan, 2015; Wilkinson, 2022). However, the implicit assumption is that social scientists studying and theorising religions and development do not share the worldviews of their research participants. The tendency of Euro-North American social science to separate the (superior) 'secular' knowledge producer from the (inferior) 'religious Other' (Barnes, 2020; Tayob, 2020) is therefore rarely problematised, and little space is made for the 'religious' subject to theorise from their own experience or intellectual tradition (Istratii, 2021, p. 14). Although religions and development scholars request that researchers interrogate their positionality (Deneulin and Rakodi, 2011; Wilkinson, 2022), they do not necessarily engage in deep reflection on their own *ontological* positioning, as opposed to *sociological* positioning and its theoretical implications.

Decolonising the development-education-religion nexus

Scholars have applied a postcolonial critique to CIE/EID by arguing that "modern forms of education with their roots in western cultures and civilizations have been deeply implicated in and provide a common thread between European imperialism and colonialism and the new imperialism" (Tikly, 2004, p. 188). Indeed, schooling was a powerful tool of colonial administrations as a form of discipline which led to 'colonisation of the mind' (Ngũgĩ wa Thiong'o, 1986), split loyalties among the colonised (Fanon, 1952) and contributed to epistemicides, linguicides, culturecides and alienation (Ndlovu-Gatsheni, 2018). Although schooling could be a site of anti-colonial resistance and an escape from 'traditional' hierarchies through social mobility, it was also a key mechanism for the 'reciprocal assimilation' of local elites, namely benefitting emerging or existing elites by granting restricted access to status, wealth and a shared identity (Tikly, 2001).

In the present day, mass education systems in post-colonial contexts, including Senegal, still bear the hallmarks of the colonial encounter in that they lack relevance to local socioeconomic, cultural and religious realities. Such systems fail to: recognise endogenous knowledge systems; exhibit persistent Euro-North American centric biases in formal curricula, pedagogy and assessment; and have language of instruction policies that favour 'global' (typically Europhone) languages (Crossley and Tikly, 2004; Brock-Utne, 2006; Rudolph, Sriprakash and Gerrard, 2018; Sriprakash, Tikly and Walker, 2020; Kalyanpur et al., 2022). State actors certainly bend development assistance to their own economic and political interests, but the influence of donor conditionalities on education policy is nonetheless a powerful mechanism through which colonialist relations and asymmetrical flows of power and capital are rearticulated in the context of globalisation (Tikly, 2004; Rizvi, Lingard and Lavia, 2006). For instance, although EFA reflects the interests of various multilateral agencies with competing agendas, it is nonetheless dominated by Northern/Western voices and is part of a wider 'regime complex' that keeps the African continent at the periphery of the world economy (Tikly, 2016).

By locating my research within CIE/EID, I therefore add to the voices of a growing number of scholar-activists who demand that we interrogate the disciplines' intellectual and practical entanglements with colonisation and its violent legacies (Takayama, Sriprakash and Connell, 2017). They have argued that many CIE researchers uncritically employ concepts or (re)produce discourses – such as 'school effectiveness' (Tikly, 2001), the 'learning crisis' (Sriprakash, Tikly and Walker, 2020) or 'powerful knowledge' (Rudolph, Sriprakash and Gerrard, 2018) – which reflect these powerful global interests and modernist values. Even the term 'education' is often used unquestioningly by CIE/EID scholars and policy-makers working within an EFA framework to refer to 'the school' derived from the Euro-North American historical and cultural context and recognised by modern nation-states, implicitly framing other knowledge and learning systems as inferior 'alternatives' (Anderson-Levitt, 2003). In contrast, throughout this book I use the wider and more neutral definition of education provided by anthropologist Hervé Varenne (2008, p. 22), namely:

> The deliberate, systematic, and sustained effort to transmit, evoke or acquire knowledge, attitudes, values, skills or sensibilities, and any learning that results from the effort, direct or indirect, intended or unintended.

This definition of education encompasses a wide range of individuals, relationships, institutions and contexts that extend far beyond 'the school'.

This situation raises the urgent need to reconsider the CIE and EID canons and theoretical perspectives and to re-narrativise educational dynamics from the perspectives and priorities of global 'peripheries' (Crossley and Tikly, 2004; Newman, 2022b). With that in mind, in the next chapter I consider in more depth the underlying links between coloniality and secularism and how to theorise the DER nexus 'from the margins', offering a challenge to the modernist and secularist binaries that inform current scholarship.

Structure of the book

Given the aforementioned, it is clear that, if the fields of comparative/international education are to move forward, there is an urgent need for a post-secular approach informed by decolonial principles which would enable us to appreciate the influence of other-than-secular worldviews – and understandings of knowledge – on educational engagement. In Chapter 2, I describe in greater detail what the conceptual and methodological foundations of such an approach could be, namely a deconstruction of the secular/religious binary and its assumptions. This is a necessary step for opening up spaces for more theorising by people who experience the world through other-than-secular cosmologies and who participate in non-Western intellectual traditions.

Part 1 of the book illustrates how this postsecular approach to educational engagement can be deployed in practice, first by constructing a history of the evolution of education systems in Islamic West Africa and second by analysing how the EFA agenda marginalises colonialist histories of educational transformation. Chapter 3 takes a deep dive into the evolution of 'Islamic' and 'secular' education in Senegal, as well as dominant trends in parents' and youths' educational preferences, from the eighteenth century to the early 2000s. To do this, I coin the notion of an *ontological regime complex* which refers to the evolving relationships among worldviews, understandings of knowledge and values on the one hand, and power, material resources and social inequalities on the other including – but not limited to – those rooted in coloniality. In Chapter 4, I pivot to discussing the main characteristics of the contemporary Senegalese eduscape based on analysis of grey literature and interviews with development practitioners in Dakar. I show how colonial critiques of Qur'anic schools re-emerge within EFA debates which leads, in turn, to forms of education provision which fail to address the needs and priorities of a large proportion of the population.

Part 2 investigates patterns of educational engagement in northern Senegal based on ethnographic research and interviews with youth, parents and education providers. I uncover how the inhabitants of one village, Medina Diallobé, sought to acquire the various knowledges that they considered valuable when none of the schools on offer fully met all of their needs. In short, individuals' educational projects were constrained by the fact that national education policy was characterised by secular Eurocentrism and the demands of the racialised global capitalist economy. Meanwhile, local Islamic schools were structured according to local hierarchies based on gender and race.

Chapter 5 starts by reporting on the preference for Qur'anic schools amongst parents and youth in Medina Diallobé. It reveals the secular shortcomings of theoretical frameworks traditionally used in the Euro-North American social sciences for understanding preference for 'strong' faith-based schools, including Bourdieu's concepts of field, capital and habitus (Bourdieu and Nice, 1977). The chapter makes the case for postsecular frameworks which can capture and articulate the value of Qur'anic schools from parents' and students' own cosmological perspectives.

Chapter 6 considers the cases of men who were barred from advanced education in Qur'anic schools due to descent-based/racialised hierarchies based on lineage and caste and how they attempted to overcome these hurdles regardless. Using Anya Topolski's concept of race-religion constellation (2018), my analysis embeds an appreciation of religious worldviews within debates on race in development. In particular, I show how European, Islamic and West African logics of racialisation combined to restrict access to powerful knowledges and how these inequalities shape contemporary trends in educational engagement.

Chapter 7 considers women who were excluded from Qur'anic schools due to their gender. I show how women in Medina Diallobé pursued Islamic knowledge through informal means, using a theoretical framework tailored to the forms of agency shown by African Muslim women. This intersectional framework overcomes the Middle Eastern-centrism of literature on Islamic feminisms and the Afrocentric race-religion constellations of some African feminist/womanist scholarship (Edwin, 2016). I argue that what is 'empowering' for women reflects the context-specific ontological regime complex that informs the values that people ascribe to particular knowledges, as well as their priorities and agency.

Chapter 8 moves beyond Islamic knowledges to show how youth in my study attempted to overcome the limitations of both Qur'anic and state schools by 'doing both', namely getting the best of each offer through a combination of formal and informal learning. Islamic and secular schools may have reflected radically different worldviews at the outset, but I reveal how youth show themselves to be *ontologically creative subjects* who move between learning spaces to their advantage. However, their abilities to do so were constrained by widening socioeconomic inequalities and secular biases within education policy. These dynamics constitute a barrier to the goal of 'educational pluralism' (D'Agostino and Callizo, 2022) informed by decolonial principles.

Finally, in Part 3 or Chapter 9, I combine the insights of the previous chapters to reiterate the importance of a postsecular approach to the study of other-than-secular worldviews and their influence on educational engagement. I unpack the concrete implications that this approach has for decolonising knowledge production in development studies, Comparative and International Education, as well as in defining policies and programmes tailored to the priorities and values of Muslims in West Africa.

Notes

1 Many Muslims use the noun and verb 'revert' to describe the person/process whereby an individual not born or raised as Muslim decides formally to enter into the religion. In the interests of accessibility, throughout this book I have preferred to use the term 'convert' to describe my experience as I think it will be more comprehensible to an audience unfamiliar with Islamic terminology.

2 Throughout this book I use 'post-colonial' to refer to the historical period after colonisation or societies which achieved political independence from colonial powers. I use 'postcolonial' to refer to a political and epistemological perspective which centres the legacies of colonisation in its analysis.

References

Abidogun, J.M. (2020) 'Introduction: African education's multiple systems', in J.M. Abidogun and T. Falola (eds) *The Palgrave Handbook of African Education and Indigenous Knowledge*. Cham, Switzerland: Palgrave Macmillan, pp. xvii–xxii.

Abidogun, J.M. and Falola, T. (2020) *The Palgrave Handbook of African Education and Indigenous Knowledge*. Cham, Switzerland: Palgrave Macmillan.

Abu-Lughod, L. (2002) 'Do Muslim women really need saving? Anthropological reflections on cultural relativism and its others', *American Anthropologist*, 104(3), pp. 783–790.

Ahmed, F. (2012) 'Tarbiyah for shakhsiyah (educating for identity): Seeking out culturally coherent pedagogy for Muslim children in Britain', *Compare – A Journal of Comparative and International Education*, 42(5), pp. 725–749.

Ahmed, F. (2018) 'An exploration of Naquib al-Attas' theory of Islamic education as ta'dīb as an "indigenous" educational philosophy', *Educational Philosophy and Theory*, 50(8), pp. 786–794.

Ahmed, F. (2021) 'Authority, autonomy and selfhood in Islamic education – Theorising Shakhsiyah Islamiyah as a dialogical Muslim-self', *Educational Philosophy and Theory*, 53(14), pp. 1520–1534.

Anderson-Levitt, K. (2003) 'Introduction. A world culture of schooling?', in K. Anderson-Levitt (ed) *Local Meanings, Global Schooling: Anthropology and World Culture Theory*. New York: Palgrave Macmillan, pp. 1–26.

Andrabi, T., et al. (2006) 'Religious school enrollment in Pakistan: A look at the data', *Comparative Education Review*, 50(3), pp. 446–477.

Asad, T. (2003) *Formations of the Secular: Christianity, Islam, Modernity*. Stanford, CA: Stanford University Press.

Ball, S.J. (2007) 'Big policies/small world: An introduction to international perspectives in education policy', in B. Lingard and J. Ozga (eds) *The Routledge Falmer Reader in Education Policy and Politics*. London: Routledge, pp. 119–130.

Bano, M. (2012) *The Rational Believer: Choices and Decisions in the Madrasas of Pakistan*. Ithaca, NY and London: Cornell University Press.

Bano, M. and Kalmbach, H. (eds) (2012) *Women, Leadership, and Mosques: Changes in Contemporary Islamic Authority*. Leiden and Boston, MA: Brill.

Barnes, J. (2020) *Stories, Senses and the Charismatic Relation: A Reflexive Ethnography of Christian Experience*. London: Routledge.

Bourdieu, P. and Nice, R. (1977) *Outline of a Theory of Practice*. Cambridge: Cambridge University Press.

Bradley, T. (2009) *The Relationships Between Religion and Development: Views from Anthropology*. Birmingham: International Development Department, University of Birmingham.

Brock-Utne, B. (2006) *Whose Education for All? The Recolonisation of the African Mind*. London: Routledge.

Bryant, K.D. (2020) 'Education and politics in colonial French West Africa', *Oxford Research Encyclopedia of African History* [Preprint]. https://doi.org/10.1093/acrefore/9780190277734.013.679.

Butler, J. (1990) *Gender Trouble: Feminism and the Subversion of Identity*. New York: Routledge.

Carr, D. (1998) 'Introduction: The post-war rise and fall of educational epistemology', in D. Carr (ed) *Education, Knowledge and Truth: Beyond the Postmodern Impasse*. London and New York: Routledge, pp. 1–15.

Chilisa, B. and Ntseane, G. (2010) 'Resisting dominant discourses: Implications of indigenous, African feminist theory and methods for gender and education research', *Gender and Education*, 22(6), pp. 617–632.

CIA (2024) *Senegal, Africa Demographic Atlas*. Langley, VA: Central Intelligence Agency. https://www.cia.gov/the-world-factbook/special-product-files/.

Clarke, G. (2007) 'Agents of transformation? Donors, faith-based organisations and international development', *Third World Quarterly*, 28(1), pp. 77–96.

Connell, R. (2007) *Southern Theory: Social Science and the Global Dynamics of Knowledge*. Cambridge: Polity Press.

Crockett, C. (2018) 'What is postsecularism?', *American Book Review*, 39(5), pp. 6–14.

Crossley, M. and Tikly, L. (2004) 'Postcolonial perspectives and comparative and international research in education: A critical introduction', *Comparative Education*, 40(2), pp. 147–156.

D'Agostino, A. and Callizo, I.G.I. (2022) 'Toward understanding the global landscape of educational pluralism', *Journal of School Choice*, 16(3), pp. 365–387.

Deneulin, S. and Bano, M. (2009) *Religion in Development: Rewriting the Secular Script*. London and New York: Zed Books.

Deneulin, S. and Rakodi, C. (2011) 'Revisiting religion: Development studies thirty years on', *World Development*, 39(1), pp. 45–54.

Dunne, M., et al. (2017) *Troubling Muslim Youth Identities: Nation, Religion, Gender*. London: Palgrave Macmillan.

Edwin, S. (2016) *Privately Empowered: Expressing Feminism in Islam in Northern Nigerian Fiction*. Evanston, IL: Northwestern University Press.

Escobar, A. (1995) *Encountering Development: The Making and Unmaking of the Third World*. Princeton, NJ: Princeton University Press.

Evans-Pritchard, E.E. (1937) *Witchcraft, Oracles, and Magic Among the Azande*. Oxford: Clarendon Press.

Fanon, F. (1952) *Peau noire, masques blancs*. Paris: Seuil.

Favret-Saada, J. (1977) *Les mots, la mort, les sorts: La sorcellerie dans le Bocage*. Paris: Gallimard.

Fennell, S. and Arnot, M. (2008) 'Decentring hegemonic gender theory: The implications for educational research', *Compare – A Journal of Comparative and International Education*, 38(5), pp. 525–538.

Furseth, I. and Repstad, P. (2006) *An Introduction to the Sociology of Religion: Classical and Contemporary Perspectives*. Aldershot: Ashgate Publishing Ltd.

Gandolfi, S. (2003) 'L'enseignement islamique en Afrique noire', *Cahiers d'études africaines*, XLIII(169–170), pp. 261–277.

Grosfoguel, R. (2007) 'The epistemic decolonial turn', *Cultural Studies*, 21(2–3), pp. 211–223.

Hall, B.S. (2011) *A History of Race in Muslim West Africa, 1600–1960*. Cambridge: Cambridge University Press.

Hefferan, T. (2015) 'Researching religions and development', in E. Tomalin (ed) *The Routledge Handbook of Religions and Global Development*. London: Routledge, pp. 36–52.

Hickling Hudson, A. (2004) 'Towards Caribbean "knowledge societies": Dismantling neo-colonial barriers in the age of globalisation', *Compare: A Journal of International and Comparative Education*, 34(3), pp. 293–300.

Hoechner, H. (2018) *Quranic Schools in Northern Nigeria: Everyday Experiences of Youth, Faith, and Poverty*. Cambridge: Cambridge University Press.

Hountondji, P.J. (1997) *Endogenous Knowledge: Research Trails*. Dakar: CODESRIA.

Human Rights Watch (2010) *Off the Backs of the Children: Forced Begging and other Abuses Against Talibés in Senegal*. New York: Human Rights Watch.

Hunt, F. (2008) *Dropping Out from School: A Cross Country Review of Literature*. Edited by T. and E. Create Consortium for Research on Educational Access. Falmer: University of Sussex, Centre for International Education.

Istratii, R. (2021) *Adapting Gender and Development to Local Religious Contexts: A Decolonial Approach to Domestic Violence in Ethiopia*. London: Routledge.

Jones, B. and Petersen, M.J. (2011) 'Instrumental, narrow, normative? Reviewing recent work on religion and development', *Third World Quarterly*, 32(7), pp. 1291–1306.

Kalyanpur, M., et al. (2022) *The Politics of English Language Education and Social Inequality Global Pressures, National Priorities and Schooling in India*. London and New York: Routledge.

Kane, O.O. (2016) *Beyond Timbuktu: An Intellectual History of Muslim West Africa*. Harvard University Press.

Kapferer, B. (2001) 'Anthropology: The paradox of the secular', *Social Anthropology*, 9(3), pp. 341–344.

Khalaf-Elledge, N. (2021) *The Religion–Gender Nexus in Development: Policy and Practice Considerations*. London: Routledge.
Khoja-Moolji, S. (2018) *Forging the Ideal Educated Girl: The Production of Desirable Subjects in Muslim South Asia*. Oakland, CA: University of California Press.
Kothari, U. (2006a) 'An agenda for thinking about "race" in development', *Progress in Development Studies*, 6(1), pp. 9–23.
Kothari, U. (2006b) 'Critiquing "race" and racism in development discourse and practice', *Progress in Development Studies*, 6(1), pp. 1–7.
Launay, R. and Soares, B.F. (1999) 'The formation of an "Islamic sphere" in French colonial West Africa', *Economy and Society*, 28(4), pp. 497–519.
Maluleka, K.J. (2023) 'Strategies to realise the decoloniality of the Comparative and International Education curriculum in South African higher education', *South African Journal of Higher Education*, 37(3), pp. 125–139.
Maniam, V. (2016) 'An Islamic voice for openness and human development in education: The relevance of Ibn Khaldun's ideas to Australian teacher education programmes today', *Postcolonial Directions in Education*, 5(1), pp. 111–129.
Marshall, K. (2010) 'Education for all: Where does religion come in?', *Comparative Education*, 46(3), pp. 273–287.
Marx, K. (1844) *Contribution to the Critique of Hegel's Philosophy of Right*. Cambridge: Cambridge University Press.
Mazrui, A.A. (1986) *The Africans: A Triple Heritage*. London: BBC Publications.
Mbembé, J.-A. (2002) 'African modes of self-writing', *Public Culture*, 4(1), pp. 239–273. Translated by Rendall, S.
McCarthy Brown, K. (1991) *Mama Lola: A Voodoo Priestess in Brooklyn*. Berkeley, CA: University of California Press.
MEN (2009) *Plan stratégique de développement des daara*. Dakar: Ministère de l'Education Nationale (MEN) Sénégal.
Mignolo, W.D. (2002) 'The geopolitics of knowledge and the colonial difference', *South Atlantic Quarterly*, 101(1), pp. 57–96.
Modood, T. and Sealy, T. (2022) 'Beyond Euro-Americancentric forms of racism and anti-racism', *The Political Quarterly*, 93(3), pp. 433–441.
Mohanty, C.T. (1984) 'Under Western eyes: Feminist scholarship and colonial discourses', *boundary 2*, 2(3), pp. 333–358.
Ndlovu-Gatsheni, S.J. (2015) 'Ali A Mazrui on the invention of Africa and postcolonial predicaments: "My life is one long debate"', *Third World Quarterly*, 36(2), pp. 205–222.
Ndlovu-Gatsheni, S.J. (2018) *Epistemic Freedom in Africa: Deprovincialization and Decolonization*. London and New York: Routledge.
Newman, A. (2020a) '"Getting the best of both worlds": Aspirations and agency in relation to marriage and schooling among Haalpulaar women in northern Senegal', *Compare – A Journal of Comparative and International Education*, 51(8), pp. 1157–1173.
Newman, A. (2020b) 'Honour, respectability and "noble" work: Descent and gender-based obstacles to the education and employment of young Haalpulaar women in northern Senegal', *Children's Geographies*, 18(6), pp. 654–666.
Newman, A. (2021) 'How descent-based hierarchies and youth culture shape secondary school engagement in Senegal', *Anthropology & Education Quarterly*, 52(4), pp. 412–429.
Newman, A. (2022a) *Making Sense of Qur'anic School Preference in West Africa: The Challenges of Secular Bias and Ontological Injustice in Scientific Theories of Educational Decision-Making, International Research Network for the Study of Science and Belief in Society (INSBS)*. Available at: https://scienceandbeliefinsociety.org/2022/09/20/making-sense-of-quranic-school-preference-in-west-africa/ (Accessed: 6 June 2023).
Newman, A. (2022b) 'Revisiting "eduscape" through a postcolonial lens: The influence of globalisation and migration on educational offer and demand in Senegal',

in A. North and E. Chase (eds) *Education, Migration and Development: Critical Perspectives in a Moving World*. London: Bloomsbury Press, pp. 111–128.
Newman, A. (2023) 'Decolonising social norms change: From "grandmother-exclusive bias" to "grandmother-inclusive" approaches', *Third World Quarterly*, 44(6), pp. 1230–1248.
Ngũgĩ wa Thiong'o, J. (1986) *Decolonizing the Mind: The Politics of Language in African Literature*. Oxford: James Currey.
Nkurunziza, E. (2007) *An Overview of Development Studies: Background Paper for the Religions and Development Research Programme. Working Paper* 2. Birmingham: International Development Department, University of Birmingham.
Pew Research Center. (2010) *Tolerance and Tension: Islam and Christianity in Sub-Saharan Africa*. Washington, DC: Pew Research Center.
Rizvi, F., Lingard, B. and Lavia, J. (2006) 'Postcolonialism and education: Negotiating a contested terrain', *Pedagogy, Culture & Society*, 14(3), pp. 249–262.
Rudolph, S., Sriprakash, A. and Gerrard, J. (2018) 'Knowledge and racial violence: The shine and shadow of "powerful knowledge"', *Ethics and Education*, 13(1), pp. 22–38.
Sommer von Würden, J. (2015) 'Islamic and educational knowledge in Zanzibar schools: Jinns as a case', unpublished talk given at the *6th European Conference on African Studies*. Paris.
Spratt, R. and Coxon, E. (2020) 'Decolonising "context" in comparative education: The potential of Oceanian theories of relationality', *Beijing International Review of Education*, 2, pp. 519–536.
Sriprakash, A., Tikly, L. and Walker, S. (2020) 'The erasures of racism in education and international development: re-reading the "global learning crisis"', *Compare: A Journal of Comparative and International Education*, 50(5), pp. 676–692.
Stambach, A. (2006) 'Revising a four-square model of a complicated whole: On the cultural politics of religion and education', *Social Analysis*, 50(3), pp. 1–18.
Stambach, A. (2010) 'Education, religion, and anthropology in Africa', *Annual Review of Anthropology*, 39, pp. 361–379.
Stambach, A. (2011) 'Religion, education, and secularism in international agencies', *Comparative Education Review*, 55(1), pp. 111–142.
Stambach, A. (2020) 'Where religion and education meet in Africa', in J.M. Abidogun and T. Falola (eds) *The Palgrave Handbook of African Education and Indigenous Knowledge*. Cham, Switzerland: Palgrave Macmillan, pp. 703–714.
Stark, R. and Finke, R. (2000) *Acts of Faith: Explaining the Human Side of Religion*. London and Berkeley, CA: University of California Press.
Stewart, C. (2001) 'Secularism as an impediment to anthropological research', *Social Anthropology*, 9(3), pp. 325–328.
Stoller, P. and Olkes, C. (2013) *In Sorcery's Shadow: A Memoir of Apprenticeship Among the Songhay of Niger*. Chicago, IL: University of Chicago Press.
Takayama, K., et al. (2016) 'Doing Southern theory: Towards alternative knowledges and knowledge practices in/for education', *Postcolonial Directions in Education*, 5(1), pp. 1–25.
Takayama, K., Sriprakash, A. and Connell, R. (2017) 'Toward a postcolonial comparative and international education', *Comparative Education Review*, 61(S1), pp. S1–S24.
Tamari, T. (1991) 'The development of caste systems in West Africa', *The Journal of African History*, 32(2), pp. 221–250.
Tayob, A. (2020) *The Promise of Decolonization for the Study of Religions, Contending Modernities*. Available at: https://contendingmodernities.nd.edu/decoloniality/promise-of-decolonization/ (Accessed: 30 November 2022).
Thorsen, D. (2012) *Children Begging for Qur'ānic School Masters: Evidence from West and Central Africa*. Dakar: United Nations Children's Fund (UNICEF).

Tikly, L. (2001) 'Globalisation and education in the postcolonial world: Towards a conceptual framework', *Comparative Education*, 37(2), pp. 151–171.

Tikly, L. (2004) 'Education and the new imperialism', *Comparative Education*, 40(28), pp. 173–198.

Tikly, L. (2014) 'Review: The World Bank and education', *Comparative Education Review*, 58(2), pp. 344–355.

Tikly, L. (2016) 'Education for all as a global regime of educational governance: Issues and tensions', in S. Yamada (ed) *Post-Education-for-All and Sustainable Development Paradigm: Structural Changes with Diversifying Actors and Norms*. Emerald Group Publishing Ltd, pp. 37–65.

Todd, Z. (2016) 'An indigenous feminist's take on the ontological turn: "Ontology" is just another word for colonialism', *Journal of Historical Sociology*, 29(1), pp. 4–22.

Tomalin, E. (2015) 'Gender, development, and the "de-privatisation" of religion: Reframing feminism and religion in Asia', in P. Fountain, R. Bush and R.M. Feaner (eds) *Religion and the Politics of Development*. Palgrave Macmillan, pp. 61–82.

Topolski, A. (2018) 'The race-religion constellation: A European contribution to the critical philosophy of race', *Critical Philosophy of Race*, 6(1), pp. 58–81.

UNESCO (2021) *Global Education Monitoring Report 2021/2022. Non-State Actors in Education: Who Chooses? Who Loses?* Paris: United Nations Educational, Scientific and Cultural Organization (UNESCO).

UNICEF (2012) *Partnering with Religious Communities for Children*. New York: UNICEF.

Unterhalter, E. and Kadiwal, L. (2022) 'Education, decolonisation and international development at the Institute of Education (London): A historical analysis', *London Review of Education*, 20(1), pp. 1–16.

Van Binsbergen, W. (1991) 'Becoming a Sangoma: Religious anthropological fieldwork in Francistown, Botswana', *Journal of Religion in Africa*, 21, pp. 309–344.

Varenne, H. (2008) 'Difficult collective deliberations: Anthropological notes toward a theory of education', in H. Varenne and E.W. Gordon (eds) *Alternative Anthropological Perspectives on Education: Perspectives on Comprehensive Education*. New York: The Edwin Mellen Press, pp. 21–50.

Vizcaíno, R. (2021) 'Secular decolonial woes', *The Journal of Speculative Philosophy*, 35(1), pp. 71–92.

Ware, R.T. (2004) *Knowledge, Faith and Power: A History of Qur'anic Schooling in 20th Century Senegal*. PhD thesis. Department of History, University of Pennsylvania.

Ware, R.T. (2014) *The Walking Qur'an: Islamic Education, Embodied Knowledge, and History in West Africa*. Chapel Hill, NC: The University of North Carolina Press.

Weber, M. (1904) *The Protestant Ethic and the Spirit of Capitalism*. New York: Scribner's Press.

White, S.C. (2002) 'Thinking race, thinking development', *Third World Quarterly*, 23(3), pp. 407–419.

Wilkinson, O. (2022) 'Re-framing common themes in religions and development research', *The Review of Faith & International Affairs*, 20(4), pp. 91–106.

Wilson, K. (2012) *Race, Racism and Development: Interrogating History, Discourse and Practice*. London and New York: Zed Books.

Wright, Z.V. (2013) 'Islam and decolonization in Africa: The political engagement of a West African Muslim community', *The International Journal of African Historical Studies*, 46(2), pp. 205–227.

Yountae, A. (2020) *A Decolonial Theory of Religion, Contending Modernities*. Available at: https://contendingmodernities.nd.edu/decoloniality/a-decolonial-theory-of-religion/ (Accessed: 29 November 2022).

2 A postsecular decolonial approach: Breaking the binaries

In Chapter 1, I identified a number of under-explored manifestations of coloniality of secularity and secular erasure in Euro-North American scholarship and policy discourses on Islamic education and the development-education-religion (DER) nexus more generally. The disciplines of CIE and development studies still reflect these flaws to a large extent, which I described in terms of stereotypes, silences and secular theoretical biases. In contrast, the literature I describe in this chapter allows us to develop a postsecular approach with which to understand educational engagement in countries under aid regimes where the majority of the population adheres to 'religious' worldviews. By outlining the advantages of such a postsecular approach, I hope to demonstrate how decolonial theory and praxis can be taken up within comparative/international education and development. The first step is to introduce decolonial theory, the second is to unpack how it has been applied to the study of religion, and the third is to consider how these frameworks can expand our understanding of educational dynamics.

Introducing decolonial theory

My starting point was the terms 'decolonisation' and 'decolonial'. Here I am indebted to the work of scholars associated – or in dialogue – with the Latin American modernity/coloniality/decoloniality (MCD) programme, otherwise known as the international decolonial collective, which focused on critiquing Eurocentric 'colonial modernity' and highlighting non-Eurocentric forms of knowing and being (Mignolo and Escobar, 2009). These scholars using decolonial theory begin from the understanding that European 'colonialism' entailed the processes, policies and ideologies used by metropoles to establish, conquer, settle, govern and economically exploit colonies. The geopolitical, economic and cultural legacies of colonialism persist, as we have seen, in the form of 'coloniality' (Quijano, 2007). Ramón Grosfoguel (2002) has described coloniality as 'heterarchies of power' which Sabelo Ndlovu-Gatsheni (2015) clarifies refers to "the complex vertical, horizontal, and crisscrossing invisible entanglements in the configuration of the modern global power structure that emerged from colonial encounters" (ibid., p. 486). Compared

DOI: 10.4324/9781003172475-2

to postcolonial studies which focused narrowly on the period of European colonisation proper, decolonial theorists pull the frame of analysis back to the conquest of the Americas in the fifteenth century, arguing that the origins of coloniality lie in the Atlantic commercial circuit (Dussel, 1998; Mignolo, 2002, p. 60). In the following section, I explore the concepts of coloniality and decoloniality and my own positionality in relation to them.

Defining coloniality and decoloniality

Decolonial theorists argue that coloniality has multiple overlapping facets which persist, despite never being totalising and always shifting, given the context and forms of local contestation (Lugones, 2007, p. 192; Tlostanova, 2015, p. 40). They distinguish among coloniality of (a) power, (b) being, (c) gender and (d) knowledge. 'Coloniality of power' entails unequal control over wealth and political authority, whether in the contexts of imperialism, colonisation or global neoliberal extractivist capitalism (Mignolo, 2007, p. 478; Quijano, 2007, p. 171). Second, 'coloniality of being' – or 'ontological Othering' – hierarchically orders human beings on the basis of language, ethnicity or culture – or through processes of racialisation. Such ordering leads even to the point of excluding certain groups from definitions of personhood entirely, thus justifying genocide, slavery and colonisation (Maldonado-Torres, 2007, p. 246; Mignolo, 2007, p. 479; Quijano, 2007, p. 171). Religion and/or secular worldviews constitute one of the important axes according to which human beings are classified and ultimately valued unequally (Yountae, 2020; Vizcaíno, 2021).

The third element, 'coloniality of gender', captures how the hierarchical dichotomies and categorical logics of patriarchy, heterosexualism and cisnormativity, informed by Euro-North American norms, intersect with processes of Othering to become key structuring principles of post-colonial societies (Lugones, 2007). Finally, 'coloniality of knowledge' refers to "epistemological issues, politics of knowledge generation, as well as questions of who generates which knowledge and for what purpose" (Ndlovu-Gatsheni, 2015, p. 490). This aspect reflects coloniality of being and gender, as bodies considered inferior by the logics of Eurocentric evolutionary thinking were also assumed to carry inferior intelligence (Mignolo, 2009, p. 178). Coloniality of knowledge also captures how Euro-North American centric worldviews and values, which underpinned global imperial designs of racialised capitalism, continue to shape cognitive models, scientific and international policy discourse and the organisation of academic disciplines (Tlostanova, 2015, p. 41).

Coloniality can be considered the 'dark side' of Western modernity (Mignolo, 2011), a project intellectually consolidated in the Age of Reason and the Enlightenment in the seventeenth and eighteenth centuries (Mignolo, 2007, pp. 459–460). Modernist thinking divides the world into essentialised binary categories. In fact, modernity as an ideal and a set of interlinked projects is underpinned by the rhetorics of progress, civilisation, emancipation and development. Yet, it is always constructed in relation to its supposedly inferior opposite, 'tradition'. Born in the crucible of European imperialism, modernity was defined on the basis of: White race; Euro-North American location, language and socio-cultural values; Christian and later secular worldviews; Euro-North American centric patriarchal, hetero- and cisnormative norms; and capitalist extractive economy (Mignolo, 2002, p. 60, 2007, p. 472). Modernity's enduring epistemic power stems from the fact that, despite emanating from a specific cultural and historical context, it claims to be universal, delocalised, disembodied and the sole claim to truth. Meanwhile, knowledges derived from other locations or standpoints, namely the position of 'colonial difference' (Mignolo, 2002, p. 58), are labelled as local, particular or unscientific and are suppressed, denigrated or appropriated (Castro-Gómez, 2007; Tlostanova, 2015, pp. 40–41).

It is important to note that earlier scholarship by some members of the MCD collective has been critiqued for suggesting, if at times implicitly, that all contemporary hierarchies can be traced back to coloniality. Leon Moosavi describes this tendency as 'nativist decolonisation' (2020, pp. 347–348) which assumes that no inequalities existed within 'subaltern' or 'Indigenous' societies prior to European contact. However, to a greater extent, this limitation has been addressed in recent years. For instance, Madina Tlostanova has centred this problematique within her work on post-Soviet Russia, coining the term 'external imperial difference' to describe how 'subaltern empires' can find themselves in a position of colonial difference relative to Euro-North American modernity/coloniality yet exercise imperialistic domination over their own internal 'Others' (2015, p. 47). In my research I apply similar logics to West African Islamic societies by paying attention to the (pre-colonial) foundations of their contemporary internal hierarchies and how these interact with coloniality. In short, I illustrate how all worldviews and education systems show both liberatory and oppressive potential. The challenge, therefore, is to demonstrate how these competing forces interact, in tension, in specific contexts, without silencing the influence of one tendency in favour of the other.

Decolonial theory differs from earlier postcolonial theory through its advancement of the notion of 'decoloniality' (Sandoval, 2000; Walsh and Mignolo, 2018) which is a concrete political project with three main characteristics. First, in contrast to modernity, decoloniality neither privileges one epistemic position from which to achieve universality nor imposes one model to follow. Rather, it reflects a family of diverse positions, a pluriversity of standpoints and worldviews, united by the perspective that coloniality represents the fundamental problem of the modern age (Ndlovu-Gatsheni, 2015, p. 492; Walsh and Mignolo, 2018, pp. 2–3). To contribute to epistemic decolonisation, thinkers are called to be explicit about their and others' locus of enunciation – or positionality and standpoint – to situate knowledges in specific historical, cultural and political contexts, as a challenge to universalising epistemic tendencies (Grosfoguel, 2007, p. 213). Second, decoloniality entails *critiquing* conceptions of knowledge that underpin colonialist hierarchies and *dismantling* the structures and power relations that sustain them (Quijano, 2007, p. 177). Third, decoloniality involves *re-building* a world that is just, inclusive, diverse and devoid of supremacy (Ndlovu-Gatsheni, 2015), including by disassembling hierarchies whose origins lie outside of Euro-North American coloniality.

In effect, decoloniality involves re-distributing resources, including material wealth and political power (Tuck and Yang, 2012). However, 'epistemic decolonisation' is first needed "to clear the way for new intercultural communication, for an interchange of experiences and meanings" (Quijano, 2007, p. 177). This requires challenging the teaching of 'knowledges of equilibrium' (Ake, 1979) which serve current global power asymmetries. Epistemic decolonisation "means to produce, transform and disseminate knowledge that is not dependent on the epistemology of North Atlantic modernity" and "the norms of the disciplines and the problems of the North Atlantic" (Mignolo, 2002, p. 80). Rather, it embraces the "contributions of racialized and colonized subjectivities in the production of knowledge and critical thinking" (Maldonado-Torres, 2007, p. 262). Inspired by Gloria Anzaldúa's theorising in *Borderlands/La Frontera: La Nueva Mestiza* (1987), Walter Mignolo further suggests that epistemic decolonial struggles require 'border thinking' which is an "epistemology from a subaltern perspective" (2002, p. 71). Such epistemologies are 'de-linked' from Euro-North American modernity, meaning that they draw on alternative standpoints, knowledge traditions and languages of expression. Hence, "de-linking means to change the terms of the conversation, and above all, of the hegemonic ideas of what knowledge and understanding are" (Mignolo, 2007, p. 459).

Between lake and mountain: My positionality

These broad conceptualisations are stimulating because they question who – or how – one can produce knowledges which can contribute to decoloniality. Within the modernity/coloniality/decoloniality collective, emphasis has understandably been placed on including people with "subaltern" standpoints who can contribute to knowledge production grounded in pluriversity (Grosfoguel, 2007, p. 212). Distinctions are often made between standpoints reflecting 'Northern' and 'Southern' perspectives which can map onto other binaries like coloniser/colonised or core/periphery (Rosa, 2014). Mignolo (2007, p. 466) proposes the following metaphor to illustrate how standpoint affects how people experience modernity (and coloniality) differently:

> A lake looks different when you are sailing on it than when you are looking at it from the top of the mountains surrounding it. Different perspectives on modernity are not only a question of the eyes, then, but also of consciousness and of physical location and power differential – those who look from the peak of the mountain see the horizon and the lake, while those inhabiting the lake see the water, the fish and the waves surrounded by mountains but not the horizon.

Within the field of comparative/international education, scholars have tended to refer to Raewyn Connell's book *Southern Theory: Social Science and the Global Dynamics of Knowledge* (2007) to grapple with these issues. According to Connell, 'theory' "connects solidly with experience and also leads fruitfully beyond it" in order to "provide a bridge between realities" and can be undertaken by non-academic thinkers (2014, p. 539). Meanwhile, although the 'South' is often used as a "geographical and temporal marker" to "denote the regions of the world . . . that have histories of colonial oppression and anti-colonial, post-colonial and de-colonizing struggles" (Takayama et al., 2016, p. 5), in Connell's framing, the 'South' can also refer more broadly to "an epistemic location that *sits on the margin, if not entirely outside,* of the global hegemony of Northern modernity" (ibid., p. 6, my italics). In Connell's view, theory from the 'South' constitutes "a source of unique knowledge in that it has emerged directly out of the experience of various forms of oppression" (ibid., p. 6).

It is important to recognise that the proposals of the MCD collective – and Raewyn Connell's articulation of Southern Theory – have been critiqued. Here I focus on four limitations, namely: the overly strict division between 'North' and 'South' as epistemic locations; the excessively inclusive definition of 'South' or 'Southern'; the essentialising tendency among some decolonial scholars to assume that sociological positioning equates to epistemological positioning; and the inadequate unpacking of the relative significance of different activities which can contribute to decolonial knowledge production.

First, the North/South binary can, arguably, prevent us from exploring global forms of oppression that cut across it (Takayama et al., 2016, p. 7) or the reality of the many 'Souths' within the global North or 'Norths' within the global South (Moosavi, 2020, p. 346). Moreover, the North/South binary is inadequate for "capturing the complexities or all forms of exclusion that coloniality generates in academia" (ibid., p. 345) which can also include education, gender, (dis)ability, class, nationality, ethnicity, language proficiency or type of employment contract. If we unpack Mignolo's metaphor, he assumes that there are only two possible standpoints: the view from the lake and the top of the mountain. In contrast, one could include additional vantage points like the view from the shore or at the base of the mountain.

Second, Connell considers herself to belong to the 'South' because, she argues, Australian academia is positioned in a 'peripheral' position relative to knowledge production sites in the US and Britain (Rosa, 2014, p. 859). Moosavi (2020, p. 347) has argued that this reflects an overly inclusive use of the terms 'South/Southern' which is itself a product of the simplistic North/South binary:

> Connell's classification of Australia as Southern diverts us from the connotations of poverty, dependency, and underdevelopment that are associated with the Global South, none of which characterise Australia, which is linguistically, culturally, economically, politically, religiously, institutionally, and socially on a par with the Global North. Yet, given

> the binary dichotomy between the way in which decolonial scholarship may speak about intellectual decolonisation, it is understandable that in the choice between Northern and Southern, Connell would categorise Australia as Southern.

Third, Grosfoguel has warned that there is not always a neat correspondence between *sociological* positioning and *epistemological* positioning. He argues that "the fact that one is socially located in the oppressed side of power relations, does not automatically mean that he/she is epistemically thinking from a subaltern epistemic location" (2007, p. 213). In turn, plenty of White and Northern-based scholars have arguably contributed immensely to exposing the violences of coloniality. Yet, Moosavi shows that an insidious manifestation of nativist decolonisation is when decolonial scholars "make the mistake of glorifying Southern scholarship or scholars just because they are from the Global South" and, alternatively, show "a distrust in Northern scholarship just because it is Northern" (2020, pp. 347–348). Furthermore, both our sociological and epistemological positions can change over time. To an extent, we can move back and forth among lake, shore and mountain at different points in our lives as our identities evolve or as a result of our relationships and journeys of (un)learning. Alternatively, because of intersectionality, we are situated at the lake in some contexts and on the shore or the mountain in others. In other words, we can be disadvantaged by one form of coloniality yet privileged by another. To overcome these challenges, Moosavi (ibid., p. 346) proposes a conceptual move toward:

> 'Centre/semi-periphery/periphery' rather than 'centre/periphery'. This would allow for a realisation that colonial hierarchies produce a spectrum of exclusion which silences various groups in similar albeit different ways rather than thinking in simplistic binary terms.

To further this agenda, I find the work of Serbian gender studies scholar Marina Blagojević to be particularly useful for theorising semi-peripheral epistemological standpoints. In her book *Knowledge Production at the Semiperiphery: A Gender Perspective* (2009, pp. 37–38) she argues that:

> In a comparison to the core, the semiperiphery is in a condition of 'being different, but not being different enough', while from the perspective of the periphery, the semiperiphery is 'different, and not similar enough'. . . . From the perspective of the periphery, the semiperiphery is 'too white', too industrial, too developed and it does not share the colonial experience, at least not in the sense of how the concept [periphery] is dominantly used when referring to the 'South'.

Blagojević speaks from the perspective of Eastern/post-Soviet/post-communist Europe and her understanding of semi-peripheral positioning is rooted in this geography. Yet, her theorising has broader theoretical implications because she recognises "that there are other semiperipheral societies, as well as . . . semiperipheral epistemic communities in the core societies" (ibid., p. 185). She proposes that semi-peripheral positioning – or "in-betweenness" – has "numerous local interpretations and meanings" (ibid., p. 37) and, in turn, important epistemological implications (ibid., pp. 39–40):

> The epistemic consequences of these ontological characteristics of the semiperiphery are enormous. This is what is certainly validating a need for the specific paradigms, coming from the semiperiphery itself, in the form of contextual knowledge, and often in the form of grounded theories. In other words, it would be unreasonable to claim that knowledge created at the center could 'cover' the realities from the semiperiphery. . . . However, from 'the below' only a few things could be understood as well, so it is equally limited.

Of central importance to my argument, Blagojević argues that (ibid., p. 43):

> what is essential from the epistemological point of view is that the semiperiphery is not some unimportant residual category, but that [the] semiperipheral condition creates deep needs for very different knowledge paradigms.

In other words, far from being 'inferior' to either a 'Northern' or 'Southern' perspective, the view from the semi-periphery (or 'the shore' to refer back to Mignolo's metaphor) provides a different and insightful vantage point from which to theorise social hierarchies. Later, I unpack my own semi-peripheral positioning and how it has underpinned the insights of this book.

Finally, there is a danger within CIE research, including Connell's *Southern Theory,* that privileged scholars can focus their activities on "serving as a 'curator' or 'translator' of neglected intellectual work produced in/of the South so that those discredited/disenfranchised knowledges are re-acknowledged and resuscitated" (Takayama et al., 2016, p. 11). Whilst well intentioned, Nirmal Puwar (2020) explains that because coloniality shapes the bestowal of prestige in academia, such initiatives can result in centring "ambassadors from the North" (2020, p. 542) rather than the thinkers and traditions they supposedly seek to promote. Although "Connell has undertaken transnational academic collaborations with scholars from the South", Puwar argues that "it is not they but Connell who has become the global spokesperson of theories from the Global South" (ibid., p. 548). Moreover, Connell's selection of Southern theories is presented like a smorgasbord tailored to the palate of Euro-North American scholars, from which they can pick and choose as suits their appetite (Moosavi, 2020, p. 344). If space is not made for Southern thinkers to participate on equal terms within the academy – which requires Northern scholars to step back to an extent – this approach risks erasing the ecologies, relationships of reciprocity and accountability, and ongoing political struggles and problem-solving dynamics that produced 'Southern' knowledges in the first place (Todd, 2016).

To chart a course through these competing opinions, I draw on Mignolo's argument that "there are gradations of decolonisation which mean that not all attempts to decolonise are as valuable as each other" (Moosavi, 2020, p. 339). To address this challenge, I propose a return to the three stages of epistemic decolonisation articulated by members of the MCD collective presented earlier. I am of the opinion that *critiquing* coloniality and *dismantling* its structures are important first steps but that the ultimate goal is *re-building* to include a pluriversity of perspectives. In dismantling the structures, more privileged scholars can play a useful role in promoting or supporting the struggles of marginalised thinkers. However, in the first and third stages of the decolonial project, it is imperative to centre the voices and theorising of people experiencing (the legacies of) colonial hierarchies. Moreover, the third stage absolutely demands full inclusion of those intimately familiar with non-Western knowledge traditions in order to enable border thinking (Mignolo, 2002, p. 71). We therefore need to assess critically efforts towards intellectual decolonisation and remain vigilant that the process is not dominated or co-opted by privileged interests.

In my case, the process of positioning myself within these debates – and in relation to the themes of this book – involved a considerable amount of self-reflection, especially on my position as a White Muslim. Sociologists who study European converts to Islam have revealed that we can be positioned at times as "a double stranger" and occupy a space that is "in between . . . born Muslim communities and a non-Muslim majority" (Sealy, 2022, pp. 96–97), which echoes Blagojević's description of semi-peripheral standpoints in terms of "in-betweenness" (2009, p. 37). Here I unravel how I have navigated this "in-betweenness" in my experience of academia and in writing this book.

First, my experience of academia is largely shaped by privilege. As a White woman born to comfortable middle-class British parents and who grew up within an ex-pat community in Brussels, I benefitted from prestigious education in an international school in Brussels, followed by degrees at the universities of Oxford, Sussex and the Institute of Development Studies in the UK and generous postdoctoral contracts at the Université Libre de Bruxelles and Ghent University in Belgium. While my conversion to Islam in my twenties positioned me as an 'Other' in a majority White and secular-but-historically-Christian social imaginary, I am 'secular-passing' and experience the world as a Muslim who is not necessarily read as such by others. Hence, I have considerable privilege within academia compared to individuals experiencing secular bias in combination with additional forms of colonial difference (Mignolo, 2002, p. 58). Examples would include Muslims facing far more vicious and racialised Islamophobia or Arabophobia due to their name, appearance, belonging to a particular ethnic or national group or those living in contexts of current or former (settler) colonialism (Allen, 2023; Durrani and Ghabrial, 2024; Mahmud and Islam, 2023; Shaheen, 2024; Wind, 2024). Moreover, despite my being Muslim, I will continue to benefit from the privileges of race, class, English mother tongue, educational trajectory, academic publication record and because I fit the stereotype of the 'good Muslim' within contemporary discourse (Sparkes, 2021).

Yet, my positioning and appearance also mean that I sometimes experience derision or suspicion from 'born Muslims' that I am not a 'proper' Muslim or those who assume that my practice is 'superficial'. Alternatively, a small number of people of colour can insinuate that White people convert to Islam 'for attention', as a form of cultural appropriation or to benefit from 'a victim status'. Indeed, Moosavi has described how, in White converts' interactions with 'born Muslims', "whiteness can signal subordination rather than dominance, marginality rather than normativity, and disadvantage rather than privilege" (2015, p. 1930).

For the purposes of this book, I argue that my semi-peripheral perspective, which is shaped by the protective cloak of secular-passing and Whiteness, has important implications for epistemic decolonisation precisely because I have access to spaces where people 'say what they really think' because they assume that everyone in the room is an atheist. In my case, this has included subtle yet disparaging comments by colleagues that all religious perspectives reflect 'the opium of the masses' or dismissing the study of religious communities from an insider perspective as 'epistemologically problematic'. As Zoe Todd, a White-passing Indigenous anthropologist from Canada argues, "This is a space that must be acknowledged and problematised, for it is a space that deeply influences how Euro-Western thought is produced within the academy" (2016, p. 12). Todd argues that experiences of such spaces, where "insecurities and hostilities" (ibid., p. 12) are laid bare when people believe that no one is watching, can provide valuable insights into the workings of coloniality in elite sites of knowledge production.

However, this book is not just about secular erasure in academic spaces; it is equally a record of my attempts at understanding the experiences of Senegalese Muslims and 'translating' some basic aspects of West African Islamic constructions of knowledge to a Euro-North American audience in comparative/international education. Once again, my appreciation of these issues is indirect and derives from my reading, my conversations with my research participants and particularly my marriage to a Senegalese man. Through him, I have intimate but indirect knowledge of formal Islamic education in Senegal, the poverty and political oppression there, prejudice and structural racism in Europe, and the experiences of undocumented people and their struggles to navigate migration regimes. Yet, my knowledge of these issues can never compare to the experiences of people, like my husband, whose bodies bear the scars of these everyday struggles against colonialist oppression. Hence, I do not claim that what I am doing reflects border thinking, an "epistemology from a subaltern perspective" (Mignolo, 2002, p. 71) or proficiency in a non-Western intellectual tradition. In my view, such border thinking can only be undertaken by – or through direct collaboration *with* and *for* – the people who hail from non-Western societies so that their worldviews, agendas and priorities directly shape the knowledge production process from the beginning.

Carrying this complex semi-peripheral positioning, I describe a postsecular approach to the study of the DER nexus which has informed my data analysis and writing – albeit not my research design or data collection. In particular, this approach offers a 'cognitive turn' in the study of religion.

Ontology and epistemology: 'With these threads, we weave the world'

Let me first take a moment to define some key terms which I use throughout this book, to analyse the different worldviews and constructions of knowledge that I found in Senegal, which arguably overcome colonialist binaries. It is important to note that Euro-North American social scientists, from Edward Evans Pritchard (1937) onwards, have endeavoured to challenge the modernist assumption that there exist profound cognitive differences between people holding 'religious' and 'secular' worldviews, with the latter usually assumed to be more rational (Day, 2020). However, in reality, different analytical frameworks are used to study the 'secular' and 'religious'. From the 1980s onwards, the Euro-North American study of religion in sociology and anthropology has reflected a "material and sensory-affective turn" which insists that "practice was prior to belief, and materiality was inseparable from and indispensable to spirituality" (Scheer, Johansen Schepelern and Fadil, 2019, p. 1). In contrast, the 'secular' has been studied primarily as a cognitive, philosophical formulation devoid of "affective or emotional textures" which therefore emphasises "neutrality, impartiality, factuality, rationality and reason as its constitutive features" (ibid., p. 2).

This differential treatment that the 'secular' and 'religious' receive in Euro-North American social science is grounded in other modernist/colonialist oppositions such as science/superstition, modern/primitive, reason/emotion, Western/non-Western, culture/nature, male/female and White/racialised bodies (Wilson, 2017). Some scholars (for example, Scheer, Fadil and Johansen Schepelern, 2019) have challenged this distinction by studying how the body, emotions and rituals are implicated in 'formations of the secular' (Asad, 2003). My approach is somewhat different, involving a combination of the older focus on embodiment and affect in the study of 'religion' with a 'cognitive turn' (Pool, 2020, p. 1043) more characteristic of studies of the 'secular'.

My starting point is that I think of worldviews using terms from philosophy, namely 'ontology' and 'epistemology', which allow us to see how "religion is no longer an exotic 'other' to the secular; both are ontological positions including both immanent and transcendent sources" (Pool, 2020, p. 1043). These terms, ontology and epistemology, have received increased attention within the social sciences since postcolonial and decolonial scholars talk of 'ontological injustice' and 'epistemic violence'. Yet, they are not necessarily familiar to an audience in development studies and CIE.

For the purposes of this book, I define ontology – derived from the Latin *ontologia* and the Ancient Greek word for 'to be' (Killam, 2013, p. 7) – as an understanding of the nature of being. Sometimes used interchangeably with 'worldview', 'cosmology', or 'metaphysics', ontology can be understood as "assumptions (which may be implicit or explicit) about what kinds of things do or can exist" (Blaser, 2009, p. 877). Ontological assumptions include "what human beings are, their fundamental characteristics, their relationships to one another, nature, the divine or supernatural (if it exists), and to themselves" (Wilson, 2017, p. 1083). Meanwhile, epistemology comes from the Greek words *episteme*, meaning knowledge, and *epistanai,* meaning to understand or to know (Killam, 2013, p. 8). Epistemology is the understanding of the nature of knowledge, including what it is possible – or not possible – to know, the criteria for assessing the validity of knowledge, and the means through which knowledge can be acquired (Ogunnaike, 2020, p. 421).

As these concepts are quite abstract, I follow the example of philosopher of education Barbara Thayer-Bacon who, in her book *Relational Ontologies* (2017), proposed a useful metaphor for understanding them. Thayer-Bacon was inspired by William James, psychologist and philosopher of religion, who argued in *A Pluralistic Universe* (1909) that the world we experience is far more than we can ever describe. Rather, the concepts and theories we develop to capture and organise the "open, flowing universe" are inevitably "incomplete, open and imperfect", as "the universe continually escapes beyond our artificial boundaries" (Thayer-Bacon, 2017, p. 16). Thayer-Bacon invites us to imagine this 'pure experience' through the metaphor of an Ocean, which she capitalises in order "to honor and underscore the spiritual quality" of what she describes (ibid., p. 1). In order to understand the universe, "we must design nets to help us catch up our experience of this vast Ocean and make sense of it". These nets are woven with warp threads representing "our theories of knowledge (our epistemology)" and weft threads signifying "our theories of being (ontology)" (ibid., p. 2).

Importantly, the things that we catch and name using our nets – such as fish, seaweed or plastic bags – represent ideas, words or concepts. They are useful to us but "if we just focus on what is in our nets, we lose sight of the moving, teeming Ocean that continues on around us" as well as the nature of the net, and how it caught some things but not others (ibid., p. 19). I share Thayer-Bacon's own epistemological position which is that "none of us can know what is True or Real, in a universal sense" (ibid., p. ix). Hence, there are many kinds of ontological and epistemological nets that humans can weave, potentially an infinite variety. Yet, no matter which net we use, "there is so much more in this vast Ocean of experience than our nets can catch" (ibid., p. 2).

Characteristics of onto-epistemologies

For the purposes of my research, I identify three important characteristics of ontologies and epistemologies – or *onto-epistemologies* as I refer to them in combination. What is important to our understanding of educational engagement are: their association with values; their subjective, fluid and often vague nature; and their material implications. Last, I consider how we might define an ontology or epistemology as 'Islamic'.

First, values are inseparable from onto-epistemological frameworks. Ontologies are imbued with moral judgements about the ideal relationships between the different entities, or forces, that are understood to exist. These shape ethical frameworks that guide humans' attitudes towards each other and the phenomena they encounter. Epistemologies also include value judgements about who should be able to seek knowledge, how and for what purposes. Both ontology and epistemology therefore have wide-ranging impacts on the design of education systems and research methodologies (Thayer-Bacon, 2017, pp. 4–10).

Second, ethnographic research shows that onto-epistemologies cannot be considered static and fixed but are constantly shifting and co-created through mundane practices and interactions (Blaser, 2009). Even young children can be actively involved in this process (Ahmed, 2012; Pedersen, 2017; Ridgely, 2017). In turn, individuals are often exposed to multiple onto-epistemological systems and draw upon them in their understandings of the world. Hence, even people co-inhabiting the same environment rarely share identical onto-epistemological positions; there is often a degree of disagreement, contestation and incompatible views (Graeber, 2015). Therefore, one cannot speak, in an essentialising way, of 'Western epistemology' or 'traditional African ontology', which would imply an identical and uncontested worldview across a bounded group (Enslin and Horsthemke, 2015). As I strive to do throughout this book, it is essential to identify the common characteristics of the onto-epistemological framings shared by a population in a given time and place, while equally acknowledging the extent of internal divergence and debate (Blaser, 2009; Graeber, 2015; Pool, 2020).

Moreover, onto-epistemologies are deeply ingrained in our 'common-sense' understandings of the world and are rarely consciously or explicitly articulated (Blaser, 2009). They are not necessarily coherent and bounded, as there is often a large degree of vagueness captured in statements like "we don't know how or why, it just is". Yet, it is precisely this vagueness that makes onto-epistemologies flexible enough to take account of uncertainty and uneasily explained phenomena (Graeber, 2015). Expressions of onto-epistemological understandings are, therefore, often articulated in stories, myths and metaphors or embodied, enacted or expressed in forms beyond discourse (Blaser, 2009; Barnes, 2020).

Third, while it may never be possible for humans to understand the true nature of the universe or 'pure experience' in a realist sense, onto-epistemologies nonetheless have very tangible implications as per the axiom that "if men [sic] define situations as real, they are real in their consequences" (Baber, 2010, p. 241). Onto-epistemologies provide frameworks which inform people's practical reasoning as well as visceral or affective habitus and are the means through which they perceive and engage with the world (Pool, 2020, p. 1047; Istratii,

2021, p. 13). Because onto-epistemologies shape reasoning and behaviour, they also shape social relations, physical space and the distribution of power and resources. As a result, manifestations of onto-epistemologies cannot be dissociated from wider material phenomena including social, economic and political inequalities.

Indeed, differences in status, power and wealth shape the dynamics of onto-epistemological contestation both within and between groups. Anthropologist Mario Blaser refers to this process as 'political ontologies', namely "the conflicts that ensue as different worlds or ontologies strive to sustain their own existence as they interact and mingle with each other" (2009, p. 877). Thayer-Bacon (2017, p. 8) adds that encounters between people using different onto-epistemological nets can be productive because:

> Following experiences with the world and others including those with different nets, we can unweave and reweave our nets to make better sense of our experiences and serve our needs.

However, in contexts of slavery, colonisation and imperialism, the nets of dominant groups are likely to be imposed on those on the receiving end of colonialist hierarchies. This process has harmful consequences, as the latter ways of understanding and living in the world are not framed as valuable or legitimate (Thayer-Bacon, 2017, p. 108). Coloniality of secularity and secular erasure of the sort that I discussed earlier are, therefore, some of the consequences that ensued once secular onto-epistemologies were imposed on the world through scientific and policy discourse.

One final detail is important for the purposes of this book, namely, the question 'what is *Islamic* about an Islamic onto-epistemology?' Social scientists have long debated how to define 'Islam' and frequently follow anthropologist Talad Asad's (1986) framework of a 'discursive tradition'. Asad coined this term in an attempt to overcome the distinctions made by Euro-North American academics between a supposedly 'pure' or 'universal' Islam on the one hand, and the plurality of local manifestations on the other. These differences were often framed in terms of modernist binaries like orthodox/unorthodox, high/low and scripturalist versus popular/folk and mapped on to social distinctions like urban/rural, educated/uneducated, literate/illiterate. Instead, Asad proposed that "a practice is Islamic because it is authorized by the discursive traditions of Islam" (ibid., p. 21) which includes "the founding texts of the Qur'an and the Hadith" (ibid., p. 20).

However, the concept of discursive tradition has been critiqued by feminist scholars for privileging "intellectual debate and argumentation over religious practice" and suggesting that "religion is coherent and consistent" (Janson, 2014, p. 11). For instance, Marloes Janson (2014) prefers to use the term 'ortho*praxy*' to analyse how Islam is done by youth in The Gambia. There, doctrinal debate over 'proper' practice, ortho*doxy*, took second place – or was even discouraged – in favour of a focus on everyday cultivation of Islamic dispositions. Moreover, this process was characterised by "contradiction, ambivalence, and struggle" (ibid., p. 12).

Rather than stake a firm position in relation to this debate, in my work I follow decolonial principles that multiple approaches towards conceptualisation have advantages in particular times and places, but defining Islam 'once and for all' might reflect a modernist preoccupation which sometimes shuts down rather than opens up debate. In my view, seeing Islam whether in terms of a discursive tradition or orthopraxy has different advantages depending on the empirical context. My decision to focus on Islam's ontological and epistemological aspects reflects the educational concerns of my research participants in Senegal. It is also likely shaped (perhaps unconsciously) by my positionality because, like many other White converts, I experience Islam more as a worldview and spiritual orientation than as the basis of my community or racial/ethnic identity (Sealy, 2022).

With these characteristics of onto-epistemologies in mind, my intention is that this book illustrates why it is so important for scholars and practitioners alike to pay greater attention to them. I hope to demonstrate that this is relevant when attempting to understand people's engagement with education in countries under aid regimes (usually referred to as 'developing countries'). Appreciating diverse worldviews should be an end it itself, but it can also be a stepping stone for informing education provision which honours a greater diversity of perspectives than is currently the case. This objective takes on a sense of urgency as the challenges facing our planet suggest that we need to do more to encourage "reciprocal valorisation among knowledge systems" (Hountondji, 1997, p. 13) and collectively support 'relational ontologies' (Thayer-Bacon, 2017; Nye, 2019) which foster relationships and practice that encourage peace, well-being and sustainability.

To use Thayer-Bacon's analogy (2017), we need to un-weave and re-weave our onto-epistemological fishing nets, slowly unravelling the colonialist threads. In relation to this project, religion has featured in the scholarship of the members of the modernity/coloniality/decoloniality (MCD) collective. In particular, they have acknowledged that Christian theology and later secular philosophy intersected with capitalism, Eurocentric evolutionary thinking, and the binary rhetorics of modernity to oppress racialised and colonised peoples (Mignolo, 2007, p. 471). However, relative to other questions like race, religion has received minimal attention from decolonial theorists. In the next section, I consider what this theoretical 'unravelling' of assumptions about religion might look like from a decolonial perspective.

Decolonial perspectives on the study of religion

As recently as 2020, decolonial scholar of religion An Yountae decried the "general lack of engagement with religion in the field of decolonial theory" including in its scholars' constitution of modernity/coloniality both past and present (2020, p. 3). Indeed, decolonial theorists can be guilty of 'decolonial woes', which philosopher Mariana Ortega describes as "the silences enacted by the very decolonial practitioners who call out other silences" (2017, p. 504). Rafael Vizcaíno draws inspiration from Ortega to argue that a '*secular* decolonial woe' is "a disregard for the potential that spirituality comprises for advancing the project of decolonization" (2021, p. 73) among some decolonial theorists.

As a first step, decolonising the study of 'religion' involves acknowledging that terms and approaches employed in its study are steeped in legacies of European colonialism and racial hierarchies. This has led some critics, like religious studies scholar Malory Nye, to ask "is the study of religion a rotten fruit of the poisoned tree of colonialism?" (2019, p. 2). Indeed, the term 'religion' – and associated concepts like spirituality, faith, ritual, belief and God – have specific histories rooted in the White European intellectual tradition (Topolski, 2018) but are often presented in academic and policy discourse as if they were universal and timeless (Fitzgerald, 2020; Maldonado-Torres, 2020). A common framing is the separation between 'sacred/religious' and 'profane' spheres of life, which reflects a Protestant belief system and is a distinction other religious communities are unlikely to make. Therefore, Nye argues that we cannot attempt to study 'religion' – or the 'secular' – in some abstract sense. Rather, we need to consider "how particular ideas (and discourses)" of religion/secularity are "practiced and operationalized in various contexts" (2019, p. 15). Indeed, Asad (2003) argues that the defining feature of secular onto-epistemology is that there exists a 'secular/religious binary' at all. A postsecular decolonial approach requires that we recognise that the concepts of 'secular' and 'religious' are not fixed categories but are, instead, socially constructed in relation to one another, in specific contexts.

In relation to international development, Erin Wilson has taken Asad's observations and used them to argue that the secular/religious binary constitutes a "globalized agglomeration of ideas and practices that vary locally". Yet, she suggests that, regardless of location, this binary shows 'family resemblances' based on six core, often overlapping, value-laden assumptions (2017, pp. 1079–1080):

1) something called 'religion' can be clearly distinguished from the 'secular';
2) 'religion' should be separated from other areas of human activity, like politics or education, that are defined as 'secular';
3) a 'religious' worldview is subjective and irrational while a 'secular' perspective is neutral and universal;
4) 'religion' is one of the primary causes of violence and intolerance;
5) 'religion' should be kept out of the 'public' sphere and confined to the 'private' to maintain peace and stability; and
6) even if 'religion' can contribute positively to society, the 'secular' should be dominant and 'religious' interventions should be regulated by 'secular' authorities.

It is the dominance of secular onto-epistemology in elite sites of knowledge production in academia and development and the six manifestations of the secular/religious binary that I refer to when I use the term coloniality of secularity. I also agree with Vizcaíno that the "problematic epistemic frame (the secular/religious divide) . . . has had a vital role in the solidification and preservation of the coloniality of knowledge" (2021, p. 76).

Following on from this, the stereotypes, silences and secular biases in theorising and policy-making in relation to the DER nexus (covered in the previous chapter) can be clearly seen to reflect this binary in one way or another. In relation to the first assumption, that the 'secular' can be clearly distinguished from 'religion', critical theorists in the field of religions and development often repeat that it is essential to study religion as infusing all aspects of people's lives rather than something that can be bracketed off from 'secular' life (Deneulin and Bano, 2009; Deneulin and Rakodi, 2011; Hefferan, 2015). Yet, the 'religions and development' framing continues to imply that there is something called 'secular' development that is separate from the 'religious' idiom. One solution here could be to shift our analytical focus away from 'religion' – typically understood as values, actors and institutions – to context-specific onto-epistemologies which are frameworks for perceiving, reasoning about and acting in the world that draw on a range of influences (Wilson, 2017; Pool, 2020; Istratii, 2021). We could start talking about 'ontologies and development' or 'worldviews and development' which enables us to break down the strict distinction between 'secular' and 'religious' phenomena which is so central to coloniality of secularity described in Chapter 1.

Furthermore, while scholars in the field of religions and development have invested significant efforts in demonstrating that a neat distinction between 'secular' and 'faith-based' organisations (FBOs) does not hold in practice (Deneulin and Rakodi, 2011; Tomalin, 2012; Wilson, 2017), with few exceptions (Pool, 2020; Stambach, 2020), they have been slow to acknowledge the reality of blurry ontological boundaries in relation to education. For instance, anthropologist Amy Stambach argues that, instead of studying 'religion' and 'education' in Africa as distinct institutionalised phenomena, everyday behaviour can be imagined more as "a dynamic matrix of relations defying easy fixity in either of the two categories" (2020, p. 713). Indeed, the distinction that economists posit between 'faith' and 'economics' fails to capture the interpenetration of 'religious' worldviews, economies and class formation at society-wide levels (Samson and LeBlanc, 2022). These dynamics have been theorised by anthropologists through concepts such as 'occult economies' (Comaroff and Comaroff, 1999) or 'spiritual economies' (Rudnyckyj, 2009).

The second assumption of the secular/religious binary, that 'religious' and 'secular' phenomena should be kept separate, gives rise to the silences around religion in literature on the DER nexus. Meanwhile, positivist approaches dominate in most development studies disciplines which assume that 'religion' and 'religiosity' can be bracketed off from 'secular' phenomena, objectively defined and measured, and correlated with other social variables. Such an approach also encourages the impression that 'religions' are monolithic and static sets of doctrines, which ignores lived religion and internal contestation (Wilkinson, 2022). Yet, scholars using qualitative and interpretivist approaches, which are more conducive to overcoming modernist binaries and value judgements, are still a minority voice in the religions and development field (Deneulin and Rakodi, 2011; Hefferan, 2015).

This assumption has also had a profound influence on the structure of academic disciplines. 'Secular' disciplines such as law, politics, international relations and education have tended to ignore religion until relatively recently. Meanwhile, philosophy, sociology and theology have typically studied religions formerly framed as 'modern', 'European' and 'rational', and religious studies has looked at the major 'world religions'. Finally, anthropology traditionally looked at 'local' manifestations of 'magic' or 'witchcraft', formerly framed as 'traditional', 'primitive', 'pagan' or 'irrational' (Nye, 2017). These disciplinary divisions and value judgements have had significant implications for the study of religion in the Islamic world, as will be demonstrated in later chapters. In particular, they have led to the side-lining of the 'esoteric sciences' or 'occult' practices within Islamic studies, development studies and comparative/international education because they are usually dismissed as unorthodox or associated with 'magic' and superstition in Euro-North American thought. This bias persists despite the pervasive nature of these practices throughout Muslim societies past and present, including in Senegal.

The third assumption, that 'religious' perspectives are subjective while a 'secular' ontology is objective, stems from functionalist sociology. Emile Durkheim (1912) first imagined 'religion' as a 'sacred canopy' which envelops its members so that they cannot think rationally outside of its discourse, compared to 'secular' ontology framed as neutral. This distinction has led to another strict separation of the academic disciplines which study 'religion' into another binary. On the one hand is 'social science' informed by secular epistemology and, on the other, is 'theology' which allows for theorising from other-than-secular ontological perspectives (Tayob, 2020). The dominance of secular epistemology in the social sciences means that it is usually assumed that an 'outsider' is better placed to produce authoritative knowledge on religion than an 'insider'. As Istratii argues, if a social scientist is "also a believer or a theologian, suddenly the fear for confessionalist bias prevails" (2021, p. xi). This fear is often "stronger than any concern that an 'outsider' or secular researcher might entirely misconstrue the local religious tradition and experience" (ibid., p. xi). Hence, social scientific research on 'religion' tends to focus on discourse and observable behaviour. It thereby excludes the subjective experiences, and particularly the theorising, of people who subscribe to other-than-secular ontologies on the grounds of monitoring the intrusion of theology into social science (Barnes, 2020, pp. 6–10).

The fourth and fifth assumptions of the secular/religious binary (that 'religion' is primarily a force of discord and violence, an obstacle to development and should be bracketed off from the 'secular' public sphere) have had a considerable influence over development theory and practice, as explained in the previous chapter. It manifests in the tendency of policy-makers to associate Islamic schools with terrorism while ignoring the geopolitical factors, especially Euro-North American colonisation and imperialist foreign policies, that have contributed to the rise of Islamic extremist movements in the first place (Deneulin and Bano, 2009; Bano, 2012; Hoechner, 2018). It is also evident in Orientalist stereotypes that Islam is inherently oppressive to women and that Muslim girls in the global South can be 'saved' by secular education (Khoja-Moolji, 2018).

Sixth, the assumption that 'religion' should be judged according to 'secular' values is prevalent within the development industry, as attempts to instrumentalise Islamic schools to meet EFA reveal (e.g. Marshall, 2010). These instrumentalising logics reflect the broader 'Two Faces of Faith Approach' (Hurd, 2015) among development organisations, namely the idea that 'religion' contains 'positive' aspects that can be harnessed for achieving secular ends. Based on secular onto-epistemologies and Euro-North American cultural norms, it is argued that religions' 'negative' aspects should be suppressed (Wilson, 2017, pp. 1080–1081). This reflects a broader distinction between 'good' and 'bad' religion – the first supposedly tolerant and able to conform to demands of rational discourse, the latter oppressive and superstitious – which abounds in academic and policy discourse (Crockett, 2018). The result is an instrumentalist orientation among researchers, donors and practitioners whose logic is to ask "what can religion do for development?" rather than aiming to understand other-than-secular onto-epistemologies – and their perspectives on development – on their own terms (Deneulin and Bano, 2009; Jones and Petersen, 2011; Wilkinson, 2022). This approach to other-than-secular onto-epistemologies reflects the fact that academic discourse on 'religion' was, from the outset, implicated in colonial projects involving global expansion and socio-political control (Nye, 2019; Maldonado-Torres, 2020).

We can understand several of these manifestations of coloniality of secularity in relation to the DER nexus by using the concept of secular erasure which I referred to earlier in Chapter 1. My use of this term draws inspiration from Vizcaíno's notion of 'secularizing erasure' but is also distinct from it. To clarify, Vizcaíno describes 'erasure' as "a normative project of silencing where a line is drawn between those subjects deemed worth studying or engaging, and those that are . . . 'not talked about'" (2021, p. 75). He uses 'secularizing erasure' to refer specifically to a "colonial impulse" among decolonial theorists who neglect "the potential that spirituality has to be a source of transformative theory and praxis" (ibid., p. 75). Vizcaíno (ibid., p. 75) further argues that secularizing erasure:

> in its policing of what is considered rigorous critical thinking, colludes with the coloniality of knowledge that has constituted the modern disciplinary production of knowledge.

My use of secular erasure differs from Vizcaíno's concept in two respects. First, my term refers to a broader process beyond the academic pursuit of epistemic decolonisation. Instead, it refers to tendencies among academics, policy-makers, development practitioners and media commentators more generally to render invisible the central relevance of other-than-secular worldviews in people's everyday lives and to silence and marginalise their perspectives. Second, Vizcaíno focuses on elevating our appreciation of "the extent that spirituality has been a vital component in the resisting life-worlds of colonized peoples" (2021, p. 71). While I embrace this principle, other-than-secular onto-epistemologies have also been responsible for (re)producing social hierarchies. I therefore use secular erasure to also include the silencing of such processes, including by decolonial theorists who romanticise Indigenous or subaltern communities through nativist decolonisation (Moosavi, 2020, p. 347), as these hierarchies also need to be dismantled as part of decolonial projects.

Finally, with this decolonial understanding, I developed a postsecular approach for the study of educational engagement. A postsecular approach to the DER nexus – and questions of educational engagement specifically – requires that research design, methodologies, analysis and dissemination shift away from the premises of secular epistemological superiority. When analysing my data, I took the view that such an approach needs to draw on insights from the standpoints of people who engage with the world through other-than-secular worldviews (Fitzgerald, 2020). The production of new knowledge needs to be informed by border thinking (Mignolo, 2002, p. 71) which draws on intellectual traditions that de-link from Western modernity including histories of struggle against the material, epistemic and ontological violence of coloniality. Therefore, the following section considers how I attempted to provide a foundation for such projects on educational engagement. Later, I demonstrate how this emerged and how it could be applied to Islamic West Africa.

Stories and senses: A postsecular approach to educational engagement in Islamic West Africa

Anthropologists defend participant observation, embedded in long-term relationships of trust and reciprocity, because rapport and empathy enable the process of entering another's perceptual world (Wikan, 1992; Jackson, 1998). This can be further enhanced by shared embodied experience because "there are a great many things that we understand only with our bodies, at a sub-conscious level without having the words to say them" (Bourdieu, 1988, p. 160). When conducting research for my doctorate in anthropology, the 'obvious' assumption was that I would use participant observation and present my data as ethnography.

However, while I found the ethnographic method very insightful, my immersion in Senegalese Muslim communities had a bigger impact on my perception of the world than is usually expected within the discipline. In truth, my affective experiences pushed me to question and re-work my own onto-epistemological theories which had influenced my thinking, reasoning, values, actions and habitus. It was only as a result of having had this transformative experience myself – and having lived and reflected on my life as a Muslim for the last decade – that I came to appreciate that so much of what underpins people's educational preferences in northern Senegal is felt and alluded to, rather than explicitly articulated. It was also this experience that revealed to me that this deeper level of onto-epistemology is lacking from current theorising about educational decision-making.

The beginning of this realisation came over the course of my stay in Senegal. At first, Muslims would ask me why I had not converted to their religion. I prepared an answer that I hoped would satisfy them: "When you want to buy a house, you have to check the contract to know what you're signing up for", I explained. "And you should go inside the house and take a look, not just trust what the seller on the outside tells you". No one was ever convinced by the house metaphor, not least because it was not culturally relevant as few Senegalese buy houses – they tend to buy land and build their own house on it! After 18 months, even I had abandoned that analogy. A Sufi *shaykh* in Medina Diallobé village asked me again when I was going to convert, and this time I answered, "Do you ask the mango when it is going to ripen? No, because the mango doesn't decide – the sun shines on the mango and, when the time is right, it ripens – and then it is at its sweetest". The *shaykh* gave a huge smile, and asked if the mango was ripening. We both knew the answer.

My shift from the house metaphor to the mango allegory reflected a deeper transformation in my onto-epistemological understanding of the world that had taken place during my time in Senegal. The first metaphor revealed a rationalist worldview where I had imagined my ontological positioning as an autonomous choice that was based on my weighing up arguments for and against, reading the sacred texts and experiencing life within a Muslim community. In contrast, the ripening mango analogy reflected my understanding of ontological transformation in terms of a shift whose course was directed by a higher power as much as my own decisions. In describing the ripe mango as sweet, I tried to communicate both the values and affective experiences that accompanied and motivated the transformation. Little by little, my original onto-epistemological net had been unravelled and re-woven to include Sufi threads. Needless to say, this metaphor resonated with the *shaykh* because we shared the worldview wherein the analogy 'made sense' on a ontological, symbolic, moral and affective basis.[1]

What I came to realise was that onto-epistemological understandings are grounded in affective, embodied experiences which are difficult to articulate through discourse to those who do not share those experiences or cultural background (Blaser, 2009; Thayer-Bacon, 2017; Barnes, 2020). The decolonial turn has undoubtedly opened up more space within academia for people experiencing and theorising the world from other-than-secular ontological perspectives. And yet, communicating such experiences remains a challenge as we might not want to share them publicly, and they cannot be easily captured in words (Barnes, 2020). Hence, ethnography "puts something into words, which did not exist in language before" and has to translate "the unspeakable, the pre-linguistic, and the indescribable" (Hirschauer, 2006, p. 413).

This unspoken thing that ethnography tries to communicate is often affect, which refers to "bodily, sensory, inarticulate, nonconscious experience" (Gould, 2009, p. 24). Affect can be distinguished from emotion, which is the attempt to 'capture' and approximate affect in gesture or language, whether literal or metaphorical. Scholars of education increasingly explore how affect and emotions influence educational phenomena, to counteract overly rationalist explanations or those based solely on discourse and representations (Probyn, 2004; Dernikos et al., 2020). However, comparative/international education as a field often fails to engage sufficiently with the implications of cultural diversity and ontological plurality for studies of affect in relation to education (c.f. Nxumalo and Villanueva, 2020).

In contrast, Christian anthropologist Jamie Barnes (2020, pp. 47–49) powerfully argues that studies of 'religious' experience *must* appreciate that different cultures construct the 'sensorium' in diverse ways, defined as understandings of the human sensory apparatus as well as the 'seat of sensation' where perceptions are experienced and interpreted (Howes, 2009, pp. 1–6). Hence, when exploring affect, we need first to appreciate the cultural and ontological 'contexts of perception', namely, how different senses and the relationships between them are understood (Jackson, 1989). Yet, Euro-North American education scholarship risks only noticing and acknowledging sensations and emotional states which resonate with their own material understandings of the sensorium (namely Aristotle's five senses of sight, hearing, smell, taste and touch) and the narrow range of possibilities that it allows for. This is particularly likely to be the case when other-than-secular worldviews are involved, as they entail an expanded conception (beyond the material or biological) of what can be sensed and how (Barnes, 2020, pp. 47–49). For instance, Sufis consider the heart (*qalb*) to be an important sensory organ because it is the place where one experiences God (Wright, 2018, p. 154).

While I do not support the essentialising proposition that all theorising of other-than-secular ontologies can and even must only be undertaken by people sharing these ontologies, the lack of 'perspectival variation' (Stewart, 2001, p. 327) in the Euro-North American social sciences nonetheless poses an obstacle to decolonising the study of the DER nexus. In my view, the task of investigating the influence of other-than-secular worldviews on educational engagement would be enabled by the inclusion of more theorising by people 'of faith' who are typically "fluent in both secular and religious vernacular" (Wilson, 2017, p. 1090). Moreover, researchers who do have personal experience of the affective and embodied underpinnings of other-than-secular worldviews are well placed to engage in self-study such as auto-ethnography (Barnes, 2020). They can translate this knowledge and insight into research design and methodologies that enable their research participants to communicate their experiences more effectively and inform the design of adapted development programmes (Istratii, 2021). With this critical awareness, I unpack in the following sections my own approach to data collection, analysis and writing.

Research methodologies, data sources and fieldwork context

The development of this book has occurred over the course of two broad phases: (a) an initial stage of intensive ethnographic data collection and inductive thematic analysis (Howell, 2018) during my doctoral research from 2010 to 2015 supplemented with complementary follow-up interviews between 2016 and 2018 and (b) a later process of auto-ethnographic reflection, grounded theory development (Babchuk and Hitchcock, 2013) and writing informed by postcolonial and decolonial theory from 2020 to 2024. The following chapters combine insights gleaned from both phases to communicate the complex relationships between Islamic onto-epistemologies and education in Senegal.

In the first phase, I collected most empirical data through interpretivist qualitative fieldwork in Senegal over 19 months from 2010–2012. I split my time between the capital Dakar and a village of 5,000 inhabitants that I call by the pseudonym of Medina Diallobé, located in the Senegal River valley basin. According to contemporary administrative divisions, this area lies within the department of Podor in the region of Saint-Louis and the department of Matam in the region of the same name (see Figure 2.1). However, the Senegal River valley zone has been referred to by its inhabitants from the sixteenth century as the Futa Tooro. Its population largely belongs to the Haalpulaar ethnic group (noun: Haalpulaar'en), which is part of the larger Pulaar-speaking group which makes up 24% of the Senegalese population (ANSD and ICF International, 2012, p. 2).

Because I was interested in EFA and how local communities responded to campaigns stressing the desirability of state schooling and the increase in school provision at primary and secondary level, I wanted to focus on families' and youths' preferences for non-accredited Islamic education. A serendipitous visit to Medina Diallobé through a contact of a contact gave me that opportunity. There, people continued to prefer Qur'anic schools despite access to state schools having increased during the 2000s. To understand these dynamics, in Dakar I conducted semi-structured interviews with staff of INGOs and NGOs working on education which I complemented with a discourse analysis of grey literature on Qur'anic schools. In Medina Diallobé, I engaged in ethnography involving participant observation in everyday activities and casual conversations with inhabitants. I saw that their patterns of educational preference diverged from the negative stereotypes about Qur'anic schools and Muslims

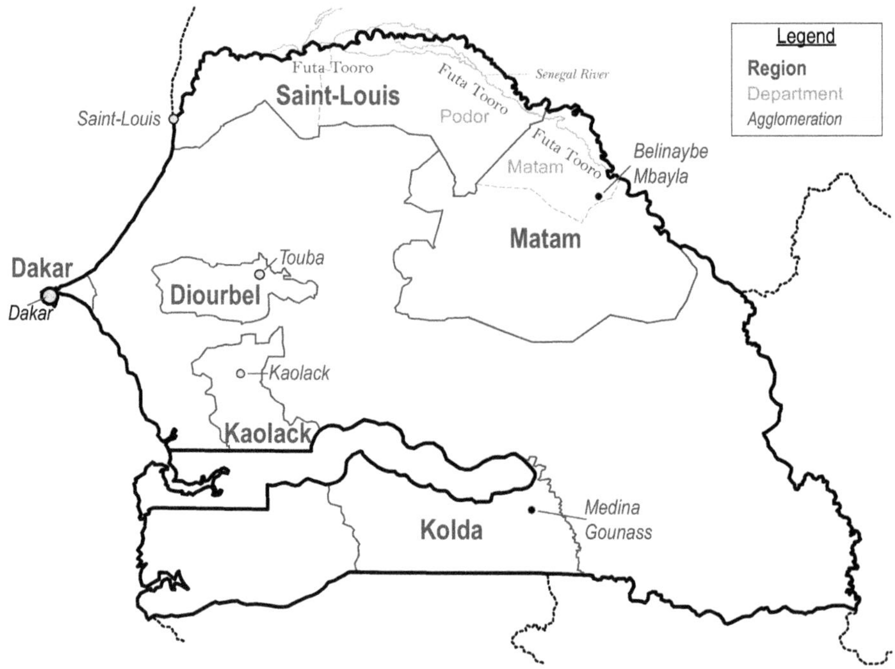

Figure 2.1 **Map of Senegal**. Includes the regions, departments, agglomerations and natural features mentioned in this book.

Credit: Anneke Newman and Isabelle Renneson.

that I had encountered among development actors in Dakar. As my research progressed, I came to understand the important epistemological implications of their decision-making logics and made a long-term commitment to communicate their perspectives to an audience in comparative/international education and development studies.

The data from this phase consisted of transcripts of 30 formal interviews as well as over 500 daily fieldwork journal entries including observations, interactions and semi-structured interviews with around 150 individuals (for more details on sampling, methods and analysis see Chapter 5). Using NVivo, I began an inductive process of identifying broad themes by open-coding the text. I focused particularly on the explanations people gave for opting for state and Islamic schools and whether their answers reflected or made reference to hierarchies based on gender, descent and socioeconomic status. I structured the chapters of my doctoral thesis according to these broad themes and used existing theoretical concepts to make sense of these dynamics, namely: 'the identity of the educated person' (Levinson and Holland, 1996); the 'cultural production of educational utility' (Demerath, 1999) and Pierre Bourdieu's (1986) framework of field, capital and habitus.

While they proved useful, I was not satisfied with these concepts as I felt that they failed to account sufficiently for profound epistemological differences in understandings of knowledge and legacies of colonisation in educational decision-making and knowledge production – but I did not have the language or confidence to articulate this argument at the time. Issues that I felt unable to write about were the fact that, before conducting fieldwork in Senegal, I had noticed discrimination against people of faith and biases against Islam and Muslims within academia and development praxis. Moreover, despite my anthropological training in ethnographic methods, I was not prepared for the fact that the relationships and affective states I experienced in Senegal would lead to my gradual adoption of a Sufi worldview over the course of my fieldwork. These processes prompted shifts in my research relationships, understandings of knowledge and everyday engagement with the world – but I felt obliged to censor those experiences. These understandings have been further informed over the years by my experiences, reading and relationships with other Muslims, particularly my Senegalese husband and members of our Sufi community in Dakar.

It was not until 2020 that I engaged with decolonial theory when attending a course on Decolonising Anthropology hosted by Goldsmiths, University of London. It was this theoretical exposure that enabled me to 'make sense' of my experiences and misgivings about dominant theories and which sparked the second phase of the book's development. I decided to use my ethnographic data in Senegal combined with auto-ethnographic introspection on my own experiences as a Muslim to engage in a process of grounded theory (Babchuk and Hitchcock, 2013), advancing concepts that could support a postsecular decolonial approach to educational decision-making.

To an extent, my desire to advance a decolonial approach was made complicated by the way I had undertaken my original ethnography. I feel that the overall thrust of my research conducted over a decade ago was compatible with an epistemic decolonisation agenda in that my overarching objective was to confront development stereotypes with perspectives grounded in Islamic worldviews. Indeed, my research participants always seemed pleased when I explained that I hoped to write a book that would reveal to a Euro-North American audience the reasons why participants valued Qu'ranic schools and Islam generally. However, once I started to read postcolonial and decolonial theory, I realised that the ethnographic research I had conducted was, in reality, quite traditional, as it involved research *about* rather than *with* my research participants – and thus risked reproducing extractivist modes of knowledge production (Moosavi, 2020, pp. 342–343). In Chapter 9, I unpack how I might do research on Islamic education in West Africa differently in future, in line with the decolonial principles I outlined earlier.

These limitations notwithstanding, I have used these data and have combined them with subjective auto-ethnographic introspection (Barnes, 2020) regarding my own onto-epistemological transformation. I often try to communicate my experiences and perceptions through creative means including through stories or metaphors. Barnes argues that 'people of faith' often employ metaphors to communicate which are collectively understood by members of their community who share a common lifeworld, cultural background and experiences. Yet, these metaphors can be poorly appreciated by researchers who hail from different cultural contexts and/or subscribe to a secular ontology if they focus their attention at the level of discourse rather than the affective experiences underpinning it (Barnes, 2020, pp. 38–45; Vizcaíno, 2021). My appropriation of metaphorical modes of writing also nods to classical scholars of Islam who see the Qur'an as consisting of literal, apparent or exoteric meanings (*al-zahir*) and deeper, inner, secret or esoteric meanings (*al-batin*). The latter are allegorical and accessible through advanced study, divine contemplation and mystic experience (Ogunnaike, 2020). My use of metaphors – ripening mangoes, oasis gardens and onto-epistemological fishing nets – are therefore my attempts at communicating an approximation of aspects of my worldview, whilst allowing for the fact that "much of what we experience remains unnamed and cannot be reduced to its articulated meanings" (Thayer-Bacon, 2017, p. 28).

Metaphors can capture deeper layers of meaning that are not explicitly articulated and therefore communicate that not everything is – or should be – knowable. They invite the reader to exercise 'epistemic humility', namely an awareness of the limits and contingencies of all of our onto-epistemological frameworks and the realities of silence and ambiguity (Vizcaíno, 2020, p. 2). Such forms of expression are rarely recognised in policy-making debates. Nonetheless, some scholars in comparative/international education, like Stephen Carney (2019), have recently argued in favour of creative writing styles, like poetry, to embody the complexity of the impacts of global education reform.

Finally, I draw on secondary literature which aims to communicate the realities of classical Islamic education in West Africa from its teachers' and learners' perspectives. I do not wish to diminish the valuable contributions of culturally and historically-sensitive research by non-Muslims, Euro-North American social scientists or those trained in the global North. Indeed, I have drawn on a great deal of such scholarship produced by such researchers in African and Islamic studies. However, there are at least four, overlapping and overlooked, categories of scholarship that I have made efforts to draw upon because they provide additional perspectives which can help address colonialist biases in research on the DER nexus.

The first are texts written by (or verbatim interviews with) members of the religious scholarly elite trained in the classical Islamic tradition in West Africa, North Africa or the Middle East, from the pre-colonial period to the present, who communicate(d) in Arabic or African languages. The works of these 'non-Europhone intellectuals' (Kane, 2012), which can be said to be de-linked from Western modernity (Mignolo, 2007, p. 459), have long been ignored by Euro-North American academics not proficient in these languages. Fortunately, these texts are increasingly being studied and translated into French or English to enable this endeavour (Cohen and Timéra, 2022, pp. 838–839).

The second category consists of texts in French, targeted to a largely francophone West African audience and written by intellectuals writing from a

West African Muslim perspective but who have not enjoyed an advanced Islamic education. Such authors have existed since the colonial period, but their scholarship has enjoyed a resurgence following the establishment of independent presses in the 2000s (Cohen and Timéra, 2022, pp. 839–841). The third group are West African scholars, particularly Muslims, based at universities on the African continent or in the global North, writing in French and English for academic audiences. The fourth category (to which I belong) are Muslim academics who are not Senegalese but are affiliated with Senegalese Sufi orders, who hail from diverse races and nationalities and are based at global North universities and write primarily in English. When describing West African Islamic knowledge traditions, most often I cite the literature of the scholars in the third and fourth categories, although they are not mutually exclusive as they themselves frequently cite scholars of the first and second categories.

My triangulation of these three sources – ethnography, creative introspection and secondary literature – is intended to synthesise findings from data derived from distinct methodologies and grounded in different disciplinary conventions. I use them in combination to support my own project of grounded theory (Babchuk and Hitchcock, 2013) and development of a postsecular decolonial approach. It aims at a 'theoretical synergy' which, according to Ali Meghji (2020, p. 652), is anchored in:

> The premise that social reality can be studied from different theoretical viewpoints, and that this theoretical pluralism is essential for understanding certain phenomena in their full complexity.

Meghji stresses that theoretical 'synergy' is not 'synthesis', meaning that it does not aim to combine theoretical approaches into one meta-theory which inevitably involves subordinating one paradigm's onto-epistemological logic to that of another. Rather, theoretical synergy is a decolonial approach to social theory which (ibid., p. 659):

> Acknowledges that different paradigms can comprehend different aspects of social life, and that to do minimal 'violence' with our conceptual scalpel, we ought to embrace a theoretical pluralism.

Nonetheless, I reiterate that I see my project as one which *critiques* coloniality of secularity and Euro-North American centric biases in current understandings of engagement with Islamic education in West Africa. It therefore corresponds to the first, more limited, step of epistemic decolonisation (Quijano, 2007, p. 177). In my view, approaches to CIE/EID theory and praxis that go further by *dismantling* power hierarchies in knowledge production and *building* more inclusive alternatives can only be achieved through collaborative projects *with and for* the people, whether teachers or learners, who are embedded within those knowledge traditions.

Conclusion

Taking into account the nature of the fields of CIE/EID and my concern to address from a decolonial perspective the question of educational engagements in Islamic African contexts, I have proposed a postsecular approach which takes epistemological distance from the assumptions of the secular/religious binary. This approach, as I have demonstrated here and in the previous chapter, demands critical engagement with coloniality and secularist logics of classification as a starting point for producing new knowledge about 'religion' (Maldonado-Torres, 2020). It also involves investigating and celebrating the spiritual grounding of local alternatives which overcome the violence of coloniality of secularity. My understanding of what constitutes a decolonial postsecular approach also entails re-imagining the study of 'religion' from the standpoints of people who experience the world through other-than-secular worldviews (Fitzgerald, 2020). This approach requires enabling border thinking by individuals and communities whose intellectual traditions are de-linked from colonialist logics. To harness Thayer-Bacon's metaphor (2017), we need to unravel and re-create our existing ontological and epistemological nets so as to pull out and replace the colonialist threads. In the next chapter I start implementing this approach by weaving a history of education provision in Senegal which does justice to Islamic worldviews and the onto-epistemological violence of the colonial encounter.

Note

1 Sufis in West Africa have applied the metaphor of 'sweetness' to the experience of acquiring Islamic knowledge, particularly mystic experiences, for centuries. Rudolph Ware (2014, p. 254) quotes Usman Dan Fodio, Sufi founder of the Sokoto Caliphate in what is now northern Nigeria, describing mystical enlightenment thus: "God removed the veil from my sight, and the dullness from my hearing and smell, and the thickness from my taste . . . I was able to . . . smell the scent of him who worshipped God, sweeter than any sweetness". Zachary Wright also reports how contemporary Sufis in Senegal often told others who were considering joining their order that "the religion was like a candy: one could hear many times how delicious the candy would be, but the only way to know directedly was to taste it oneself" (2018, p. 140).

References

Ahmed, F. (2012) 'Tarbiyah for shakhsiyah (educating for identity): Seeking out culturally coherent pedagogy for Muslim children in Britain', *Compare – A Journal of Comparative and International Education*, 42(5), pp. 725–749.

Ake, C. (1979) *Social Science as Imperialism: The Theory of Political Development*. Ibadan: University of Ibadan Press.

Allen, C. (2023) 'Everyday experiences of Islamophobia in university spaces: A qualitative study in the United Kingdom', *Education, Citizenship and Social Justice*, pp. 1–13. https://doi.org/10.1177/17461979231210996.

ANSD and ICF International (2012) *Senegal Demographic and Health and Multiple Indicator Cluster Survey (EDS-MICS) 2010–2011*. Rockville, MD: Agence Nationale de la Statistique et de la Démographie and ICF International.

Anzaldúa, G. (1987) *Borderlands/La Frontera: La nueva mestiza*. San Francisco, CA: Aunt Lute Books.

Asad, T. (1986) *The Idea of an Anthropology of Islam. Occasional.* Washington, DC: Center for Contemporary Arab Studies, Georgetown University.

Asad, T. (2003) *Formations of the Secular: Christianity, Islam, Modernity*. Stanford, CA: Stanford University Press.

Babchuk, W.A. and Hitchcock, R.K. (2013) 'Grounded theory ethnography: Merging methodologies for advancing naturalistic inquiry', in *Adult Education Research Conference*. Available at: https://newprairiepress.org/aerc/2013/papers/5.

Baber, Z. (2010) 'Racism without races: Reflections on racialization and racial projects', *Sociology Compass*, 4(4), pp. 241–248.

Bano, M. (2012) *The Rational Believer: Choices and Decisions in the Madrasas of Pakistan*. Ithaca, NY and London: Cornell University Press.

Barnes, J. (2020) *Stories, Senses and the Charismatic Relation: A Reflexive Ethnography of Christian Experience*. London: Routledge.

Blagojević, M. (2009) *Knowledge Production at the Semiperiphery: A Gender Perspective*. Belgrade: Institut za kriminološka i sociološka istraživanja.

Blaser, M. (2009) 'Political ontology: Cultural studies without "cultures"?', *Cultural Studies*, 23(5–6), pp. 873–896.

Bourdieu, P. (1986) 'The forms of capital', in J. Richardson (ed) *Handbook of Theory and Research for the Sociology of Education*. New York: Greenwood Press, pp. 241–258.

Bourdieu, P. (1988) 'Program for a sociology of sport', *Sociology of Sport Journal*, 5(2), pp. 153–161.

Carney, S. (2019) 'Writing global education policy research', in M. Parreira do Amaral, G. Steiner-Khamsi and C. Thompson (eds) *Researching the Global Education Industry*. London: Palgrave Macmillan, pp. 251–271.

Castro-Gómez, S. (2007) 'Decolonizar la universidad: La hybris del punto cero y el diálogo de saberes', in S. Castro-Gómez and R. Grosfoguel (eds) *El giro decolonial: Reflexiones para una diversidad epistémica más allá del capitalismo global*. Bogotá: Siglo del Hombre Editores, pp. 79–92.

Cohen, A. and Timéra, M. (2022) 'Tentations d'islam et écrits d'élites europhones au Sénégal. Quelle production de nouvelles normativités islamiques?', *Cahiers d'études africaines*, 248(4), pp. 829–857.

Comaroff, J. and Comaroff, J.L. (1999) 'Occult economies and the violence of abstraction: Notes from the South African postcolony', *American Ethnologist*, 26(2), pp. 279–303.

Connell, R. (2007) *Southern Theory: Social Science and the Global Dynamics of Knowledge*. Cambridge: Polity Press.

Connell, R. (2014) 'Rethinking gender from the South', *Feminist Studies*, 40(3), pp. 518–539.

Crockett, C. (2018) 'What is postsecularism?', *American Book Review*, 39(5), pp. 6–14.

Day, A. (2020) *Sociology of Religion: Overview and Analysis of Contemporary Religion*. London and New York: Routledge.

Demerath, P. (1999) 'The cultural production of educational utility in Pere Village, Papua New Guinea', *Comparative Education Review*, 43(2), pp. 162–192.

Deneulin, S. and Bano, M. (2009) *Religion in Development: Rewriting the Secular Script*. London and New York: Zed Books.

Deneulin, S. and Rakodi, C. (2011) 'Revisiting religion: Development studies thirty years on', *World Development*, 39(1), pp. 45–54.

Dernikos, B.P., et al. (2020) 'Feeling education', in B.P. Dernikos et al. (eds) *Mapping the Affective Turn in Education: Theories, Research, and Pedagogies*. New York: Routledge, pp. 1–25.

Durkheim, E. (1912) *The Elementary Forms of Religious Life*. London: Allen & Unwin.

Durrani, M. and Ghabrial, S. (2024) 'The War on Terror Never Ended', *Inside Higher Ed*. Available at: www.insidehighered.com/opinion/views/2024/02/20/anti-muslim-racism-fuels-academic-freedom-attacks-opinion (Accessed 10 September 2024).

Dussel, E. (1998) 'Beyond Eurocentrism: The world-system and the limits of modernity', in F. Jameson and M. Miyosi (eds) *The Cultures of Globalization*. Durham, NC: Duke University Press, pp. 3–31.

Enslin, P. and Horsthemke, K. (2015) 'Rethinking the "Western tradition"', *Educational Philosophy and Theory*, 47(11), pp. 1166–1174.

Evans-Pritchard, E.E. (1937) *Witchcraft, Oracles, and Magic among the Azande*. Oxford: Clarendon Press.

Fitzgerald, G. (2020) *Introduction to Decoloniality and the Study of Religion, Contending Modernities*. Available at: https://contendingmodernities.nd.edu/decoloniality/introdecolonial/ (Accessed: 30 November 2022).

Gould, D.B. (2009) *Moving Politics: Emotion and ACT UP's Fight Against AIDS*. Chicago, IL: Chicago University Press.

Graeber, D. (2015) 'Radical alterity is just another way of saying "reality": A reply to Eduardo Viveiros de Castro', *Hau: Journal of Ethnographic Theory*, 5(2), pp. 1–41.

Grosfoguel, R. (2002) 'Colonial difference, geopolitics of knowledge and global coloniality in the modern/colonial capitalist world-system', *Review*, 25(3), pp. 203–224.

Grosfoguel, R. (2007) 'The epistemic decolonial turn', *Cultural Studies*, 21(2–3), pp. 211–223.

Hefferan, T. (2015) 'Researching religions and development', in E. Tomalin (ed) *The Routledge Handbook of Religions and Global Development*. London: Routledge, pp. 36–52.

Hirschauer, S. (2006) 'Puttings things into words. Ethnographic description and the silence of the social', *Human Studies*, 29(4), pp. 413–441.

Hoechner, H. (2018) *Quranic Schools in Northern Nigeria: Everyday Experiences of Youth, Faith, and Poverty*. Cambridge: Cambridge University Press.

Hountondji, P.J. (1997) *Endogenous Knowledge: Research Trails*. Dakar: CODESRIA.

Howell, S. (2018) 'Ethnography', in F. Stein (ed) *The Open Encyclopedia of Anthropology*. Facsimile of the first edition in *The Cambridge Encyclopedia of Anthropology*. http://doi.org/10.29164/18ethno.

Howes, D. (2009) 'Introduction: The revolving sensorium', in D. Howes (ed) *The Sixth Sense Reader*. Oxford: Berg, pp. 1–6.

Hurd, E.S. (2015) *Beyond Religious Freedom: The New Global Politics of Religion*. Princeton, NJ: Princeton University Press.

Istratii, R. (2021) *Adapting Gender and Development to Local Religious Contexts: A Decolonial Approach to Domestic Violence in Ethiopia*. London: Routledge.

Jackson, M. (1989) *Paths Toward a Clearing: Radical Empiricism and Ethnographic Inquiry*. Bloomington, IN: Indiana University Press.

Jackson, M. (1998) *Minima Ethnographica: Intersubjectivity and the Anthropological Project*. Chicago, IL: Chicago University Press.

James, W. (1909) *A Pluralistic Universe*. London and Lincoln, NE: University of Nebraska Press.

Janson, M. (2014) *Islam, Youth and Modernity in The Gambia: The Tablighi Jama'at*. Cambridge: Cambridge University Press.

Jones, B. and Petersen, M.J. (2011) 'Instrumental, narrow, normative? Reviewing recent work on religion and development', *Third World Quarterly*, 32(7), pp. 1291–1306.

Kane, O.O. (2012) *Non-Europhone Intellectuals*. Dakar: CODESRIA.

Khoja-Moolji, S. (2018) *Forging the Ideal Educated Girl: The Production of Desirable Subjects in Muslim South Asia*. Oakland, CA: University of California Press.

Killam, L.A. (2013) *Research Terminology Simplified: Paradigms, Axiology, Ontology, Epistemology and Methodology*. Sudbury, ON: Laura Killam.

Levinson, B.A. and Holland, D.C. (1996) 'The cultural production of the educated person: An introduction', in B.A. Levinson, D.E. Foley, and D.C. Holland (eds) *The Cultural Production of the Educated Person*. Albany, NY: State University of New York Press, pp. 1–56.

Lugones, M. (2007) 'Heterosexualism and the colonial/modern gender system', *Hypatia*, 22(1), pp. 186–209.

Mahmud, A. and Islam, M. (2023) 'Intersectional oppression: A reflexive dialogue between Muslim academics and their experiences of Islamophobia and exclusion in UK Higher Education', *Sociology Compass*, 17(2), pp. 41–52.

Maldonado-Torres, N. (2007) 'On the coloniality of being', *Cultural Studies*, 21(2–3), pp. 240–270.

Maldonado-Torres, N. (2020) *Religious Studies in/and the Decolonial Turn, Contending Modernities*. Available at: https://contendingmodernities.nd.edu/decoloniality/religiousstudiesdecolonialturn/ (Accessed: 30 November 2022).

Marshall, K. (2010) 'Education for all: Where does religion come in?', *Comparative Education*, 46(3), pp. 273–287.

Meghji, A. (2020) 'Towards a theoretical synergy: Critical race theory and decolonial thought in Trumpamerica and Brexit Britain', *Current Sociology*, 70(5), pp. 647–664.

Mignolo, W.D. (2002) 'The geopolitics of knowledge and the colonial difference', *South Atlantic Quarterly*, 101(1), pp. 57–96.

Mignolo, W.D. (2007) 'Delinking: The rhetoric of modernity, the logic of coloniality and the grammar of de-coloniality', *Cultural Studies*, 21(2–3), pp. 449–514.

Mignolo, W.D. (2009) 'Epistemic disobedience, independent thought and decolonial freedom', *Theory, Culture & Society*, 26(7–8), pp. 159–181.

Mignolo, W.D. (2011) *The Darker Side of Western Modernity: Global Futures, Decolonial Options*. Durham, NC: Duke University Press.

Mignolo, W.D. and Escobar, A. (2009) *Globalization and the Decolonial Option*. London: Routledge.

Moosavi, L. (2015) 'White privilege in the lives of Muslim converts in Britain', *Ethnic and Racial Studies*, 38(11), pp. 1918–1933.

Moosavi, L. (2020) 'The decolonial bandwagon and the dangers of intellectual decolonisation', *International Review of Sociology*, 30(2), pp. 332–354.

Ndlovu-Gatsheni, S.J. (2015) 'Decoloniality as the future of Africa', *History Compass*, 13(10), pp. 485–496.

Nxumalo, F. and Villanueva, M.T. (2020) '(Re)storying water: Decolonial pedagogies of relational affect with young children', in B.P. Dernikos et al. (eds) *Mapping the Affective Turn in Education: Theories, Research, and Pedagogies*. New York: Routledge, pp. 208–228.

Nye, M. (2017) *Some Thoughts on the Decolonization of Religious Studies, Medium*. Available at: https://medium.com/religion-bites/decolonisation-of-religious-studies-993727c6d1bc (Accessed: 30 November 2022).

Nye, M. (2019) 'Decolonizing the study of religion', *Open Library of Humanities*, 5(1), pp. 1–45.

Ogunnaike, O. (2020) 'Islamic philosophies of education in Africa', in J.M. Abidogun and T. Falola (eds) *The Palgrave Handbook of African Education and Indigenous Knowledge*. Cham, Switzerland: Palgrave Macmillan, pp. 421–450.

Ortega, M. (2017) 'Decolonial woes and practices of un-knowing', *Journal of Speculative Philosophy*, 31(3), pp. 504–516.

Pedersen, M.H. (2017) 'Becoming Muslim in a Danish provincial town', in A. Strhan, S.B. Ridgely, and S. Parker (eds) *The Bloomsbury Reader in Religion and Childhood*. London and New York: Bloomsbury Publishing, pp. 131–137.

Pool, F.W. (2020) 'Development within a religious ontology? The argument from Islamic dharma', *European Journal of Development Research*, 32, pp. 1038–1056.

Probyn, E. (2004) 'Teaching bodies: Affects in the classroom', *Body & Society*, 10, pp. 21–43.
Puwar, N. (2020) 'Puzzlement of a déjà vu: Illuminaries of the global South', *The Sociological Review*, 68(3), pp. 540–556.
Quijano, A. (2007) 'Coloniality and modernity/rationality', *Cultural Studies*, 21(2–3), pp. 168–178.
Ridgely, S.B. (2017) 'Faith co-creation in US Catholic churches: How first communicants and faith formation teachers shape Catholic identity', in A. Strhan, S.B. Ridgely, and S. Parker (eds) *The Bloomsbury Reader in Religion and Childhood*. London and New York: Bloomsbury Publishing, pp. 139–145.
Rosa, M.C. (2014) 'Theories of the South: Limits and perspectives of an emergent movement in social sciences', *Current Sociology Review*, 62(6), pp. 851–867.
Rudnyckyj, D. (2009) 'Spiritual economies: Islam and neoliberalism in contemporary Indonesia', *Cultural Anthropology*, 24(1), pp. 104–141.
Samson, F. and LeBlanc, M.N. (2022) 'Repenser les religiosités islamiques en Afrique: classes sociales et manières de se montrer musulman.e', *Cahiers d'études africaines*, 4(248), pp. 679–695.
Sandoval, C. (2000) *Methodology of the Oppressed*. Minneapolis, MN: University of Minnesota Press.
Scheer, M., Fadil, N. and Johansen Schepelern, B. (2019) *Secular Bodies, Affects and Emotions: European Configurations*. London: Bloomsbury Publishing.
Scheer, M., Johansen Schepelern, B. and Fadil, N. (2019) 'Secular embodiments: Mapping an emergent field', in M. Scheer, N. Fadil and B. Schepelern Johansen (eds) *Secular Bodies, Affects and Emotions: European Configurations*. London: Bloomsbury Publishing, pp. 1–14.
Sealy, T. (2022) 'The betweenness of the double stranger: British converts to Islam and patterns of belonging', *Social Compass*, 69(1), pp. 95–112.
Shaheen, M. (2024) 'Islamophobia in higher education environments', *New Directions in Higher Education*, 206, pp. 41–52.
Sparkes, J.I. (2021) Decolonizing the left and the right: Muslim mistrust of foxes and wolves. *TheMaydan.com*. Available at: https://themaydan.com/2021/02/decolonizing-the-left-and-the-right-muslim-mistrust-of-foxes-and-wolves/ (Accessed: 15 May 2022).
Stambach, A. (2020) 'Where religion and education meet in Africa', in J.M. Abidogun and T. Falola (eds) *The Palgrave Handbook of African Education and Indigenous Knowledge*. Cham, Switzerland: Palgrave Macmillan, pp. 703–714.
Stewart, C. (2001) 'Secularism as an impediment to anthropological research', *Social Anthropology*, 9(3), pp. 325–328.
Takayama, K., et al. (2016) 'Doing Southern theory: Towards alternative knowledges and knowledge practices in/for education', *Postcolonial Directions in Education*, 5(1), pp. 1–25.
Tayob, A. (2020) *The Promise of Decolonization for the Study of Religions, Contending Modernities*. Available at: https://contendingmodernities.nd.edu/decoloniality/promise-of-decolonization/ (Accessed: 30 November 2022).
Thayer-Bacon, B.J. (2017) *Relational Ontologies*. New York: Peter Lang Incorporated, International Academic Publishers.
Tlostanova, M. (2015) 'Can the post-Soviet think? On coloniality of knowledge, external imperial and double colonial difference', *Intersections*, 1(2), pp. 38–58.
Todd, Z. (2016) 'An indigenous feminist's take on the ontological turn: "Ontology" is just another word for colonialism', *Journal of Historical Sociology*, 29(1), pp. 4–22.
Tomalin, E. (2012) 'Thinking about faith-based organisations in development: Where have we got to and what next?', *Development in Practice*, 22(5–6), pp. 689–703.
Topolski, A. (2018) 'The race-religion constellation: A European contribution to the critical philosophy of race', *Critical Philosophy of Race*, 6(1), pp. 58–81.

Tuck, E. and Yang, K.W. (2012) 'Decolonization is not a metaphor', *Decolonization: Indigeneity, Education & Society*, 1(1), pp. 1–40.

Vizcaíno, R. (2020) *On Epistemic Decolonization: Praxis Beyond Metaphors, The Peace Chronicle: The Magazine of the Peace and Justice Studies Association*. Available at: www.peacejusticestudies.org/chronicle/article-6-vizcaino/ (Accessed: 8 September 2022).

Vizcaíno, R. (2021) 'Secular decolonial woes', *The Journal of Speculative Philosophy*, 35(1), pp. 71–92.

Walsh, C.E. and Mignolo, W.D. (2018) 'Introduction', in W.D. Mignolo and C.E. Walsh (eds) *On Decoloniality: Concepts, Analytics, Praxis*. Durham, NC and London: Duke University Press, pp. 1–12.

Ware, R.T. (2014) *The Walking Qur'an: Islamic Education, Embodied Knowledge, and History in West Africa*. Chapel Hill, NC: The University of North Carolina Press.

Wikan, U. (1992) 'Beyond the words: The power of resonance', *American Ethnologist*, 19(3), pp. 460–482.

Wilkinson, O. (2022) 'Re-framing common themes in religions and development research', *The Review of Faith & International Affairs*, 20(4), pp. 91–106.

Wilson, E.K. (2017) '"Power differences" and "the power of difference": The dominance of secularism as ontological injustice', *Globalizations*, 14(7), pp. 1076–1093.

Wind, M. (2024) *Towers of Ivory and Steel: How Israeli Universities Deny Palestinian Freedom*. London and New York, NY: Verso Books.

Wright, Z. V (2018) *Living Knowledge in West African Islam*. New York and Accra: Fayda Books.

Yountae, A. (2020) *A Decolonial Theory of Religion, Contending Modernities*. Available at: https://contendingmodernities.nd.edu/decoloniality/a-decolonial-theory-of-religion/ (Accessed: 29 November 2022).

Part I

Secular bias in education policies: From colonisation to Education for All

3 The evolution of Islam and education in West Africa

The field of comparative/international education can sometimes make assumptions that the 1980s onwards represents the first true example of globalisation, although postcolonial scholars push the frame back to European colonisation (Tikly, 2001; Crossley and Tikly, 2004). In contrast, decolonial scholars stretch our lens back even further when they argue that global connections pre-date European imperialisms by centuries and that we need to situate current phenomena in the context of these regional "macro-histories" (Wright, 2018, p. 5). Qur'anic schools in Senegal, for example, have existed in West Africa for a thousand years and share the majority of their teaching practices with the earliest Islamic schools in Arabia (Ware, 2014; Ogunnaike, 2020). These schools hearken back to an era before the rise of European empires when Islamic civilisations were at their apogee. Far from being considered a 'periphery' in global knowledge production, West Africa was a highly respected centre of intellectual excellence which attracted thinkers from across the Islamic world. Scholarly towns, like Timbuktu, "created fertile ground for linking and cementing ties between scholars from across the region" (Hima, 2020, p. 474) (see Figure 3.1).[1]

Hence, in the words of Islamic studies Professor Ousmane Kane, "no study of the history of education or knowledge production in West Africa will be complete unless it pays attention to this intellectual tradition" (2016, p. 18). Yet, critical CIE scholars argue that scholarship on education and development is characterised by a "lack of historical reflexivity" as well as an absence of "knowledge of ongoing anti-racist, anti-colonial struggle" (Sriprakash, Tikly and Walker, 2020, p. 687) which eclipses such histories. Later I counter this trend by providing an historical account of relationships between Islam and education in West Africa (with a focus on Senegal) which embeds Qur'anic schools in the intellectual history of the Islamic world before, during and after the violence of colonial occupation.

For two decades, anthropologists, historians and religious studies scholars of Islamic West Africa (e.g. Brenner, 2000; Kane, 2012, 2016; Ware, 2014; Launay and Ware, 2016; Ogunnaike, 2020) have analysed the differences in content and pedagogy across school types in the region, especially

DOI: 10.4324/9781003172475-4

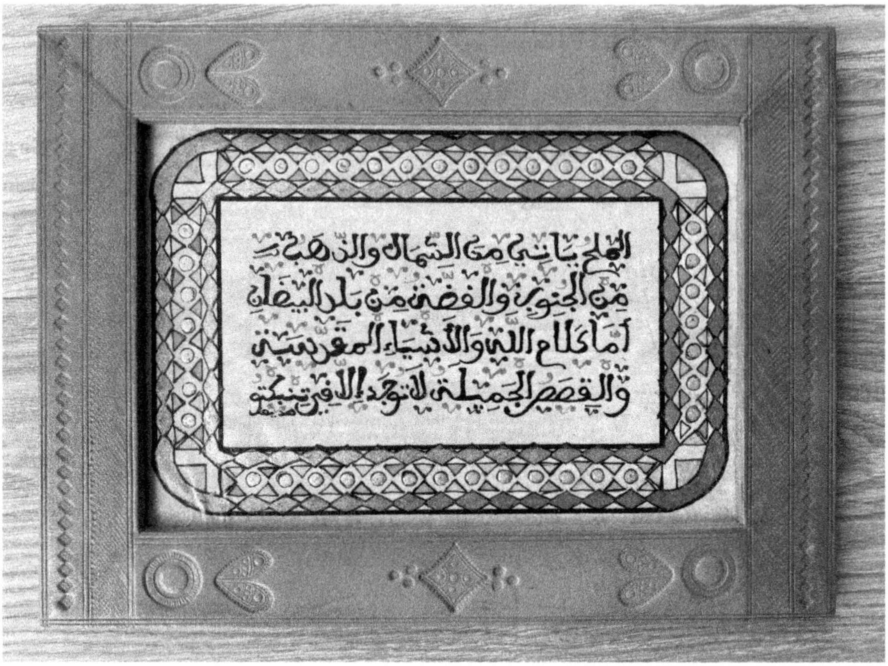

Figure 3.1 **Islamic calligraphy from Timbuktu, Mali.** By artist Boubacar Sadek. *Credit:* Anneke Newman.

the particularities of Qur'anic schools, through the lens of epistemology. Drawing on this rich literature, I offer an account of the content and pedagogy of Qur'anic schools in West Africa and the Sahel[2] grounded in an understanding of both classical Islamic worldviews and the social hierarchies specific to the region. In the second section, I move to consider how European colonial administrators across the Islamic world positioned Qur'anic schools as an obstacle to their attempts to draw local populations into their civilising mission and extractivist economic projects. Their policies involved denigrating Qur'anic education and imposing their own schools to bring the population under control. I then zoom in on the specific policies of the colony of *Afrique Occidentale Française* (AOF) or French West Africa, which encompassed what is now Senegal, in order to show the varied responses of Muslim education providers and parents to this rupture in their understandings of knowledge and valued forms of transmission. Such responses ranged from those who preferred colonial school models, the offer from Muslim reformists who re-shaped their curricula and pedagogies when inspired by such schools, to providers of Qur'anic schools who aimed to sustain a classical Islamic epistemology – including as a form of resistance.

To understand these complex processes, I coin the notion of an *ontological regime complex* to capture differences in school models and demand across the region but also their representations in academic and policy literature. My definition of a *regime* is inspired by anthropological usage (Costa, 2019), namely a set of practices, both material and symbolic, through which norms and rules are established, including who or what is considered to be valuable, legitimate or authoritative. A regime *complex* is a system in which multiple regimes co-exist, intersect or conflict to produce a distinct outcome. An *ontological* regime complex in relation to education refers to the ways in which onto-epistemological understandings and moral values intersect with social, political and economic dynamics to influence education supply and engagement, as well as representations of these phenomena. Finally, my use of this concept takes as given that our understanding of the power relations informing these dynamics inevitably demands a decolonial perspective.

In line with a postsecular and decolonial approach to the study of 'religion' (Nye, 2019; Fitzgerald, 2020; Vizcaíno, 2021), to construct this historical narrative I have made sure to draw on the work of scholars who explicitly challenge the modernist/colonialist logics and Eurocentrism embedded in both colonial education policies and subsequent Euro-North American academic accounts of Islamic education. I also draw on theorising from West African and Sufi Muslim standpoints and/or researchers who draw on sources by scholars embedded within African Islamic intellectual traditions who communicate(d) in Arabic and African languages rather than Europhone languages. In so doing, I address the relative side-lining of African thinkers within decolonial debates (Ndlovu-Gatsheni, 2018). My starting point is the content and pedagogy of Qur'anic schools in the region of West Africa. These characteristics date back many centuries but I describe them in the present tense where they are still applicable today.

Content and pedagogy of classical Qur'anic schools

The content and pedagogy of Qur'anic schools in West Africa have received significant criticism from European observers since the colonial period. Louis Brenner first argued, based on an historical and ethnographic study of Islamic schools in Mali (2000), that these criticisms are grounded in the fact that classical Qur'anic and secular European schools were based on what he described, following Foucault, as fundamentally different *epistemes.* Later theorists (e.g. Ware, 2014; Launay, 2016; Ogunnaike, 2020) refer to these assumptions about knowledge as *epistemologies.* Later I describe the content of a classical Qur'anic school education, its principal pedagogies and why understanding them requires an appreciation of both their Islamic epistemology and the socio-economic and political characteristics of the region in which they emerged. From a pedagogic point of view, the key elements I describe are memorisation and recitation, moral and spiritual transformation, and practical and livelihood skills.

Memorisation and recitation

The core 'curriculum' of Qur'anic schools in West Africa is correct pronunciation and memorisation of the Qur'an – at minimum a few short verses for prayers, at most the entire text (Diallo, 2013). Qur'anic education is therefore central to being a Muslim because the second pillar of the Islamic faith involves performing the five mandatory daily prayers (Hima, 2020, p. 500). Importantly, in Sub-Saharan Africa, the spread of Islam was not accompanied by arabisation and Qur'anic schools used African languages as their language of instruction (LOI). Hence, students learned 'Qur'anic literacy' (Diallo, 2013, p. 95), a form of literacy which entails learning to both recognise and eventually reproduce Arabic script and to identify and produce equivalent sounds in order to recite verses. Students would eventually learn the 'gist' of the verses' meanings but not necessarily their exact nuanced meanings. In contrast, 'Arabic literacy' – namely learning to read, understand and write the Arabic language – was only taught once Qur'anic memorisation was completed and only in a smaller number of specialised schools (ibid., p. 95).

Comparative educationalist Helen Boyle has argued that, within much academic and policy discourse, memorisation is associated with mindless rote learning and indoctrination – hence the opposite of understanding and critical thinking (2006, p. 480). However, based on a review of classical Islamic scholarship and ethnography in Qur'anic schools in Yemen, Nigeria and Morocco in the 2000s, Boyle argued that Qur'anic literacy is a "far more learner-oriented and meaningful process than is typically described" (ibid., p. 480). This is because, within classical Islamic understandings of knowledge, memorisation of the Qur'an was considered the first step towards understanding and reasoning, not a substitute for them (ibid., p. 488).

In fact, Islam places huge importance on knowledge (*'ilm*) which is the third-most-mentioned term in the Qur'an after Allah (God) and Rabb (Lord) (ibid., p. 485). Knowledge is divided into two types: 'revealed knowledge' which comes directly from God, versus that derived from the material universe including human reason or empirical study. While both are considered essential, revealed knowledge, of which the Qur'an is considered the highest example, is held to be superior – hence the importance of committing it to memory. Furthermore, contrary to schools with age-graded classrooms, Qur'anic schools group students together according to their level of proficiency who then learn at their individual pace (ibid., p. 487).

Moral and spiritual transformation

Memorisation of the Qur'an serves a deeper moral and spiritual purpose. Through an ethnography with Sufi clerics in Senegal, Rüdiger Seesemann (2017) concluded that, within classical Islamic epistemologies, values and knowledge were considered inseparable. The acquisition of religious disposition (*adab*) or comportment, as well as good actions (*'amal*) – and the power of the intellect (*'aql*) – were understood to be mutually reinforcing. Based on in-depth interviews with Senegalese Sufi practitioners and reading texts by renowned historical Sufis, religious studies scholar Oludamini Ogunnaike showed that the Qur'anic school's primary aim is to impart a moral education designed to transform students into a living example of the revelation. In other words, the schools moulded students who could apply Islamic values to any context (2020, p. 426). Strong emphasis is, therefore, placed on seeking knowledge for the right reasons, as is the imperative to translate knowledge into virtuous practice for the benefit of self and society, in the present and hereafter (ibid., p. 422). Memorisation of the Qur'an has several pedagogical justifications built around the classical Islamic principle of "learn *adab* before you acquire knowledge" (Seesemann, 2017, p. 25) since Muslim clerics fear that, until an individual has acquired moral virtues, it is dangerous that they engage in Qur'anic interpretation.

Teaching values through discursive means (*ta'lim*) is only one method through which this transformation is achieved. Other methods like consuming the Qur'an, strict discipline and imitation of the clerics' exemplary behaviour are also important (2014). Rudolph Ware's research, which compares autobiographical accounts by Qur'anic students in Senegal in the colonial period and participant observation in Qur'anic schools in the 2000s, reveals how the moral development of the student was – and continues to be – premised on a profound physical and metaphysical transformation. These pedagogies cannot therefore be understood without appreciating classical Islamic worldviews based on God's oneness and the unity of His creation (*tawhid*). Such ontologies make no hard distinction between mind and body, the material and spiritual, the moral and intellectual, this life and the afterlife (Ogunnaike, 2020). As Halimatou Hima explains, "Islamic education holds a metaphysical character. It is a space where the familiar meets the mystical. . . . There is a spiritual element to learning" (2020, p. 479). These elements are important to stress because they underpin the Qur'anic schools' value in the eyes of West African Muslims – a value which can be largely hidden from those experiencing the world from a secular perspective.

Moreover, revealed knowledge – particularly the Qur'an – possesses value not only as a literal text but also because it is imbued with a sacred force or God's grace, known as *baraka* (Ogunnaike, 2020, p. 436). *Baraka* cleanses the heart, soul and thus intellect. Acquiring *baraka* – and incorporating it into one's body – otherwise known as embodiment – is therefore an essential aspect of a student's moral education in the Qur'anic school. Once embodied it would act like a magnet or moral compass, nudging the individual in the direction of God (Boyle, 2006, pp. 491–493). Embodying the Qur'an's *baraka* is considered to be optimally achieved through recitation, but other methods are also used. Qur'anic verses are written on to wooden tablets using ink made from soot, and *baraka* can be acquired by drinking or bathing in the liquid created by washing the ink off the wooden tablets (Ware, 2014, p. 9).

Other elements of the Qur'anic pedagogies which Arab and European observers alike have long documented include the strict discipline that Qur'anic school students in West Africa receive, which can include beatings (Kane, 2016, p. 10). Such discipline is used to instil respect for the text and protect it from mispronunciation. Higher cognitive faculties like reason are also considered to require mental and physical discipline (Boyle, 2006, p. 489). The classical Qur'anic schools also require that students endure physical and psychological hardship. During the pre-colonial period they were typically based on a residential model whereby students were conferred to the clerics' care for several years from childhood onwards, a phenomenon which endures today. Students also beg for alms from the local community, a practice that today appears mainly restricted to West Africa (Macleod, 2021, p. 26). These pedagogies are considered to teach *adab* including humility, generosity and the ability to withstand difficult life conditions (Ware, 2014, pp. 45–47). Despite the hardships students endured, before colonisation such an education was considered a sign of privilege and the best way to become a good Muslim (ibid., p. 90). Yet, despite these apparently harsh methods, classical scholars also stressed how children should be allowed to rest and play (Ogunnaike, 2020, p. 437).

Another notable element in the spiritual transformation of students in Qur'anic schools is the close relationship between student and teacher which often endures throughout life (Kane, 2016, pp. 12–14). This is because clerics are revered not only for their knowledge but also for being model Muslims whose example students learn through socialisation (*tarbiya*) and imitation (*taqlid*). Hence, imitation of the teacher's behaviour and mannerisms was as central a part of the education process as the texts that students were expected to read (Ware, 2014, p. 49). Clerics can also pass their *baraka* on to their students through physical touch or prayer. Indeed, "in much of West Africa, the *marabout* or *malam* is thought to have powers that transcend human understanding" (Hima, 2020, p. 479). For these reasons, individualised instruction is valued over knowledge acquired through disembodied, written texts. The written qualification to become a teacher – or *ijaza* – is accorded to those who memorised key texts in respected Qur'anic schools and who show exemplary religiosity (Ogunnaike, 2020, p. 421).

Practical and livelihood skills

Discussions about Qur'anic schools within comparative/international education literature and policy reports often end here, after unpacking their formal curriculum based on memorisation. They therefore tend to conclude that their value, if any is recognised at all, is spiritual and social (Boyle, 2006). However, this ignores how Qur'anic schools constitute the most basic level of Islamic education. Qur'anic interpretation (*tafsir*), legal sciences (*fiqh*), Islamic history, poetry and lively debate on these topics are taught at advanced levels. Moreover, Qur'anic schools are integrated into the economic activities of religious communities, so students learn skills relevant to livelihoods in farming or trade (Kane, 2016, pp. 13–14). This process of skills acquisition is part of the Qur'anic schools' informal or 'hidden' curriculum.

Students who live in Qur'anic schools in rural areas work the clerics' fields and, in return, receive knowledge and *baraka* but also agricultural skills (Ware, 2014, pp. 225–230). Advanced students could also become teachers, jurists, or receive income for officiating at life-cycle ceremonies (Kane, 2016, pp. 13–14). In West Africa, from the eighteenth century onwards, the longstanding model of Qur'anic students working for Muslim clerics started to overlap with affiliation of student-disciples to Sufi leaders who were part of institutionalised Sufi orders. In Senegambia especially, Sufi orders became the dominant form of Islamic social and economic organisation. These orders were characterised by strong networks of reciprocity based on ties both biological and spiritual and organised around a hub of agriculture, trade and religious services (Ware, 2014, p. 187).

Qur'anic schools also confer additional practical skills useful in Islamic contexts. As Abdullahi El-Tom explains, classical Islamic onto-epistemologies understand that Qur'anic verses – and Arabic letters and numerals – have properties that act upon the material world (1987, p. 243). The 'esoteric sciences' (Soares, 2005, p. 127) refer to knowledge of the secret meanings of Qur'anic verses and how to manipulate Arabic letters and numerals to ensure good fortune, heal, bring rain or protect others from dangerous natural and supernatural forces – a skill I refer to as 'esoteric literacy'. Esoteric sciences can also encompass Islamic astrology, numerology, geomancy, divination, dream interpretation or exorcism of malevolent spirits or *jinn* (Brenner, 2007). Muslim clerics often participate in the 'prayer economy', namely, "an economy of religious practice in which substantial gifts are exchanged for blessings, prayers and intercession with God" (Soares, 2005, p. 11) or sell products of the esoteric sciences, including amulets and medicines, to supplement their incomes (Ware, 2014, p. 79). While "the mode of transmission of amulets and other forms of 'secret' knowledge is often kept separate from (formal) religious education" (Launay, 2016, p. 10), advanced students can acquire it over time (Brenner, 2007; Kane, 2016).

Finally, in addition to Qur'anic, Arabic and esoteric literacy, Qur'anic schools in West Africa can also encourage *Ajami* literacy. Meikal Mumin explains that *Ajami* is the practice of employing Arabic script to write languages other than Arabic and has been documented for at least 80 African languages, from the tenth century onwards (2014, pp. 41–46) (see Figure 3.2). This phenomenon has only received significant attention from Euro-North American historians, anthropologists and linguists during the last 20 years or so. According to linguists Friederike Lüpke and Sokhna Bao-Diop, *Ajami* "is (near to) invisible to educators, language planners and development activists" (2014, p. 86). Sometimes *Ajami* literacy is taught deliberately, and there is evidence from Guinea, for instance, that a catechism was used in the nineteenth century to teach students *Ajami* literacy after they completed Qur'anic memorisation (Huméry, 2014, p. 185). However, *Ajami* literacy is not always part of the

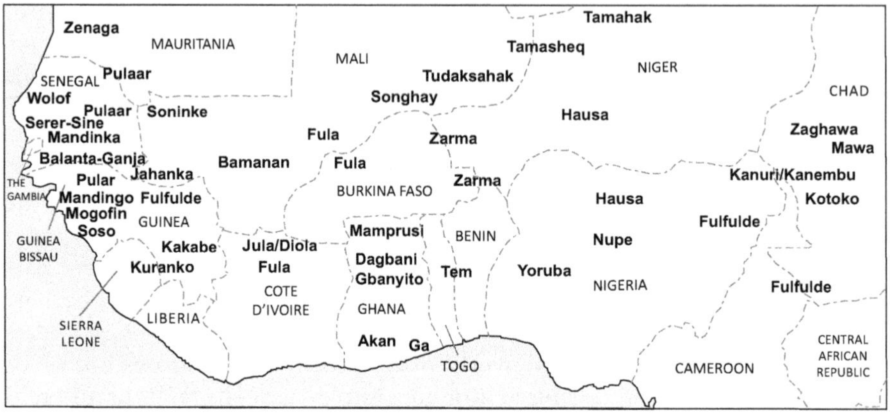

Figure 3.2 **West African languages for which *Ajami* use is attested**. Based on Mumin (2014, p. 45).

Credit: Anneke Newman and Isabelle Renneson.

formal Qur'anic school curriculum. Rather, advanced learners and clerics often appropriate(d) the Arabic script in ad hoc ways to write for personal purposes, both religious and secular (Diallo, 2013; Mumin, 2014). Nonetheless, by the eighteenth century, *Ajami* literacy was thoroughly embedded in West African Muslim societies, particularly the Sufi empires in what are now Guinea, Mali, Senegambia, northern Nigeria and Cameroon (Huméry, 2014; Lüpke and Bao-Diop, 2014).

Despite the "colonial myth" that "literacy was introduced to Africa by European settlers and missionaries", *Ajami* in fact represented a "powerful intellectual revolution" (Diallo, 2013, pp. 92–93) which enriched African languages and created a common regional Islamic culture and identity. It was used for religious, political, administrative, poetic and personal texts. Sufi leaders in the eighteenth and nineteenth centuries even taught it through mass literacy campaigns to people, such as women and slaves, who had limited access to formal Qur'anic education (Huméry, 2014; Lüpke and Bao-Diop, 2014). Furthermore, colonial powers were aware – yet suspicious – of *Ajami*, and they deliberately suppressed its use by promoting the writing of African languages using Roman/Latin script instead (Lüpke and Bao-Diop, 2014, p. 90). In fact, Mamadou Sall (2020, pp. 552–553) shows, from colonial archives, that in the early twentieth century the French used *Ajami* to communicate with the masses in AOF by employing it on banknotes and in correspondence. However, they soon suppressed communication with local Muslims in *Ajami* as well Arabic on the basis of the theory of *islam noir* and favoured use of Roman/Latin script instead.

Social hierarchies and knowledge-power

My account of Qur'anic school content and pedagogy has so far stressed the importance of classical Islamic worldviews which have endured until the present, but it is equally important to consider how socio-political dynamics have also shaped knowledge transmission. Historians like Rudolph Ware and Sylviane Diouf have shown how educated Muslims from Senegambia were powerful advocates for social justice in the eighteenth and nineteenth centuries, mobilising their knowledge, spiritual power, and military skills to challenge the enslavement of Africans during the Transatlantic slave trade. This phenomenon proved determinant during the slave rebellions in Saint Dominique, now Haiti (Diouf, 1998), and Muslim reformers from Senegal even inspired the Quaker abolitionists in England (Ware, 2014, pp. 115–118). These historians argue that such phenomena demand a renewed focus on Islam in the struggles of Africans and Africa's diasporas, which has often been eclipsed by an emphasis on African Traditional Religions and Christianity. Such arguments are a powerful example of what it means to re-narrativise world history from the perspectives of colonial peripheries (Crossley and Tikly, 2004) and regional macro-histories (Wright, 2018, p. 5) which connect and draw inspiration from margin-to-margin movements of anti-imperial resistance.

Yet, as Africanist anthropologist Jean-François Bayart argues, there is a risk of romanticising anti-imperialistic movements if we ignore their own internal hierarchies (2010). Qur'anic schools in Senegambia emerged in a context characterised by hierarchies along the axes of age, gender and descent. They were similar to pre-colonial African systems of education more generally in that they were "to mold character and prepare for a specific occupation" as well as "maintain social 'harmony' and hierarchies" because "children often studied and received instruction in line with their forefathers' occupation and mothers' roles" (Hima, 2020, p. 469). Hence, justification of long-term memorisation to form moral persons notwithstanding, this pedagogy also reflected how young people were subordinate to the power of elders, men in particular.

In the mid-2000s, Marloes Janson showed from ethnography in The Gambia that young people are still expected to defer to the authority of elders, and knowledge is framed as something produced by elders and acquired by youth. The latter are considered to lack advanced faculties of understanding (*fahm*) and reason (*'aql*) (2010). While Islamic knowledge is, in theory, public and available to everyone, in reality its acquisition takes time and dedication. This is even more the case for esoteric sciences: given the power and prestige this knowledge confers, teachers will only impart their secrets to family members or students after they show years or even decades of sufficiently virtuous behaviour (Brenner, 2007, pp. 11–12).

In addition, in West Africa and the Sahel, Qur'anic school education has also reflected local forms of racialised distinction based on descent. Scholars have documented how, from the twelfth and thirteenth centuries, West

African Muslims had developed into a distinct clerical class making a living from Qur'anic teaching and the esoteric sciences (Willis, 1978). These communities inserted themselves into the social structure across the region which divided people into freeborn, artisan/musician and slave ranks which were largely endogamous and observed social segregation. Each group within these ranks was associated with a hereditary occupation which required both technical and mystic knowledge or, in the words of anthropologist Roy Dilley, 'lore' or 'knowledge-power' (Dilley, 2004, p. 4). In such a context, Islam functioned almost as a hereditary craft (Launay and Soares, 1999; Brenner, 2000). Even in societies where everyone was Muslim, outward demonstrations of piety – such as praying, fasting and abstaining from alcohol – were usually practiced by members of clerical lineages who were associated with the professions of teacher, jurist, healer and purveyor of Islamic esoteric sciences. Islamic knowledge underpinned the clerics' group identity and livelihood and was therefore closely guarded (Brenner, 2000; Dilley, 2004). Generally, members of artisan/musician and slave lineages were barred from Qur'anic schools entirely, and other freeborn lineages were excluded from advanced Islamic education (Willis, 1978; Dilley, 2004; Ware, 2014). This trend still persists in some parts of Senegambia as the ethnographic chapters of this book later demonstrate.

Gender norms also structured knowledge acquisition in the Qur'anic schools. Norms across different Muslim communities differed but, generally, from the Medieval period onwards, men tended to exclude women from the most powerful forms of Islamic knowledge (Kalmbach, 2012). Several historians have shown that, during the pre-colonial period, women from clerical families in West Africa could learn the Qur'an and even advanced Islamic sciences at home (Mack and Boyd, 2000; Robinson, 2000). However, generally women did not attend residential or boarding rural Qur'anic schools and tended to only learn basic verses for praying at home or as day students (Hima, 2020, p. 478). However, accounts by Senegalese observers in the 1920s note that such girls also learned *Ajami* literacy for domestic purposes (Ware, 2014, p. 159). Women also had less access to powerful forms of esoteric Islamic knowledge. Moreover, anthropologists working in Mali (Soares, 2005) and Senegal (Mueller, 2013) have shown that female spheres of esoteric knowledge, particularly relating to spirit possession, were characterised by male clerics as non-Islamic, immoral and potentially dangerous.

In conclusion, before European colonisation "Qur'anic schools . . . were socially embedded institutions of learning which, even if often rudimentary in appearance, were highly developed" (Hima, 2020, p. 473). They were also "complementary in the formation of personhood found in traditional African education" (ibid., p. 477) in that they reproduced a strong sense of community but also social hierarchies. Whilst the pedagogies of Qur'anic schools in West Africa have developed from within over time, including expanding access for women and individuals from subordinate castes, an understanding of the history of their treatment under colonisation is also vital to any interpretation of contemporary school preferences among Senegalese parents and their children.

Race, religion, capitalist extraction: Colonial schools and education policy

The evolution of classical Qur'anic education was affected by European colonisation which profoundly transformed Islamic West African societies from the nineteenth century onwards. This section demonstrates how the region was sucked into the orbit of racialised capitalism accompanied by the imposition of what Barbara Thayer-Bacon would call an onto-epistemological net (2017) underpinned by Eurocentric, rationalist and modernist logics. Policies towards Qur'anic schools – and the implantation of new school systems with a profoundly different form and purpose – were central to the colonial project. From this period onwards, the educational landscape in West Africa saw the development of an ontological regime complex in which school models reflecting vastly different worldviews and understandings of knowledge came to compete for legitimacy. Qur'anic schools in Senegal were drawn into this struggle, their providers reacting in diverse ways to pressures to reform according to secular Eurocentric ontological and epistemological norms. In the following sections, I map some of those pressures, starting with French colonial policy.

French colonial policy towards Qur'anic schools and Islamic education

European colonial administrations differed in their constructions of the ideal role of religion in public schools. In British, Portuguese and Belgian colonies, Christian mission schools were encouraged (White, 1996; Madeira, 2005). In contrast, as Christopher Harrison (1988) has shown through an analysis of French government policies towards Islam in the colony of *Afrique Occidentale Française* (AOF) (see Figure 3.3), religion was progressively excluded from public schools from the early twentieth century onwards. This was due to the model of *laïcité* – or strict division between church and state – enshrined in French law in 1905 (1988, p. 59). These differences between colonial powers notwithstanding, "Islamic education has never had a positive reception in the West since colonial times" (Loimeier, 2009, p. 8) and "the central bone of contention was the very nature of knowledge and its transmission" (Launay, 2016, p. 10).

During the colonial period, the classical Qur'anic schools' focus on memorisation before literal understanding was strongly criticised by colonial administrators. Using archives in Nigeria, Senegal and Zanzibar, Roman Loimeier concludes that "in both British and French colonies, learning in Qurānic schools was often characterized as being 'without pedagogic value' or was simply referred to as 'parrot talk'" (2009, p. 8). Moreover, the idea that the Qur'anic text could hold intrinsic properties able to act upon the world through the recitation of verses or wearing of amulets was considered, as one

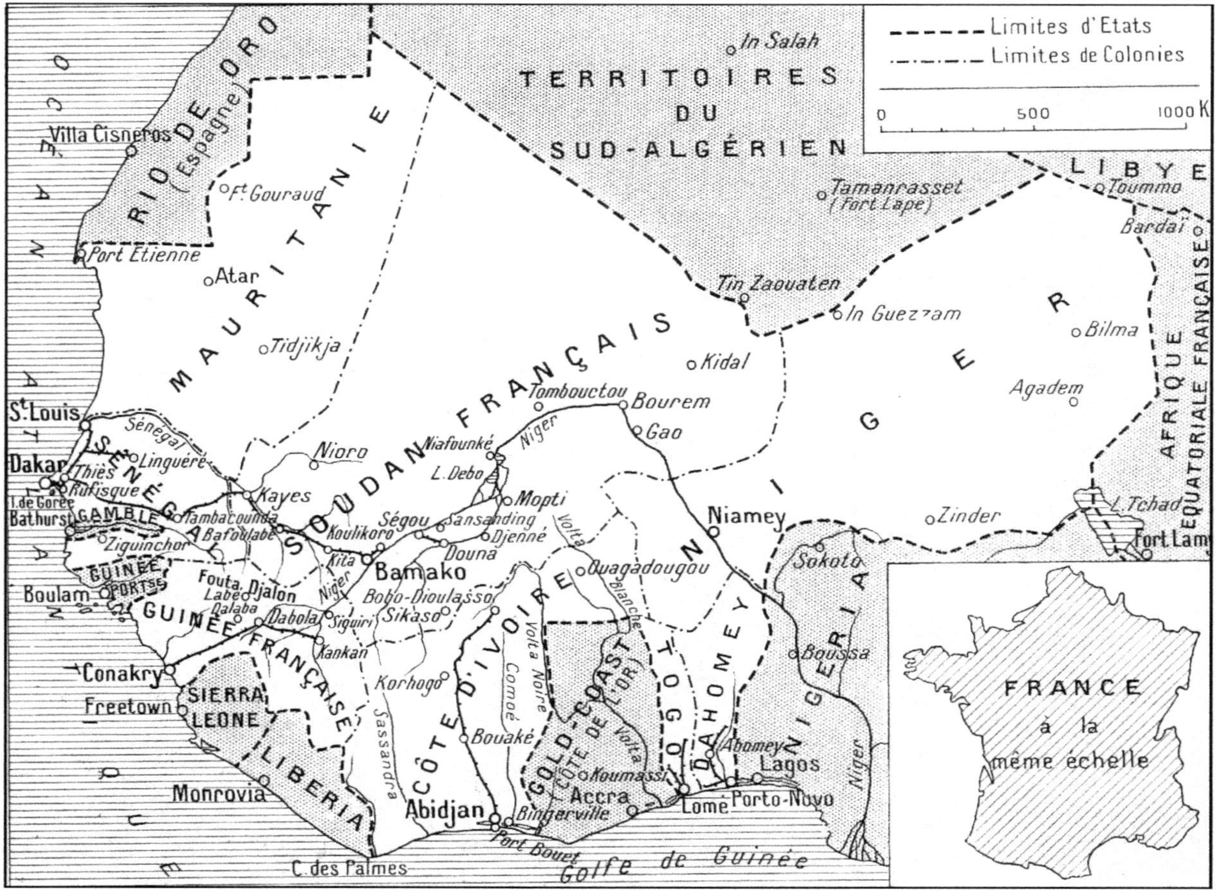

Figure 3.3 **The eight colonies of *Afrique Occidentale Française* (AOF) 1895–1958**. From L'Illustration: L'oeuvre de la France en Afrique occidentale, n°4852. 29 February 1936, p. 261.

French administrator in the 1900s put it, "ridiculous superstitions" (Harrison, 1988, p. 47). The norms surrounding hygiene, corporal punishment and begging were also criticised, which ignored the classical Islamic epistemological foundations of these pedagogies or the realities of living conditions more generally. One report from AOF in 1911 stated that Qur'anic schools were "only a pretext to exploit the religious sentiment of the masses by using the boys which are confided to them to beg" (Ware, 2014, pp. 239–240). The French first attempted to prohibit students from begging in 1857 but with little success (Macleod, 2021, p. 41). Furthermore, the morality of teachers was considered irrelevant to knowledge transmission. Their legitimacy to instruct was granted through state-granted diplomas, not *ijaza* testifying to their morality (Harrison, 1988; Ware, 2014).

Colonial administrators in Muslim contexts evaluated the utility of Islamic education more broadly according to their economic and political objectives, not just their secular values. As one administrator in AOF argued in 1917, "the first requirement of the education which we give in our colonies should be one of practical utility, first of all for us and then for the natives" (Harrison, 1988, p. 57). Qur'anic schools were perceived as a barrier to enrolment in government-provided schools and, by extension, colonial influence and interests. Hence, some administrations created 'hybrid' government-controlled Islamic schools or incorporated those elements of Islamic knowledge which they perceived as useful into mainstream schools. Such policies were pursued to undermine the Muslim clerics' power and instrumentalise the Muslim population. According to Gregory Starrett, British archives in Egypt in the 1920s and 30s reveal that "what counted as real religion could now be defined by its social utility", with anything falling outside of this sphere considered " 'superstition', targeted for elimination through centralized programs of scientific modernization" (1998, p. 71). As a result, colonial educational objectives were "for religious instruction . . . to be 'secular,' forming a part of the cultural background of the cultivated individual, and nothing more" (ibid., p. 66).

Two processes enabled colonial educators to package Islam within a European-style school curriculum alongside other subjects. The first was 'objectification' (Eickelman and Piscatori, 1996) whereby, as a result of modernisation and rationalisation processes, Islam as well as other religions came to be seen as bounded and coherent systems of beliefs and practices. Hence, differences in opinion were minimised without acknowledging the subtlety of contextual and historical factors affecting interpretation. As Starrett notes in relation to curriculum design in colonial schools in Egypt, 'knowing' Islam hence became "being able to articulate the religion as a defined set of beliefs such as those set down in textbook presentations" (1998, p. 9).

The second aspect of this modernisation/rationalisation process was 'functionalisation', namely a "translation in which intellectual objects from one discourse come to serve the strategic or utilitarian ends of another discourse" (Starrett, 1998, p. 9). In this context, the newly systematised forms of Islam were appropriated through mass education to serve colonial interests. In AOF, the main 'marketable skills' (Loimeier, 2009) that Islamic education had to offer were Arabic literacy to prepare men for positions as civil servants and interpreters and *fiqh* to train judges for tribunals sympathetic to the colonial endeavour (Harrison, 1988, p. 61).

The fact that the various colonising nations differed in their commitment towards Islamic education reform has had a significant impact on the relative abundance of Qur'anic schools in different parts of the Muslim world today. Openness to including religion in public schools meant that the British – and French in North Africa – engaged in a systematic incorporation of Qur'anic schools and clerics into the public education system. They also created extensive networks of 'hybrid' schools combining Islamic subjects in Arabic with 'secular' subjects in European languages (Starrett, 1998; Ware, 2004; Loimeier, 2009). In such contexts, classical Qur'anic schools and pedagogical methods went into serious decline from the 1920s onwards (Ware, 2014, p. 202).

In contrast, the French in West Africa hardly integrated Islam into the government education system because of their commitment to principles of *laïcité*, and a particular race-religion constellation (Topolski, 2018) developed in this context. As Robert Launay and Benjamin Soares explain, the French considered Islam to be a "potentially disruptive element" around which colonised peoples could mount resistance across ethnic and racial boundaries (1999, p. 503). In the 1910s, Paul Marty, an influential colonial administrator in AOF, overcame this paranoia of the "Islamic menace" by constructing the notion of *islam noir*, "a 'Black Islam' . . . tinged with heterodox elements" such as divination, spirit possession, talismanic uses of the Qur'an and supposedly blind popular allegiance to charismatic Sufi clerics. The concept was based on the logic that such supposed "syncretism . . . rendered Islam both more accessible and acceptable to the 'African character'" (ibid., p. 53). According to the logics of *islam noir*, the French aimed to co-opt the West African Sufi clerics and isolate them, as a protective measure, against the supposedly more menacing 'White' or 'Oriental' varieties of Islam of North Africa, Egypt or Arabia (ibid., p. 504). *Islam noir* had a pervasive influence despite being a "serious misrepresentation" (Launay and Soares, 1999, p. 504) of reality which read Islam in Sub-Saharan Africa through the lenses of European racial classification schemes. To provide a sense of the flawed assumptions underpinning *islam noir*, Islam had been implanted in Africa for over a millennium and was no more 'syncretic' or accommodating of local customs than anywhere else (ibid., p. 504). Moreover, many of the practices considered to be 'African' modifications of Islam, like spirit possession and use of amulets based on the Qur'anic text, appear to have been introduced to the continent by Arabs rather than vice versa (Ware, 2014, p. 4).

Islam noir strongly informed French education policy in AOF. To illustrate, policy-makers initially experimented with '*médersas*' combining Arabic, Islamic sciences and 'secular' subjects in French to form a pro-colonial clerisy, as they had done in Algeria. Initial implantation of government schools was accompanied by forced conscription of the sons of noble families and aggressive policies to control the opening of Qur'anic schools. A decree from 1922 ruled that religious schools could only be recognised by the government as 'educational establishments' – and win eligibility for subsidies – if they taught in French (Ware, 2004, p. 276). However, French policy towards Qur'anic schools soon shifted as *islam noir* made them seem much less threatening. By the 1920s they had abandoned the *médersa* project on the basis that, in the words of one administrator, "amongst African blacks islamisation is synonymous with social breakdown" (Harrison, 1988, p. 149). Moreover, "instead of trying to actively intervene in and regulate them, officials prioritized limiting contact between West African and North African Muslims" by supporting Sufi leaders who they perceived as helpful to their cause (Bryant, 2020, p. 5). Ironically, French policy during this period enabled Islam to spread rapidly. Several new Sufi orders emerged in Senegal between the 1850s and 1930s whose leaders become a powerful force able to resist the colonial administration (Launay and Soares, 1999; Ware, 2014). Furthermore, "the joint expansion of Islam and Western European colonization . . . made resistance on the basis of religion an important unifying factor for the struggle for sociocultural independence and political autonomy" (Hima, 2020, p. 476).

In conclusion, because the French administration did not attempt to integrate Qur'anic schools into their school system in West Africa, these schools proliferated throughout AOF during the colonial period. Because of their contemporary geographical association with West Africa, the distinctive characteristics of Qur'anic schools – such as close teacher-student relationships, begging, corporal punishment, esoteric sciences and intimate links to Sufi orders – are often attributed by Euro-American scholars and Muslims alike to *islam noir* or the syncretic mixing of Islam with African customs. In contrast, Ware shows that these schools reflect the persistence of classical Islamic onto-epistemologies and pedagogic traits whose origins can been traced to the earliest Muslim communities in Arabia but which have mainly survived only in West Africa – ironically due to *islam noir* (Ware, 2014, p. 202).

Colonial schools

By the late nineteenth century, European colonial administrations considered implanting school systems a priority in order to control and train subjects in ways useful to the extractivist economy. At the time, there was a "broad consensus among French colonizers" that Africans were " 'primitive', 'backwards', indeed 'childlike' compared to Europeans". However, there was disagreement regarding whether Africans could assimilate according to the European "evolutionary trajectory" or were fixed in their current state (Launay and Soares, 1999, p. 502).

Differences notwithstanding, colonial schools were designed to create an entirely different kind of person to Qur'anic schools. Teaching followed a timetable based on Christian rest days and the European agricultural calendar, unlike Qur'anic schools adjusted to the local agricultural calendar and Islamic celebrations. Learning took place within state-constructed buildings with children sitting in rows at desks in front of a teacher and a blackboard, rather than sitting on the ground in the home of the cleric. Ultimately, these schools would inculcate allegiance to the state rather than to a community or God (Bryant, 2020, p. 3). As Haalpulaar novelist Cheikh Hamidou Kane wrote (1972, pp. 71–72):

> The new school shares at the same time the characteristics of the cannon and the magnet. From the cannon it draws its efficacy as an arm of combat. Better than the cannon, it makes conquest permanent. The cannon compels the body, the school bewitches the soul.

Notably, in AOF, schooling "was to imbue children with French values with the intention of producing loyal and trustworthy colonial subjects", who would be trained as teachers or "for positions in . . . the lower echelons of the Colonial Administration" (Brenner, 2000, pp. 51–52). Moreover, schooling on the French model played a key role in "reshaping Senegambian approaches to knowledge" (Ware, 2014, p. 195). Hence, "rationalism was the supreme orienting principle of all (French) education" (ibid., p. 195) and "colonial education inculcated a whole new conception of literacy centered on the disenchantment of the word" (Launay, 2016, p. 15). Therefore, school knowledge was to be associated with the intellect, its purest form considered to be abstract, written and objectifiable. The value of a text was considered to be its literal meaning and literacy was therefore considered a skill of utmost importance (Ware, 2014, p. 205).

Furthermore, as Kelly Bryant shows, in AOF "the racism inherent in colonial education" was stark, most notably in "three levels of schooling with separate curricula" (2011, pp. 299–300). French Republican ideals encouraged assimilationist rhetoric at the outset, but by the 1900s, the French colonial school system was structured in tiers according to racist logics. A top tier provided an education equivalent to the metropole. It was accessible to 'Whites (*blancs*)' and 'mixed-race *métis*'. 'Whites' was used interchangeably with 'Europeans' to refer to "people who had only European (usually French) ancestry" who "maintained a European lifestyle, spoke French at home, and were secular or Christian". *Métis* belonged to families that "had at least one European male ancestor, enjoyed French citizenship, spoke French and Wolof, and were Catholic or secular". A second tier of schools aimed to train a corps of teachers, interpreters and civil servants to undertake executive tasks. It was open to '*assimilés*', "a category which . . . mostly referred to Africans recognized as having assimilated French values, styles of dress, Catholic religion, and language". A third level of 'village' schools trained farmers and artisans in rudimentary French and maths. These schools targeted 'natives (*indigènes*)' who were "Africans, predominantly Muslim, who spoke Wolof or other African languages more than French, and who . . . did not adopt a French lifestyle" (ibid., p. 301).

From the nineteenth century, *assimilés* increasingly demanded diplomas and jobs equivalent to metropolitan standards, although politics of parity were only adopted in 1949. While an important anti-colonial cultural movement, *la négritude*, emerged in the 1930s, the Senegalese elite resisted the integration of African culture and languages into the state school system as part of a political struggle against educational apartheid (Jézéquel, 2007, p. 20). The system therefore remained strictly secular and taught in French. Since children were never taught French as a foreign language, many simply memorised lessons without understanding (Diallo, 2011).

The French colonial administrators also assumed low utility in girls' schooling. Historian Diane Barthel showed that, "throughout the first thirty years of the [twentieth] century, total enrolment of indigenous girls at public primary schools in Senegal vacillated between 200 and 500, while comparable figures for boys climbed into the 2,500–5,000 range" (1989, p. 143). It was not until the 1930s that the *assimilés* demanded further investment in girls' education to socialise their daughters and wives into European middle-class gender norms (ibid., p. 145).

Despite French colonial intentions, the administration's schools never rivalled Qur'anic schools in terms of student numbers. In 1914, in Senegal there were "1385 recorded Qur'anic schools with 11,451 students", versus "seven regional [French] schools and fifty rural schools" in the entire AOF which hosted "4014 students" (Hima, 2020, pp. 473–474). Nevertheless, colonisation wrought a massive re-organisation of political and economic relations and re-defined the relationships among knowledges, onto-epistemologies, power and status relations (Brenner, 2000; Ware, 2014; Launay, 2016). This had a complex impact on educational engagements, and two broad trends can be identified.

On the one hand, despite French efforts to the contrary, the colonial period ushered in a new Islamic public sphere (Launay and Soares, 1999) characterised by a more standardised form of Islam less differentiated along the lines of lineage or descent. The account of slavery in France's West African colonies by Martin Klein (1998) documents the rise of attempts at abolition during the 1900s and the disappearance of formal (although not domestic) slavery by the 1930s. As a result, freed people migrated to towns and the Sufi orders' agricultural hubs to work and re-define themselves free of stigma. Because the most prestigious definition of the educated person had thus far rested on Islamic education, attending a residential, rural Qur'anic school became an important strategy for these people to reclaim their dignity (Ware, 2014, pp. 168–174). The new Sufi orders which had emerged during the colonial period also made their schools accessible to all regardless of origin (Klein, 1998; Launay and Soares, 1999). Qur'anic schools located in towns, which tended to be day-schools rather than residential boarding schools, also opened up to girls. In the early decades of the twentieth century, enrolment in such schools among daughters of the new urban middle-classes rose far faster than in government schools, and girls often represented as much as half of day students (Ware, 2014, pp. 174–175).

However, government school diplomas led to the most significant economic and political opportunities in the new colonial order. Hence, a parallel trend emerged whereby parents' preferences shifted towards colonial rather than residential Qur'anic schools or towards new ways of combining the two. In towns, the popularity of a colonial education among parents led to strategies to combine it with the Qur'anic school rather than choose one over the other. One option was sending children to Qur'anic schools as day students from a younger age before they started at a government school. Another option was to send children to Qur'anic schools in the early morning and evening or during government schools' holidays (Ware, 2014, p. 193). Day students in Qur'anic schools did not have time to work for the cleric or beg so had to pay their tuition in colonial currency, requiring that their family have a cash surplus. As a result, simultaneously attending both schools became a sign of privilege, and evaluations of pedagogies associated with long-term residential Qur'anic study (like begging and working for the cleric) shifted accordingly among the emergent middle-class. Affluent urban dwellers portrayed day study as a better-quality education because students were not 'distracted' by work, although the time spent learning the Qur'an was halved. They also depicted begging and hardship as signs of genuine poverty. Elite families were therefore able to maintain their social status associated with Islamic piety while simultaneously benefitting economically from colonial schools (ibid., p. 190).

Islamic modernities and education reform

In this final section, I consider how the suppression of the ontological and epistemological principles underpinning Qur'anic schools came to be reinforced through coloniality of power. The rise of state school diplomas became the main route to social mobility in the new social order. Hence, Muslim families who were influenced by colonial discourses started to understand knowledge and education in a different way because their onto-epistemological nets were re-woven to include modernist threads. They were increasingly likely to challenge the classical modes of Islamic education I described earlier and to devise school models which strategically combined the perceived benefits of both Islamic and colonial school systems. The result would be a radical departure from the epistemology of the classical Qur'anic schools.

To appreciate these changes in Islamic onto-epistemologies, we need to understand Salafism, a reform movement "that advocated a return by Muslims to pure and simple Islam" by following the example of the rightly-guided Companions of the Prophet or *salaf* (Shahin, 2009). Salafism emerged in the Medieval period. Its proponents advocated a revival of the 'true' form of Islam by purging it of heretical innovation (*bid'ah*) which, in the Salafis' view, included the fabrication of amulets and excessive veneration of Sufi *shaykhs* that they thought amounted to polytheism (*shirk*) (ibid., 2009). From the eighteenth century, the Islamic world saw a number of 'pre-modern' Salafi movements emerge as resistance to European imperialism, the most famous being the Wahhabiyya in Arabia but which also included *jihads* led by Sufi leaders in West Africa (Robinson, 2000). The 'modern' Salafi movement crystallised in the early twentieth century and represented an even more radical shift (Shahin, 2009). Its architects were not usually educated in the classical Islamic education system and "sought to end European domination by imitating, perfecting, and Islamizing European modernity" (Kobo, 2012, p. 30).

In the words of Launay and Ware, "the single most important epistemic difference distinguishing adherents of the classical approach [to Islamic education] from [modern Salafi] reformists is that the former are convinced of the opacity of signs, the latter of their transparency" (2016, p. 261). Hence, while classical scholars understood that students had to be morally and spiritually transformed before engaging in Qur'anic interpretation, Salafis saw the value of the Qur'anic text as the literal meaning of its words, which they inferred could be understood by anyone who mastered Arabic literacy (Ogunnaike, 2020, p. 442). Meanwhile, as Ware describes (2014, p. 67), Salafis appropriated the Cartesian dualism of Eurocentric modernist thought which separates and elevates mind from body and therefore preferred pedagogies which transmitted knowledge through discourse over older methods focused on embodiment:

> The educational approach in most secular schools and many modern Islamic educational institutions . . . rests on a Cartesian divide between the mind and the body. A teacher acts primarily on the intellect, and when religious ideas are understood, the mind of the believer will compel the body to apply them. The mind orders the body, and the body responds. The idea that one could "learn" through osmosis makes no sense in this understanding.

The Salafis considered that the traditional method of teaching through personalised transmission, including students' learning *adab* through imitation of clerics' behaviour, had allowed Islam to be "corrupted by the accretion of errors and heretical beliefs" (Ogunnaike, 2020, p. 441). They argued instead that "the masses could interpret the Qur'an and sunna for themselves without the intermediaries of scholars or Sufi masters" and proposed "a more 'democratic' episteme in which anything could potentially be known by any one, regardless of his or her spiritual qualifications" (ibid., p. 441). Moreover, emphasis on acquiring *baraka* which would act directly upon the heart – through memorisation and recitation of the Qur'an, receiving prayers and *baraka* from a cleric or drinking or bathing in liquid derived from the Qur'anic text – were considered by reformists as "outdated superstition" and an unreliable means of forming moral persons (ibid., p. 441).

'Modernising' Islamic education, by creating a standardised 'hybrid' school system on the European model, became a key element of the Salafi reformists' strategies for social transformation throughout the Islamic world in the late nineteenth and twentieth centuries (Ware, 2014, p. 207). Their schools retained some memorisation of the Qur'an and moral education but Arabic literacy and learning the meaning of verses were greatly prioritised (ibid., p. 67). Arabic was taught as a foreign language from the start, with the intention that it become the language of instruction. In their hybrid school systems, reformists appropriated colonial school pedagogies with age-graded classrooms, a school day divided into subjects taught during specific time-slots, blackboards, desks and standardised exams (Brenner, 2000, p. 54). Like colonial schools, the reformists' offer was intended to be functional, including more marketable skills. Reformists also promoted a more democratic approach to knowledge acquisition with the consequence that more pupils were given access to Islamic knowledge. This led to a 'fragmentation of authority' whereby new Muslim intellectuals, who had rarely benefitted from a classical Qur'anic education, destabilised the monopoly of interpretation held by the classical clerical elite (Eickelman and Piscatori, 1996, p. 30).

Reformist onto-epistemologies and school models spread quickly throughout most of the Islamic world during the early twentieth century. However, the French in AOF were, according to Ware (2014, p. 214), so paranoid about what they saw as a 'Wahhabi' threat to *islam noir* that they suppressed any Salafi-inspired reformist groups until the 1940s. As a result, the Qur'anic schools thrived in Senegal relative to the schools of Salafi-inspired reformist associations. It was only from the 1940s onwards that reformist schools emerged in the Senegalese eduscape, and it was not until the 1970s that they started to gain significant ground (Loimeier, 2003, pp. 243–244).

However, modifications to the Qur'anic school system were not limited to schools created by anti-Sufi Salafi reformists. In the first half of the twentieth century, Sufi leaders and more ordinary Muslim clerics also started to reform their pedagogies. Their onto-epistemological nets still reflected classical Islamic principles and they recognised embodied, personalised and esoteric forms of knowledge acquisition. They continued to prioritise memorisation and employ pedagogies which involved physical hardship and transmission of *baraka*. However, they accepted the necessity to incorporate discursive forms of knowledge, like Arabic literacy and Islamic sciences, at earlier stages of instruction than was typical in the classical Qur'anic schools (Brenner, 2000, pp. 75–76). Some also taught European languages and secular subjects to benefit from government accreditation and to meet popular demand for these skills given their economic utility (Ogunnaike, 2020, p. 244). They also made Islamic education more accessible to girls and members of artisan/musician and slave lineages (Launay, 2016, p. 21). These new 'hybrid' school types, which endure today, include (a) 'Arabo-Islamic institutes' which teach study of Islamic scripture alongside Qur'anic memorisation and (b) 'Franco-Arab schools' which combine the study of Arabic and Islamic texts with French language and sometimes additional secular subjects (Loimeier, 1998; Ware, 2014).

By the time of Senegal's independence in 1960, the Qur'anic schools had also diversified into a variety of other forms which still persist today (see Table 3.1). Classical Qur'anic schools dedicated to memorisation of the Qur'an, where students beg at neighbours' houses and work the clerics' fields, are still widespread in rural areas. However, Qur'anic schools have further evolved into three broad types. They consist of: (a) day-schools where students learn at the cleric's home as a form of pre-school, or outside of public-school schedules, for a small fee; (b) itinerant schools where students travel with the cleric from rural locations to urban centres where they beg to support their tuition; and (c) boarding or *internat* Qur'anic schools where students study full-time and parents pay a sizeable tuition and maintenance fee (D'Aoust, 2013). Given this diversity of provision amongst Qur'anic and Islamic schools, by the early 2000s, there was a wide range of different types of schools in the country. As Table 3.1 indicates, their differences related as much to their longevity in the Senegalese landscape, language of instruction, subject coverage and inclusion of religion as to their pedagogic strategy.

From independence in 1960 to the early 2000s, there were two additional trends: proliferation and convergence. Structural adjustment programmes (SAPs) and the liberalisation of public services in the 1980s, combined with pressure to meet EFA and universal primary education, led to an explosion of non-state funders and providers of education including Western NGOs, transnational Islamic NGOs and local Muslim entrepreneurs (Dilger and Schulz, 2013). In a parallel trend, from the 1970s to 1990s, multilateral Islamic donors, NGOs and Arab states – Saudi Arabia especially – provided aid to African countries and associations to build schools and funded scholarships for students to attend universities in the Arab world. This was explicitly to promote Salafi/Wahhabi doctrine, yet the degree to which such ideologies were followed by African aid recipients is debatable. Furthermore, in response to popular demand, the pedagogies and content of both public and private schools have increasingly converged to feature combinations derived from both Islamic and European onto-epistemological origins (Loimeier, 2000). There has also been greater dialogue and collaboration between 'Sufis' and 'Salafi-inspired reformists', with doctrinal divides much less stark than during the colonial period (Ware, 2014, pp. 230–233).

Unfortunately, these various school types and their student numbers are not systematically quantified. When I interviewed the director of UNICEF Senegal in 2011, he estimated that there were around 15,000 Qur'anic schools compared to 8,000 state primary schools. In the late 90s, the number of children attending Qur'anic schools was estimated at between 600,000 and one million

Table 3.1 Types of schools in Senegal by the year 2000 in chronological order of emergence.

School type	*Dates from*	*Level*	*Language of instruction*	*Formal curriculum*	*Current fees*	*Government accreditation of diplomas*
Classical residential Qur'anic schools in rural areas	Tenth century	Elementary	African languages	Memorisation of the Qur'an, moral education, Islamic rituals, sometimes *Ajami* literacy	Gifts in kind, students' labour or begging, nominal cash payment	No
Advanced classical Islamic schools	Tenth century	Advanced	African languages + Arabic	Arabic language and Islamic subjects	Gifts in kind, students' labour, nominal cash payment	No
Private Catholic schools	Mid-nineteenth century	Elementary + advanced	French	State syllabus within a Catholic ontological framework	Medium-high cash payment	Yes
Public secular schools	Late nineteenth century	Elementary + advanced	French	Secular state syllabus, few hours of religious instruction and Arabic language since 2002	Nominal cash payment	Yes
Day-time Qur'anic schools	Early twentieth century	Elementary	African languages	Memorisation of the Qur'an, moral education, Islamic rituals, sometimes *Ajami* literacy	Nominal cash payment	No
Arabo-Islamic institutes	1940s	Advanced	African languages + Arabic	Memorisation of the Qur'an, Arabic language, advanced Islamic subjects	Medium-high cash payment	No
Private Franco-Arab schools	1940s	Elementary + advanced	African languages, Arabic + French	Arabic and French language, religious and secular subjects	Medium-high cash payment	No

(*Continued*)

Table 3.1 (Continued)

School type	*Dates from*	*Level*	*Language of instruction*	*Formal curriculum*	*Current fees*	*Government accreditation of diplomas*
Itinerant Qur'anic schools which migrate with children from rural to urban centres	1960s	Elementary	African languages	Memorisation of the Qur'an, moral education, Islamic rituals, sometimes *Ajami* literacy	Gifts in kind, students' begging	No
Boarding Qur'anic schools (*internat*)	1960s	Elementary	African languages	Memorisation of the Qur'an, moral education, Islamic rituals	Medium cash payment	No

(Charlier, 2002, p. 65). Recently, Shona Macleod has explained that attempts at quantifying Qur'anic schools over the last two decades vary wildly in methodology and results, with estimates of students begging in itinerant schools ranging from 6,840 to 100,000 children depending on the source (Macleod, 2021, pp. 29–32).

In terms of evolving patterns of school preference among the population, hybrid Islamic schools placing high value on literacy – and especially those which integrated secular subjects and European languages – became popular among fathers educated in West Africa's colonial schools. Later, they also appealed to young Senegalese intellectuals who followed their schooling with advanced education in Arabia or North Africa, which tended to be informed by a Salafi reformist perspective. They disagreed with the authority of the classical Muslim clerical elite and wished to reconcile their religion with 'modern' lifestyles (Loimeier, 2003, pp. 242–243). However, the schools also attracted members of the Muslim clerical elite, including leaders of Sufi orders, who sent their sons because they were attracted to the new pedagogies and wished to improve their own practice but still within a classical Islamic or Sufi paradigm (Ware, 2004, pp. 305–306; Kane, 2016, p. 444). Today, in cities and regions with a strong history of Arabo-Islamic and Franco-Arab schools, many Muslim clerics have themselves had an educational trajectory combining Qur'anic schools with these other types (Ware, 2014, pp. 224–228).

Conclusion

This chapter has provided an overview of the competing ontological regimes that have structured education provision and engagement in West Africa over the last 300 years. Essentially, there were two characteristics of the Senegalese ontological regime complex that are consistent across the multiple accounts reviewed. These features are essential to appreciate if we are to understand popular engagement with Islamic education in the contemporary context. First, under European colonialism, "epistemological change was driven by ideological attacks in the context of dramatic imbalances of power" (Ware, 2014, p. 196). Second, many African Muslims re-wove their 'onto-epistemological nets' (Thayer-Bacon, 2017) by appropriating elements of European modernity and subsequently created 'hybrid' Islamic schools. Yet, "this hybridization was never on equal terms" and often "came at the price of the whole scale adoption of the habitus of the colonial school" (Launay, 2016, p. 16). In colonial and post-colonial contexts, government schools came to embody the promise of social mobility while classical Qur'anic schools were increasingly considered by political and economic elites as relics of a bygone age.

Understanding educational dynamics in this context requires sensitivity because the epistemological perspectives held by European colonial intellectuals – and appropriated by Salafi-inspired reformist Muslim scholars – have shaped not only school provision but also academic scholarship.

The Salafi reformers appropriated the "Enlightenment dichotomy of reason versus superstition" which "overtly shuns the occult sciences and largely dismisses Islamic esoteric currents, deemed as embarrassing and backward superstitions" (Saif and Leoni, 2021, p. 11). Meanwhile, as I explained in Chapter 1, contemporary Euro-North American scholarship on Islam in Africa often reproduces the assumptions of *islam noir*. Indeed, Islamic studies literature often imposes a distinction between 'religion' as orthodoxy, while 'magic' supposedly refers to the syncretic and heterodox "modification of pre-Islamic and non-Islamic magical models and genres" (ibid., p. 18). This has resulted in the marginalisation of serious study of the Islamic esoteric sciences in disciplines such as history, Islamic studies and anthropology until the last decade (ibid., p. 11), including in relation to education. This framing fails to appreciate the fact that, before colonisation, Muslim scholars considered the study of the esoteric sciences to be reputable and on par with other natural sciences (ibid., pp. 2–4), and these practices continue to be extremely prevalent within contemporary Islamic societies (Brenner, 2007, p. 7). Inspired by decolonial debates, Saif and Leoni therefore advocate for "the value of studying and researching the occult sciences as *an integral part* of the vibrant Islamicate intellectual and scientific enterprise" (my italics, ibid., p. 7) in ways that avoid reproducing modernist value judgements.

The following chapter unpacks how negative colonial assumptions about Qur'anic schools and classical Islamic worldviews (including their denigration of the esoteric sciences and Sufi practices) have now been reproduced, relatively unquestioned, within global EFA debates and contemporary education policies in West Africa. The second half of the book turns to see how parents and youth perceive and engage with the different schools available in the midst of this ontological regime complex.

Notes

1 Translated into English, the calligraphy reads: "Salt comes from the north, gold from the south, money from the White man's country; but God's words, holy things, interesting tales, we can find them only in Timbuktu".

2 The Sahel is an uninterrupted stretch of land which connects Africa south of the Sahara to the Maghreb, and covers the countries of Mauritania, Senegal, The Gambia, Guinea, Mali, Niger, Burkina Faso, Nigeria, Cameroon and Chad. The region's name is derived from the Arabic *sahil*, meaning shore or coast, and it represents both a bridge and a frontier (Hima, 2020, p. 463).

References

Barthel, D. (1989) 'Senegal', in *International Handbook of Women's Education*. New York: Greenwood Press, pp. 65–83.

Bayart, J.-F. (2010) 'Les très fâché(e)s des études postcoloniales', *Sociétés Politiques Comparées*, 23, pp. 1–12.

Boyle, H.N. (2006) 'Memorization and learning in Islamic schools', *Comparative Education Review*, 50(3), pp. 478–495.

Brenner, L. (2000) *Controlling Knowledge: Religion, Power and Schooling in a West African Muslim Society*. Bloomington, IN and Indianapolis, IN: University of Indiana Press.

Brenner, L. (2007) 'Introduction', in C. Hamès (ed.) *Coran et talismans: Textes et pratiques magiques en milieu musulman*. Paris: Karthala, pp. 7–15.

Bryant, K.D. (2011) '"The color of the Pupils": Schooling and race in Senegal's cities, 1900–10', *The Journal of African History*, 52(03), pp. 299–319.

Bryant, K.D. (2020) 'Education and politics in colonial French West Africa', *Oxford Research Encyclopedia of African History* [Preprint]. https://doi.org/10.1093/acrefore/9780190277734.013.679.

Charlier, J.-É. (2002) 'Le retour de Dieu: L'introduction de l'enseignement religieux dans l'École de la République laïque du Sénégal', *Education et Sociétés*, 10(2), pp. 95–111.

Costa, J. (2019) 'Introduction: Regimes of language and the social, hierarchized organization of ideologies', *Language & Communication*, 66, pp. 1–5.

Crossley, M. and Tikly, L. (2004) 'Postcolonial perspectives and comparative and international research in education: A critical introduction', *Comparative Education*, 40(2), pp. 147–156.

D'Aoust, S. (2013) 'Écoles franco-arabes publiques et daaras modernes au Sénégal: hybridation des ordres normatifs concernant l'éducation', *Cahiers de la recherche sur l'éducation et les savoirs*, 12, pp. 313–338.

Diallo, I. (2011) '"To understand lessons, think through your own languages." An analysis of narratives in support of the introduction of indigenous languages in the education system in Senegal', *Language Matters*, 42(2), pp. 207–230.

Diallo, I. (2013) 'Qur'anic and Ajami literacies in pre-colonial West Africa', *Current Issues in Language Planning*, 13(2), pp. 91–104.

Dilger, H. and Schulz, D. (2013) 'Politics of religious schooling: Christian and Muslim engagements with education in Africa. Introduction', *Journal of Religion in Africa*, 43, pp. 365–378.

Dilley, R.M. (2004) *Islamic and Caste Knowledge Practices Among Haalpulaar'en in Senegal: Between Mosque and Termite Mound*. Edinburgh: Edinburgh University Press.

Diouf, S.A. (1998) *Servants of Allah: Muslim African Enslaved in the Americas*. New York: New York University Press.

Eickelman, D.F. and Piscatori, J. (1996) *Muslim Politics*. Princeton, NJ: Princeton University Press.

El-Tom, A. (1987) 'Berti Qur'anic amulets', *Journal of Religion in Africa*, 17(3), pp. 224–244.

Fitzgerald, G. (2020) *Introduction to Decoloniality and the Study of Religion, Contending Modernities*. Available at: https://contendingmodernities.nd.edu/decoloniality/introdecolonial/ (Accessed: 30 November 2022).

Harrison, C. (1988) *France and Islam in West Africa 1860–1960*. Cambridge: Cambridge University Press.

Hima, H. (2020) '"Francophone" education and intersectionalities: Gender, language, and religion', in J.M. Abidogun and T. Falola (eds) *The Palgrave Handbook of African Education and Indigenous Knowledge*. Cham, Switzerland: Palgrave Macmillan, pp. 463–525.

Huméry, M.-È. (2014) 'Fula and the Ajami writing system in the Haalpulaar society of Fuuta Tooro (Senegal and Mauritania): A specific "restricted literacy"', in M. Mumin and K. Versteegh (eds) *The Arabic Script in Africa: Studies in the Use of a Writing System*. Leiden: Brill, pp. 173–198.

Janson, M. (2010) 'The battle of the ages: Contests for religious authority in the Gambia', in *Being Young and Muslim: New Cultural Politics in the Global South and North*. Oxford: Oxford University Press, pp. 95–111.

Jézéquel, J.-H. (2007) '"Grammaire de la distinction coloniale" L'organisation des cadres de l'enseignement en Afrique occidentale francaise (1903-fin des années 1930)', *Genèses*, 69(4), pp. 4–25.

Kalmbach, H. (2012) 'Introduction: Islamic authority and the study of female religious leaders', in M. Bano and H. Kalmbach (eds) *Women, Leadership, and Mosques: Changes in Contemporary Islamic Authority*. Leiden and Boston, MA: Brill, pp. 1–27.

Kane, C.H. (1972) *An Ambiguous Adventure*. London: Heinemann.

Kane, O.O. (2012) *Non-Europhone Intellectuals*. Dakar: CODESRIA.

Kane, O.O. (2016) *Beyond Timbuktu: An Intellectual History of Muslim West Africa*. Harvard University Press.

Klein, M. (1998) *Slavery and Colonial Rule in French West Africa*. Cambridge: Cambridge University Press.

Kobo, O.M. (2012) *Unveiling Modernity in Twentieth-Century West African Islamic Reforms*. Leiden and Boston, MA: Brill.

Launay, R. (2016) 'Writing boards and blackboards: Introduction', in R. Launay (ed) *Islamic Education in Africa: Writing Boards and Blackboards*. Bloomington, IN: Indiana University Press.

Launay, R. and Soares, B.F. (1999) 'The formation of an "Islamic sphere" in French colonial West Africa', *Economy and Society*, 28(4), pp. 497–519.

Launay, R. and Ware, R.T. (2016) 'How (not) to read the Quran? Logics of Islamic education in Senegal and Côte d'Ivoire', in R. Launay (ed) *Writing Boards and Blackboards: Islamic Education in Africa*. Indianapolis, IN: Indiana University Press, pp. 255–267.

Loimeier, R. (1998) 'Cheikh Touré, un musulman sénégalais dans le siècle: du réformisme à l'islamisme', in O.O. Kane and J.-L. Triaud (eds) *Islam et Islamismes au sud du Sahara*. Paris: Karthala, pp. 155–168.

Loimeier, R. (2000) 'L'Islam ne se vend plus: The Islamic reform movement and the state in Senegal', *Journal of Religion in Africa*, 30(2), pp. 168–190.

Loimeier, R. (2003) 'Patterns and peculiarities of Islamic reform in Africa', *Journal of Religion in Africa*, 33(3), pp. 237–262.

Loimeier, R. (2009) *Between Social Skills and Marketable Skills: The Politics of Islamic Education in Twentieth Century Zanzibar*. Leiden: Brill.

Lüpke, F. and Bao-Diop, S. (2014) 'Beneath the surface? Contemporary ajami writing', in K. Juffermans, Y.M. Asfaha and A. Abdelhay (eds) *African Literacies: Ideologies, Scripts, Education*. Newcastle: Cambridge Scholars Publishing, pp. 88–117.

Mack, B.B. and Boyd, J. (2000) *One Woman's Jihad: Nana Asma'u, Scholar and Scribe*. Bloomington, IN: University of Indiana Press.

Macleod, S.L. (2021) *Daaras and Development Discourses: Three Interventions Targeting the Practice of Begging by Talibés in Urban Senegal*. PhD thesis, Department of Development Studies, School of Oriental and African Studies (SOAS), University of London.

Madeira, A.I. (2005) 'Portuguese, French and British discourses on colonial education: Church–State relations, school expansion and missionary competition in Africa, 1890–1930', *Paedagogica Historica*, 41(1–2), pp. 31–60.

Mueller, R. (2013) *The Spirits Are My Neighbours: Women and the Rab Cult in Dakar, Senegal, Anthropology Honours Projects: Paper 18*. Anthropology Department, Macalester College.

Mumin, M. (2014) 'The Arabic script in Africa: Understudied literacy', in M. Mumin and K. Versteegh (eds) *The Arabic Script in Africa: Studies in the Use of a Writing System*. Leiden: Brill, pp. 41–76.

Ndlovu-Gatsheni, S.J. (2018) *Epistemic Freedom in Africa: Deprovincialization and Decolonization*. London and New York: Routledge.

Nye, M. (2019) 'Decolonizing the study of religion', *Open Library of Humanities*, 5(1), pp. 1–45.

Ogunnaike, O. (2020) 'Islamic philosophies of education in Africa', in J.M. Abidogun and T. Falola (eds) *The Palgrave Handbook of African Education and Indigenous Knowledge*. Cham, Switzerland: Palgrave Macmillan, pp. 421–450.
Robinson, D. (2000) 'Revolutions in the Western Sahara', in N. Levtzion and R.L. Pouwels (eds) *The History of Islam in Africa*. Oxford: James Currey, pp. 131–152.
Saif, L. and Leoni, F. (2021) 'Introduction', in L. Saif et al. (eds) *Islamicate Occult Sciences in Theory and Practice*. Leiden: Brill, pp. 1–40.
Sall, M.Y. (2020) 'African ajami: The case of Senegal', in J.M. Abidogun and T. Falola (eds) *The Palgrave Handbook of African Education and Indigenous Knowledge*. Cham, Switzerland: Palgrave Macmillan, pp. 545–557.
Seesemann, R. (2017) ''Ilm and Adab revisited: Knowledge transmission and character formation in Islamic Africa', in M. Kemper and R. Elger (eds) *The Piety of Learning: Islamic Studies in Honor of Stefan Reichmuth*. Leiden: Brill, pp. 13–37.
Shahin, E. el-D. (2009) 'Salafiyah', in J.L. Esposito (ed) *The Oxford Encyclopedia of the Islamic World*. Oxford: Oxford University Press.
Soares, B.F. (2005) *Islam and the Prayer Economy*. Edinburgh: Edinburgh University Press.
Sriprakash, A., Tikly, L. and Walker, S. (2020) 'The erasures of racism in education and international development: Re-reading the "global learning crisis"', *Compare: A Journal of Comparative and International Education*, 50(5), pp. 676–692.
Starrett, G. (1998) *Putting Islam to Work: Education, Politics and Religious Transformation in Egypt*. Berkeley, CA: University of California Press.
Thayer-Bacon, B.J. (2017) *Relational Ontologies*. New York: Peter Lang Incorporated, International Academic Publishers.
Tikly, L. (2001) 'Globalisation and education in the postcolonial world: Towards a conceptual framework', *Comparative Education*, 37(2), pp. 151–171.
Topolski, A. (2018) 'The race-religion constellation: A European contribution to the critical philosophy of race', *Critical Philosophy of Race*, 6(1), pp. 58–81.
Vizcaíno, R. (2021) 'Secular decolonial woes', *The Journal of Speculative Philosophy*, 35(1), pp. 71–92.
Ware, R.T. (2004) *Knowledge, Faith and Power: A History of Qur'anic Schooling in 20th Century Senegal*. PhD thesis. Department of History, University of Pennsylvania.
Ware, R.T. (2014) *The Walking Qur'an: Islamic Education, Embodied Knowledge, and History in West Africa*. Chapel Hill, NC: The University of North Carolina Press.
White, B.W. (1996) 'Talk about school: Education and the colonial project in French and British Africa (1860–1960)', *Comparative Education*, 32(1), pp. 9–26.
Willis, J.R. (1978) 'The torodbe clerisy: A social view', *The Journal of African History*, 19(2), pp. 195–212.
Wright, Z.V. (2018) *Living Knowledge in West African Islam*. New York and Accra: Fayda Books.

4 Coloniality of secularity and Education for All

In one of my first interviews with development actors in Dakar in 2010, an education specialist at an INGO told me that:

> Learning the Qur'an isn't quality education by the definition of EFA or the Human Rights of the Child. . . . Children only learn the Qur'an and hence miss out on literacy, numeracy and personal development.

This trope, that Qur'anic schools did not constitute 'quality education' but that state schools did, was widespread among personnel in both NGOs and INGOs. Yet, as I found in my research, local parents and youth in Medina Diallobé often held the opposite view, particularly as they had observed that the standard of teaching in state schools had declined following massification of schooling during the 2000s under EFA. I had to wonder, why was there such a chasm between different actors' definitions of 'quality education'? Why were the assumptions that underpinned policies related to EFA so divorced from Muslim parents' and youths' perceptions? And to what extent did such stereotypes reproduce colonial assumptions about Islam, *islam noir* and Islamic education described in the last three chapters?

The starting point for considering these questions is 1990, when the World Declaration on EFA was signed in Jomtien, Thailand. This declaration was committed to ensuring that "every person – child, youth and adult – shall be able to benefit from educational opportunities designed to meet their basic learning needs". These needs were defined both in terms of 'tools' like "literacy, oral expression, numeracy and problem-solving" and 'content' such as "knowledge, skills, values and attitudes" (UNESCO, 1990, p. 3). Article 1 of the framework acknowledged that "the scope of basic learning needs and how they should be met varies with individual countries and cultures" (ibid., p. 3). The preamble even recognised that "traditional knowledge and indigenous cultural heritage have a value and validity in their own right and a capacity to both define and promote development" (ibid., p. 2).

In 2000, the Framework for Action and EFA targets were subsequently agreed at the World Education Forum in (coincidentally) Dakar, Senegal

DOI: 10.4324/9781003172475-5

and extended the goals for another 15 years while combining them with the MDGs (Tikly, 2016). In its preamble, the Regional Framework for Action on Sub-Saharan Africa specified that the authors "recognize that African indigenous knowledge systems, languages and values should be the foundation for the development of African education systems" (UNESCO, 2000, p. 27). It was argued that such systems should include, among other things, "curriculum reform toward locally relevant subjects" and "use of mother tongue as the language of instruction" (ibid., p. 26). The EFA agenda was further consolidated in alignment with the SDGs, signed in 2015, which include SDG 4 that combines both EFA debates and global discourses on sustainability in its aim to "ensure inclusive and equitable quality education and to promote lifelong learning opportunities for all" (Tikly, 2020, p. 8).

Whilst noting the progressive nature of these EFA ideals, scholars have critiqued the agenda's operationalisation. The influence of rights-based and sustainability approaches notwithstanding, classical HCT has shaped understandings of the value of investing in universal primary education (UPE). Consequently, because EFA intersects with the regimes of international large-scale assessments (ILSAs), the MDGs and the SDGs, the achievement of universal, measurable, quantitative goals arguably has taken precedence over qualitative factors and a context-dependent approach (Tikly, 2016). Coloniality of power and knowledge also structure the EFA agenda as "centre-periphery dynamics" are reproduced whereby "northern actors play leadership roles" (Tikly, 2016, p. 52). Indeed, Kenneth King (2007, p. 380) has argued:

> If we were to summarize the role of southern governments, researchers and NGOs in affecting substantially the content of the Jomtien Declaration and Framework for Action, it was minor, if not minimal.

Hence, while education is presented as being the key to development, countries reliant on foreign aid have little sovereignty to define national educational priorities (Tikly, 2017, p. 46).

Critical comparative/international education scholars have argued that coloniality of power in their field reproduces coloniality of knowledge. We can see this in debates around the 'quality' of education which has enjoyed a strong emphasis under the EFA agenda (Sriprakash, Tikly and Walker, 2020, p. 683) as illustrated through UNESCO's Global Education Monitoring (GEM) Reports[1] which have tracked progress to meet EFA since 2002. The report dedicated to discussions of quality, *Education For All: The Quality Imperative,* included a lengthy and critical discussion of the concept and drew particular attention to the question of 'relevance' (UNESCO, 2005, p. 31):

> The notion of relevance has always attended debates about the quality of education. In . . . developing countries, imported or inherited curricula have often been judged insufficiently sensitive to the local context and to learners' socio-cultural circumstances.

Ten years later, the GEM Report *Education For All 2000–2015: Achievements and challenges* also stressed that "quality is a relative, value-laden and dynamic concept" (UNESCO, 2015, p. 68). Yet, in reality, quality is measured using indicators such as "government spending on education, pupil/teacher ratios, teacher qualifications, test scores and the length of time pupils spend in school" (UNESCO, 2004, p. 21). Hence, concepts and measurements central to debates on 'quality education' within EFA are presented as neutral and 'universal', whilst in reality they privilege knowledges grounded in Euro-North American worldviews and relevant to global formal capitalist economies. EFA discourse is underpinned by assumptions about "what learning is (the ontology of learning) and how we come to know what learning is (the epistemology of learning)" that are "rarely made explicit" (Tikly, 2015, p. 237). These discourses tend to reflect the positivist empiricism of economists and cognitive neuro-scientists who believe that their observations are objective and neutral and fail to acknowledge their own biases and assumptions. These include the notions that "learning outcomes can be improved through the use of neo-liberal market mechanisms" (ibid., p. 242) or that learning can be "implicitly equated with standardised test scores" (ibid., p. 248). The 'particularity' of 'local' perspectives – and knowledges valued in those contexts – are thus discredited. This reflects a form of racial erasure whereby academics and policy-makers promote "colour-blind and technocratic approaches" to global educational inequalities "that erase histories of racial domination" (Sriprakash, Tikly and Walker, 2020, p. 684).

While these arguments complement my own, I would argue that EFA debates also reflect secular erasure, a term I coined in Chapter 2 to refer to the tendency for academic scholarship – and policy and public discourse – to render invisible the contributions of other-than-secular worldviews and associated knowledge systems to people's everyday lives. In this chapter, I address this lacuna by submitting these contemporary global education discourses on EFA, particularly their assumptions about Qur'anic schools in West Africa, to critical scrutiny. Ultimately, such education debates – which are framed as neutral and evidence-based – are, in fact, based on secular and Eurocentric worldviews similar to those which underpinned historical colonialist assumptions about the role, effects and dangers of Islam. As a result, contemporary education policies fail to honour the ethos of the EFA declarations which advocated for the embrace of knowledges grounded in African worldviews and which argued for recognition of types of education provision rooted in local realities and priorities.

My argument here builds on the findings of Chapter 3, namely that the European colonial installation of secular public schools in Muslim majority contexts – and the attempted regulation of Qur'anic schools – represented an epistemological rupture in countries in West Africa. Contemporary Qur'anic schools reflecting classical Islamic onto-epistemologies had to compete – against a backdrop of enormous political and economic inequalities – with schools that were grounded in secular worldviews, as well as 'hybrid' Islamic schools based on rationalist interpretations of Islam. It is true that Muslim education providers and parents incorporated threads of secular European worldviews into their onto-epistemological nets and that this agency must be acknowledged. Yet, this occurred as colonisation ushered in what I described in Chapter 3 as an ontological regime complex whereby educational norms and standards informed by modern/colonialist logics came to dominate in political and economic terms. In this chapter, I show how the secular ideology and Orientalist assumptions of colonial powers has lived on within contemporary policy debates about Qur'anic schools in Senegal under EFA. I develop this argument by unpacking three examples: persistent negative stereotypes among development actors about Qur'anic students' begging; unfounded assumptions that Qur'anic schools fail to confer literacy, numeracy and economic opportunities compared to secular schools; and instrumentalist attempts to 'reform' Qur'anic schools to meet EFA goals.

The '*talibé* problem': Development critiques of child begging

"*Marabouts*[2] [Muslim clerics] ought to be banned – it's disgusting how they are permitted to abuse children". In 2010, this opinion was shared with me by a Japanese intern who worked for an INGO in Dakar, during an informal conversation. Her desire to ban Muslim clerics entirely was an extreme position. Yet, the impression that many (if not most) Qur'anic school teachers were abusive towards the students in their care (known in Senegal as *talibés*) – and that Qur'anic schools were harmful to children's well-being – was nonetheless common amongst the INGO staff that I met. The Wolof word *talibé* means any student of Islam, but in Senegal the term is narrowly associated with young boys whom Muslim clerics bring from rural areas to itinerant *daaras* (the Wolof word for Qur'anic schools) in urban centres (Ware, 2004). These young boys can be found begging in the streets for food and small change to support their education and lodging.

From the early 1990s, UNICEF and a host of national and international NGOs pushed the government to reform or control the Qur'anic schools under the banner of child protection, particularly itinerant types which have led to the visible phenomenon of child begging in urban settings (Ware, 2014, pp. 223–225). A policy brief undertaken by Dorte Thorsen (2012) for UNICEF illustrates how significant investment has been made by NGOs, ministries and the international community to end corporal punishment, unhygienic living conditions and other dangers to which *talibés* in poorer establishments can be exposed, like substance and sexual abuse. Begging in the streets for money receives particular attention from development actors on the basis that it exposes children to risks like car accidents. Similarly, such children can be beaten severely by the cleric for not bringing back a defined daily quota. Such practices are described as taking excessive time away from Qur'an study and enabling clerics to get rich through exploiting children. Two dominant strategies are used to prevent such practices which I describe in the following sections.

Tackling talibé *begging: From 'trafficking' to 'vulnerable schools'*

In an ethnographic study of NGOs in Senegal in the 2010s, Sara Lahti (2019) identified two principal development discourses framing *talibé* begging as a significant problem. They consisted of the 'anti-trafficking' discourse – which grew out of child protection and UN anti-slavery conventions – and the 'vulnerable schools' discourse linked to wider international education and development debates and EFA mandates. These discourses differ in their framing of the '*talibé* problem', its causes and hence solutions.

The anti-trafficking discourse frames all movement of children from one location to another where they work or beg on arrival, as in itinerant *daaras*, as trafficking and hence a crime. A neat binary is made between the child as a victim without agency and the Muslim cleric as an exploitative perpetrator seeking to make a profit. It blames clerics, as well as *talibés'* supposedly 'complicit' parents and the 'negligent' state, rather than implicating wider social and structural circumstances. Lahti (2018) argues that it is transnational human rights organisations, INGOs, IGOs and the global media who typically subscribe to this discourse. Their strategies often consist of aggressive 'shock and shame' human rights advocacy tactics which involve condemnation of 'guilty' parties and demands for stronger domestic laws and punitive implementation of legal frameworks.

A report by Human Rights Watch (HRW), titled *Off the Backs of the Children: Forced Begging and other Abuses against Talibés in Senegal* (2010), is an illustrative example. Rudolph Ware (2014) provides a scathing critique of this report, arguing that it is based on generalisations and stereotypes that are not supported by empirical evidence. It also fails to appreciate the classical Islamic onto-epistemologies underpinning begging and corporal punishment, or the moral values like humility or generosity that these pedagogies are designed to teach. It ignores the views of parents and the majority of students themselves, including those interviewed for the report, who valued Qur'anic schools in their current form (ibid., pp. 89–90). As noted in Chapter 3, attempts at quantifying *daaras* over the last two decades vary enormously, but figures in the upper range are predictably mobilised by organisations like HRW for advocacy purposes (Macleod, 2021, pp. 29–32). Moreover, the plight of a small minority of *talibés* in the worst conditions are exaggerated for instrumentalist ends because, in reality, most urban *daaras* now rely on tuition fees from parents instead of begging. Ware (2014, p. 39) concludes by saying that:

> HRW's [Human Rights Watch] depiction of Qur'an schooling . . . conveys the notion that *daaras* offer no education worthy of the name and are sites only of child endangerment, abuse, and neglect. In such portrayals, Qur'an teachers are accused of the most cynical forms of exploitation. . . . In most cases, the outrage is certainly sincere and motivated by a desire to protect children, but it is based on a shallow understanding of what Qur'an schooling means to – and does for – African Muslims.

Ware continues by tracing the genealogy of these stereotypes from the colonial period to the present day (ibid., pp. 39–40):

> This kind of caricature of the *daara* did not originate with human rights groups. Senegalese colonial and postcolonial archives are full of government reports – beginning in the 1850s – that resemble *Off the Backs of the Children*. Attacks on Qur'an schools were a major component of French assimilation policy and the colonial *mission civilisatrice* (civilizing mission) in Africa.

It is worth noting that, since the publication of *Off the Backs of the Children*, HRW has released a number of additional reports on *talibés*. To a greater extent, it has acknowledged the diverse nature of Qur'anic schools and Muslim clerics, even occasionally showcasing those working to find sustainable solutions to child protection concerns (Human Rights Watch, 2014, pp. 23–25). However, the reports continue to reflect the other dominant tropes of the anti-trafficking discourse, namely that child begging and the migration of children to itinerant *daaras* are unequivocally harmful and that abetting these practices constitutes trafficking and/or exploitation and is or should be a criminal offence (Human Rights Watch, 2014, 2019a, 2019b).

In contrast, proponents of the vulnerable schools discourse show a shift in framing away from colonial legacies by recognising Qur'anic schools as legitimate educational establishments, even nodding to the pedagogical and spiritual benefits of begging. They present the poor conditions of contemporary itinerant *daaras* – and widespread child begging – as the results of rural poverty, mass urbanisation and a lack of state and international recognition of – and investment in – Qur'anic education (Lahti, 2019). This framing situates *talibés* who beg within a "meta-narrative of large-scale structural forces that have 'tainted' local culture and rendered it dysfunctional". It avoids apportioning individual blame to clerics and parents and thus side-steps accusations of cultural imperialism (Perry, 2004, p. 50).

Given their divergent causal narratives, these discourses propose different solutions to *talibé* begging. Anti-trafficking discourse supports 'rescue-repatriation-reintegration' of *talibés* where they are taken off the streets by NGOs and sent back home. Vulnerable schools discourse promotes financial support for *daaras* and encourages Muslim clerics to conform to definitions of 'quality education' that are embedded in the EFA aspirations (Macleod, 2021, p. 205). However, despite their differences, both local and transnational development actors agree on one ultimate goal: the elimination of 'forced' child begging (Lahti, 2018). In an ethnographic account of NGO work with street children, Shona Macleod (2021, p. 51) summarises how Senegal banned forced begging in 2005, but then-president Abdoulaye Wade only enforced the law for the first time in 2010 after international pressure catalysed by the *Off the Backs of the Children* HRW report. However, Wade backed down two months later following resistance from the National Federation of Qur'anic Teachers'

Associations (FNAECS) who were offended at not having been consulted, despite having worked with the government to end *talibé* begging for several years. Occasionally, individual clerics are prosecuted on charges relating to begging or extreme mistreatment of children, including manslaughter, but cases are rare and sentences disturbingly lenient.

These debates occasionally make it into the GEM Reports: two mention the issue of begging *talibés* in West Africa. Both reproduce the flaws outlined earlier whereby Qur'anic schools are presented as undesirable barriers to EFA which parents should be coaxed away from. *Migration, Displacement and Education: Building Bridges not Walls* (UNESCO, 2019) includes a text box dedicated to Qur'anic schools in northern Nigeria. It starts off well by explaining that "the main challenge remains tackling the socio-economic challenges that sustain the almajiri [classical Qur'anic school] system" which is mainly favoured by poor families (ibid., p. 25). It then argues that efforts at integrating the Qur'anic schools into the formal system of basic education are impeded "if parents have concerns about the quality of formal secular schools" (ibid., p. 25). Yet, instead of addressing the limitations of the formal schools, acknowledging the relative advantages of the Qur'anic schools in their current form, or alleviating the poverty faced by many families, the report promotes a policy focus on "efforts to increase the demand [for the state system] and gain the trust of students, parents and teachers who prefer the existing non-formal education system" (ibid., p. 25). More recently, *Non-state Actors in Education* (UNESCO, 2021, p. 85) includes a text box outlining the limitations of religious education around the world which features a mention of abuses faced by *talibés* in Senegalese Qur'anic schools. It is largely derived from HRW reports and sensationalist media articles, again failing to situate these phenomena in a wider social or historical context.

Ontological obstacles to begging bans

Critics have pointed out that there are various flaws in these anti-trafficking and vulnerable schools discourses which help to explain why progress to curb *talibé* begging has proven so slow. Narratives about the causes of *talibé* begging rely on the stereotypical view that clerics exploit victimised children and 'force' them to beg. Yet empirical evidence shows that *talibés* have been found to voice preferences for a Qur'anic education involving begging (Einarsdóttir et al., 2010) including because they are sometimes able to save any alms they collect beyond their daily quota (Bianchin, 2020, p. 87). The discourses also reflect simplistic binaries, like 'good but poor' versus 'greedy charlatan' *marabouts*, or 'begging *talibés*' versus 'begging street children' not affiliated with Qur'anic schools. These categories of persons demand different policy responses but are often difficult or impossible to differentiate in practice (Macleod, 2021, p. 118). Intervention strategies, particularly sudden begging bans, aggressive international shock and shame advocacy campaigns (Lahti, 2018) and misguided rescue-and-repatriation missions (Einarsdóttir et al.,

2010) are often unsustainable. *Talibés* are often 'repatriated' against their will which is extremely distressing for them and their families and undermines relationships among local NGOs, the state, religious leaders and community members. Yet, critics of the discourses around *talibé* begging nonetheless argue that the practice could be banned effectively if only development organisations shared a coherent, accurate discourse and mission statement and sufficient funding (Lahti, 2018, p. 640).

As Ware's argument shows, these critiques of *talibé* begging fail to appreciate how Euro-North American and secular ontological biases underpin these discourses, particularly the apparently unquestioned negative assessments of child begging. Indeed, the development discourses encircling begging appear to be attempts to justify an already-taken policy decision, the need to ban *talibés* from begging for alms, which first emerged in the 1850s (Macleod, 2021, p. 41). It is underpinned by a set of onto-epistemological assumptions that align to form a consensus that begging is always harmful to children. These underpinnings can be summarised as: charity encourages dependency (Nieuwenhuys, 2001, pp. 543–544); the urban poor, including beggars, constitute undesirable "human clutter" (Ware, 2004, p. 520); all forms of child labour are categorically harmful (Macleod, 2021, pp. 67–68); and, from a rationalist perspective, classical Islamic pedagogies are harmful and superstitious (Ware and Launay, 2009; Ware, 2014).

Another major reason why efforts to ban *talibé* begging have failed is not just, as is often assumed, because widespread poverty encourages the practice. Rather, begging has broad support from religious leaders, the wider population and even children because they share an onto-epistemological understanding that both alms-seeking and alms-giving are beneficial for society. They either represent *zakat* which is one of the five pillars of the Muslim faith or *sadaqa* which can be translated as charity or sacrifice. These donations enable the acquisition of *baraka* for both giver and receiver and constitute a recognised pedagogy through which *talibés* acquire moral values (Ware, 2004, p. 521) and other transferable skills (see later mention).

It is not my intention to romanticise this worldview which also has its downsides. It is embedded in a social hierarchy built on religious authority that makes it difficult for community members, including even the police and the government, to challenge clerics who abuse children. Pro-begging discourse can risk legitimising child abuse through reference to religious and cultural tradition (Lahti, 2018, pp. 629–630). Nonetheless, the more effective solutions to ensuring *talibé* well-being appear to be local grassroots movements or close collaborations between NGOs and community members including Muslim clerics. In these initiatives, community members organise to satisfy some of the needs that begging fills for both givers and receivers by, for instance, donating the profits of their economic activities directly to *daaras* or cooking meals for *talibés* (Cochrane, 2020, p. 9; Macleod, 2021, p. 249). More details on the practicalities of supporting such community-level projects are discussed in Chapter 9.

Assumptions about Qur'anic schools and 'quality education'

During the 2000s, these development critiques of Qur'anic schools shifted away from their previous articulation around child protection towards concerns that the schools present a barrier to 'quality' universal primary education (UPE). These critiques went beyond itinerant *daaras* that encouraged *talibé* begging to encompass boarding *daaras*, where students pay tuition fees and therefore do not beg, because their full-time schedules mean that they cannot attend state-recognised schools (Binaté and Hugon, 2019). In the following sections I unpack the logics underpinning the assumptions of development actors that Qur'anic schools do not constitute a 'quality education'. Two major reasons are put forward, namely: (a) their supposed neglect of foundational cognitive skills including literacy and numeracy and (b) their neglect of transferable and technical/vocational skills and consequent inability to enable the professional insertion of *talibés*. I unpack how these assumptions are not necessarily underpinned by empirical evidence and neither are the parallel presuppositions that the government-accredited secular schools do teach these skills effectively.

Literacy, numeracy and cognitive skills

Within EFA debates, a core element of a 'quality education' is understood to be the imparting of skills in literacy and numeracy. The GEM Report *Education For All: The Quality Imperative* stresses its importance by noting that "literacy is a critical tool for the mastery of other subjects and one of the best predictors of long-term learning achievement" (UNESCO, 2004, p. 17). Target 4.6 of the SDGs is "Universal literacy and numeracy" which aims to ensure, by 2030, "that all youth and a substantial proportion of adults, both men and women, achieve literacy and numeracy" (UNESCO, 2021, p. 308). However, because the formal curriculum of West African Qur'anic schools is memorisation of the Qur'an and moral education with the language of instruction (LOI) being African languages, not Arabic (see Chapter 3), development actors have tended to assume that students do not acquire literacy or numeracy skills in such schools. In contrast, they assume that secular schools do teach these skills effectively. These ideas were echoed by the Senegalese education specialist quoted at the start of this chapter. However, as I will show, these assumptions are not necessarily founded on empirical evidence.

As the previous chapter showed, the historical prevalence of writing African languages in Arabic script (*Ajami* literacy) is well documented, and the following map (Figure 4.1) shows that the phenomenon has been recorded in most countries of the continent. Although the contemporary weight of *Ajami* is less well understood (Mumin, 2014), surveys in the early 2000s found *Ajami* literacy rates of over 70% in Pulaar-speaking Guinea including among 20–25% of women, 70% in parts of Wolof and Pulaar-speaking Senegal and over 80% in Hausa-speaking Niger and Nigeria (Ngom, 2015, p. 333). *Ajami* literacy is not taught within state schools but is, instead, associated with Qur'anic schools.

Figure 4.1 **Countries in Africa where *Ajami* use has been recorded**. Based on Verde (2011) and Mumin (2014, p. 45).

Credit: Anneke Newman and Isabelle Renneson.

The case of Touba is illustrative. Touba is Senegal's second-largest city and the holy city of the Mouride Sufi order, where no French-medium state schools are permitted by its religious leaders. Given the high density of Qur'anic schools, the surrounding region of Djourbel has the lowest state school enrolment ratio in the country with only 32% of 6–12-year-olds enrolled (Management Systems International and USAID Senegal, 2017, p. 12). Yet, linguists

Friederike Lüpke and Sokhna Bao-Diop (2014) found that writing Wolof in *Ajami*, a phenomenon called Wolofal, was very common. In fact, it was far more common than literacy in Roman/Latin script, presumably because *daaras* taught children to read Sufi poetry written in Wolofal (2014, p. 99). Moreover, studies of Qur'anic school students tend to focus on the 10% of those who complete memorisation, ignoring what the remaining 90% do with their education (Mumin, 2014, p. 55). Yet, another study conducted in Senegal in the 1990s found that Qur'anic school students developed very good *Ajami* reading skills after only 2–4 years, and 60% acquired writing ability (Ware, 2014, p. 245).

On the numeracy front, Fallou Ngom further draws our attention to "the centrality of numeracy among *Ajami* users" which, he argues, is "largely overlooked in the literature" (2015, p. 343). Ngom explains that numeracy can involve Arabic numerals which are considered to have spiritual potency and are hence widely used for esoteric purposes in amulets, Islamic medicine, numerology, divination or prayers. Practitioners of esoteric sciences also use Roman/Latin numerals, for instance to write down instructions of how to use the medicine, including how many times to recite a specific Qur'anic verse to bring about a desired outcome (ibid., pp. 343–344). Indeed, Roman/Latin numerals are frequently used for 'secular' purposes, evidenced by the fact that "many successful business people, shopkeepers, farmers, fishermen, and merchants in African Muslim communities are *Ajami* users with good numeracy skills" (ibid., p. 344). Indeed, Ngom (ibid., p. 344) interviewed an archivist in Touba called Sam Niang and paraphrased his observations thus:

> Though the traditional Qur'anic schools do not teach numeracy as a subject matter, students generally acquire numeracy in western numerals through a process that could be termed "currency-derived numeracy", i.e. through their sustained exposure to the currency used in their communities.

Ngom adds in a footnote that "this fascinating 'currency-derived numeracy' among Murid *Ajami* users begs for further scholarly inquiry" (ibid., p. 344). I would go a step further to hypothesise that, in a significant stroke of irony, the begging that *talibés* engage in – so much maligned by development agencies – is actually teaching children significant numeracy skills useful in their everyday contexts.

Despite such evidence, the importance of *Ajami* literacy – and, I would add, currency-derived numeracy – and their intimate association with Qur'anic schools is largely ignored by development actors (Mumin, 2014, p. 84). Over the last two decades, the African Academy of Languages (ACALAN) of the African Union has proposed to strengthen African languages through literacy in order to replace European languages. Fifteen regional lingua franca, such as Swahili, have been proposed for the continent, but the fact that most of these had/have writing traditions in *Ajami* has never been recognised because only

Roman/Latin script is promoted (ibid., p. 56). The GEM Reports are also illustrative of this tendency to ignore *Ajami*. The report dedicated to literacy, *Literacy for Life* (UNESCO, 2005), includes a section on the global importance of the Arabic language (ibid., p. 201) and the historical legacy of Qur'anic schools for normalising formal schooling (ibid., p. 193) and sustaining a 'literate environment' or 'literate society' which encourages lifelong learning (ibid., p. 190). The report also mentions non-formal programmes teaching African languages in Roman/Latin script (ibid., p. 198), script diversity and Indigenous scripts in Africa (ibid., p. 201) and the challenges for education policy of multilingualism and language diversity (ibid., pp. 163, 204–205). Yet, it fails to acknowledge *Ajami* and instead repeats statistics that "in sub-Saharan Africa, literacy rates are extremely low" particularly "in Benin, Burkina Faso, Chad, Mali, Mozambique, the Niger, Senegal and Sierra Leone" (ibid., p. 168). Not surprisingly, most of these countries show evidence of strong contemporary *Ajami* use. Not a single subsequent GEM Report has mentioned *Ajami* either.

Therefore, the association of Islamic Africa with low levels of literacy within development discourse is no coincidence and reflects profound biases in statistical measurement based, arguably, on secular erasure and negative assumptions about African Qur'anic schools. Despite UNESCO's standardisation of *Ajami* scripts in Senegal in 2002, no official literacy statistics give an overview of *Ajami's* contemporary importance (Lüpke and Bao-Diop, 2014, p. 105). Critically, UNESCO statistics on literacy, including those included in the GEM Reports, draw on national surveys and assessments which do not recognise "literacies . . . in vernacular languages and non-Roman scripts" (Lüpke, 2004, pp. 93–94) In fact, Lüpke and Bao-Diop hypothesise that most comparative/international education scholars and practitioners are totally unaware that *Ajami* even exists and therefore confuse *Ajami* for Arabic. They cite a background paper drafted for *Literacy for Life* which described the literacy environment in Dakar but failed to mention *Ajami*. The paper's author assumed that Arabic script on a shop front was Arabic, when it was almost certainly Wolofal (see Figure 4.2 of a shop front[3] using Wolof written in *Ajami* in Touba, Senegal) (Lüpke and Bao-Diop, 2014, p. 95). Even Arabic literacy is not always recognised as literacy within international statistics, which raises serious questions about their validity (Mumin, 2014, p. 47). Meanwhile, academic scholars of education often take these statistics for granted, thus reproducing the trope that literacy rates in West Africa are low. For instance, the book *Troubling Muslim Youth Identities*, based on a comparative study of Lebanon, Pakistan, Nigeria and Senegal, states uncritically on the basis of a UNESCO report (2016), that in Senegal "the youth literacy rate . . . is the lowest of our four country cases at 56%" (Dunne et al., 2017, p. 134).

Meikal Mumin (2014) further argues that this devaluing of *Ajami* can be traced back, once again, to the colonial period. As an influential French administrator in AOF, Maurice Delafosse, stated: "The Muslims of West Africa do not make use of Arabic characters to write the indigenous languages". According to Mumin, this view "influenced the opinion of a large share if not the

Figure 4.2 **A shop front in Touba, Senegal, using Wolof written in Arabic script (*Ajami*).**

Credit: Fallou Ngom.

entire French academic tradition" for most of the twentieth century (2014, p. 46). Alternatively, *Ajami* was acknowledged but erroneously understood to be restricted to a small number of specialists for strictly religious purposes (ibid., pp. 48–49). Meanwhile, Africanist linguists have tended to exclude Islamic Africa from their analyses. They have, therefore, ignored how African languages were shaped for centuries by Arabic and Islamic discourse (Abdelhay, Asfaha and Juffermans, 2014, p. 35).

While I have problematised the assumption that Qur'anic schools fail to impart any literacy or numeracy skills, the parallel argument, that secular state schools do teach these skills effectively, also deserves attention. In order to unpack these discourses, we need to situate Qur'anic schools within the broader Senegalese educational landscape. African anti-colonial nationalist movements from the 1930s onwards demanded public schooling for all and newly-independent states and tried to adapt school systems inherited from the colonial period to meet this demand. However, as Ogunnaike (2020, p. 440) has argued:

> While some nations modified their curricula after independence, the basic structures, pedagogical and disciplinary techniques, bureaucracy, and epistemologies of these school systems have remained virtually the same.

Halimatou Hima further explains that, in West Africa, "countries had become 'Francophone' because the African elites were and because France said so" (2020, p. 468). Given the low importance that the French gave to mass education, "when Senegal attained independence in 1960, enrolment rates were at only 36% for boys and zero for girls, and only 11% of Senegalese people were able to write French" (Diallo, 2011, p. 211). Despite tweaks made from the 2000s onwards, the mainstream public school system in this context still reflects its original assimilationist purpose to create a small elite of francophones imbued in French cultural norms to manage the colonial civil service.

Importantly, only 0.3% of the Senegalese population have French as their mother-tongue, and less than 30% use French for everyday communication. Everyone else uses an African language – mainly Wolof, followed by Pulaar – for socialisation and everyday communication (Guiliano Sarr, 2020, p. 103). African languages are the LOI of basic Qur'anic education, while Arabic is the LOI of advanced Islamic education and national religious debate (ibid., p. 109). Yet, although Senegal recognises African languages as 'national' languages, French is the only 'official' language in which all state functions are undertaken. Since the 1990s, sporadic pilot studies have used African languages as the LOI in primary schools, and in the 1960s Arabic was introduced as an optional foreign language in secondary school. However, the mainstream public school system still uses French as the LOI at all levels (ibid., p. 102). Therefore, Senegal's situation is one shared by other former French colonies whereby full enjoyment of citizenship is contingent on being francophone despite French only being spoken fluently by an elite minority (Albaugh, 2014).

Based on qualitative fieldwork in Senegal, Ghana and Cameroon, Ericka Albaugh (2014) found that LOI policies in Africa are largely dictated by bilateral foreign aid from former colonial powers. From the 1990s, France had started to support, in rhetoric if not yet in practice, a system of progressive bilingualism in its former West African colonies. Primary school would start using African languages of instruction, then teach French as a foreign language and progress to operating in French as the LOI by the end of primary schooling (ibid., p. 117). The official narrative was that this move would improve education quality in line with empirical linguistic evidence on language acquisition and international advocacy around language rights. However, as Albaugh argues, this shift was mainly motivated by France's colonialist desire to keep West Africa francophone as part of its geopolitical resistance to what it perceived as global anglophone hegemony (ibid., p. 108).

Observers have long documented how the majority of primary school students in Senegal struggle to understand or speak French because they do not use it at home which, in turn, impedes their acquisition of literacy and numeracy skills. In fact, the PASEC standardised assessment of learning outcomes in ten francophone Sub-Saharan African countries found that, in Senegal, by the end of primary schooling 25.3% of children had not attained the minimum proficiency level in French and 35% did not attain it in maths (PASEC,

2020, pp. 73, 77). French LOI therefore functions as "a gateway for children from privileged socioeconomic backgrounds (and likely to speak French) and a gatekeeper for the majority who only hear French in the classroom" (Hima, 2020, pp. 494–495).

Of note, the GEM Reports do acknowledge the importance of LOI as a component of 'quality education', as *Education For All: The Quality Imperative* argues ((UNESCO, 2004, p. 17):

> The choice of the language of instruction used in school is of utmost importance. Initial instruction in the learner's first language improves learning outcomes and reduces subsequent grade repetition and dropout rates.

Yet, the underlying assumption within the GEM Reports is that literacy is best learned in formal 'Western-style' schools inherited from the colonial period. If language planners are aware of *Ajami* at all, it stills tend to be disregarded as it is seen as a by-product of Qur'anic schooling rather than its formal curriculum. Yet, we should not forget that these schools have produced mass movements of literacy in African languages, including among marginalised groups like women and slaves, which is something education systems inherited from the colonial period have not necessarily achieved to this day (Mumin, 2014, p. 56).

Ajami*: Ignored by 'colonial', 'autonomous' and 'global' literacies*

The persistent invisibilisation of *Ajami* literacy raises the important question of why there is such a disconnect between local realities and policies under EFA in West Africa. New Literacy Studies (NLS) provides a useful framework to understand this situation. Developed by ethnographers of education in the 1980s, proponents of NLS argue that there are multiple literacies, of which 'school' literacy is only one type. Literacies are not individual technical skills but rather social practices associated with specific communities, institutions and motivations for their use (Abdelhay, Asfaha and Juffermans, 2014, p. 15). Moreover, NLS takes an explicitly "ideological approach to literacy" (Street, 1995, p. 29) which acknowledges institutional and discursive power. While there are multiple literacies in any given context, relationships between them "cannot be adequately grasped without the interpretive plane of language ideologies" (ibid., 2014, p. 16) whose impact is to serve moral and political interests and normalise social hierarchies. Some NLS scholars have also added numeracy to the mix, coining the concept of 'street numeracies' and observing from ethnography that "numeracy in real life is always integrated with literacy" (Gebre et al., 2009, p. 122).

Crucially for our discussion about Qur'anic schools and EFA, anthropologist Brian Street draws attention to the fact that development policy is informed by an 'autonomous model' of literacy (1995, p. 1) which assumes that literacy is a neutral, technical skill that can be measured comparably across contexts. Importantly, the literacy that 'counts' under the autonomous model is "based upon the particular uses and associations of literacy in recent European and North American history" (ibid., p. 14). Street also coins the concept of 'colonial literacy' which is when "members of an outside culture introduced their particular form of literacy to a colonized people as part of a much wider process of domination". Local people obviously "find pragmatic ways of adopting elements of the new ideology, or of the new forms in which literacy is introduced, to indigenous belief and practice" (ibid., p. 36). Yet, the shift involves a one-sided transfer of " 'western' values" and "deeper aspects of ideology, culture and even epistemology" (ibid., p. 30) to the extent that other uses of writing have been marginalised and, in some cases, destroyed.

In post-colonial contexts such as Senegal, these power hierarchies are reproduced, as the main agents of literacy policy tend to be "national governments and indigenous experts . . . drawn from a narrow class or cultural base" who are "often wedded to major features of western culture and style", not to mention "economically dependent on the western economic order" (Street, 1995, p. 37). This situation of 'internal domination' within post-colonial contexts gives rise to language ideologies which privilege 'dominant literacy' (ibid., pp. 36–37). Dominant literacies and numeracies are not always useful to ordinary people, but they carry status in society while non-dominant forms do not (Gebre et al., 2009, p. 123).

In a more recent contribution to NLS debates, Camilla Addey (2018), a comparative education scholar and former UNESCO employee, argues that, since the 1990s, the autonomous model of literacy has become further entrenched by the rise of international large-scale assessments (ILSAs), particularly the OECD's "psycho-metric based measuring of learning outcomes" through standardised tests with randomly sampled households (2018, pp. 319–320). Most current statements on education therefore reflect the idea of 'literacy as numbers' or literacy as "an internationally comparable, countable skill" (ibid., p. 315). This discourse Addey refers to as 'global literacy', namely a process whereby "a chosen set of materials and texts, contexts and content, procedures and strategies have been elected to represent a universal, global literacy" (ibid., p. 326).

Addey argues that global literacy defined by ILSAs "has come to dominate the epistemological pluralisms of literacy" (ibid. p. 316). Moreover, the standardised test is "an artificial literacy practice" which does not resemble "common everyday life practice of literacy, with its real-life contexts, purposes and processes" (ibid., p. 325). Crucially, she demonstrates that locally relevant literacy practices are ignored by policy-makers as "low levels and gaps between those who have the desired literacy and those who do not become the policy problem and priority, rather than a discussion of what literacies people need" (ibid., pp. 326–327). Addey summarises her view of the current situation by asserting that "global literacy has not derived a global consensus on what literacy should be from democratic, universal debates on what literacy represents". Rather, "everyday literacy is no longer all literacy practices, but everyday literacy to compete in a global capitalistic world" (ibid., p. 329).

It is worth noting that some authors of UNESCO's GEM Reports are aware of these challenges. *Education For All: The Quality Imperative* notes that (UNESCO, 2004, p. 31):

> Increased monitoring and regulation of education systems and . . . a flourishing industry of cross-national learning assessment using comparative benchmarks . . . may contribute to the standardization of cognitive skills informed by a set of culturally exclusive principles and knowledge. Recent research has shown that even skills as basic as literacy and numeracy can be conceived and taught in quite varied ways and thus run the risk of misrepresentation by culturally insensitive assessment.

Similarly, *Literacy for Life* includes an overview of different theoretical approaches to literacy, differentiating between the autonomous "literacy as skills" approach which sees literacy and numeracy as "independent of the context in which they are acquired" versus the idea of "literacy as applied, practised and situated" more characteristic of NLS (UNESCO, 2005, pp. 147–151). Nonetheless, in practice, the GEM Reports are increasingly based on statistics from standardised household surveys which do not yet capture the diversity of languages or scripts in which people can be literate (UNESCO, 2021, pp. 303–305).

In line with the arguments of NLS proponents, scholars of *Ajami* propose that a more critical approach is needed in order to understand literacies in Africa which avoid discourses shaped by universal autonomous or global definitions of literacy which privilege one form of reading and writing even in contexts with multiple educational regimes. For instance, Ashraf Abdelhay, Yonas Asfaha and Kasper Juffermans (2014) argue that, because of the prevalence of the autonomous model in development institutions, " 'poor/low literacy rates' have ideologically become associated with specific macro-categories of identification such as Africa". The model therefore constitutes "a form of 'symbolic violence'" (ibid., p. 2). The supposedly low levels of literacy in Africa feed into its association with the so-called learning crisis because "in relation to virtually all of the indicators, Africa lags behind other regions of the world" (Tikly, 2020, p. 8). Yet, far from reflecting reality, this narrative would appear to be constructed from data and discursive tropes grounded in a long history of coloniality of knowledge which side-lines African knowledges. As Hima recently noted, "the need to re-center African languages in sites of knowledge production lingers as an unfinished undertaking of the decolonization process" (2020, p. 469). Moreover, epistemic decolonisation must address not only language but also script diversity.

Economic opportunities and transferable, technical and vocational skills

Another element of 'quality education' according to the EFA agenda is its potential to aid economic integration. Target 4.4 of the SDGs is "Relevant skills for financial success" which aims, by 2030, to "substantially increase the number of youth and adults who have relevant skills, including technical and vocational skills, for employment, decent jobs and entrepreneurship". Hence, the third dimension of the devaluation of Qur'anic schools in West Africa is the assumption among development actors that such schools do not confer technical, vocational or transferable skills which can be translated into economic opportunities. It is for this reason that the *Plan Stratégique de Développement des Daara* (Strategic Plan for Development of the *Daaras*), published by the Senegalese Ministry of Education in 2009, stated that "the *daara* sector undermines the very future of thousands of children each year" (MEN, 2009, p. 3). However, a wealth of historical accounts and recent sociological and anthropological studies show that Islamic schools often aid students' insertion into informal economies (see Daun, 2010, p. 411 for a review).

In Chapter 3, I described how Qur'anic schools were embedded in the economic activities of Muslim communities. Advanced Islamic education was required for the religious professions of teacher, imam or jurist. However, long before completing memorisation of the Qur'an, students would learn skills relevant to agriculture and trade. Meanwhile, a wealth of historical and anthropological accounts show how the Sufi orders which emerged in Senegal from the nineteenth century onwards capitalised on the colonial imposition of peanut cash cropping to expand their activities. Qur'anic schools were embedded in rural Sufi residential communities where disciples worked the fields of their leader or *shaykh* to further their spiritual development. Over time, they were given plots of land to start their own households (Ware, 2014, pp. 182–184).

Fast forward to the present, and studies continue to demonstrate that Senegalese Muslim communities have responded creatively to economic challenges as diverse as drought and agricultural decline throughout the 1970s and 80s – and SAPs in the 1980s – which provoked a massive increase in the informal sector (Cochrane, 2020). Laura Cochrane's ethnographic study of a Mouride Sufi community found an "artisanal campus, with workspaces for spinners, weavers, dyers, tailors, tanners, and welders" which "used regional craft traditions to make products for a contemporary global clientele" (2020, p. 7). She also observed that religious networks have "adapted to and used a neoliberal economy for their own needs" (ibid., p. 5). This phenomenon is not limited to rural areas. As Abdou Fall (2011) shows, through interviews with entrepreneurs from across all Senegalese Sufi orders, the relationships between disciples and their *shaykh* – and between co-disciples, which are developed through attendance in Qur'anic schools – provide significant social capital. This translates into privileged access to credit, economic collaborations and markets in a range of spheres of the informal economy from trade to construction and public transport. Moreover, these relationships span transnational borders, linking entrepreneurs in the diaspora across Africa, the Middle East, the US and Europe.

Critics might counter at this point that the economic benefits of Qur'anic schools are linked more to the networks that they foster than to their content. Yet, Ware observes that Qur'anic school students acquire significant transferable skills and values like solidarity and entrepreneurial ability which means that they often thrive in competitive market environments (2014, pp. 244–245). In addition, a recent World Bank report titled *Youth Employment in Sub-Saharan Africa* showed that social capital is an equally important factor in school graduates' professional insertion as 60% find jobs through clientelist networks (Filmer and Fox, 2014, pp. 53, 58).

Despite these well-documented links within the Africanist literature between Islamic schooling and informal economies, few similar investigations have been undertaken by development scholars. We therefore lack studies which establish links between: formal and informal curricula in Islamic schools; knowledge, skills, dispositions, values and networks acquired by students; these schools' connections to technical or vocational training opportunities; and young people's parallel or subsequent economic activities in informal economies both urban and rural. One of the few existing examples is Street's ethnography of Qur'anic schools in Iran, known as *maktabs,* undertaken in the 1970s. He showed that urban state schools taught aspirations and 'modern literacy' which did not prepare rural youth for the kinds of jobs available in their home villages (1995, p. 40). Meanwhile, *maktabs* were assumed by the state to only teach mindless rote memorisation of the Qur'an, even though students were learning "many of the hidden conventions of literacy" (ibid., p. 42). Some villagers developed a form of 'commercial literacy' – which clearly included numeracy – including writing of bills, signing cheques, labelling boxes and recording transactions in exercise books, which enabled them to "create an infrastructure for the production and distribution of village fruit to urban areas" (ibid., p. 42).

More recently, Sam Niang, archivist in Touba city in Senegal, has also made the connection between currency-derived numeracy acquired by children and later informal apprenticeships and economic activities within Mouride Sufi communities in Senegal. Fallou Ngom (2015, p. 344) interviewed Niang in the late 2000s and paraphrased his argument, stating that:

> When students leave their communities and schools later, they enhance their numeracy skills in western numerals by learning from their supervisors. Thus, an *Ajami* literate apprentice tailor will learn from his boss how to take measurements and write them correctly and a novice shopkeeper, itinerant merchant, or businessman will improve his numeracy skills in western numerals by learning from his supervisor more arithmetic, how to use modern calculators, keep financial records, and write invoices for local customers who request them.

Moreover, Leila Bianchin interviewed *talibés* in Dakar in 2020 and revealed that the students pooled their begging income so that each child made their daily quota. If they made more, they kept the profit which they remitted to their families (2020, p. 87). Similarly, in 2012, a Senegalese NGO coordinator told me that "some of the *talibés* I know in Dakar have a system where, if they make too much begging one day, they entrust it to a street vendor, and then claim it back on a day when they fall short". These practices suggest that *talibés* acquire currency-derived numeracy as a direct consequence of begging. Moreover, begging as an income-generating activity for *talibés* allows them to perceive the practice in a positive light and a source of pride since with it they can support their families (Bianchin, 2020, p. 87).

Interestingly, Street concluded from Iran that "many found that their education in the local *maktab*, or Qur'anic school, prepared them better for the new, 'commercial' literacy required of village entrepreneurs than would the new State education" (1995, p. 40). In common with Street's Iranian policy-makers, the GEM Reports reflect a similar tendency to ignore the Qur'anic schools' contributions to young people's employability in informal sectors. *Youth and Skills: Putting Education to Work* (UNESCO, 2012) stresses three important kinds of skills for employability: foundation skills including literacy and numeracy; transferable skills like problem-solving or entrepreneurialism; and technical and vocational skills associated with specific occupations (ibid., pp. 171–173). The report recognises that "almost all work in some developing countries could be viewed as informal" (ibid., p. 261) and that, based on a study of youth in West African capital cities, "returns to education and skills in the informal sector can be strong" (ibid., p. 262). It notes further that "in sub-Saharan Africa, traditional apprenticeship is the main type of skills training in the informal sector" and informal technical and vocational training opportunities in such contexts outnumber those from NGOs or public training institutions by at least tenfold (ibid., p. 271). The report continues by extolling the potential of such opportunities, arguing that they are "more flexible, cheaper, and have immediate practical relevance" and promotes the regularisation of traditional apprenticeships which "had hitherto been invisible to policy-makers" (ibid., p. 271). While these observations are fascinating, the report – and education and development scholarship and policy more broadly – unfortunately fail to appreciate how classical Qur'anic schools in West Africa *in their current form* are already providing their students with such informal training opportunities or are embedded in networks of other actors that do. Moreover, scholarship and related educational policy also overlook the supply and demand for esoteric and religious services as an informal market of major significance across the Islamic world.

The report also suggests that a limitation of 'traditional' or informal technical/vocational training opportunities is that they fail to teach foundational skills or confer recognised diplomas that could enable youth to transition into formal education or employment (UNESCO, 2012, p. 263). However, this constant focus on formal education and employment within EFA discourse is problematic. As the World Bank has noted, most schooled youth in Africa aspire to salaried formal sector jobs, yet only 16% of the labour force on the continent work in this sector and most have an upper secondary or university education (Filmer and Fox, 2014, pp. 4, 10, 17). Agriculture and informal employment therefore represent the main opportunities available for African youth (ibid., p. 15). The public school system can represent a huge investment of time and resources with few substantial social or economic returns for most, and it largely serves the urban-dwelling middle-class elite. This situation is concerning since, by promoting mass school systems in their current state, actors in development and comparative/international education risk reproducing the "power relations of colonial-modernity" which "hold the 'shine' of possibility whilst denying the 'shadow side' of colonial violence" (Rudolph, Sriprakash and Gerrard, 2018, p. 25). This 'shadow' involves encouraging unrealistic aspirations tailored to the needs of global capitalism, which cause shame and frustration when these promises are not met, while simultaneously de-skilling for local livelihoods. In contrast, Qur'anic schools encourage less ambitious but arguably more realistic aspirations.

Finally, despite the repeated assertions among development actors in Senegal that Qur'anic schools undermine children's futures, there has been little attempt to measure comparatively the trajectories of people who have attended different types of schools (Thorsen, 2012, p. 11). To my knowledge only one longitudinal study, led by Holger Daun (2010), has compared the outcomes of individuals who attended Qur'anic schools, secular schools or 'indigenous education' in Senegal. The study tracked 346 individuals from two villages in the Djourbel region. The cohort were children in 1980/1, and they were followed up with 10 and 20 years later. Daun found, predictably, that men had higher earnings than women, and state school-educated individuals had higher test scores. Yet, there were unexpectedly no significant differences in terms of material standard of living (including occupation and income), life skills, and participation in household and community decision-making between attendees of different types of education (ibid., p. 414). The exception was that men with advanced institutionalised education had higher incomes than those with 'indigenous education', but this advantage was conferred equally by both secondary state schooling and advanced Islamic education (ibid., p. 417).

These findings beg the question, how can we explain the persistent stereotypes that accredited state schools confer automatic economic opportunities while Qur'anic schools do not? There is a lack of strong empirical evidence for either assumption. In short, critical scholars have long argued that, despite massive investment in UPE to promote professional insertion and economic growth, "research reviews are uncertain about the effects of education on various features in low-income countries, both at individual level and at societal level" (Daun, 2010, p. 424). From an interactionist perspective, an analysis of formal curriculum can never linearly predict educational outcomes because interactions among schools, teachers, students and their wider environment are always unpredictable and must be situated in specific contexts (Bano, 2017, pp. 22–23). Rather, the assumptions covered here reflect the simplistic yet persistent logics that accredited schools based on the

Euro-North American model – whether secular or 'weakly faith-based' hybrid Franco-Arab schools – confer objectively measurable and universally applicable economic returns, while 'strong' classical Qur'anic schools do not (Stambach, 2006). As I argued in Chapter 1, this trope stems from the secularisation thesis reproduced within HCT (Deneulin and Bano, 2009) and reflects coloniality of secularity.

Among the personnel working for international development organisations in Senegal, I only ever met one person who was aware of these biases, namely a consultant with anthropological training that I call Sophie, whom I interviewed in 2018. She pointed out:

> I get annoyed when comparisons are made between Qur'anic schools and an imagined ideal of public school, when the comparison should be with *reality* of public school. . . . You know, no one who works for an international organisation or a ministry of education sends their child to public school – because they're rubbish! Or maybe there is a tiny number of exceptions, but still. . . . They promote public schooling based on an imagined ideal of what public school could be, not on the reality. They always arrive at this idea that everyone should be able to continue at school and go to university, but Qur'anic school trains you for reality – but if you point that out, they get offended.

Unfortunately, Sophie's appears to be a lone voice among development actors in Senegal.

The instrumentalisation of Islamic education under EFA

The assumptions that I have analysed previously have arguably undermined the embrace of Qur'anic schools within the EFA agenda and affected the ways in which they have been researched in debates about 'quality education' – with massive detrimental implications for Muslims living in Senegal and other Islamic African countries. These assumptions, as I will show, are still being reproduced within recent EFA-related policies, even those that try to include Islamic schools in order to deliver UPE. To understand this process, it is important to appreciate the diversity of schools within the post-colonial Senegalese eduscape.

Despite demands from the 1970s to the 1990s from Senegalese religious leaders and parents that Islamic schools be recognised by the government, ruling parties remained committed to *laïcité* or strict secularism. Policy-makers had argued that attendance of children in non-state-accredited schools – which in practice were often faith-based – constituted a 'barrier' to UPE (Marshall, 2010). In 2017, a survey designed by USAID quantified a trend that many on the ground had understood for decades: only 63% of children aged 6–16 in Senegal were attending state-accredited primary or secondary schools, and 70% of those who had never frequented such institutions attended a Qur'anic school instead (Management Systems International and USAID Senegal,

2017, p. 12). Yet, it was only during the 'turn to religion' in the 2000s that development actors shifted towards the wide range of Islamic schools operating in West Africa to meet EFA (Villalón and Bodian, 2012).

The increased openness towards faith-based schools among development actors ushered in a radical shift in education policy across West Africa. In Senegal, the law requiring secularism in education was changed in 2002. In the same year, the Islamic Development Bank and Senegalese government initiated a three-pronged education reform strategy to integrate more Islamic content into the public school system (see Table 4.1. for details). This involved: (a) the introduction of a few hours of religious studies into mainstream public schools which had, until then, taught no religious content, in order to make them more attractive to parents; (b) the creation of public 'hybrid' or Franco-Arab schools which combined Islamic subjects in Arabic and 'secular' subjects in French, with the possibility for private Franco-Arab schools to gain accreditation if they adopted the official curriculum; and (c) the creation of public 'modern *daaras*' (*daara moderne)* which followed a state-approved syllabus of Qur'anic memorisation combined with French and vocational skills (Binaté

Table 4.1 Islamic schools introduced or accredited by the Senegalese state after reforms in 2002.

School type	*Level*	*Language of instruction*	*Formal curriculum*	*Fees*
Private Franco-Arab schools	Elementary + advanced	African languages, Arabic + French	Arabic and French language, religious subjects, state primary/ secondary syllabus	Medium-high cash payment
Public Franco-Arab schools	Elementary + advanced	Arabic + French	Arabic and French language, religious subjects, state primary/ secondary syllabus	Nominal cash payment
Public 'modern' Qur'anic school (*daara moderne*)	Elementary	Arabic + French	Memorisation of the Qur'an, Arabic and French language, state primary syllabus, vocational training	Nominal cash payment
Private 'modernised' Qur'anic school (*daara modernisé*)	Elementary	African languages	Memorisation of the Qur'an, vocational training	Nominal cash payment

and Hugon, 2019). In addition, existing Qur'anic schools were provided with incentives such as funding and accreditation to 'modernise' by conforming to government standards, including through the ending of child begging, whereupon they could gain the label of 'modernised *daara*' (*daara modernisé*) (D'Aoust, 2013). One objective of eventually accrediting all Islamic schools was to enable routes or '*passerelles*' for pupils to transition between different school types (Binaté and Hugon, 2019).

In 2017, the UNICEF West and Central Africa Regional Office (WCARO) commissioned a major report which documented the variety of Islamic schools across the region and parents' logics in choosing them (Roy and Humeau, 2018). In 2022, when I conducted an online interview with one of the authors, Émilie Roy, she told me that the report had ushered in a greater openness towards Islamic schools among policy-makers in West Africa:

> Over the last five years, there's a world of difference in how people perceive Qur'anic education. Honestly, it's changing. . . . I supported the programmes in Côte d'Ivoire, Guinea, and Mali where they're quite far along in writing new laws that ensure that Qur'anic education is part of the education system, without fundamentally changing its nature – that's what I keep insisting to everybody, we can't change its nature. . . .
>
> It's about Qur'anic schools giving more opportunities to the children whose parents want those schools. . . . If [UNICEF's] goal is to reach as many out-of-school children with basic functional training in different careers, like mechanic repair, cellphone repair, whatever, then Qur'anic schools are actually a low-hanging fruit! There are hundreds of thousands of children who are already in an institution of some sort whose parents value education enough to put them in school.

The growing perception of the educational value of Qur'anic schools among international donors and ministries of education in some West African countries represents, in my opinion, progress compared to the negative stereotypes of earlier decades. However, despite this 'turn to religion', development discourses around Islamic school reform still reflect coloniality of secularity and Eurocentrism.

Although accrediting Islamic schools was partly a response to the demands of Muslim clerics and parents, this move also appeared to be motivated by desires to 'capture' millions of children defined as being 'out-of-school' in order to boost enrolment statistics to meet UPE (Villalón and Bodian, 2012). Government concerns to regulate the parallel systems of school provision also played a part, as did their desires to bring Sufi leaders and reformist Islamic associations under state control (Loimeier, 2000; Villalón and Bodian, 2012). Moreover, the proposed form of 'modern *daaras*' resembles almost exactly the proposals made by French colonial administrators at the turn of the twentieth century who argued for "the inclusion of 'French' subjects such as 'theory of agriculture and elementary notions of social hygiene' in the curriculum of Quranic schools" (Harrison, 1988, pp. 61–62). These patterns echo the wider tendency among secular development actors to functionalise and instrumentalise Islamic education for their own socio-political ends (Deneulin and Bano, 2009) which, as I showed in Chapter 3, is a trend which dates from the colonial period (Starrett, 1998). UNICEF WCARO's 2018 report also reproduces modernist and evolutionary logics in the way it presents Islamic schools. To illustrate, the report presents a table (see Table 4.2) of six different types of Islamic schools found across the region (Roy and Humeau, 2018, p. 19). The schools are presented across the horizontal axis, starting with the category of 'non-formal Qur'anic education' (school types 1–4) followed by the category of 'formal Islamic education' (school types 5 and 6). Hence, classical Qur'anic schools teaching in African languages (types 1–4) are placed on the left, and Arabo-Islamic institutes and hybrid Franco-Arab schools (types 5 and 6), whose format and content more closely resemble secular 'Western-style' schools, are on the right. Through this framing, the report implicitly reflects an evolutionary logic which privileges French language and literacy over Arabic (and ignores *Ajami* altogether), secular subjects over Islamic ones, and rationalist onto-epistemologies and pedagogies over classical Islamic alternatives.

The report also includes a section explaining its use of the terms 'non-formal' and 'formal' but it basically just describes the characteristics of each type of school (Roy and Humeau, 2018, p. 36). The definition is therefore tautological and is reminiscent of the observation that anthropologist Claudia Strauss made 40 years ago that "discussion and research on the formal/informal dichotomy *really* seems to be about the difference between Western-style schooling and other forms" (1984, p. 195). Hence, Western-style schools are implicitly framed as the 'ideal type', and other models of education are portrayed as more or less desirable based on their degree of deviance from that ideal. The challenges of integrating Qur'anic schools into the 'formal' education system, when the former are inevitably obliged to conform to the norms of latter, are discussed further in Chapter 8.

In addition, assumptions have been made by some development actors that parents' preferences should be nudged towards more 'secular' options (Villalón and Bodian, 2012). For example, when discussing policy regarding Islamic education in Pakistan, Matthew Nelson noted that "scholars and policy makers alike have failed to devote sufficient attention to a disinterested assessment of local educational demands" (2006, p. 701). Instead he argued that policymakers in Pakistan (ibid., p. 702):

> have demonstrated a remarkably consistent attitude in turning their attention away from what individual preferences *are* toward a politically motivated account of what . . . they *should* be.

I would argue that such dynamics apply equally to West African contexts. These tendencies among donors also reflect the Two Faces of Faith trope (Hurd, 2015), covered in Chapter 2, which distinguishes between 'good'

Table 4.2 Classification of Islamic schools in West Africa according to the UNICEF West and Central Africa Regional Office.

	Non-formal Qur'anic education				*Formal Islamic education*	
	Family or neighbourhood Qur'anic school (type 1)	*Traditional Qur'anic school (type 2)*	*Itinerant school (type 3)*	*Modern Qur'anic school (type 4)*	*Arabo-Islamic médersa (type 5)*	*Arab or Franco-Arab school/médersa (type 6)*
Primary educational objective	Memorisation of the Qur'an	Memorisation of the Qur'an	Memorisation of the Qur'an	Memorisation of the Qur'an, Islamic sciences and secular subjects	Secular and Islamic sciences	Secular and Islamic sciences
Language of instruction	Arabic and national languages	Arabic and national languages	Arabic and national languages	Arabic and national languages	Arabic and official languages	Arabic and official languages
Pedagogical method	Traditional	Traditional	Traditional	Traditional and lecture-based	Lecture-based	Lecture-based
Recognition of studies	Hafiz, ijaza	Hafiz, ijaza	Hafiz, ijaza	Hafiz, ijaza or another diploma recognised or not by the state	Diploma recognised or not by the state	State diploma or diploma recognised by the state
Physical structure	None	Non-formal	None	Formal and non-formal	Formal	Formal

Based on Roy and Humeau (2018, p. 19). Translated from French by Anneke Newman.

and 'bad' religious practice, with the latter judged according to secular onto-epistemologies, Euro-North American cultural norms and modernist logics. 'Good' religion is instrumentalised for secular ends, while 'bad' forms are pressured to become some 'modern' alternative (Deneulin and Bano, 2009).

The education practitioner Sophie again seemed uniquely aware of this problem when she made the following observation:

> UNICEF has a colonialist vision, like only one vision of what it means to be 'educated'. They won't say it explicitly – although some government officials in the ministries of education will say it explicitly – that it's not useful to learn Arabic, although there are 400 million speakers of Arabic in the world! And if it's not modern Western-style education then it's not good. Which is absurd because actually the Qur'anic schools include lots of characteristics that UNICEF supposedly values – like a needs-based approach to children's learning, one-to-one teaching, there are no benchmarks or standardised tests so each child progresses at their own pace. . . . But they don't want to know.

Development agencies appear to still hold moral judgements about the kinds of knowledge and education that people ought to value. This ignores the valid reasons that Muslims in Senegal and elsewhere – whether education providers, parents or students – might have to reject the global North as a pole of moral, intellectual or economic relevance. Crucially, few development actors appear to appreciate why so many people continue to value the Qur'anic schools *in their current form* and not just for the marketable skills of literacy, numeracy and technical/vocational skills which hold more tangible value for policy-makers. Shedding light on this question is, therefore, the objective of the second half of this book.

Conclusion

This chapter has provided an analysis of the discourses of international development actors on Qur'anic schools and EFA, juxtaposed by critical literature on EID policies by historians, anthropologists, CIE scholars and linguists. This account shows how education policies locate, placate and ultimately marginalise Qur'anic schooling and associated phenomena like *Ajami* literacy. This is because they are informed more by colonialist stereotypes and value judgements, including those reflecting coloniality of secularity, than due appreciation of communities' perspectives or sound empirical evidence.

However, in order to understand trends in school preference in Senegal and how they are shaped by Islamic worldviews, we need more information from the parents and children themselves. The chapters in Part I of this book have raised a number of issues which lead to questions regarding how parents and youth perceive the different schools available. Given the continued legacies of colonialism, including the dominance of French literacy and government-accredited diplomas for enjoyment of citizenship, how do people choose between school types in practice? What relative weight do different individuals give to moral values, worldviews, epistemologies, identities, social capital or economic opportunities when making educational decisions? Does the Qur'anic schools' historic exclusion of women – and people who do not belong to Muslim clerical lineages – shape contemporary trends in school preference? How do parents and young people feel about contested issues like begging and corporal punishment in the *daara*? Part II pivots towards answering these questions, with Chapter 5 starting by explaining the popularity of Qur'anic schools in northern Senegal.

Notes

1 From 2002 to 2015 the reports were called 'EFA Global Monitoring Reports' and from 2016 onwards 'Global Education Monitoring Reports'.

2 *Marabout* is the term most-often used in francophone academic scholarship – and among people in Senegal – for a Muslim teacher, practitioner or Sufi leader. It is a French version of the Arabic term *murabit* meaning a man of religion. However, the term *marabout* has derogatory connotations inherited from the colonial period and implies that clerics are fraudulent and self-interested (Seesemann, 2011, pp. 11–12). Although my research participants used the term *marabout*, and I use their words when citing them directly, I employ the more neutral 'Muslim cleric' or simply 'cleric'.

3 The shop front features English, French and Wolof words written in Roman/Latin script and Wolofal (Wolof written in Arabic script) which is an example of *Ajami*.

References

Abdelhay, A., Asfaha, Y.M. and Juffermans, K. (2014) 'African literacies, ideologies, scripts, education', in K. Juffermans, Y.M. Asfaha and A. Abdelhay (eds) *African Literacies: Ideologies, Scripts, Education*. Newcastle: Cambridge Scholars Publishing, pp. 1–62.

Addey, C. (2018) 'Assembling literacy as global: The danger of a single story', in M. Milana et al. (eds) *The Palgrave International Handbook on Adult and Lifelong Education and Learning*. Cham, Switzerland: Palgrave Macmillan, pp. 315–335.

Albaugh, E.A. (2014) *State Building and Multilingual Education in Africa*. Cambridge: Cambridge University Press.

Bano, M. (2017) *Female Islamic Education Movements: The Re-Democratisation of Islamic Knowledge*. Cambridge: Cambridge University Press.

Bianchin, L. (2020) *L'utilité économique de l'éducation coranique: perceptions contrastées des parents, des talibés et des acteurs du développement dans la région de Dakar, Sénégal*. Unpublished Masters thesis, Centre d'Études de la Coopération Internationale et du Développement. Brussels: Université Libre de Bruxelles.

Binaté, I. and Hugon, C. (2019) 'Les réformes de l'éducation arabo-islamique en Côte d'Ivoire et au Sénégal: dynamiques, acteurs et stratégies', *Education Comparée*, 21, pp. 55–75.

Cochrane, L.L. (2020) 'Religious networks and small businesses in Senegal', *Economic Anthropology*, pp. 1–12. https://doi.org/10.1002/sea2.12185.

D'Aoust, S. (2013) 'Écoles franco-arabes publiques et daaras modernes au Sénégal: hybridation des ordres normatifs concernant l'éducation', *Cahiers de la recherche sur l'éducation et les savoirs*, 12, pp. 313–338.

Daun, H. (2010) 'Childhood learning, life skills and well-being in adult life: A Senegalese case', *Comparative Education*, 46(4), pp. 409–428.

Deneulin, S. and Bano, M. (2009) *Religion in Development: Rewriting the Secular Script*. London and New York: Zed Books.

Diallo, I. (2011) '"To understand lessons, think through your own languages." An analysis of narratives in support of the introduction of indigenous languages in the education system in Senegal', *Language Matters*, 42(2), pp. 207–230.

Dunne, M., et al. (2017) *Troubling Muslim Youth Identities: Nation, Religion, Gender*. London: Palgrave Macmillan.

Einarsdóttir, J., et al. (2010) *Child Trafficking in Guinea-Bissau. An Explorative Study*. Reykjavik: UNICEF Iceland.

Fall, A.S. (2011) 'Les usages des liens confrériques religieux dans l'économie Sénégalaise', in M. Kaag (ed) *Islam et engagements au Sénégal*. Leiden: Centre d'Etudes Africaines, pp. 46–77.

Filmer, D. and Fox, L. (2014) *Youth Employment in Sub-Saharan Africa. Africa Development Series*. Washington, DC: World Bank.

Gebre, A.H., et al. (2009) *Everyday Literacies in Africa: Ethnographic Studies of Literacy and Numeracy Practices in Ethiopia*. Kampala: Fountain Publishers Limited.

Guiliano Sarr, K. (2020) 'Conduit and gatekeeper: Practices and contestations of language within informal and formal education in Senegal', in J.M. Abidogun and T. Falola (eds) *Palgrave Handbook of African Education and Indigenous Knowledge*. Cham, Switzerland: Palgrave Macmillan, pp. 101–126.

Harrison, C. (1988) *France and Islam in West Africa 1860–1960*. Cambridge: Cambridge University Press.

Hima, H. (2020) '"Francophone" education and intersectionalities: Gender, language, and religion', in J.M. Abidogun and T. Falola (eds) *The Palgrave Handbook of African Education and Indigenous Knowledge*. Cham, Switzerland: Palgrave Macmillan, pp. 463–525.

Human Rights Watch (2010) *Off the Backs of the Children: Forced Begging and other Abuses Against Talibés in Senegal*. New York: Human Rights Watch.

Human Rights Watch (2014) *Exploitation in the Name of Education: Uneven Progress in Ending Forced Child Begging in Senegal*. New York: Human Rights Watch.

Human Rights Watch (2019a) *'There Is Enormous Suffering': Serious Abuses Against Talibé Children in Senegal, 2017–2018*. New York: Human Rights Watch.

Human Rights Watch (2019b) *"These Children Don't Belong in the Streets": A Roadmap for Ending Exploitation, Abuse of Talibés in Senegal*. New York: Human Rights Watch.

Hurd, E.S. (2015) *Beyond Religious Freedom: The New Global Politics of Religion*. Princeton, NJ: Princeton University Press.

King, K. (2007) 'Multi-lateral agencies in the construction of the global agenda on education', *Comparative Education*, 43(3), pp. 377–391.

Lahti, S.E. (2018) 'The limits of shock and shame: An ethnographic case analysis of the naming and shaming technique to promote human rights for the taalibe Qur'anic School students of Senegal', *Human Rights Quarterly*, 40, pp. 605–640.

Lahti, S.E. (2019) 'A tale of two NGO discourses: NGO stories of suffering Qur'anic school children in Senegal', in K. Cheney and A. Sinervo (eds) *Disadvantaged Childhoods and Humanitarian Intervention: Processes of Affective Commodification and Objectification*. Palgrave Macmillan, pp. 113–134.

Loimeier, R. (2000) 'L'Islam ne se vend plus: The Islamic reform movement and the state in Senegal', *Journal of Religion in Africa*, 30(2), pp. 168–190.

Lüpke, F. (2004) 'Language planning in West Africa: Who writes the script?', *Language Documentation and Description*, 2, pp. 90–107.
Lüpke, F. and Bao-Diop, S. (2014) 'Beneath the surface? Contemporary ajami writing', in K. Juffermans, Y.M. Asfaha and A. Abdelhay (eds) *African Literacies: Ideologies, Scripts, Education*. Newcastle: Cambridge Scholars Publishing, pp. 88–117.
Macleod, S.L. (2021) *Daaras and Development Discourses: Three Interventions Targeting the Practice of Begging by Talibés in Urban Senegal*. PhD thesis, Department of Development Studies, School of Oriental and African Studies (SOAS), University of London.
Management Systems International and USAID Senegal (2017) *Etude nationale sur les enfants et les jeunes hors du système éducatif au Sénégal*. Dakar: USAID Senegal.
Marshall, K. (2010) 'Education for all: Where does religion come in?', *Comparative Education*, 46(3), pp. 273–287.
MEN (2009) *Plan stratégique de développement des daara*. Dakar: Ministère de l'Education Nationale (MEN) Sénégal.
Mumin, M. (2014) 'The Arabic script in Africa: Understudied literacy', in M. Mumin and K. Versteegh (eds) *The Arabic Script in Africa: Studies in the Use of a Writing System*. Leiden: Brill, pp. 41–76.
Nelson, M.J. (2006) 'Muslims, markets, and the meaning of a "good" education in Pakistan', *Asian Survey*, 46(5), pp. 699–720.
Ngom, F. (2015) 'Murid Ajami sources of knowledge: The myth and the reality', in M. Kominko (ed) *From Dust to Digital: Ten Years of the Endangered Archives Programme*. Open Book Publishers, pp. 331–375.
Nieuwenhuys, O. (2001) 'By the sweat of their brow? "Street children", NGOs and children's rights in Addis Ababa', *Africa*, 71(4), pp. 539–557.
Ogunnaike, O. (2020) 'Islamic philosophies of education in Africa', in J.M. Abidogun and T. Falola (eds) *The Palgrave Handbook of African Education and Indigenous Knowledge*. Cham, Switzerland: Palgrave Macmillan, pp. 421–450.
PASEC (2020) *PASEC2019: Quality of Education Systems in French-Speaking Sub-Saharan Africa. Teaching/Learning Performance and Environment in Primary Education*. Dakar: PASEC.
Perry, D. (2004) 'Muslim child disciples, global civil society, and children's rights in Senegal', *Anthropological Quarterly*, 77(1), pp. 47–86.
Roy, É. and Humeau, P. (2018) *Etat des lieux sur l'offre et les mécanismes institutionnels relatifs à l'éducation coranique et à l'enseignement islamique dans les pays de l'Afrique de l'Ouest et du Centre*. Dakar: UNICEF and Qualé.
Rudolph, S., Sriprakash, A. and Gerrard, J. (2018) 'Knowledge and racial violence: The shine and shadow of "powerful knowledge"', *Ethics and Education*, 13(1), pp. 22–38.
Seesemann, R. (2011) *The Divine Flood: Ibrahim Niasse and the Roots of a Twentieth-Century Sufi Revival*. Oxford: Oxford University Press.
Sriprakash, A., Tikly, L. and Walker, S. (2020) 'The erasures of racism in education and international development: Re-reading the "global learning crisis"', *Compare: A Journal of Comparative and International Education*, 50(5), pp. 676–692.
Stambach, A. (2006) 'Revising a four-square model of a complicated whole: On the cultural politics of religion and education', *Social Analysis*, 50(3), pp. 1–18.
Starrett, G. (1998) *Putting Islam to Work: Education, Politics and Religious Transformation in Egypt*. Berkeley, CA: University of California Press.
Strauss, C. (1984) 'Beyond "formal" versus "informal" education: Uses of psychological theory in anthropological research', *Ethos*, 12(3), pp. 195–222.
Street, B.V. (1995) *Social Literacies: Critical Approaches to Literacy in Development, Ethnography and Education*. Harlow: Pearson Education Limited.
Thorsen, D. (2012) *Children Begging for Qur'ānic School Masters: Evidence from West and Central Africa*. Dakar: United Nations Children's Fund (UNICEF).
Tikly, L. (2015) 'What works, for whom, and in what circumstances? Towards a critical realist understanding of learning in international and comparative education', *International Journal of Educational Development*, 40, pp. 237–249.

Tikly, L. (2016) 'Education for all as a global regime of educational governance: Issues and tensions', in S. Yamada (ed) *Post-Education-for-All and Sustainable Development Paradigm: Structural Changes with Diversifying Actors and Norms.* Emerald Group Publishing Ltd, pp. 37–65.

Tikly, L. (2017) 'The future of education for all as a global regime of educational governance', *Comparative Education Review*, 61(1), pp. 22–57.

Tikly, L. (2020) *Education for Sustainable Development in the Postcolonial World: Towards a Transformative Agenda for Africa.* London: Routledge.

UNESCO (1990) *World Declaration on Education For All and Framework for Action to Meet Basic Learning Needs. Jomtien, Thailand 5–9 March 1990.* Paris: United Nations Educational, Scientific and Cultural Organization (UNESCO).

UNESCO (2000) *The Dakar Framework for Action. Education for All: Meeting Our Collective Commitments. Adopted by the World Education Forum Dakar, Senegal, 26–28 April 2000.* Paris: United Nations Educational, Scientific and Cultural Organization (UNESCO).

UNESCO (2004) *EFA Global Monitoring Report 2005. Education for All: The Quality Imperative.* Paris: United Nations Educational, Scientific and Cultural Organization (UNESCO).

UNESCO (2005) *EFA Global Monitoring Report 2006. Literacy for Life.* Paris: United Nations Educational, Scientific and Cultural Organization (UNESCO).

UNESCO (2012) *EFA Global Monitoring Report 2012. Youth and Skills: Putting Education to Work.* Paris: United Nations Educational, Scientific and Cultural Organization (UNESCO).

UNESCO (2015) *EFA Global Monitoring Report 2015. Education for All 2000–2015: Achievements and Challenges.* Paris: United Nations Educational, Scientific and Cultural Organization (UNESCO).

UNESCO (2019) *Global Education Monitoring Report 2019. Migration, Displacement and Education: Building Bridges Not Walls.* Paris: United Nations Educational, Scientific and Cultural Organization (UNESCO).

UNESCO (2021) *Global Education Monitoring Report 2021/2022. Non-State Actors in Education: Who Chooses? Who Loses?* Paris: United Nations Educational, Scientific and Cultural Organization (UNESCO).

Verde, T. (2011) 'From Africa, in Ajami', *Aramco World*, 62(5), pp. 34–39.

Villalón, L.A. and Bodian, M. (2012) *Religion, demande sociale, et réformes éducatives au Sénégal.* Miami, Niamey and London: University of Florida, Laboratoire d'Etudes et de Recherches sur les Dynamiques Sociales et le Développement Local, Overseas Development Institute.

Ware, R.T. (2004) 'Njàngaan: The daily regime of Qur'ânic students in twentieth-century Senegal', *The International Journal of African Historical Studies*, 37(3), pp. 515–538.

Ware, R.T. (2014) *The Walking Qur'an: Islamic Education, Embodied Knowledge, and History in West Africa.* Chapel Hill, NC: The University of North Carolina Press.

Ware, R.T. and Launay, R. (2009) 'Comment (ne pas) lire le Coran: Logiques de l'enseignement religieux au Sénégal et en Côte d'Ivoire', in G. Holder (ed) *L'islam, nouvel espace public en Afrique.* Paris: Karthala, pp. 127–145.

Part II

Patterns of educational engagement in northern Senegal

5 Understanding Qur'anic school preference

As Chapter 4 showed, development professionals in Dakar overwhelmingly assumed that parents who opted for Qur'anic schools were poor, neglectful or religiously conservative. However, these impressions were shattered by the inhabitants of Medina Diallobé, a village in northern Senegal. My host family strongly valued *daaras* for their sons despite the accessibility of state schools, and their attitudes challenged the patronising stereotypes that I had heard from development actors.

In Medina Diallobé, parents and youth alike agreed that Qur'anic education entailed some degree of hardship but argued that this discomfort was necessary for learning. The *daaras*[1] were considered to be more effective at meeting their stated objectives than the local state schools. And neither were the members of my host family ignorant, poor traditionalists – they were relatively affluent by local standards. Several of the men had studied to advanced levels in both the state and Islamic systems and had travelled extensively to study or to work in Europe, Africa, the US and the Middle East. One had played a local leadership role in organising for the UN's annual World Interfaith Harmony Week. Many had chosen full-time Qur'anic schooling for their sons over the state school. Some boys had even dropped out of state schools, preferring to attend *daaras* instead, occasionally against their parents' wishes, and were not forced to do so by poverty or similar constraints. This experience inspired me to not only investigate why people in Medina Diallobé valued Qur'anic schools so much but also to understand why there was such a gap between their perceptions and those of development elites.

The development professionals I met all tended to take for granted, albeit unconsciously, the premises of human capital theory (HCT) and rational choice theory (RCT) by assuming that Qur'anic schools were inferior 'quality' compared to 'secular' and 'hybrid' Franco-Arab schools when it came to imparting useful knowledge and economic skills. They presumed that parents who sent their children to Qur'anic schools were too poor to support their children's upkeep or lacked access to 'quality' state schools. To illustrate this logic, in a report on Islamic schools in West Africa, Stefania Gandolfi, writing as UNESCO Chair on Human Rights and Ethics in International Cooperation and

DOI: 10.4324/9781003172475-7

Sustainable Development at the University of Bergamo, generalised across the region to assume that *daaras* only appealed to the poor without other options. She asserted that, "without adaptation, Qur'anic schools . . . risk becoming a refuge for the poor and all those who do not benefit from access to state education" (2003, p. 273). While there is a trend in West Africa whereby poorer families often opt for Qur'anic schools (Hoechner, 2018), this is not always the case – as we shall see later.

Meanwhile, if parents preferred Qur'anic schools for their children even when state schools were accessible, development actors tended to assume that they were naïve and ignorant of the *daaras*' poor standards. At worst, they were considered to be so attached to their faith that they were willing to sacrifice their children's well-being (Thorsen, 2012). Such narratives are apparent in reports like Human Rights Watch's *Off the Backs of the Children: Forced Begging and Other Abuses Against Talibés in Senegal* (2010). It states that "pressed financially, some parents send their children ostensibly to learn the Quran, but also to alleviate household expenditures". Even more accusatory, it asserts that "parents' treatment of the children they choose to send hundreds of kilometers away to marabouts [Muslim clerics] ranges from neglect to knowing complicity in abuse" (ibid., p. 85). The recent GEM Report *Inclusion and Education* (UNESCO, 2020, p. 78) also illustrates this thinking in its framing of parental preference for faith-based schools as 'self-segregation' and hence problematic:

> Self-segregation blurs the boundaries of inclusion. Special education may nominally be a parental choice. It may also reflect a preference for self-exclusion. . . This applies as well to schools that cater to specific groups, such as single-sex, minority language and religious community schools.

Much education policy in West Africa under EFA, including the reforms to integrate more religious content into the public school systems described in Chapter 4, was therefore intended to 'coax' parents away from Qur'anic schools towards 'quality' alternatives. A cornerstone of the Senegalese government's 10-year education strategy, the *Programme d'Amélioration de la Qualité, de l'Equité et de la Transparence 2013–2025* (PAQUET) includes creating state-controlled religious schools explicitly to encourage parents to move away from classical Qur'anic schools in communities labelled as "resistant" to state schooling (MEN, 2013, p. 35). Meanwhile, public 'modern *daaras*' and accredited Franco-Arab schools are supposed to appeal to parents currently sending their children to boarding Qur'anic schools (D'Aoust, 2013).

Such coloniality of secularity and Euro-North American centric value judgements impede our understanding of Qur'anic school preference because the same negative stereotypes that inform policy (analysed in Chapter 4) also creep into models of educational decision-making. As I argued previously, overcoming this problem requires a theoretical framework that avoids modern/colonialist assumptions. In the first section, I therefore review the main theories on educational engagement used in academic scholarship and their advantages and limitations. I then present the village of Medina Diallobé and situate it within a brief history of the dominant onto-epistemological, sociological and educational trends characteristic of the Haalpulaar ethnic group and Futa Tooro region in northern Senegal. This region has some of the highest rates of Qur'anic school preference in the country yet compared to the Wolof-speaking Djourbel region described in Chapter 4, it has received far less academic attention in debates on Islamic education. However, as we shall see in this chapter, the characteristics of the Futa Tooro region regarding its Islamic culture, gender dynamics and descent-based/racialised hierarchies (or 'caste') add an extra layer of complexity to our understanding of educational trends.

Coloniality of secularity in frameworks for understanding educational decision-making

Two paradigms dominate within scholarly analysis of educational decision-making in the global South. In the following sections I reveal the limitations of, first, the economic paradigms common in development studies and, second, the anthropological and sociological frameworks.

Economic paradigms

In Chapters 1 and 4, I unpacked at length the flawed assumptions that classical economists make about religious behaviour, specifically preference for faith-based schools. These biases underpin both RCT and HCT and, in turn, inform the theories of educational decision-making used in development research and policy. Essentially, economists tend to assume, on the basis of large-scale surveys and statistical modelling, that religious behaviour is not utility-maximising – with utility defined in narrowly materialistic terms – and hence evidence of irrationality or indoctrination. Alternatively, they suggest that religious behaviour provides religious rewards which are only appealing in situations of material deprivation (Bano, 2012, pp. 6–9).

An important corrective is the framework developed by Masooda Bano in *The Rational Believer: Choices and Decisions in the Madrasas of Pakistan* (2012). Bano argues that classical economists fail to acknowledge that "in order to command adherence the given belief system must have moral or practical appeal for the believer" (ibid., p. 8). Instead, she proposes a framework grounded in New Institutional Economics and informed by qualitative and ethnographic data. Bano suggests that preference for strong faith-based schools reflects "dual notions of utility" with the former resting on "the human need for material achievement" and the latter "the pursuit of ideas". According to Bano, "the constant struggle between material and ideal utility is central to the rationality of religious behavior" (ibid., p. 12). In her account of preference for *madrasas*, she explains that Islamic ontology means that

Muslims are orientated towards both "this world" and "the other world (the afterlife)" which results in a "conscious desire to endear themselves to God" (ibid., p. 113). This orientation has an important impact on school preference (ibid., pp. 105–106) although individuals differ in their "propensity towards other-worldly concerns" (ibid., p. 122). Bano describes a wide range of "religious benefits" of *madrasas* and an Islamic worldview more broadly, including the teaching of moral values (ibid., pp. 107–108, 117) and a set of "logics" which help people explain the world and face challenging circumstances (ibid., pp. 112–120).

Although Bano's work addresses many of the flaws of classical RCT/HCT, it is noteworthy that she argues that religious actors are strategic, calculating and rational and that the value of religious ontologies are the 'logics' they provide for understanding the world. In so doing, she arguably subscribes too closely to modernist value judgements that elevate individual intellect and conscious action over embodied affect, intuition or social relations. Her account of school preference has the disadvantage of ignoring the significance of sensed, embodied experiences that qualitative religious studies scholars have convincingly argued underpin people's onto-epistemologies (Barnes, 2020). Bano also side-steps how religious behaviour is often relatively unconscious and a product of group belonging and social identity, as has been long documented by anthropologists (see Noret, 2013 for a review).

From my perspective, a decolonial approach also demands that any analysis of education preference in the global South must systematically acknowledge the legacies of colonisation. Bano shows how colonial hierarchies and the imposition of secular ontology have underpinned *madrasa* reform in Southeast Asia (2012, p. 42) and that resistance to "cultural Westernisation" informed women's attendance in *madrasas* (ibid., p. 141). However, her economic framework does not provide conceptual tools for theorising how power inequalities stemming from colonisation, including in relation to ontology and epistemology, shape contemporary trends in educational engagement.

Sociological and anthropological frameworks

If rational choice and human capital theories are ubiquitous in economics and development studies, Pierre Bourdieu's framework of field, habitus and capital holds the same status in the disciplines of sociology and anthropology. This is illustrated in its widespread application to parents' and young people's engagement with state and Islamic schools in India (Jeffrey, Jeffery and Jeffery, 2008; Froerer, 2011) and West Africa (Gérard, 1992; Barnes, 2009; Hoechner, 2018) including Senegal (Lewandowski, 2011; Chehami, 2016; Bianchin, 2020).

According to Bourdieu, the social world can be thought of as a space subdivided into microcosms or 'fields', where individuals strive to acquire 'capital' valued in that field (Esquerre, 2016). Bourdieu (1986) defines capital as scarce goods and resources with his four main types being: 'economic capital' or material wealth; 'cultural capital' or valued knowledge and behaviour which exists in embodied, objectified or institutionalised forms; 'social capital' or relationships and connections with others through which other resources can be acquired; and 'symbolic capital', namely the prestige, honour or status associated with the acquisition of other forms of capital valued in a particular field. The forms of capital are to some extent convertible and their acquisition enables individuals to gain more capital, as well as power and authority. Through the cumulative effect of past experiences acquired through pursuing capital, individuals develop dispositions or 'habitus' which consists of internalised and often unconscious ways of thinking and interacting with the world (Bourdieu, 1977, p. 72).

Bourdieu's (1986) framework is useful because it highlights the multiple and inter-linked benefits that education can confer, the structural barriers to educational opportunities, and the often unconscious and affective underpinnings of patterned behaviour. The Bourdieusian approach has advantages over a framework rooted in New Institutional Economics because it highlights the collective and often unconscious nature of educational preferences and strategies and emphasises more systematically the influence of colonialist hierarchies on perceptions of schooling. Africanists using Bourdieu show that people rarely deliberate extensively when calculating costs and benefits of different schools. Rather, group-level 'social representations of education and the school' – based on personal and group experience, assumptions and emotions – often operate as mental 'short-cuts' which inform behaviour (Lange, 2003, pp. 156–157). Scholars of education in Islamic West Africa have widely recognised how colonial administrators and later post-colonial governments perceived Islamic schools as a threat to their influence, as I described in Chapter 3. Hence, many Muslims in Islamic Africa today still perceive state-run institutions to be colonialist enterprises and avoid them, even if it impedes their acquisition of economic capital (Gérard, 1997; Chehami, 2016; Hoechner, 2018, p. 77).

Bourdieusian scholarship on Islamic education nonetheless exhibits a number of secular biases which could reflect the blindspots of the researchers or the inherently materialist nature of the framework. In contrast to Bano's account which devotes attention to the 'intrinsic benefits' or 'ideal utility' of religion (2012, p. 12), Africanist scholars of Islamic education preference who use Bourdieu often gloss over religious motivations. For instance, when explaining parental preference for Qur'anic schools in Senegal, Joanne Chehami (2016) claims that such schools inculcate values and a sense of identity respected in Senegalese society and insert students into community and religious networks. Parents also derive prestige from their child's status as a *hafiz* (someone who has memorised the Qur'an). Thus, she reduces incentives to pursue religious education to expectations of social and symbolic capital. While Chehami briefly mentions *baraka* or blessing and pedagogy in the *daaras* linked to "mystical principles" associated with the Sufi orders (ibid., p. 58), there is no discussion in her work of ontology, people's religious subjectivities or affective experiences and how these might inform their decisions.

In contrast, Hannah Hoechner's book, *Qur'anic Schools in Northern Nigeria: Youth, Faith and Poverty* (2018), based on participatory ethnography with young Qur'anic students, makes significant efforts to demonstrate that "we cannot neglect the significance that religious, moral, and social considerations hold in their own right and independent of underlying material circumstances" (ibid., p. 111). Further, she argues that preference for Qur'anic schools "is not merely 'virtue made of necessity,' but also a positive choice of its own" (ibid., p. 99). However, when Hoechner speaks of "religious reasoning", she describes the value of Qur'anic schools for inculcating a habitus that confers psychological resilience and symbolic capital that can be converted to economic and social capital later down the line (ibid., pp. 112–121), rather than looking at affective or spiritual experiences and how they might shape educational motivations. In her defence, Hoechner practiced an extremely commendable standard of reflexivity. She went to great lengths to represent faithfully her research participants' voices, including through co-creating a participatory documentary (ibid., pp. 24–41) and so the child Qur'anic students in her study probably did not allude to such issues. In contrast, the research participants in my study were slightly older, the poverty in northern Senegal was less acute, and I discussed my experiences as a Sufi with them. Their narratives therefore revealed a different set of perspectives where Islamic onto-epistemologies and affective religious experiences were more explicitly discussed.

Ultimately, sociologists and anthropologists of school *engagement* in Islamic Africa have engaged little with the theoretical (as opposed to simply empirical) implications of the epistemological debates raised by scholars of Islamic education *provision* covered in Chapter 3. The latter group of researchers are also guilty of privileging the discourses of education providers and Muslim intellectuals while side-lining the views of parents and especially children (Hoechner, 2018, pp. 4–9). Furthermore, scholars using Bourdieu pay relatively little attention to the implications of people's onto-epistemologies potentially because the framework itself is resolutely secular and materialist (thus reflecting colonialist tendencies of secular erasure). A postsecular approach to understanding educational decision-making therefore requires dismantling the classical academic concepts, theories and modes of engagement underpinned by coloniality of secularity by finding alternatives that better reflect emic perspectives – a project I pursue further in Chapter 9.

In what follows, I present ethnographic data on educational trends in Medina Diallobé and how their logics expose the limitations of a Bourdieusian framework. But first, I start by presenting the fieldsite and wider region of the Futa Tooro, before describing my research study in detail.

Researching education in Medina Diallobé village

The Route Nationale 2 is an artery of asphalt which departs from the bustling city sprawl of Dakar and snakes its way northwards along the Atlantic coast to the old colonial capital of Saint-Louis before curling eastwards into the Senegal River valley basin – a region known by its Haalpulaar inhabitants as the Futa Tooro. Medina Diallobé, where I conducted my research, is one of the larger villages dotted at regular intervals along the Route Nationale 2. The historical characteristics of the Futa Tooro region, namely its distinctive Islamic culture and descent-based hierarchy, as we shall see, played out in the educational worlds of Medina Diallobé.

The Islamic culture of the Futa Tooro region

The distinctive Islamic culture of the Haalpulaar'en – and their hierarchical social structure – continue to shape trends in educational engagement. Despite the Futa Tooro's hot climate, the river floods every rainy season enabling cultivation of millet, sorghum, barley and rice in the plain (*waalo*). The highlands (*jeeri*) host rain-fed cultivation of vegetables and provide grass for the pasture of cattle, sheep and goats. The river basin's fertility means that it has been settled from at least the ninth century by several important empires. Islam was spread to the region by trans-Saharan traders in the tenth century and soon became renowned throughout the Islamic world as the cradle of Islam in West Africa (Kane, 1987, pp. 23–26, 29).

Islam in the Futa Tooro moulded to the local descent-based/racial hierarchy of three endogamous ranks, namely the freeborn, artisan/musicians and slaves – a hierarchy shared by many West African societies as described in Chapter 3. The sub-categories or 'status groups' within each rank were each associated with a hereditary occupation characterised by a specific body of both technical and mystic knowledge which anthropologist Roy Dilley calls 'lore' or 'knowledge-power' (2004, p. 4). The livelihood of teaching the Qur'an and selling products of the esoteric sciences among Muslim clerical communities in West Africa functioned like a hereditary craft. They closely guarded their knowledge and barred other freeborn groups from advanced Islamic education and excluded artisan/musician and slave ranks from Qur'anic schools altogether (Willis, 1978).

This situation evolved as Muslim clerics rose to dominate Haapulaar society. In the fifteenth century, the Portuguese established the Senegalese coast as their primary port in West Africa. While domestic slavery had long been practiced in the region, the Transatlantic slave trade brought about a massive social restructuring as intense manhunts into the interior stimulated militarisation and inter-state violence (Klein, 1998). Muslim clerics played an important social role in the Futa Tooro region but, since they were excluded from political and economic power, their communities were vulnerable to slave raids practiced or permitted by local kings (Willis, 1978). By the eighteenth century, the clerics constituted a group calling themselves the *toorobe* (singular: *toorodo*) and waged a holy war (*jihad*) to overthrow the ruling kingdom. They established an Islamic state or Almamate in 1776 headed by the cleric Abdul Qader Kane. Although Kane's assassination in 1807 marked the end of a strong centralised Islamic state in the Futa Tooro, his legacy persisted in the integration of Islam into public life, including the implantation of mosques and Qur'anic schools throughout the territory (Dilley, 2004, pp. 34–37).

The Almamate entrenched the *toorobe's* dominance in the Futa Tooro region but also increased inequality within the group. Kane allowed any man – including from the ranks of artisan/musicians and freed slaves – to be a cleric on the basis of knowledge, and the *toorodo* category swelled to become 45% of the population (Bouteiller et al., 1962 cited in Coulon, 1975, p. 34). Yet, after Kane's death, the *toorobe* closed ranks and re-defined their status group in terms of inheritance. They developed elaborate genealogies and even claims of descent from the Prophet's family, known locally as *sharif*, to justify their superior position (Dilley, 2004, p. 94). Moreover, the *toorodo* lineages who had led the *jihad* monopolised the prestigious inherited positions as imams or clerics of Qur'anic schools who wielded political as well as religious authority (*seerembe* lineages). They often appropriated the political title of village chief and re-distributed the most fertile *waalo* land, and hence primary source of wealth, among their allies. Hence, while the *toorodo* group as a whole represented almost half of the population, wealth and power was concentrated within these aristocratic lineages (Schmitz, 1986, p. 362). As the French appointed many as colonial administrators or jurists, these families have seen their socio-economic dominance reproduced in the colonial and post-colonial contexts. Later generations mobilised their families' political connections and economic wealth to secure elected positions in national and local government (Blundo, 2000).

Two final characteristics of Islamic culture in the Futa Tooro region deserve mention, namely a history of anti-colonial resistance and the dominance of a particular Sufi order. The French traded along the river from the seventeenth century and expanded into the interior in the nineteenth. The most significant resistance movement was organised by *toorodo* Cheikh Umar Tall, a Sufi leader who recruited an army to mount a *jihad* against French colonial forces in the 1850s and established an Islamic state in what is present-day Mali. Tall belonged to a long tradition of Muslim intellectuals from the Futa Tooro who studied throughout the Islamic world and used Islam to challenge social disruption linked to European encroachment. He is hailed as a hero by the Haalpulaar'en and was often mentioned by my research participants as a source of inspiration in their educational trajectories, although his violent military campaigns against fellow West Africans mean that his legacy is more contested elsewhere (Robinson, 1985). Tall was killed in 1862 and his state toppled in 1893, marking the definitive beginning of French colonial rule in Senegambia (Sall, 2000). A significant element of Tall's authority was his affiliation to the Tijaniyya[2] Sufi order. Originally, Sufi mystics formed loose associations, but in the face of European imperialism they developed stronger institutional frameworks called orders. This form of social organisation has come to define Senegambian Muslim societies (Robinson, 2000). Representing one-third of the world's Muslims today (Barnes, 2009, p. 210), Sufi orders are typically characterised by classical Islamic onto-epistemological principles (explained in Chapter 3). Each order has specific prayers and rituals designed to guide followers towards "the inner reality of God" (ibid., p. 210). Leaders – or *shaykhs* – are guides on that path. Individuals choose to be disciples – or followers – of a specific *shaykh,* and *shaykhs* may have dozens to thousands of disciples (Cochrane, 2020). The orders represent social, economic and political as well as religious networks. In rural West Africa, they were organised around agricultural production and overlapped with existing networks of Qur'anic schools. Sufi disciples and Qur'anic school students provided labour and political support; in turn they benefitted from an education, blessings, a community network and clientelistic support from the *shaykh* or cleric (Ware, 2014, p. 187). Tall's defeat stimulated an exodus of his disciples back to the Futa Tooro region where they created a dense network of Qur'anic schools affiliated with the Tijaniyya Umariyya (Umariyya meaning named after Cheikh Umar) to resist French influence (Sall, 2000).

In Chapter 3, I explained how there was a strong tradition of female textual learning and Islamic scholarship in the West African Sufi empires. Yet, the Futa Tooro region represented an exception to this trend. Rather, under Tall's militaristic *jihad,* there were fewer opportunities for female scholars, and women were relegated to roles in marriage and the home (Robinson, 2000, p. 143). If girls from clerical families studied at Qur'anic schools, it was as day students, learning the minimum of verses and how to behave according to norms of feminine piety (Ware, 2014, p. 172).

My first trip to the Futa Tooro region in 2010 holds a special place in my heart, as I remember the excitement I felt as an extremely rickety mini-bus carried us through a sparse ochre landscape of prickly acacia trees and the occasional indigo-turbaned pastoralist guiding a herd of goats. At regular intervals, we passed a cluster of brick-walled compounds or thatched-roof huts, and my Haalpulaar guide Mamadou would explain the history of that particular village. After a long day in the dusty heat, my concentration had started to wane, but I remembered him pointing out the birthplace of Cheikh Umar Tall. In the later sections and Chapter 6 we will see how the historic legacy of the wider Futa Tooro region manifests in the present – in its high density of classical Qur'anic schools, the status and honour that this education confers on Muslim clerical families, and the political dominance of the Tijaniyya Umariyya (Dilley, 2004, pp. 34–37).

Building relationships in Medina Diallobé village

In 2011, the year in which I conducted my research, Medina Diallobé had around 5,000 residents, two-thirds of whom were women due to high rates of male emigration. Haalpulaar society still exhibits the three ranks of freeborn, artisan/musicians and descendants of slaves. The freeborn rank consists of the status groups of Muslim clerics (*toorobe*), warriors, courtiers/advisors, pastoralists and fishermen. The artisan/musician rank includes leatherworkers, weavers, woodcarvers, blacksmiths, musicians and praise singers. My figures on the proportions of different status groups in Medina Diallobé in 2011 followed estimates from local government officials that *tooroɓe* made up roughly 50% of the population and descendants of slaves (*gallunkooɓe*) around 25%. The artisan/musician rank were roughly 15%, predominantly the status group of blacksmiths. The remaining 10% of inhabitants were other groups of freeborn rank. These figures were not dissimilar from the last official survey of status groups in the Futa Tooro in 1962 (Bouteiller et al., 1962 cited in Coulon, 1975, p. 34).

Demographic and Health Survey statistics found that households of the regions of Saint Louis and Matam (which correspond roughly to the Futa Tooro region) were clustered in the lowest, second and third wealth quintiles in the country (ANSD and ICF International, 2012, p. 19). Yet, these data mask disparities related to descent-based/racialised inequalities. In fact, when I conducted fieldwork there, the most affluent households in Medina Diallobé were mainly of freeborn rank whose ancestors had settled the village in the nineteenth century and who held inherited religious or political titles. They often boasted large concrete houses, a brick wall around their compound, electricity, running water and sometimes flushing toilets. Many could be considered 'lower middle-class' by African standards, namely above the poverty line but vulnerable to shocks and fluctuations in income (Samson and LeBlanc, 2022, p. 683). Their economic capital was sometimes acquired through formal sector salaries but more frequently through having any of the following: at least one migrant family member abroad sending regular remittances; successful careers in trade; clientelistic relationships with individuals with political connections; or religious professions in the case of *seeremɓe*. Poorer families had smaller houses either with an earth floor, outdoor latrines and sometimes no running water and no outside fence or just one built from woven branches. They mainly lived from, for example: farming; small-scale commerce; customary trades associated with their status group; or 'modern' professions such as mechanic, shopkeeper or restaurant owner.

Against the backdrop of the massification of state schooling under EFA, my research initially aimed to uncover how gender, descent and socioeconomic status fed into the educational preferences of parents and aspirations and trajectories of youth, relative to the state and Qur'anic schools. However, in practice, my investigations went much deeper than that. The study catapulted me into the world of Sufism and its influence on social dynamics, the personal, spiritual and social value of learning the Qur'an, and the tensions and struggles between different groups in the village.

My original objective was to talk to education providers, as well as a sample of parents and youth, in their homes and at school, starting from my *toorodo* host family and branching out through snowball sampling to their extended family and friends. I lived in the village for nine months spread across 2010 and 2012 and, after getting to know people and building trust, I conducted semi-structured interviews and life histories of educational trajectories with education providers, parents and youth to understand the values they attributed to knowledge and education. This group included 34 elders/parents, 85 youth aged between 13 and 30, five local government and 13 state school personnel, and seven religious professionals. There was a bias towards *toorobɓe* (76% of research participants) because of their numerical dominance in the village, the fact that my host family hailed from this group, and my interest in Islamic education which they monopolised (see Table 5.1). I only audio-recorded formal interviews, while informal conversations I wrote up in a diary soon afterwards and typed up later. Over the next few years, I conducted follow-up interviews by phone with closer research participants and in person during a three-week return trip to Senegal in 2018. This was to maintain interpersonal relationships and to complement the data I had already obtained particularly in relation to the evolving policy landscape.

While schooled individuals spoke French at varying levels of proficiency, Pulaar was the dominant language. Before starting data collection in Medina Diallobé, I spent three months learning Pulaar at a language school in Dakar, followed by two months' immersion in the village. Although I could manage basic conversations and follow people's discussions, I never became fluent, and I was reliant on an interpreter for complex interviews, especially with groups. I spent the first two months of fieldwork trying to find a suitable interpreter and worked with three different individuals: a schoolteacher, the head of the local youth association and the coordinator of a local NGO. I developed good relationships with all three and had insightful conversations with their families and people of the same age or status group. However, the common challenge emerged that my interpreters felt uncomfortable – or made excuses to avoid organising interviews – outside of these networks.

Fortunately, I met a local administrator whom I call Demba who became a friend and one of my closest research participants. He explained that my intepreters' discomfort stemmed from the fact that they might be concerned about maintaining *soutoura*, a concept found across Senegal meaning protecting one's own and other people's privacy, dignity and, above all, family reputation. Keeping sensitive information within 'safe' networks of trust, where they would be kept secret, is crucial to people's efforts to maintain *soutoura* (Ndiaye, 2008, pp. 156–158). Demba and I discussed the possibility of finding an interpreter from outside of Medina Diallobé to overcome this challenge but decided that introducing a third party could disturb the close relationships that I had managed to build so far. In the end, I asked friends or host family members to interpret for those present in the conversation who spoke French less well, which usually happened spontaneously without my asking. Rather than seeing this technique as problematic because of the biases it generated, I followed the premise that all interviews, whether with interpreters or without, constitute creative dialogues in which the interaction between researcher and informant shapes what people say. While this approach did restrict my access to non-French speakers to an extent, I felt confident that, because of the high levels of trust built within these relationships, the opinions that people

Table 5.1 Research participants in Medina Diallobé by age, category and status group.

Category of research participant	*Status group (all Haalpulaar'en unless indicated under 'other ethnicity')*							
	Tooroɗo *(Muslim cleric)*	Pullo *(cattle herder)*	Ceɗɗo *(warrior)*	Cuballo *(fisher)*	Baylo *(blacksmith)*	Gallunke *(freed slave)*	*Other ethnicity*	*Unknown*
Older parents/elders (> 31)								
Male	15	0	0	0	1	0	0	0
Female	17	0	0	0	1	0	0	0
Youth (13–30)								
Male	27	0	3	1	3	5	0	3
Female	37	0	0	0	2	4	0	0
Local government								
Male	3	0	0	0	1	0	1	0
Female	0	0	0	0	0	0	0	0
School personnel								
Male	2	1	2	0	1	0	3	0
Female	1	1	0	0	1	0	1	0
Religious professionals								
Male	6	0	0	0	0	0	0	0
Female	1	0	0	0	0	0	0	0
TOTAL	109	2	5	1	10	9	5	3

expressed were more honest than they might have been with a third party interpreter – even if this had meant more interactions with people who only spoke Pulaar.

My gender also shaped my interactions. In the Futa Tooro region, a stranger's relationship with their host family (*njatigi*) provides the foundation for their integration into the community (Schmitz, 2006). A guest is expected to behave appropriately, and any violation of local norms reflects badly on the host's reputation. As my relationship with my host family formed the bedrock of connections I built in Medina Diallobé, I did the utmost to behave in ways which made them proud. As a woman in my late twenties, my dress and interactions with men were two areas crucial to my maintaining an image of a respectable femininity. I always dressed according to my host family's relatively high standards of modesty by wearing a long dress with sleeves, wraparound skirt, headscarf, and outer shawl covering my arms. I was never prevented from spending time with male acquaintances, including after dark, but I made sure I had discussions in public, such as outside a shop on the main road or in the yard of the man's compound but with other family members present, to avoid gossip.

In fact, I found social norms which restricted interactions on the basis of descent-based/racial hierarchies harder to negotiate than those based on gender, which I unpack further in Chapter 6. My conversion to Islam fairly late on during fieldwork also had an impact. While I had developed close relationships long before then, my formal conversion meant that people started sharing more details about secret or esoteric Islamic knowledge which I describe later. In what follows, I share what these relationships revealed to me about school provision in Medina Diallobé and dominant trends in educational engagement.

In terms of informing people about my research and obtaining consent, I opted for a 'situated ethics' approach, grounded in self-reflexive adaption to the particular context rather than based on ethical absolutes (Simons and Usher, 2000). This approach aligns with the guidelines of the Association of Social Anthropologists of the UK (ASA) which states that "ethical decision-making has to be undertaken repeatedly throughout the research and in response to specific circumstances" (ASA, 2011, p. 1) and that "consent in ethnographic research is a process, not a one-off event, due to its long-term and open-ended qualities" (ibid., p. 5). It took me time to learn how to explain the purpose and content of my research in ways that were clear and meaningful to people. After discovering that most people did not understand what "doing research" and "writing a thesis" were, I then told them that I was "learning about Haalpulaar culture" and "writing a book about how people choose between the French school and the *daara*".

Anthropologists have noticed that, if research participants are illiterate or suspicious of formal bureaucratic procedures, seeking verbal consent can be preferable to written consent forms (ASA, 2011, p. 1), so I originally asked people if they would be comfortable 'doing an interview'. I immediately discovered that teachers, administrators and Muslim clerics were comfortable with formal interviews. However, others felt awkward and declined the proposal but were nonetheless happy to share personal information in informal conversations with full awareness of my intentions – a pattern documented by other researchers (Gill and Temple, 2014, pp. 5–7). For advice on this issue, I consulted with Senegalese university graduates and academics who agreed that many people were unfamiliar with formal interviews and the one-off, formalised giving of consent. However, they told me that people constantly gauge whether they trust someone enough to confide in them, and that I would be no exception. As one lecturer told me, "If they agree to talk to you at all, it's because they trust you. That's consent". I then focused on ensuring that no harm came to people as a result of their talking to me by protecting informants' anonymity and confidentiality. An obvious aspect of this involved not divulging sensitive information to third parties, maintaining *soutoura*, and removing as much personal information from people's narratives in written publications as possible. I have anonymised the name of the village and provided pseudonyms for the names of my research participants using common Haalpulaar names found throughout the Futa Tooro region.

School provision and educational trends

Medina Diallobé boasted three large Qur'anic schools, as well as seven smaller 'overflow' schools, run by men of the *seerembe* lineage whose ancestor was appointed to the task of Qur'anic teaching in the nineteenth century. The clerics did not quantify how many students they had, but my total of their general (and I suspect quite conservative) estimates was of at least 500 children and youth, combining live-in students from surrounding villages and day students originating from Medina Diallobé.

The first primary school was built in the 1950s. Until the 1970s, educational trends reflected status groups' customary professions such that only *toorodo* boys from the lineage of village chiefs attended the state primary school in the village. From the 1980s, demand for state primary schooling grew among parents of all status groups including for their daughters. However, secondary schools were located in cities tens, if not hundreds, of kilometres away. School attendance was greatly increased by the opening in Medina Diallobé of a *collège* in 2001, a second primary school in 2005 and a *lycée* in 2011 – all of which were linked to the promotion of school provision under EFA. It was from this point onwards that education from primary level to the award of the *baccalauréat* diploma became accessible to all of Medina Diallobé's inhabitants. According to statistics provided by the schools' directors, by 2011 there was a female majority in primary enrolment (55% girls to 45% boys), *collège* (56% girls to 44% boys) and *lycée* (54% girls to 46% boys). According to state school personnel, parents and religious teachers alike, the low rates of male enrolment in state schools were largely explained by the fact that many of the village's *toorodo* boys studied in Qur'anic schools instead (see Table 5.2 for school types and enrolment data).

Table 5.2 School types in Medina Diallobé and total enrolment for the academic year 2010/2011.

School type	*Date of implantation*	*No. of grades*	*Official age of entry*	*Qualification*	*Government accredited*	*Enrolment 2010/2011*		
						Male	*Female*	*Total*
Classical Qur'anic schools × 10 (day students and boarding)	Nineteenth century onwards	N/A	≈6	*Ijaza*	No	–	–	> 500
Primary school × 2 (*primaire*)	1950, 2005	6	6	Certificat de Fin d'Etudes Elémentaires (CFEE)	Yes	342	413	755
Lower secondary school (*collège*)	2001	4	12	Brevet des Fins d'Etudes Moyennes (BFEM)	Yes	227	296	523
Upper secondary school (*lycée*)	2011	3	15	Baccalauréat	Yes	87	103	190

The young people I interviewed all received some Qur'anic instruction regardless of gender or status group. However, live-in students (singular: *almuudo*; plural: *almuuɓe*) were all male, mainly *tooroɓe* and came from other villages. Meanwhile, most children originating from Medina Diallobé who attended *daaras* full-time were sent to other villages so that they would concentrate better. Day students were all Medina Diallobé residents, mainly male, and they usually attended the state school alongside the *daara*.

The younger students who lived in the *daaras*, aged from around six to mid-adolescence, were called *baydas*. They were colourful personalities in the village landscape. Their lives were undeniably tough; they were grubby with a few ragged clothes and often no shoes. To earn their keep, they begged at houses at breakfast and lunchtime with a metal tin or plastic pot. People would give them a few sugar cubes or a handful of rice or millet from the storeroom, or the leftovers of lunch. Sometimes villagers gave these alms asking for nothing in return, whilst at other times they gave in return for small errands like sweeping the yard or fetching groceries from the local shop. Between breakfast and lunch the *baydas* studied the Qur'an; in the afternoons they worked the cleric's fields and did chores like fetching wood for the evening fire. After sundown they studied again, from a wooden tablet or *alluwal* inked with a Qur'anic verse. Walking through the village at night, through gaps in the fences, one could catch glimpses of *almuuɓe* hunched around their fire, the smells of woodsmoke and murmur of young voices wafting out of the compound. Alternatively, they would sit reciting beneath streetlamps or under shop awnings along the main streets of the village.

If students continued their studies after late adolescence they were referred to as *sandas*. *Sandas* no longer lived in the cleric's compound, instead they found host families. They did not beg but instead were offered meals from local households or bought their own food by doing odd jobs, sometimes supplemented by pocket money from their parents. Many *sandas* worked in the clerics' fields although less intensively if they taught, as many instructed *bayda* students in the *daaras* or village children in their homes. Like giving alms to *baydas*, hosting *sandas* was a way for local people to give alms (*sadaqa)* and receive blessing (*baraka*). Many households in Medina Diallobé had a resident *sanda* – two slept in a disused building in my host family's compound, while another pair joined them to study during the day – which was a way for status groups who were barred from advanced Qur'anic schooling to gain *baraka*. Only a few students ever completed memorisation of the Qur'an. Afterwards, some learned other Islamic subjects, like jurisprudence (*sharia*) and Arabic, which involved travelling to specialised advanced *daaras* elsewhere in the Futa Tooro region. This situation was fairly typical of the region overall, as a survey of 54 *daaras* in Podor and Matam departments noted that fully memorising the Qur'an took ten years on average, and only 20% of boys continued for this length of time (MEN, 2010).

There were clear patterns regarding which families in Medina Diallobé sent their children to *daaras* and for how long. From the age of four, boys and girls of all status groups learned the Arabic alphabet, essential Qur'anic verses and how to pray, usually at home with a *sanda*. Having mastered these essentials, most children from six years of age gave up Qur'anic study to attend state school instead. In Medina Diallobé, this was the common trajectory for girls and non-*toorodo* boys. Alternatively, they continued memorising additional verses throughout middle childhood, at a *daara* or at home with a *sanda* tutor and would only stop if the burden of domestic tasks or schoolwork became too much. However, this chapter focuses on those committed to full-time, long-term study aimed at memorising most, if not all, of the Qur'an who were almost exclusively male *tooroɓe*. In the following sections I describe their and their parents' incentives for choosing a *daara* education. All the *daara* students I spoke to were male *tooroɓe* aged 12 and over, although most were *sandas* aged between 20–25.

Explaining Qur'anic school preference

What emerged from my interviews and discussions with Medina Diallobé's inhabitants was that a number of intersecting factors underpinned preference for the Qur'anic schools among *toorodo* families. As I unpack later, these factors included: (a) *baraka* or blessing, spirituality and moral values; (b) identity, status and marriage prospects for *toorodo* men; (c) material and economic returns in Senegal; and (d) internal and transnational migration.

Baraka *(blessing), spirituality and moral values*

The hum of the Qur'an being recited very much shaped our everyday soundscape. If I rose early in the morning, in the clear darkness I could hear the low melodic cadence of the *sandas* reciting on the far side of our compound. After daybreak the murmur continued, blending with the tweeting of birds around the water tap, the rhythmic *thunk-thunk* of wooden mortar in pestle, the squealing of children, and the swish of a grass broom on the concrete floor. Stillness fell during the shimmering heat of the afternoon, but the *sandas* resumed their chanting in the chill of nightfall. As we dragged our mattresses out under the stars and tucked our mosquito nets around us, they bathed us in the Qur'an. Whether it was rainy season when water hammered on the zinc roof and streamed in rivulets over the clogged sand, or dry season when the sun baked the cracked earth and we veiled our faces from the biting desert wind, the sound of the Qur'an was constant like a beating heart.

I once asked 22-year-old *sanda* Yagouba why he learned the Qur'an. He replied:

> Because it's a book written by God, brought by Mohamed. And it translates life, all the rules and the stories of the Prophets, what is and isn't forbidden – it talks about a lot of things. And it's through the Qur'an that we can pray, if you haven't learned the *surah al-fatiha* [opening

> verse of the Qur'an] you can never pray, your prayer won't be valid. If you learn the Qur'an, angels will come. If you finish, lots of angels will come and pray for you. And, the Qur'an contains secrets, BIG secrets. Everything that is hard or difficult can be cured with the Qur'an. All illnesses, problems and catastrophes can be cured with the Qur'an.

Yagouba's quote captured several of the reasons given by parents and youth for preferring full-time education in a *daara*: the opportunity to develop a close relationship with God; practical instruction for leading a pious life; and the receipt of blessings and learning invocations which influence the material world. A common thread underpinning these benefits was the pursuit of *baraka* or blessing. As explained in Chapter 3, *baraka* can be understood as divine grace and can be acquired directly from God through one's personal actions and embodied through memorising and reciting the Qur'an: "There are extraordinary benefits for those who memorise the Qur'an", explained Samba, a 40-year-old *toorodo*, "They benefit from God's mercy. When you learn the Qur'an, each time you recite it you are in a state of grace, God glorifies you and you will bear the trace of His words".

The second way that *baraka* could be accumulated was through performing pious acts – a self-enhancing cycle as *baraka* cleanses the heart, making its bearer more inclined to do more good deeds. While memorisation of the Qur'an was the main curriculum of the *daara*, students also learned moral behaviour through emulating the cleric's behaviour and receiving informal lessons about pious comportment. While students in advanced *daaras* learned *sharia* with reference to books of jurisprudence of the Maliki school of law[3] which their cleric translated orally into Pulaar, in the typical *daara*, moral values were not necessarily taught in association with *hadith* or specific quotes from the Qur'an. Instead, they reflected a body of oral lore or orthopraxy which was passed through clerics. Following the moral proscriptions of the Qur'an that were imparted in the *daara* was considered essential for one's own, and the wider community's, happiness and well-being. *Baraka* could also be received through transmission from a very pious person, like a saint or cleric. In the context of the *daara*, this was achieved through working for the cleric, as Abda, a 40-year-old *toorodo*, explained:

> Working for the cleric, there is a big notion here that you need to understand, which is *baraka*, or blessing. This goes hand in hand with knowledge. The more you work for him, when you leave, you could have the same knowledge as another student . . . but more satisfaction of the cleric, and then when he prays for you, he blesses you.

The third way in which *baraka* could be acquired was through inheritance or descent, and so members of lineages of saints, clerics and *sharif* were seen to possess more *baraka* than other people. Hence, Medina Diallobé residents preferred a cleric from a *toorodo* lineage with an inherited position as a Qur'anic teacher or imam (*seereмɓe*). Students who studied under them were seen to be more likely to acquire *baraka* over the course of their studies.

Amassing *baraka* carried significant benefits in the here-and-now and afterlife, a distinction referred to in French as '*ici*' versus '*au-delà*' ('here' and 'beyond'). Sidy, an 18-year-old *toorodo*, listed such benefits of memorising the full Qur'an:

> There's a secret inside. If you learn it off by heart you're assured of going to paradise. You can also take 500 people with you, like friends and family. Even with just a little – but it's more assured if you have it all.

In addition to benefit in the afterlife, being imbued with *baraka* made God more inclined to look favourably on someone in the current material world. Samba summarised this logic thus: "We say, if you want to succeed, you should have less knowledge and lots of *baraka*! . . . If you go into trade, or teaching, or whatever, you will succeed more". A further attribute of possessing *baraka* that people mentioned was enhanced mystical power and the ability to perform miracles.

Historian Zachary Wright suggests that, when trying to explain the popularity of Muslim clerics and Qur'anic schools in West Africa, anthropologists have placed too much emphasis on "instrumentalist causes" including clerics being "vessels of worldly 'blessing' (*baraka*)" (2018, p. 24). However, I emphasise the importance of *baraka* because my research participants mentioned it constantly – it was probably the most oft-cited explanation for Qur'anic school preference. I suggest, though, that the problem that Wright is referring to is the way that anthropologists have emphasised the ways that *baraka* resembles one of Bourdieu's capitals and hence how its acquisition resembles the logics of material accumulation (Hoechner, 2018, p. 99). As a consequence of such secular erasure, the more spiritual and sensed characteristics of *baraka* are downplayed.

To illustrate this dimension, students often described how reciting the Qur'an was "*ina weli*", from the Pulaar verb *welde* meaning 'to be sweet or tasty' or 'good' in the sense that a meal is 'good' or enjoyable in sensory terms. Moreover, several Sufis whom I have spoken to over the years describe *baraka* in terms of *feeling* or *sensing* some kind of energy around certain spiritual leaders or *shaykhs*. I asked one Sufi *shaykh* in Dakar what he thought of this idea, that *baraka* is something one can *feel*. He chuckled and replied:

> Yes, that's it, there are forces that pull, it's the force of God. If He wants you, he pulls you, it's like a magnet. . . . We can call it *baraka* because there are forces that come from God and flow through the Prophet to the *waliou* [saints], and if you associate with them, you will get the *baraka* that God gave them. . . . It's like a person who wears perfume, if you sit next to him, you will also smell of perfume.

In contrast to these sentiments, Euro-North American trained social scientists (e.g. Barnes, 2009, pp. 215–216) have tended to suggest that people infer whether a Sufi *shaykh* possesses *baraka* based on their lineage, education, social network, good deeds and reputation – which is the product of other forms of capital and social perceptions.

I stress these two examples of the spiritual and moral sensations associated with Qur'anic recitation and *baraka* precisely because I have yet to come across an anthropological account of *daara* preference in West Africa which does justice to the sensed aspects of *baraka*. These embodied experiences were definitely a factor that sustained people's adherence to Sufi onto-epistemologies – and hence patterns of educational engagement – in Senegal. Neglect of their importance is indicative of secular erasure.

Identity, status and marriage prospects

In addition to its spiritual benefits, *daara* education also conferred social status – or symbolic capital – upon *toorodo* men. "The value is so embedded, it's a prestige", explained Omar, a *toorodo* in his forties. "My son could become a bricklayer if he wants, but for me as a father, that my son memorised the Qur'an is a prestige". The seal of status for the students who finished memorising the Qur'an was a celebration called *mbaaral*. Their family would host a party where the young man recited a significant part of the Qur'an in front of a public audience, before slaughtering a sheep or cow for the guests. I attended one *mbaaral* in Medina Diallobé, in honour of the imam's 22-year-old nephew. It was a prestigious event, with easily 100 people present, including members of the village nobility and political elite. The youth received an embroidered cover for his wooden writing tablet or *alluwal*, many of which were prominently displayed in people's homes. When I met my host family in Medina Diallobé in 2010, the first things my 24-year-old brother Abderahmane showed me, with enormous pride, were his *alluwal* cover and *mbaaral* photo album from earlier that year.

Such status translated into benefits like influence in village affairs, political leverage and greater marriage prospects, as 28-year old *toorodo*, Kasim, described:

> Your family will say *mashallah* [praise to God], you're a *hafiz* [someone who has memorised the whole Qur'an]! It's noble, grandiose, extraordinary! In the past you would celebrate your *mbaaral* and your wedding on the same day. If you completed the Qur'an, the women would be queuing at your door to marry you!

While the status accorded by a *daara* education was linked exclusively to male *toorodo* identity, this connection was especially strong in the case of clerical *seerembe* lineages who comprised the traditional aristocracy or nobility among the Haalpulaar'en. Forty-year-old *toorodo* Baaba told me that, for men of such families, it was "a mark of weakness not to have learned the Qur'an". Indeed, those families in Medina Diallobé who placed most emphasis on *daara* education for their sons were the family of the imam and those appointed as clerics of Qur'anic schools. I came across a case of one 15-year-old *toorodo* called Mohamed from one of these families whose father had enrolled him in the state school, feeling that he would have more opportunities as a result. Two years after his father's death, Mohamed dropped out of the penultimate year of *collège* to attend a Qur'anic school instead. One of the reasons he gave me was "You can't say you're the son of a *marabout* [Muslim cleric] if you haven't studied the Qur'an!" Yet, because *toorodo* men stood to gain such symbolic capital from Qur'anic memorisation, they often sought to maintain a monopoly over it and restricted *daara* access to other status groups as well as women.

To an extent, choice of the *daara* also reflected a rejection of state schooling, in part because of the social representations (Lange, 2003) associated with Senegal's colonial history and the French administration's legacy of forced enrolment of students (see Chapter 3). One of Medina Diallobé's school directors told me that the Pulaar word *lekkoñ*, or faggot burned for firewood, sounded so similar to the French word for school, *l'école*, that the association between the latter and hellfire was easily made, and he remembered a cleric preaching to this effect in the 1960s. Another school administrator in his forties explained that, even in his generation, the school "was associated with the West and with Satan".

However, these explicit associations were made by middle-aged and older people rather than by members of younger generations who tended to make more nuanced connections between coloniality and state schooling. Mohamed, mentioned earlier, stated that,

> in school we learn all about Molière [seventeenth century French playwright] and René Caillé [the French explorer who 'discovered' Timbuktu in 1828] but nothing about Cheikh Umar Tall who brought good things to Senegal – he taught us about God. Instead we only learn about people who did bad things to Africa.

Moreover, parents had noticed that primary school children appeared to learn relatively little because French was the language of instruction which they did not speak at home. For instance, I overheard one 8-year-old mechanically reciting her lesson for the day: "*le-lion-est-un-carnivore-l'antilope-est-un-herbivore* . . ." [the lion is a carnivore, the antelope is a herbivore]. Her mother Hadja asked her, "What does a carnivore mean?" to which her daughter shrugged and ran off. Hadja turned to me and rolled her eyes: "See? She doesn't even know what it means, she just repeats it". Hence, memorisation without understanding was common to both the state and Qur'anic schools – but only the latter was perceived to confer long-term benefits.

Finally, the secondary schools were mired in teacher/student strikes throughout 2011 and 2012 because of overcrowded classrooms, inadequate infrastructure and government failures to pay teacher salaries – all of which were linked to the rapid expansion of schooling under EFA. The disruption of state schools stood in contrast to the steady pace of the *daaras* whose *almuuɓe* learned peacefully throughout the year. This comparison was made explicit by one *sanda* during a student protest in 2012. One morning we were roused by the sound of chanting and the banging of tam-tams. A large crowd of *collège* and *lycée* students was marching through the main streets of the village after forcing teaching to stop in both primary schools and blocking the main road of traffic. Members of my host family discussed the commotion, and one of our resident *sandas* – known for being a bit of a comedian – told me the Qur'anic school students were having a strike tomorrow. Everyone present erupted in giggles, as such an idea was unthinkable.

Material and economic returns

This brings me to the third reason why Medina Diallobé's inhabitants chose Qur'anic education. When I asked what practical use there was in memorising the whole Qur'an, many people replied that the value was not material or economic, but for the afterlife. "It's not for earning money!" Khadidiatou, a 24-year-old university student, exclaimed, "You'll use it once you're dead". However, this strict dichotomy broke down in practice, as people's discourses revealed several associations between *daara* education and practical skills which had economic utility, often acquired as part of the hidden or informal curriculum.

Several middle-aged men reported how the *daara* taught *almuuɓe* the skills for rural *toorodo* livelihoods. "You learn everything, you learn the Qur'an but you also beg, and through that you learn about the village and do odd jobs", explained one 45-year-old farmer. "So by the time you finish, you have a livelihood". A school Arabic teacher agreed: "In the *daara* you work the field for the cleric, you fix things around the house, you learn how to do lots of tasks, it teaches practical skills".

Interestingly, despite the prevalence of *Ajami* literacy associated with Qur'anic schools in Wolof-speaking parts of Senegal which I documented in Chapter 4, I did not see much evidence of its use during my time in Medina Diallobé. There are two explanations, the first being that *Ajami* was not widely used. Anthropologist Marie-Eve Humery conducted surveys on literacy practices in the Futa Tooro in the late 90s and early 2000s and found that only 1–3% of people stated that they could read and write Pulaar in *Ajami* (2014, p. 177). She argued that no public texts were circulating in *Ajami* and, rather, individuals employed it for personal use such as recording esoteric secrets, writing letters or documenting aspects of Haalpulaar culture (2014, p. 178). Huméry suggested that, unlike the Mourides who promote Wolofal, Haalpulaar clerics deliberately restricted the writing of Pulaar in Arabic script. Indeed, Cheikh Umar Tall cultivated close ties with Arabic-speaking Muslim intellectuals in North Africa and Arabia and encouraged intellectual debate in Arabic over *Ajami* (ibid., p. 185). Another explanation, however, is that the 'absence' of *Ajami* use in Medina Diallobé was a product of my own blindspots, as I only learned about its prevalence in West Africa after completing fieldwork. Indeed, Friederike Lüpke and Sokhna Bao-Diop (2014) have long argued that the limited awareness among – and identity of – White, Euro-North American researchers has led to the invisibilisation of *Ajami* as their research participants in Cameroon would only talk about it with local Muslim researchers (2014, p. 97).

However, I do remember one interesting incident attesting to *Ajami* use. A 22-year-old *sanda* called Hammadi and I agreed that he would teach me Qur'anic verses while I would coach him in French. He sounded out the verses in Arabic, and I transcribed them phonetically, as best I could, in my notebook in Roman/Latin script. Meanwhile, he did the equivalent – transcribing my French vocabulary list in his notebook using Arabic script. I found this fascinating while he just assumed it was obvious! We laughed about it at the time, but I did not press the matter further. It was only after returning home to the UK that I realised what I had witnessed. At the very least this was an example of *Ajami* literacy acquired ad hoc during the course of a Qur'anic education that Hammadi used to serve his everyday needs.

Another obvious livelihood option was for *daara* graduates to exercise religious professions. However, becoming the cleric of a *daara* was only viable for a minority of *toorodo* men, namely those with economic capital and inherited *baraka* of belonging to a *seerembe* lineage. As argued by Habib, a 40-year-old *toorodo:*

> Clerics are only respected if their father was a big cleric. It's his son who inherits the *daara*. Here in Medina Diallobé, even if you learn the Qur'an but your father isn't a big cleric, then you can't be a cleric.

In contrast to being a cleric, *daara* graduates more frequently earned a living in the prayer economy or using the esoteric sciences. Demba, a 40-year-old *toorodo* who had completed state school and tried to learn some esoteric sciences in his spare time, explained: "You see, the Qur'an contains knowledge called *batin* [from the Arabic *al-batin*] meaning hidden, or *lasarar* [from the Arabic *al-asrar*] meaning secret". Cheikhna, a 15-year-old *toorodo*, explained that learning which Qur'anic verses, invocations (*du'a*) or names of God could be recited for which purposes was therefore accorded high value:

> Even if you stay in your room and just pray and learn the Qur'an, you will have all you need, because all the *du'as* [supplication, call on God] are in there, *du'as* are to have what you want, and to protect you.

He further explained that he and other students shared what few secrets they knew between themselves in the *daara*.

A practitioner who mastered a significant amount of secret knowledge – and sold products and services derived from it – was called a *dabotoodo* (plural:

dabotooɓe). Given the power of this knowledge, 38-year-old *dabotooɗo* Abou told me that clerics did not teach it as part of the *daara's* formal curriculum. Rather, a student would have to approach a cleric and request that he teach him. The cleric might ask for money or invite the student to work for him over several years. If he found that the student was hard-working and of good character, he could impart secrets slowly as he saw fit – or he might prefer to only share such things with his family members. Indeed, few *dabotooɓe* in Medina Diallobé actually learned this way as most were taught by male kin.

People made me aware of the existence of the esoteric sciences early on during fieldwork, but once I converted to Islam they divulged much more sensitive information on the content of secret knowledge. They told me that it was forbidden for non-Muslims to hear this information and, I sensed in some cases, some wanted to impress me. One 35-year-old *dabotooɗo*, Seydou, explained that the Qur'an could be combined with other things. Once when I visited him, he was preparing a charm for a Wolof client who wanted to travel to Italy and asked if I could write down the instructions in French on how to use it. He explained that there was no Qur'anic text in this particular charm but instead a powdered plant, perfume, white kola nut, sand from outside the mosque and sand from the market, all mixed together, over which he recited a secret incantation. He explained that some of his work involved writing down parts of the Qur'an and including the paper in the charms, but other things were just "magic". Such descriptions of amulets or charms, and their contents and uses, that I encountered in Medina Diallobé were very similar to the account provided by Sudanese anthropologist Abdullahi El-Tom (1987) who found amulets there consisting of Qur'anic verses written on paper – and sometimes additional ingredients – sewn into leather pouches or sealed in metal rings or bracelets (see Figure 5.1).[4]

In addition, *dabotooɗo* Abou from Medina Diallobé also explained that his work involved healing illnesses caused by spirits or *jinn*, which required communicating and developing relationships with them:

> Theirs is a parallel world, like ours, there are nice people and nasty people. [. . .] You need to know what family a *jinn* [spirit] is from, and how to call them, or send a calm *jinn* to talk to a boisterous one. You need to test a *jinn's* behaviour to see if you can work with them. Sometimes you might even need to work with a nasty *jinn* in order to cure someone.

Moreover, El-Tom has argued that the contents of amulets "may be written by non-human beings through human mediums" and their contents are therefore "believed to be unintelligible to human beings" (1987, p. 225). The skills required for these practices I refer to as 'esoteric literacy and numeracy', a form of situated literacy with the important characteristic that the exact or literal meaning of the Qur'anic text is secondary to the knowledge of how to manipulate it for specific purposes. While *Ajami* literacy is widely ignored by scholars working on international education and development, esoteric

Figure 5.1 **A Senegalese amulet.**

Credit: Anneke Newman.

literacy is totally off their radar. Yet, anthropologist Amber Gemmeke explains that several historians of West Africa "believe that the magic of writing and manipulating Qur'anic verses is the main reason that Islam was easily accepted by many people in Africa" (2009, p. 131).

Muslims and scholars of Islam have long debated the 'Islamicness' and morality of associating with *jinn* and 'mixing' the Qur'anic text with other things in the context of the esoteric sciences. Their analyses are often coloured by judgements that these practices are 'African', 'pre-Islamic' and immoral – which do not always reflect historical evidence or local people's interpretations (Gemmeke, 2009, p. 130). These practices were certainly debated in Medina Diallobé with some of my research participants expressing suspicion – although not of their efficacy but, rather, of their licitness. *Dabotooɓe* Seydou and Abou justified them on the basis that they were performed with good intent for beneficial purposes. Demand for this kind of service was widespread in Medina Diallobé and, indeed, throughout Senegal. For instance, when Gemmeke (2009, p. 136) interviewed a female *marabout* in Dakar the latter explained that her father:

> Blessed me and gave me a big silver ring with a *turabu* [Qur'anic verses written on paper] that I always wear. He also gave me one of his jinni.

> Because of this ring and because of my inherited djinn, all that I do for clients works.

Meanwhile, anthropologist Rachel Mueller found that, among the Lébou ethnic group on the west coast of Senegal, spirit possession and Islam were considered totally complementary and she documented a close collaboration between an imam and a *marabout* who worked with spirits (2013, p. 73). Mueller suggested that, because everyone in Senegal believes in spirits, practices involving them are widely tolerated because they serve a healing purpose (ibid., p. 103). Importantly, humans do not always choose to have relationships with spirits (ibid., pp. 79–80), which demands that we nuance our understanding of agency and 'social capital' when theorising people's interactions with other-than-human entities and their impact on knowledge-seeking behaviour.

Despite trying over the years, I have found it difficult to convince audiences in international education or development of the economic significance of the esoteric sciences or prayer economy – probably, I expect, because of secular and Orientalist perceptions that such practices are superstitious and embarrassing. Yet, the scale of this economy is spectacular. The Musée de l'Homme and Eco-anthropologie lab at Université Paris Cité host the 'Collection ALEP',[5] a treasure trove of amulets and magico-religious objects found by garbage collectors in Dakar from 1983 to 2018, numbering in the tens of thousands (Eco-anthropologie (EA), 2024).

I know of only two studies that have attempted to quantify household expenditure on esoteric sciences in West Africa – both surveys in Benin where individuals of all faiths widely believe that severe misfortunes are caused by witchcraft or sorcery involving evil spirits and offensive charms. People pay to see diviners to diagnose the problem – often in collaboration with a *vodoun* spirit – and propose solutions such as amulets, charms or baths using spiritually potent ingredients (Lang, LeMay-Boucher and Tomavo, 2019, p. 157). The survey in 2006 found that 48% of household heads had made such an investment in the last year which represented an average of 5.6% of monthly household expenditure (ibid., p. 158). The survey in 2014 corroborated these findings and, with the exception of lower spending among the poorest households, found little difference in spending by gender, age, religion or income. Moreover, people often invested in such practices without wholeheartedly believing in them but 'just in case' to cover all possibilities (ibid., p. 160). This is important because it shows how a dominant collective ontology shapes economic dynamics and social norms independent of individual ontology.

Meanwhile, much qualitative evidence speaks to the returns on the esoteric sciences and prayer economy for their practitioners in Senegal. Islamic studies professor Ousmane Kane (2016, p. 201) notes that his home city of Kaolack has changed beyond all description over the course of the twenty-first century because:

> Mansions worth hundreds of thousands of dollars have mushroomed there. Those houses are equipped with all the modern amenities, including big-screen TVs, luxury furniture, and satellite connections, and their owners drive expensive cars. . . . From where do they derive the resources to maintain such a lavish lifestyle? The prayer market! Many come seeking a blessing, professional advancement, prosperity, fertility, or healing and will pay fees in exchange for petitionary prayers.

Kaolack is the holy city of the Tijaniyya Niassiyya Sufi order but my evidence from Medina Diallobé shows that earning a good livelihood from the esoteric sciences, especially if it represents one income stream among several, is by no means restricted to elites.

As noted in the previous chapter, the World Bank's report *Youth Employment in Sub-Saharan Africa* argued that, despite youths' preference for waged employment, by 2020 most new jobs in Africa would be informal and in non-farm household enterprises like trade in commodities and services (Filmer and Fox, 2014, p. 15). The GEM Report *Youth and Skills: Putting Education to Work* (UNESCO, 2012) also stressed that policy-makers in the global South should support existing 'traditional' technical and vocational training opportunities tailored to the informal sectors (ibid., pp. 260–273). In that case, the esoteric and prayer economies should be included in development definitions of informal economic activity – that they are totally ignored reflects secular erasure on the part of development economists.

Internal and transnational migration

Finally, most *toorodo* parents I interviewed assumed that, after completing Qur'anic schooling, their sons would migrate, whether to other African countries, the US or Europe sometimes as undocumented workers – which is a dynamic I unpack in more detail in several other publications (Newman, 2019, 2022). Some *tooroɓe* perceived that Qur'anic schools taught transferable skills or dispositions directly useful for migrating such as self-discipline and the ability to withstand hardship – thus applying a long-standing characteristic of the Qur'anic school (Ware, 2014, pp. 45–47) to a novel transnational context. Interestingly, another popular option was working as an imam or *dabatoodo* catering to Muslims overseas, whether in Arab states or the African diaspora. Indeed, the transnational appeal of West Africa's esoteric practitioners has been widely documented. Kane notes that the banning of such practices in Saudi Arabia by the Wahhabi regime, which frames them as un-Islamic and *haram,* ironically "created a vacuum that was filled by divines from West Africa, who made huge fortunes offering talismanic services to Arab princes" (2016, p. 202). Moreover, the demand for Islamic esoteric sciences is not restricted to Muslims. Many Africanists have documented the market for these services among non-Muslims in the West (see for example: Gemmeke, 2009, p. 129; Mueller, 2013, p. 68; Kane, 2016, p. 201). For example, I frequently receive fliers in my letterbox from individuals proposing these services in Brussels, Belgium[6] (see Figure 5.2). In contrast to other neighbourhoods of the city that are associated with Sub-Saharan or North African communities, most inhabitants of my quarter are of diverse European nationalities. The fact that we regularly receive large volumes of publicity from a number of esoteric practitioners suggests that there is potentially a clientèle here beyond the African and Muslim communities.

However, not everyone in Medina Diallobé considered that Qur'anic schooling bestowed knowledge that was useful abroad since graduates, once overseas, found themselves undertaking manual work for which there were few returns on any type of formal education. Therefore, migration represented a 'fall-back option', as a school Arabic teacher explained:

> Often your studies don't link to a profession, whether it's French school or Qur'anic school. People here go to university, but then they migrate and become taxi drivers. I have an uncle who was a physics and chemistry teacher, he had a Masters' degree. He went to the US and now he's a taxi driver.

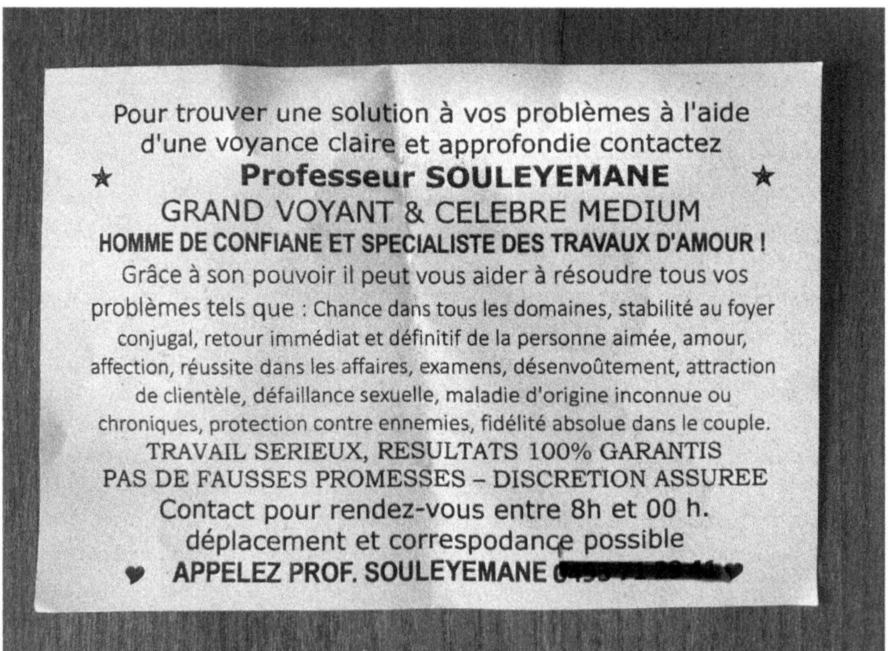

Figure 5.2 **Flier in French offering clairvoyant and esoteric services, Brussels, Belgium.**

Credit: Anneke Newman.

This logic reflects the well-documented phenomenon whereby school diplomas from low-income countries do not necessarily translate into high-skilled and well-paid employment in high-income contexts where, instead, migrants have no option but to do jobs below their skill level (Newman, 2019, p. 221).

Choosing the Qur'anic school: An increasingly complex decision

Despite the reasons that people gave for preferring classical Qur'anic schools, by the time of my study, these reasons had become more contested due to concerns about child protection and economic constraints.

Medina Diallobé's inhabitants widely subscribed to the onto-epistemological position that begging and living in hardship were good for *almuuɓe* for their moral education and acquisition of *baraka* and that giving was also beneficial for the alms-givers. Meanwhile, adolescent boys proudly showed me scars on their legs that they had received from beatings when studying at *daaras*. They argued that the education was meant to be hard as that was how *baraka* was earned, echoing similar testimonies from former *talibés* in Wolof-speaking parts of Senegal (Perry, 2004). However, parents also made a distinction between levels of hardship they considered 'acceptable' versus what was 'excessive' – and the local Qur'anic schools were sometimes perceived to fall short. I return to such challenges – and possible solutions – in Chapters 8 and 9.

Furthermore, while the spiritual and social benefits conferred by Qur'anic schools still applied, the rising costs of living meant that youth without the privileges of inherited *baraka*, a family Qur'anic school, economic capital or the possibility to migrate were likely to re-consider how to reconcile an Islamic education with other forms of knowledge acquisition which conferred additional income-generating skills. For instance, one 35-year-old *toorodo* told me that "a person cannot live from *dabaade* alone" and that he only used it to supplement his main income from agricultural cultivation. Hoechner documents a similar phenomenon in northern Nigeria noting that "the market in 'spiritual security services' has become increasingly crowded" rendering "livelihoods in the 'prayer economy' precarious and unpredictable" (2018, p. 183). Indeed, the *toorodo* men in Medina Diallobé who sustained their households solely through the esoteric sciences claimed direct descent from the Prophet or his Companions (*sharif*) and were perceived as possessing exceptional quantities of *baraka*. They could, therefore, request large donations (*addiya*) in return for blessings.

For men without these privileges, the decision over how to school their children had become more complicated. For instance, Seydou, the 35-year-old *dabotoodo* mentioned earlier, experienced financial difficulties which caused him great anxiety and created strain within his extended family. These tensions shaped Seydou and his wife Rabia's views about their children's education. Seydou explained to me how important it was to know God and why he had therefore sent his son, aged five, to the *daara*. When I asked Rabia about it separately, she sighed and said: "Ibrahima doesn't go to school. He just does the Qur'an. But my second son will do both, *inshallah* [God willing]".

The perceived inability to balance spiritual and economic desires was a significant source of stress for some. Twenty-five-year-old *toorodo* Malik had studied in a boarding *daara* in Dakar for eight years before moving home to Medina Diallobé once his father could no longer afford the fees. When I met Malik, he was studying *sharia* in an advanced *daara* in the Futa Tooro region and was constantly preoccupied by the social pressures to support his family:

> Once your studies are finished, you're like a newborn. And they say 'find work', and that's your baptism. . . . If I could, I would teach what I know, about the *sharia*, like my *marabout* [Muslim cleric]. But it doesn't lead to anything specific, I need to earn money. . . . It's hard to find work here. You need to have a father with connections or whatever. . . . These days everyone does *dabaade* [esoteric sciences], but it's not feasible, not everyone can make a living off that, and you don't get much.

These difficulties notwithstanding, Malik hoped that his younger brother would grow up to memorise the Qur'an as he had, as God might make his circumstances easier. However, I encountered several examples of such challenges leading to a shift in preference away from Qur'anic schooling among youth. One was Kasim, a 28-year-old *toorodo* who had abandoned the *daara* as a teenager. He stressed that there was significant status associated with *daara* but that he would prefer the state school for his sons:

> You gain respect, but aside from that . . . Feeding your family is more important! You can't work with the Qur'an. . . . Before, your parents would take care of you, and you would work the fields. People were under their parents' care for a long time, it was the collective life. The world has changed, things cost a lot more, and we are forced to change with it. But people cling to their traditions, it's so embedded. It's hard to suggest anything different.

The influence of migrants in Europe and the US also shaped families' re-evaluations of Qur'anic school education, as 40-year-old Moussa explained:

> Lots of migrants are now demanding that their younger siblings and cousins go to [state] school, as a condition for sending money. My cousin in the US does this. They went to the *daara* and then to the US. They weren't [state] schooled, and realised that they have to do manual labour while those with [state] schooling, who can read, can be a team supervisor and sit at a desk all day.

Therefore, while Medina Diallobé's inhabitants still sought out *baraka* and valued the classical Qur'anic school, the realities of the global capitalist economy were provoking greater differentiation between the *toorodo* group. Preference for Qur'anic education used to dominate among all but the lineage of village chiefs. Yet, from the 2000s onwards, it had become increasingly restricted to *seerembe* religious lineages whose livelihoods through religious professions were more secure. In Chapter 8, I return to the perceived limitations of the classical Qur'anic schools among Medina Diallobé's inhabitants. I show how parents and youth, when faced with these challenges, attempted to 'do both' using creative strategies to acquire knowledges associated with both Islamic and state schools.

Conclusion

In this chapter, I have not only described my research study but have started to unpack why certain *toorodo* families in Medina Diallobé preferred that their sons memorise the full Qur'an in a classical *daara* in the Futa Tooro region over attending accessible state schools implanted in the village as a result of the EFA agenda. This account of educational decision-making is sensitive to dominant Sufi onto-epistemologies, the historical and sociological characteristics of the Futa Tooro region and Haalpulaar ethnic group, and the coloniality embedded in the state school system. In short, the choice of a classical Qur'anic education happened when an alignment was perceived to occur across the three forms of benefit this education was seen to confer. The first benefit was *baraka* – or blessing – and moral values acquired through memorisation and recitation of the text. The second was the social status or sense of identity, tied to constructions of *toorodo* masculinity, that were conferred through full memorisation of the Qur'an. The third advantage consisted of material and economic returns, largely obtained through the hidden curriculum, including: skills relevant to the local agricultural economy; *Ajami* literacy for personal use; and esoteric literacy and numeracy for the local and transnational prayer economies. Finally, Qur'anic schooling was also attractive to families whose sons had the possibility to engage in transnational migration to Africa, the Middle East, Europe and the US, including as undocumented workers, which represented a fall-back livelihood option.

Crucially, the convergence of these benefits was becoming attainable only to *toorodo* men from *seerembe* lineages who held prestigious inherited religious positions such as imam or Qur'anic school teacher, claimed inheritance from the Prophet or his Companions (*sharif*), or had clientelistic relationships with other politically powerful and affluent *toorodo* families. Those who lacked these privileges perceived the Qur'anic school option to be associated with diminishing economic returns. Some parents also expressed concern about the safety of children in the classical *daaras*. For these individuals, choosing the *daara* had become an increasingly complex decision – although it remained an option nonetheless. I continue this analysis in Chapters 6 and 7 which unpack in more detail how the Muslim clerics' exclusion from Qur'anic schools of men specifically from non-*toorodo* status groups and women, continued to be maintained. This allows me to consider the implications of these trends for reinforcing social hierarchies and the attempts people made to acquire Islamic knowledge to challenge these forms of discrimination.

Finally, my analysis of school preference revealed several secular limitations of the Bourdieusian framework of field, capital and habitus which anthropologists and sociologists largely employ to understand educational decision-making involving Islamic schools. In contrast to Bourdieu's concept of social capital which refers narrowly to relationships with other human beings, a number of significant other-than-human entities shaped the knowledge-seeking activities of Medina Diallobé's inhabitants, namely God and spirits (*jinn*). Moreover, when Africanists have studied *baraka* in West Africa, they have tended to focus on its capital-resembling characteristics and have thus reduced the reasons for its pursuit to economic logics. In contrast, my conversations with Senegalese Sufis revealed that sensed aspects of *baraka* also played an important role in sustaining their onto-epistemologies and underpinned their educational preferences. These dynamics demand a postsecular theory of educational decision-making, and, in Chapter 9, I re-imagine Bourdieu's framework along such lines.

Notes

1 The Pulaar word for Qur'anic school is *dudal*, but, with the exception of older people who spoke only Pulaar, my research participants in Medina Diallobé usually used the Wolof term *daara* especially when speaking in French. I use *daara* throughout this book for the sake of simplicity.
2 Sufi orders are generally named after their founder: the Tijaniyya by Cheikh Ahmad Al-Tijani from Morocco in the eighteenth century; the Umariyya branch of the Tijaniyya by Cheikh Umar Tall, etc.
3 There are four major Sunni schools of religious law (*fiqh*), namely the Hanafi, Maliki, Shafi'i and Hanbali. Most jurists align themselves with a particular school. In North and West Africa the Maliki school is dominant.
4 This amulet was gifted to my infant daughter for her protection. It is designed to be worn around the waist.
5 The Collection ALEP is named after Alain Epelboin, Senior Researcher at the French National Centre for Scientific Research (CNRS), who originally coordinated the project.
6 Translated into English the flier promises marital stability, fidelity in relationships, protection against enemies, success in business and exams and cures for witchcraft, sexual dysfunction and chronic or unexplained illness.

References

ANSD and ICF International (2012) *Senegal Demographic and Health and Multiple Indicator Cluster Survey (EDS-MICS) 2010–2011*. Rockville, MD: Agence Nationale de la Statistique et de la Démographie and ICF International.

ASA (2011) *Ethical Guidelines for Good Research Practice, Association of Social Anthropologists of the UK and the Commonwealth (ASA)*. Available at: www.theasa.org/downloads/ASA ethics guidelines 2011.pdf (Accessed: 27 October 2015).

Bano, M. (2012) *The Rational Believer: Choices and Decisions in the Madrasas of Pakistan.* Ithaca, NY and London: Cornell University Press.

Barnes, J. (2020) *Stories, Senses and the Charismatic Relation: A Reflexive Ethnography of Christian Experience.* London: Routledge.

Barnes, S.G. (2009) 'Religion, social capital and development in the Sahel: The Niass Tijaniyya in Niger', *Journal of International Affairs*, 62(2), pp. 209–221.

Bianchin, L. (2020) *L'utilité économique de l'éducation coranique: perceptions contrastées des parents, des talibés et des acteurs du développement dans la région de Dakar, Sénégal.* Unpublished Masters thesis, Centre d'Études de la Coopération Internationale et du Développement. Brussels: Université Libre de Bruxelles.

Blundo, G. (2000) 'Elus locaux et courtiers en développement au Sénégal: Trajectoires politiques, modes de légitimation et stratégies d'alliance', in T. Bierschenk, J.-P. Chauveau and J.-P. Olivier de Sardan (eds) *Courtiers en développement: Les villages africains en quête de projets.* Paris: Karthala, pp. 71–100.

Bourdieu, P. (1986) 'The forms of capital', in J. Richardson (ed) *Handbook of Theory and Research for the Sociology of Education.* New York: Greenwood Press, pp. 241–258.

Bourdieu, P. (1977) *Outline of a Theory of Practice.* Translated by Nice, R. Cambridge: Cambridge University Press.

Bouteiller, J., Cantrelle, P., Causse, J. Laurent, C. and N'Doye, T. (1962) *La moyenne vallée du Sénégal.* Paris: Ministère de la Coopération.

Chehami, J. (2016) 'Les familles et le daara au Sénégal: Entre facteurs macrosociaux, stratégies collectives et choix individuels', *Afrique Contemporaine*, 257(1), pp. 77–89.

Cochrane, L.L. (2020) 'Religious networks and small businesses in Senegal', *Economic Anthropology*, pp. 1–12. https://doi.org/10.1002/sea2.12185.

Coulon, C. (1975) 'Pouvoir oligarchique et mutations sociales et politiques au Fouta-Toro', in J.-L. Balans, C. Coulon and J.-M. Gastellu (eds) *Autonomie locale et intégration nationale au Sénégal.* Paris: Pedone, pp. 23–80.

D'Aoust, S. (2013) 'Écoles franco-arabes publiques et daaras modernes au Sénégal: hybridation des ordres normatifs concernant l'éducation', *Cahiers de la recherche sur l'éducation et les savoirs*, 12, pp. 313–338.

Dilley, R.M. (2004) *Islamic and Caste Knowledge Practices Among Haalpulaar'en in Senegal: Between Mosque and Termite Mound.* Edinburgh: Edinburgh University Press.

Eco-anthropologie (EA) (2024) *Collection AlEp, Amulettes et objets magiques ouest-africains, collectés dans les décharges à ordures du Sénégal de 1983 à 2018.* Available at: www.ecoanthropologie.fr/fr/collection-alep-6227 (Accessed: 26 January 2024).

El-Tom, A. (1987) 'Berti Qur'anic amulets', *Journal of Religion in Africa*, 17(3), pp. 224–244.

Esquerre, A. (2016) *Compte Rendu. Pierre Bourdieu, Sociologie générale. Volume 1. Cours au Collège de France 1981–1983.* Paris: Le Seuil.

Filmer, D. and Fox, L. (2014) *Youth Employment in Sub-Saharan Africa. Africa Development Series.* Washington, DC: World Bank.

Froerer, P. (2011) 'Education, inequality and social mobility in central India', *European Journal of Development Research*, 23(5), pp. 695–711.

Gandolfi, S. (2003) 'L'enseignement islamique en Afrique noire', *Cahiers d'études africaines*, XLIII(169–170), pp. 261–277.

Gemmeke, A.B. (2009) 'Marabout women in Dakar: Creating authority in religious knowledge', *Africa: Journal of the International African Institute*, 79(1), pp. 128–147.

Gérard, E. (1992) *L'école déclassée. Une étude anthropo-sociologique de la scolarisation au Mali. Cas des sociétés malinkés.* PhD thesis. Université Paul Valery, Montpellier III.

Gérard, E. (1997) *La tentation du savoir en Afrique: Politiques, mythes et stratégies d'éducation au Mali*. Paris: Karthala.

Gill, P.R. and Temple, E. (2014) 'Walking the fine line between fieldwork success and failure: Advice for new ethnographers', *Journal of Research Practice*, 10(1), pp. 1–12.

Hoechner, H. (2018) *Quranic Schools in Northern Nigeria: Everyday Experiences of Youth, Faith, and Poverty*. Cambridge: Cambridge University Press.

Human Rights Watch (2010) *Off the Backs of the Children: Forced Begging and other Abuses Against Talibés in Senegal*. New York: Human Rights Watch.

Huméry, M.-È. (2014) 'Fula and the Ajami writing system in the Haalpulaar society of Fuuta Tooro (Senegal and Mauritania): A specific "restricted literacy"', in M. Mumin and K. Versteegh (eds) *The Arabic Script in Africa: Studies in the Use of a Writing System*. Leiden: Brill, pp. 173–198.

Jeffrey, C., Jeffery, R. and Jeffery, P. (2008) 'School and madrasah education: gender and the strategies of Muslim young men in rural north India', *Compare: A Journal of Comparative and International Education*, 38(5), pp. 581–593.

Kane, M.M. (1987) *A History of Fuuta Tooro, 1890s–1920s: Senegal Under Colonial Rule: The Protectorate*. PhD thesis. Department of History, University of Michigan.

Kane, O.O. (2016) *Beyond Timbuktu: An Intellectual History of Muslim West Africa*. Harvard University Press.

Klein, M. (1998) *Slavery and Colonial Rule in French West Africa*. Cambridge: Cambridge University Press.

Lang, A., LeMay-Boucher, P. and Tomavo, C.C. (2019) 'Expenditures on malevolent magico-religious powers: Empirical evidence from Benin', *African Studies Review*, 62(4), pp. 154–180.

Lange, M.-F. (2003) 'École et mondialisation: vers un nouvel ordre scolaire?', *Cahiers d'études africaines*, 43(169/170), pp. 143–166.

Lewandowski, S. (2011) 'Politiques de lutte contre la pauvreté et inégalités scolaires à Dakar: Vers un éclatement des normes éducatives?', *Autrepart*, 59(3), pp. 37–56.

Lüpke, F. and Bao-Diop, S. (2014) 'Beneath the surface? Contemporary ajami writing', in K. Juffermans, Y.M. Asfaha and A. Abdelhay (eds) *African Literacies: Ideologies, Scripts, Education*. Newcastle: Cambridge Scholars Publishing, pp. 88–117.

MEN (2010) *Étude de la situation de référence des structures d'accueil, des structures de formation, des daaras, des enfants de la rue, des talibés, des associations de maîtres coraniques et d'autres acteurs pour les régions de Dakar, Louga, Saint-Louis et Matam*. Dakar: Ministère de l'Education Nationale (MEN) Sénégal et Emergence Consulting.

MEN (2013) *Le Programme d'Amélioration de la Qualité, de l'Équité et de la Transparence du secteur de l'Éducation et de la Formation (PAQUET). Secteur Education Formation 2013–2025*. Dakar: Ministère de l'Education Nationale (MEN) Sénégal.

Mueller, R. (2013) *The Spirits Are My Neighbours: Women and the Rab Cult in Dakar, Senegal, Anthropology Honours Projects: Paper 18*. Anthropology Department, Macalester College.

Ndiaye, K. (2008) *When Soutoura (Dignity, Respect, and Privacy) Matters Most: Understanding and Assessing HIV/AIDS Stigma in the Family Context in Senegal*. PhD thesis. The Graduate School, College of the Liberal Arts, Pennsylvania State University.

Newman, A. (2019) 'The influence of migration on the educational aspirations of young men in northern Senegal: Implications for policy', *International Journal of Educational Development*, 65(3), pp. 216–226.

Newman, A. (2022) 'Revisiting "eduscape" through a postcolonial lens: The influence of globalisation and migration on educational offer and demand in Senegal', in A. North and E. Chase (eds) *Education, Migration and Development: Critical Perspectives in a Moving World*. London: Bloomsbury Press, pp. 111–128.

Noret, J. (2013) 'Autour du fait religieux: La théorie du choix rationnel et ses limites', in P.J. Hountondji (ed) *L'ancien et le Nouveau: La production du savoir dans l'Afrique d'aujourd'hui*. Langaa RPCIG, pp. 103–120.

Perry, D. (2004) 'Muslim child disciples, global civil society, and children's rights in Senegal', *Anthropological Quarterly*, 77(1), pp. 47–86.

Robinson, D. (1985) *The Holy War of Umar Tal: The Western Sudan in the Mid-Nineteenth Century*. Oxford: Clarendon Press.

Robinson, D. (2000) 'Revolutions in the Western Sahara', in N. Levtzion and R.L. Pouwels (eds) *The History of Islam in Africa*. Oxford: James Currey, pp. 131–152.

Sall, I.A. (2000) 'La diffusion de la tijâniyya au Fuuta Tooro (Mauritanie-Sénégal)', in J.-L. Triaud and D. Robinson (eds) *La Tijâniyya: une confrérie musulmane à la conquête de l'Afrique*. Paris: Karthala, pp. 367–392.

Samson, F. and LeBlanc, M.N. (2022) 'Repenser les religiosités islamiques en Afrique: classes sociales et manières de se montrer musulman.e', *Cahiers d'études africaines*, 4(248), pp. 679–695.

Schmitz, J. (1986) 'L'état géomètre: les leydi des Peul du Fuuta Tooro (Sénégal) et du Maasina (Mali)', *Cahiers d'études africaines*, 103(XXVI–3), pp. 349–394.

Schmitz, J. (2006) 'Des "aventuriers" aux "notables" urbains. Economies morales et communautés transnationales des gens du fleuve Sénégal. FASOPO', in J.-F. Bayart and F. Adelkhah (eds) *Migration et Anthropologie du voyage et migrations internationales*. Paris: FASOPO.

Simons, H. and Usher, R. (2000) 'Introduction: Ethics in the practice of research', in H. Simon and R. Usher (eds) *Situated Ethics in Educational Research*. London: Routledge, pp. 1–11.

Thorsen, D. (2012) *Children Begging for Qur'ānic School Masters: Evidence from West and Central Africa*. Dakar: United Nations Children's Fund (UNICEF).

UNESCO (2012) *EFA Global Monitoring Report 2012. Youth and Skills: Putting Education to Work*. Paris: United Nations Educational, Scientific and Cultural Organization (UNESCO).

UNESCO (2020) *Global Education Monitoring Report 2020. Inclusion and Education*. Paris: United Nations Educational, Scientific and Cultural Organization (UNESCO).

Ware, R.T. (2014) *The Walking Qur'an: Islamic Education, Embodied Knowledge, and History in West Africa*. Chapel Hill, NC: The University of North Carolina Press.

Willis, J.R. (1978) 'The torodbe clerisy: A social view', *The Journal of African History*, 19(2), pp. 195–212.

Wright, Z.V. (2018) *Living Knowledge in West African Islam*. New York and Accra: Fayda Books.

6 Racial hierarchies and Islamic education: From exclusion to resistance

In Chapter 5 I unpacked how classical Qur'anic schools in the Futa Tooro region were monopolised by the Muslim clerical status group, the *tooroɓe*, who dominated the local caste-like hierarchy. This education contributed particularly to the prestige of men of families of the old aristocracy who enjoyed inherited religious professions, known locally as *seereemɓe* lineages. This chapter shifts to look at the 'dark side' of this situation, namely the exclusion from *daaras* of men from other groups, especially from the ranks of artisan/musicians and descendants of slaves, and their attempts to overcome this form of descent-based/racialised discrimination. In Medina Diallobé, I found that many *tooroɓe* – although certainly not all – held derogatory views about other status groups. One quote from a 26-year-old *toorodo* woman illustrates this view:

> The *ñeeñɓe* [artisan/musicians] do all kinds of jobs like blacksmith and weaver, they don't respect the religion much, they wear God knows what. Then there are nobles, we just learn and teach the Qur'an. The nobles took the *maccuɓe* [derogatory term for slaves] as servants. It's like in the past, there was *homo sapiens* who didn't wear clothes and so on – those people are still like that, they know nothing, they don't even know how to pray.

Having risen to political dominance in the Futa Tooro region in the eighteenth century, despite their humble origins and history of resistance against colonial oppression, the *tooroɓe* have promoted a descent-based hierarchy in which they position themselves as morally and intellectually superior to other groups. While children of all groups could obtain a basic Qur'anic education involving memorisation of verses for obligatory daily prayers, the *tooroɓe* maintained a monopoly over long-term Qur'anic education leading to full memorisation of the Qur'an. This was an important component of their racial ideology as it reinforced the *tooroɓe*'s claims over the piety, knowledge and religious authority that justified their superiority.

Far from being an isolated case in northern Senegal, descent-based hierarchies are a widely documented phenomenon in which membership by birth, inherited profession, endogamy, discrimination and restrictions on social

DOI: 10.4324/9781003172475-8

relations organise people's identities and everyday lives (Human Rights Watch, 2001, p. 2). Anthropologist of development David Mosse argues that descent plays a role in determining the life opportunities of 20–25% of the world's population yet is not accorded the same importance in policy debates compared to gender, age, ethnicity or religion (2018, p. 423). Mosse defends his argument using the example of the caste system in India which is quite familiar to a Euro-North American audience. Yet, few development scholars or practitioners appreciate that, on the African continent, there are also two types of groups that are marked by descent: endogamous occupation-based groups of artisans, musicians and praise-singers sometimes called 'castes', and slaves or descendants of slaves. Elsewhere, I have shown how anthropologists have documented the presence of one or both of these groups among 21 ethnicities in 27 countries largely in West Africa and the Sahel (Newman, 2021, pp. 414, 427). I have therefore made a conservative estimate, on the basis of census data on each ethnicity available on Wikipedia, that 218 million people, or 17% of the continent's population, live in societies structured by this form of social differentiation.

While the scale of this phenomenon seems generally not to be known to many development scholars or policy-makers, including those working in international education and development, neither are its social ramifications. In contrast, Africanists have long documented the links between such hierarchies and a range of ensuing inequalities which undermine people's rights to citizenship including in relation to political participation, legal rights, economic opportunities, land tenure and choice of marriage partner. These scholars also document that the consequences of deviating from such established norms range from ostracisation and fear of mystic retribution to verbal harassment and physical violence (Human Rights Watch, 2001; Schmitz, 2009; Pelckmans, 2011; Séhou, 2019; Regnier, 2020).

Importantly, with few exceptions (Einarsdóttir and Boiro, 2016; Newman, 2019, 2020, 2021), there has been little investigation into the links between descent-based inequalities in Africa and educational engagement under EFA. While UNESCO's GEM Reports list a number of forms of inequality and marginalisation that can disadvantage learners including gender, disability, caste (referring to South Asian contexts), ethnicity, religion, race and socioeconomic status (UNESCO, 2010, 2020), descent-based hierarchies in African contexts are never mentioned. In contrast, in one rare study, Jónína Einarsdóttir and Hamadou Boiro (2016) found that Fula[1] parents in Guinea-Bissau who were descendants of former slaves sent their favourite sons to itinerant Qur'anic schools in Senegal to increase their social status. The parents were outraged by the actions of development organisations who classified such practices as 'child trafficking' (see Chapter 4) and found the repatriation of their boys back home to be "degrading and criminalising" and "proof of discrimination" (ibid., p. 857).

In the conclusion of his seminal account of slavery in the French colony of *Afrique Coloniale Française* (AOF), Martin Klein (1998, p. 251) argued that the narratives of slaves and their descendants in West Africa are stories that still urgently need to be told:

> The real heroes of this story are those who sought freedom, people who made the long march to distant homes, sought freedom in the new towns and cities and people who struggled to assert their autonomy. In North America, we honor those who rose above slave origins, people like Frederick Douglass, Harriet Tubman, Booker T. Washington or George Washington Carver, whose accomplishments are all the more remarkable when their modest roots are considered. Their West African counterparts are invisible. . . . In 1848, both Gorée and Saint-Louis [on the west coast of Senegal] were cities with heavy slave majorities, and in the century after 1848, the cities were clearly an important destination for former slaves. . . . It is certain that a large part, perhaps a majority of the population of Dakar, Conakry and Bamako was of slave origin until very recently. There is thus a dramatic story here which will never be told in full.

Fortunately, this situation has changed during the last 25 years, as a wealth of historical and anthropological scholarship has documented the experiences of slaves and their descendants in West Africa (e.g. Rossi, ed. 2016), including documentaries that enable people to speak for themselves (Hahonou and Strandsbjerg, 2011; Rodet, 2014; Thioub, N'Gaïde and Seck, 2014; Rodet and Maximin, 2020). However, in Medina Diallobé, the everyday discrimination faced by other groups, especially blacksmiths of the artisan/musician rank, could be just as pernicious as that faced by descendants of slaves – as observed by other anthropologists of the Haalpulaar'en (N'Gaïde, 2003; Dilley, 2004, p. 71). Yet, Africanist scholars tend to focus only on the struggles of descendants of slaves but not on how 'casted' groups are impacted by these descent-based/racialised hierarchies.

Given this context, in this chapter I unpack how negotiating access to education was an integral element of the ongoing constitution of descent-based/racialised distinction among the Haalpulaar'en in the Futa Tooro region. Access to Islamic knowledge represented the 'final frontier' in epistemic struggles for honour and social mobility among those disadvantaged by these hierarchies. Specifically, I focus on the ways that men from non-*toorodo* status groups strived to overcome these barriers by acquiring Islamic knowledge and challenging the logics of difference and inferiority. Because this form of social inequality is intimately tied up with local Islamic onto-epistemologies, its neglect by education and development scholars and policy-makers can be seen as constituting another form of secular erasure.

Related to this, it is important to note that many of the scholars who have celebrated the role of Islam in Africans' anti-colonial struggles – and who have critiqued how Islam in Africa has been misinterpreted due to Euro-North American coloniality (which I reviewed in Chapter 3) – have, in my view, tended to under-emphasise the imperialistic practices of Muslim elites. To give an example, as Ahmadou Séhou (2019, p. 5) shows, slavery in Adamaoua in Cameroon was introduced during the course of the Sufi Muslim *jihads* starting with Usman Dan Fodio in the early eighteenth century and was "unknown in the region before the Fulani conquests, at least in its institutionalised form". In Séhou's view, Islam was "just a pious pretext to justify all ambitions" imposed through "cruelty and violence" (ibid., p. 4) (my translation from French). Hence, as Africanist anthropologist Jean-François Bayart argues, some post-colonial literature – and arguably decolonial literature – risks side-lining how "the plural history of the colonization of Africa is also . . . the history of the multiple collisions between European and Arab empires, and the myriad dynastic states and cultures of Africa" (2010, p. 6).

Decolonial theorists have started to engage with such complexity but, in general, it remains under-theorised within this intellectual community. Madina Tlostanova's concept of 'external imperial difference' (2015, p. 47) is a positive example in the right direction. Based on the Russian case, Tlostanova coined this term to capture how 'subaltern empires' can find themselves in a position of colonial difference relative to Euro-North American influences yet also exercise imperialistic domination over their own internal 'Others'. Such external imperial difference as developed from the Russian case is not necessarily applicable to West Africa. I mention it, rather, to suggest that this kind of theorising is needed to make sense of current dynamics, especially in debates in comparative/international education and development on the liberatory potential of non-Western epistemologies. This is because, as I show in this chapter, in political and onto-epistemological terms, Muslim elites can display characteristics of both coloniser and colonised.

Before diving back into the stories of my research participants, I first provide a theoretical framework for making sense of the influence of descent-based hierarchies on education and, second, present the practical challenges of researching such dynamics in Medina Diallobé.

Understanding descent-based inequalities in Islamic West Africa

The important influence in Senegal of descent-based hierarchies which pre-date European colonisation by centuries is of significant relevance to current debates around race and Education and International Development (EID). As noted in Chapter 1, both educationalists and scholars of 'race and development' have tended to side-line the importance of religion or what Topolski (2018) calls the 'race-religion constellation' in the constitution of European racial hierarchies. Consequently, in Chapter 3, I explained that we cannot understand the logics behind colonial education policies in the colony of AOF without appreciating how they were informed by the nineteenth-century European race-religion constellation of *islam noir* which combined anti-Black stereotypes with Orientalist attitudes towards Islam (Launay and Soares, 1999).

Furthermore, to understand popular engagement with schooling in Senegal from the colonial period onwards, one must also appreciate how *islam noir* was layered upon local forms of racialisation which originated before – and have persisted long after – the Transatlantic slave trade and colonisation. In order to understand these dynamics in the Futa Tooro, I needed (a) a theoretical framework that could capture the intersections of these different hierarchies and (b) to overcome the methodological challenges which emerged when investigating them at the local level.

Race-as-descent: Theorising African histories of race

Scholars who argue for the acknowledgement of racial hierarchies in EID (Rudolph, Sriprakash and Gerrard, 2018; Sriprakash, Tikly and Walker, 2020) overwhelmingly employ a definition of 'race' tied to nineteenth-century European classification schemes focused on biological inheritance, specifically phenotypic markers of "skin tone and hair color and texture" (Bonilla-Silva, 1997, p. 474). While this framework enables us to understand some of the French colonial logics that underpinned *islam noir,* it fails to encapsulate the ongoing influence of local descent-based hierarchies and racialisation frameworks derived from Middle Eastern and North African Muslim communities. Historian of race in the Sahel, Bruce Hall (2011) has argued that, when descent-based hierarchies in West Africa feature anti-Black subordination, they often owe their origins to the Islamic intellectual traditions of Arabia and North Africa. Only later did they come to overlap with European colonial classificatory frameworks. In line with this evidence, we should not forget that "there are African histories of race that do not obey colonial logics" (ibid., p. 2).

To theorise these intersections, I turned to the work of sociologists of race, like Zaheer Baber, Tariq Modood and Thomas Sealy, who critique dominant framings of race used in Critical Race Theory (CRT) (Baber, 2010, 2022; Modood and Sealy, 2022) which informs the scholarship on race and development. In contrast, these sociologists argue that defining race and racialisation solely on the basis of the North American experience risks "extrapolating a common and universal structure to racism which remains essentially the same, outside of its specific historical location" (Hall, 1980, p. 337). Instead, they propose that categories can be considered 'racial' when based on "perceived or attributed descent" (Modood and Sealy, 2022, p. 435). They argue that, even in Euro-North American cases, descent is always shaped by the 'dual logics' of 'biological' characteristics and 'cultural' markers. Biological traits, whether alleged or real, can be inferred on the basis of visible differences in phenotype but equally via genetics or family and lineage which are not necessarily immediately discernible from someone's appearance. Meanwhile, 'inherited' cultural markers include religion, language and regional or ethnic lifestyle differences (Baber, 2010).

These sociologists stress "the operation of perceived or attributed descent in the notion of racism" because, without this emphasis, "racism could not be distinguished from other forms of groupism such as nationalism or sexism" (Modood and Sealy, 2022, p. 435). They propose that this broad definition of racialisation as based on descent rather than phenotype *per se* better reflects the historical and anthropological data on the evolution of European racial categories and phenomena like anti-Semitism and Islamophobia – as documented by Topolski (2018) for example. Modood and Sealy also propose that this framing overcomes the 'Eurocentric myopia' of decolonial debates which have focused on the racial legacies of European empires while ignoring "other empires and the legacy of their racial hierarchies today, as well as the development of new forms of racism outside the West" which are rooted in different logics, genealogies and onto-epistemologies (ibid., p. 438).

I find that this definition of racialisation, which positions descent as opposed to phenotype as the overarching characteristic of racial categories, is empirically useful for studying the Senegalese case. Zaheer Baber (2022) argues that this theoretical framework has the advantage in that we can compare diverse phenomena traditionally referred to in the Euro-North American social sciences by terms other than 'race' or 'racism', for example by the terms 'caste', 'descent-based hierarchies' or 'xenophobic othering' (2022, pp. 152–153). By studying them together, we observe that they actually bear significant 'family resemblances' to Euro-North American forms of anti-Black racism in both their underlying logics and consequences (Modood and Sealy, 2022, p. 435).

These contemporary debates are relevant to the work of anthropologists who have long documented how boundaries between ranks and status groups among the Haalpulaar'en continue to be maintained because of ideas about descent. Members subscribe to an essentialising ideology which assumes that identity and associated traits are fixed at birth (N'Gaïde, 2003). Significantly, the symbolic boundaries are upheld by a classification system that associates dominant groups with honour and purity/cleanliness and subordinate groups with shame and dirt/pollution (Klein, 2005). Being a member of a particular group is understood as "a way of being, a . . . moral and physical constitution of persons', of sharing an 'essence', or being of the same 'kind'" (Dilley, 2000, p. 150). In-group endogamy is also widespread, underpinned as it is by this 'indigenous discourse of difference' (ibid., pp. 149–150).

Descent-based hierarchies based on the constructs of honour/shame were well-entrenched in West Africa by the twelfth century (Tamari, 1991). However, only later were Sahelian societies influenced by race-religion constellations emanating from the Middle Eastern and North African Islamic intellectual traditions. The latter associated nobility with Islamic faith, cultural norms and 'Whiteness' (which meant Arab, not European, descent) and servility with 'Blackness' and non-Muslim religion (Hall, 2011). Later still, during colonisation, European race-religion constellations were layered on top of these forms of racialisation, including in the form of *islam noir* (Launay and Soares, 1999).

It goes without saying that the specific logics of different forms of racialisation must be unpacked and their interactions situated in specific times and places. For example, I observed that, in Medina Diallobé, differentiation between ranks and status groups was ubiquitous and mapped onto socioeconomic and political inequalities. To an extent, these hierarchies were linked to phenotype in the sense that some *toorodo* families claimed ancestry from the Prophet's family which carried associations of superiority on the basis of their religiosity and 'White' (Arab) race. However, in reality people in Medina Diallobé rarely inferred someone's status group membership based on their appearance; rather, they deduced it on the basis of their surname, profession or lineage. This situation appears to contrast with Sahelian contexts further north, like Mauritania or northern Mali, where the presence of communities of Arab and Berber heritage means that phenotypic diversity is more pronounced and hence prominent in racialisation processes (Hall, 2011). Using this definition of race-as-descent, I unpack later several distinct historical race-religion constellations that have emerged in the Futa Tooro region over the last 300 years and the evolving relationships between them and education in the present.

However, before moving back to the data from Medina Diallobé, it was equally important for me to think through not just *what* race is but to consider *how* racial divisions and ensuing inequalities might be (re)produced. For this task, I followed Falguni Sheth (2009) and Alana Lentin (2022) who understand racial ideology as a *technology* that naturalises difference, conceals the constructed nature and implications of this difference and instrumentalises this difference to discipline something (people, behaviours, traits) that elites perceive as threatening to the social and political order. As Alexander Weheliye adds, specific constructions of racial difference and racial ideology are reproduced through "ongoing sets of political relations" that are constantly perpetuated through "institutions, discourses, practices, desires, infrastructures, languages, technologies, sciences, economies, dreams, and cultural artifacts" (2014, p. 3). With this framing in mind, I not only show later how religious leaders, including Muslim clerics of Qur'anic schools in Medina Diallobé, contributed to (re)producing a racial ideology in their discourses and practices – but also how Islamic education created resources and spaces where these constructions could, to an extent, be resisted (Rudolph, Sriprakash and Gerrard, 2018; Sriprakash, Tikly and Walker, 2020).

Despite these dynamics, discussion of descent-based hierarchies is almost entirely absent from development research and policy debates in Africa, with the exception of scholarship on social movements organised by descendants of slaves (Ould Ahmed Salem, 2009; Pelckmans and Hahonou, 2011; Thioub, N'Gaïde and Seck, 2014; Pelckmans and Hardung, 2015). This may be because people from these societies are often ashamed to discuss these hierarchies openly, outsiders unfamiliar with these contexts can struggle to discern them, and no official statistics are collected on people's group membership. It is to these realities – and the ensuing methodological challenges – that I now turn.

The challenges of researching descent-based hierarchies

The context in which I aimed to explore racialised descent-based hierarchies posed a number of empirical challenges. First, in 1905 the French banned trade in persons in AOF, yet structural and symbolic vestiges of slavery endured. In particular, slaves' inferior position was underlain by the customary codes of honour/shame which framed the freeborn as brave, generous and modest, while slaves were considered as lacking honour (Klein, 2005). Hence, even once freed, slaves and their descendants continued to endure stigma and subordination. Because of socioeconomic constraints, today descendants of slaves in the Futa Tooro region often maintain clientelist relationships with their former masters' lineages (N'Gaïde, 2003).

Second, in many West African societies, it is considered inappropriate to speak publicly about a person's status group membership, and individuals of artisan/musician or slave descent are often ashamed to reveal their status, particularly if they have managed to disguise it through migrating (Pelckmans, 2011). Hence, outsiders to these communities can only discern the influence of descent-based hierarchies after developing relationships of trust and through sensitive observation of individuals' interactions and embodied behavioural styles (Pelckmans, 2015; Regnier, 2020). In Senegal, it has been illegal since independence to refer to someone's status group origins given the stigma associated with caste and slave status (Dilley, 2004, p. 202). Thus, even academics hesitate to admit, out of embarrassment, that such 'traditional' hierarchies still persist (Mbow, 2000, p. 74). As a result, no official statistics or large-scale data are collected on descent-based hierarchies in Senegal which could form the basis of a comparison of descent with variables like education level or socioeconomic status. This problem is common to other countries in West Africa and the Sahel.

Third, in terms of classifications, French colonial administrators had solidified descent-based relationships, imagining them to be more fixed than was necessarily the case. They labelled the respective groups according to a European gaze, namely primary producers as 'freeborn' or 'nobles' evoking the feudal system of Medieval Europe and the artisan/musicians as 'caste' groups inspired by the segregation and endogamy of the Hindu system (Conrad and Frank, 1995; Dilley, 2004, p. 27). These terms continue to be appropriated into local use, including in Medina Diallobé. However, there are pitfalls to be aware of here. When presenting my research participants' narratives, I quote their own words to designate people of slave descent, usually *maccuɗo* (plural: *maccuɓe*). But this word is considered derogatory (Dilley, 2000, p. 152), so in my analysis I use the more neutral term *gallunke* (plural: *gallunkooɓe*) to signify someone of slave decent (Schmitz, 2009, p. 96).

Finally, this situation posed other even more difficult challenges for my investigation into the influence of descent-based hierarchies on educational engagement in Medina Diallobé. Barring the quote at the beginning of this chapter, few of my *toorodo* research participants made explicit their views about other groups. Yet, I could infer such attitudes by observing their attempts to reinforce their superiority – and enforce symbolic boundaries between themselves and others – by controlling young people's everyday interactions. For instance, several *tooroɓe* advised me against visiting the houses of blacksmiths saying that I would get sick or be attacked with sorcery. When I occasionally fell ill, usually with diarrhoea, these individuals made haughty remarks along the lines of "I told you so" – clearly suggesting that my discomfort was a consequence of my social misadventures. I also remember hearing a *toorodo* man proudly compliment his wife saying, "See her beautiful aquiline nose? You can see that she is of Arab descent!" While her skin colour was not noticeably lighter than the average in the community, such a discourse nonetheless revealed relationships often made by *tooroɓe* between phenotypic traits associated with Arab (not European) 'Whiteness', nobility, beauty and moral or spiritual superiority.

Therefore, despite my observations confirmed by one research participant that "caste is central to everything", making explicit reference to someone's status group in Medina Diallobé was considered tactless or unbecoming. Nevertheless, many people obliquely referred to status group dynamics by talking about 'racism' or 'hierarchies'. Having experienced the weight of such hierarchies in my own interactions (as I described in Chapter 5 when my interpreters refused to organise interviews outside of their status groups), I could pick up on these references. I found generally that if I asked people with whom I had developed relations of trust, in a private and discreet place, they tended to open up about the topic.

One strategy I employed to try to ascertain the influence of caste on dynamics within state schools was to ask school directors to prepare a list of teachers, the subjects they taught, and their qualifications. I only did this once I had already gotten to know them well over several months and judged that they would feel comfortable discussing sensitive topics. I later met with them to discuss the data and at the end of the conversation broached the subject of teachers' 'origins' – whether ethnic group or status group – and whether this had an impact on schooling. With one director, whilst our initial discussions had been clear and open, once questions of origins arose his voice dropped in volume so that, over the whir of the electric fan, no one in the adjoining staffroom could overhear us:

> I don't ask about this sort of thing you know, it doesn't interest me. But you hear, you know, you overhear conversations . . . so-and-so lives in this neighbourhood, is related to so-and-so . . . and you find out that way.

It was only several months later, when we shared a meal at his home, that he discussed more explicitly how descent shaped the dynamics between pupils in the classroom, which I unpack later.

Given this context, I set about finding out if and how educational institutions and providers in Medina Diallobé directly or indirectly contributed to processes of racialisation in their discourses and practices. Later I reveal, through a combination of literature review and empirical data, that state schools in the Futa Tooro region have represented a significant set of resources and spaces for groups disadvantaged by the descent-based hierarchy to enjoy social mobility, which in some cases was an opportunity for them to resist their subordinate status positioning. Yet, Islamic education remained the 'final frontier' whereby their access to powerful knowledge continued to be denied.

Knowledge-power, education and social mobility: An evolving relationship

In a previous article (Newman, 2021), I reviewed the anthropological and historical scholarship which showed how education has been implicated in the constitution of status group identities among the Haalpulaar'en for centuries. Each status group was associated with a body of 'lore' specific to its customary profession which "encompassed not only the technical aspects of the craft or occupation but also the oral traditions and the magical procedures necessary for its successful conduct". The discourse of difference between groups was thus "symbolically elaborated in terms of bodies of knowledge and competing systems of power" (Dilley, 2000, p. 149) and groups upheld these distinctions by closely guarding their secrets. In addition to their lore, families would inculcate and monitor the acquisition of values and behaviours specific to their status group among their children, such as leadership for *toorobe* and humility and obedience for *gallunkoobe* (N'Gaïde, 2003).

However, the new ontological regime complex and state schools implanted during the colonial period had had a profound impact on relationships between status group identity, knowledge and social mobility. In line with their own racial ideology, the French wanted the aristocratic freeborn lineages to enrol their children in state schools to train and co-opt them as Indigenous administrators. Yet, fearing colonial influence, such families often sent the sons of their slaves instead. State schooling therefore became a route for men from families of artisan/musician and *gallunkoobe* ranks to obtain positions of authority in the colonial administration (Coulon, 1975). The degree of social mobility conferred by state schools in the late colonial period and shortly after independence in 1960 was such that some formerly disenfranchised groups were able to overtake the freeborn in terms of economic and political advantages (Schmitz, 2009; Pelckmans, 2012). However, once the freeborn in the Futa Tooro region realised the value of state schooling in the 1960s and 70s, they tried to monopolise its benefits by, for instance, opposing policies to make school mandatory and hence accessible to all (Coulon, 1975, p. 56). Furthermore, when artisan/musicians and *gallunkoobe* attended state schools alongside the freeborn, discrimination played out within the school space (Thioub, N'Gaïde and Seck, 2014). More recently, non-formal educational opportunities provided by NGOs in the 1990s, such as Pulaar literacy classes, have provided an opportunity for artisan/musicians and *gallunkoobe* to obtain employment with NGOs – a form of social mobility that was subsequently co-opted by *toorobe* (Huméry, 2012, pp. 303–305).

In several publications I have shown how, following the expansion of school provision under EFA in recent years, people's engagement with state schools in Medina Diallobé both reproduce these historical dynamics and reveal new trends (Newman, 2020, 2021). I found that some *toorodo* parents socialised their children into logics of superiority which some students reproduced in the classroom by treating members of subordinate status groups in disrespectful ways. However, other *toorodo* youth used spaces associated with the school to enact more egalitarian relationships by refusing to treat others differently contrary to their parents' attitudes. Meanwhile blacksmith and *gallunke* parents told me that, from the 1980s onwards, whilst still teaching the lore associated with their customary livelihoods, they had invested in state schooling to improve their children's social mobility. This meant that *lycée* and university graduates from these groups far outnumbered those of *toorobe* and by the 2010s they dominated formal employment in local administration, teaching and healthcare. At this point, *toorobe* parents had realised that they risked falling behind and were increasingly sending their children to state schools instead of Qur'anic schools. The massification of schools and the declining value of diplomas under EFA also meant that some blacksmith and *gallunke* youth attended school less for diplomas and more in order to promote their status group through popular culture and socialising with peers (Newman, 2021). In addition, the ideals associated with status group identity could still be constraining in particular for young female *toorobe* who struggled to convert their lower secondary school diplomas into employment. The only options available to them were in vocational spheres which their families considered 'shameful' given their 'noble' status (Newman, 2020).

Despite the fact that state schools presented a degree of opportunity for subordinate status groups to challenge their social position, Qur'anic schools in the Futa Tooro region still excluded them. Later I describe how Islamic education therefore came to represent the 'final frontier' in terms of equal access to knowledge which had historically been monopolised by the dominant *toorodo* group to reinforce hierarchical racial logics and, arguably, its onto-epistemological values and preferred pedagogies.

Islamic education in the Futa Tooro region: The 'final frontier'

Until the colonial period, the freeborn rank of the Haalpulaar'en consisted of primary producers who lived from agriculture, fishing and animal husbandry, while the artisan/musician rank were secondary producers who subsisted through clientelist relationships with freeborn lineages. Such relationships were originally characterised by interdependence, with artisans and bards respected for their crafts if also feared for their lore's connection to occult forces. In West Africa, the ability to work iron has long been attributed to relationships with powerful supernatural entities, and blacksmiths in particular were both respected and feared (Conrad and Frank, 1995).

However, the spread of Islam made the social structure more hierarchical. The Muslim clerical lineages imposed an onto-epistemological net (Thayer-Bacon, 2017) and race-religion constellation (Topolski, 2018) which framed their lore as *halal* or licit (Dilley, 2004, p. 4). In contrast, artisan/musicians' knowledge was associated with dirt, pagan or immoral (*haram*) practices and supernatural danger (Ware, 2014, p. 82). As the previous chapter explained, during the *toorodo jihads* in the Futa Tooro region in the late eighteenth and nineteenth centuries, their leaders Abdul Qader Kane and Cheikh Umar Tall tried to challenge the prevailing race-religion constellation by privileging knowledge over lineage when defining membership in the *toorodo* clerisy. However, following these leaders' deaths, once the *toorobe* ascended to political power, the Muslim clerical group became increasingly endogamous. They barred artisan/musicians and slaves from Qur'anic schools (Ware, 2014, pp. 168–171) and excluded other freeborn lineages from advanced Islamic education (Dilley, 2004).

During colonisation, the relationship between Islamic education and status group identities had notably shifted in other parts of Senegambia to reflect more inclusive race-religion constellations. The newly founded Sufi orders expanded their educational offer to include other groups, including slaves after abolition who sought out a prestigious live-in Qur'anic education to cast off their stigma and regain their honour (Ware, 2014, p. 188). Yet, the *toorobe* in the Futa Tooro region who were affiliated to the Tijaniyya Sufi order founded by Cheikh Umar Tall (the Tijaniyya Umariyya), continued to exclude other groups from their Qur'anic schools thus monopolising the knowledge underpinning their dominance (Coulon, 1975; Schmitz, 2009). The *toorobe* here subscribed to – and reproduced – a narrow race-religion constellation whereby Islamic knowledge and education – and supposedly piety and moral superiority – were restricted to their status group. Prestigious inherited positions conferring religious authority and hence discursive power, like imam or cleric of a Qur'anic school, were further limited to those with the *baraka* (inherited blessing) of belonging to an established *seerembe* lineage (Willis, 1978).

However, during the colonial and post-colonial periods, these exclusionary habits of the *toorobe* in the Futa Tooro region were challenged as new Islamic communities attempted to promote a more inclusive race-religion constellation which uncoupled lineage from Islamic knowledge and authority. For example, in 1936, a Haalpulaar disciple of the Tijaniyya Umariyya named Mohammed Seydou Ba founded a new Sufi community in the village of Medina Gounass in the region of Kolda in southern Senegal near The Gambia (Wane, 1974). Contrary to the clerics in the Futa Tooro region, Medina Gounass expanded access to Qur'anic schooling to members of non-*toorodo* lineages. Such individuals have subsequently migrated there from the Futa since at least the 1970s to obtain an Islamic education free from descent-based barriers (Coulon, 1975, pp. 76–77).

In Chapter 3, I explained how the colonial period also saw the emergence of reformist movements inspired by Salafi ideology whose onto-epistemological nets borrowed elements from European modernist worldviews. They challenged the monopoly that the classically educated

Muslim clerics held over Islamic education by advocating for a more democratic school system. This movement also reached the Futa Tooro region in the 1930s. A Haalpulaar called El Hajj Mahmud Ba learned the Qur'an and undertook advanced Islamic study in the Futa Tooro and Mauritania despite coming from a *fulɓe* (pastoralist) family which was not a clerical *toorodo* lineage. Ba, who was exposed to Salafism while on pilgrimage (*hajj*) to Mecca in the 1930s, opened the first of a chain of schools in 1941 called Al-Falah in the Futa Tooro. Like other Salafi-inspired reformists of the time, Ba's onto-epistemological position included rejection of Sufism and the framing of esoteric practices as superstition and unlawful innovation (*bid'ah*). The Al-Falah schools borrowed European norms by teaching the Qur'an and Arabic using blackboards and according to a strict weekly timetable (Kane, 1997).

In less than a decade, graduates of Ba's schools had created 60 similar schools in the Futa Tooro region, southern Mauritania and western Mali. Young men and those of subordinate status groups were particularly receptive to Ba's reformist agenda as it offered an education and interpretation of Islam beyond the *toorodo*-dominated Sufi path (Kane, 1997). This trend dovetails with many anthropological accounts of reformist movements throughout the Islamic world from the nineteenth century to the present. Scholars have found that these movements are never just about differences in onto-epistemologies or moral debates over what practices are correct. Rather, contestations over religious authority are also political, as divisions between clerics of the establishment on the one hand and reformist intellectuals on the other tend to coincide with entrenched lines of social inequality which shape access to power and resources. These distinctions include age and gender (Masquelier, 2001; Cantone, 2012; Janson, 2014) and, in this case, descent-based racial hierarchies.

However, the crackdown on Ba's Al-Falah movement was harsh and swift. Influenced by the logics of *islam noir*, the French colonial administration in AOF were suspicious of the Salafis' agenda of social change. They saw them as a pan-Islamic anti-colonial menace and an attack on the Sufi clerics whose support they had carefully cultivated. Cheikh Umar Tall's grandson, Seydou Nourou Tall, vilified Ba as a dangerous extremist and allied with the French to prevent him from opening new schools. Ba was forced into quasi-exile in Cameroon in the 1960s (Kane, 1997). Hence, it has only been as a result of urbanisation, globalisation and the fragmentation of Sufi orders in the 2000s that new Islamic movements began to pose a serious challenge to *toorodo* clerical authority and the Tijaniyya Umariyya in the Futa Tooro region (Jourde, 2012).

By the twenty-first century in Medina Diallobé, people's Islamic onto-epistemological nets were being re-woven and race-religion constellations debated, as men from non-*seeremɓe* families strove to acquire and use Islamic knowledge to challenge the *toorodo* clerics' exclusionary practices. It is to these resistances that I now turn.

Using Islamic knowledge to resist racialised exclusion

In the previous chapter, I showed that it was *toorobe* who showed the greatest preference for full-time education for boys in the Futa Tooro's Qur'anic schools. Consequently, many of Medina Diallobé's inhabitants whom I interviewed attributed low attendance of other groups merely to a lack of interest linked to their customary professions. For instance, a state-school teacher told me:

> The *pullo* [pastoralist] doesn't have time to learn or teach the Qur'an, he has his cows to herd. The *baylo* [blacksmith] has his occupation, so no time for the Qur'an. The fisherman fishes, he has no time for the Qur'an. The *toorodo* works his fields and teaches the Qur'an, that's his profession. . . . Everyone can learn the Qur'an – but to make a living out of it, a profession, is different. . . . Technically the Qur'an doesn't 'belong' to anyone, but it's having the time. . . . Others had their own professions.

However, other inhabitants framed the pattern of *daara* attendance in less neutral terms, stressing discrimination on the part of *toorobe*. These individuals were either not *toorobe* or were *toorobe* who had lived elsewhere and had developed a more critical perspective on Haalpulaar customs. For instance, 45-year-old *toorodo* Omar, who grew up in Dakar, said: "The *daaras* are a system for *toorobe*", he stated. "If you know the cleric, and you send your children there, you will help him, he will help you. It's a bit like a mafia. The other categories won't be treated the same". Adama, a 50-year-old Wolof administrator, argued that the clerics had constructed the authority to teach the Qur'an as dependent on the inherited *baraka* of *seerembe toorodo* lineage. He argued that non-*toorodo* men did not invest in Islamic education not just because they preferred their own customary profession but due to the weight of this exclusionary ideology:

> In the Haalpulaar context, the first to learn the Qur'an were *toorobe*. . . . So that's how it spread and the situation has continued to this day. And then their position of . . . well, dominance in the society has meant that is has become their 'property' in a sense. A non-*toorodo* can learn and have knowledge, but he will never be of the same status as a *toorodo*.

Souleye, a 22-year-old university student in Dakar who was of the blacksmith status group, argued that it was clerics especially who reinforced the Indigenous discourse of difference between status groups by stressing how important endogamy was for social stability.

Given how *toorodo* clerics in the Futa Tooro region tended to exclude men from other status groups from advanced *daaras*, there were few such individuals in Medina Diallobé who had attended an Islamic school on a full-time basis. However, during my fieldwork I came across several non-*toorodo* men in Medina Diallobé who had studied Islam formally outside the village. Their trajectories reflected the two main options documented earlier: a Salafi-inspired reformist school or the Sufi community of Medina Gounass. The first individual was Kalidou, a 24-year-old *ceďďo* (warrior status group of the freeborn rank) in his final year of *lycée*. After completing state primary school, his father had enrolled Kalidou in a boarding Arabo-Islamic school of Salafi orientation in the town of Saint-Louis where he studied the Qur'an and Arabic. Kalidou then moved back to Medina Diallobé as a teenager where he attended the state secondary school. The second individual was Ahmed, a blacksmith who had fully memorised the Qur'an when studying in Medina Gounass. I never met Ahmed personally but his story was relayed to me by his friend Hamidou. The third case I heard about was a group of three men who had attempted to challenge the *toorodo* clerics' exclusionary race-religion constellation in the early 2000s – namely, a *toorodo* named El Hajji and two *gallunkooɓe* called Demba and Youssouf. They had either died or left the village by the time of my fieldwork and their stories were told to me by their friends and family. The following experiences of Kalidou, Ahmed, El Hajji, Demba and Youssouf illustrate just how influential the *tooroɓe*'s exclusionary race-religion constellation could be but also how resistance against it can take shape.

Life as politics: Quiet encroachment in The Little Mosque

Kalidou explained, in his characteristically poetic style, how his educational trajectory was very unusual for a member of his status group in the Futa Tooro region:

> My family are members of the *ceďďo* caste. In the past they were warriors, they weren't even concerned with Islam. Rather, it was their own magic [lore] that interested them. They would get together and sing and talk of their horse and their rifle. But it was my father's Islamic faith which led me to learn the Qur'an. . . . The fact that our caste couldn't learn the religion was a myth, a myth propagated as much by ourselves as by others, through fear and laziness – but we have broken through it. It's not about being Black or White which makes you superior, or your caste, or who your father is. . . . Before, some castes were held to be superior, and even I used to call people *maccuɓe* [a derogatory term for slaves] and so on – but I have since learned from the Qur'an that this is bad.

Not only did Kalidou and Ahmed buck the dominant trend by pursuing a formal Islamic education, but they actively strove to challenge exclusionary orthopraxy and the authority of the *toorodo* clerics in Medina Diallobé. "There is a proverb that you need to know, to understand the Futa", my friend *toorodo* Yaya once told me. "'*Yimbe fof ngara mosquée, kono toorodo woni yeeso*' which means 'Everyone goes to the mosque, but the *toorodo* is always in front'". Mosques were the main places in which Kalidou, Ahmed, El Hajji, Demba and Youssouf tried to carve out a space for themselves. Like many larger villages in the Futa Tooro region, Medina Diallobé had a number of mosques catering to its population. The largest and oldest was creatively named The Big Mosque (*la grande mosquée*) which was centrally located and where inhabitants of surrounding villages came to attend collective prayer on Fridays. It held a dominant position as a site of religious influence, as one of the most powerful inherited religious positions in the village was the imam of The Big Mosque. There were also several smaller mosques in Medina Diallobé including one predictably called The Little Mosque (*la petite mosquée*). It was built in the 1990s partly by funding from Saudi Arabia during the heyday of Gulf petrodollar investment in African Islamic infrastructures. It was in The Little Mosque that Kalidou and Ahmed tried to challenge dominant orthopraxy.

To consider Kalidou's case first, he explained how he had challenged local traditions that 'the *tooroɓe* always pray in front':

> At first, in The Little Mosque I felt awkward, as if I'm not meant to be there as a *ceddo* [warrior status group], it was all *tooroɓe* there. They have a kind of monopoly over the religion and I daren't say anything. Then there was one day when we were all in line to pray and I was in the front row. And someone from the family of the imam [of The Big Mosque] came in late, and someone tried to push me aside to make room for him – but I refused. After we had prayed I said, 'You don't have the right to push me aside, we're all here to worship God', and they said 'Yes that's true . . . but the wise ones have the right to a place at the front', or whatever. They agreed, though, that what I said was correct in the religion. People here have a tendency to continue tradition as a routine, in a way that goes unchallenged. But then there were some instances when I just couldn't keep quiet anymore, things that I just had to correct.

Kalidou told me that his erudition in Arabic and intimate knowledge of the Qur'an and *hadith* (traditions of the Prophet), had convinced the *tooroɓe* of his authority such that they had acquiesced and allowed him to lead prayer in The Little Mosque. However, things were not so easy for blacksmith Ahmed, as his friend Hamidou explained. Ahmed had also attempted to lead prayer in The Little Mosque, which he argued was his right not least because of his advanced education and knowledge. However, Ahmed's experience had ended quite differently to Kalidou's, following a challenge by an elderly *toorodo* man, Modou:

> The *baylo* [blacksmith], called Ahmed, led prayer next door at The Little Mosque. But the old man [who lives nearby], Modou, came and started asking questions, like 'Where are you from?' Ahmed said Medina Gounass, but Modou asked about his family, and found out that he was a *baylo*, and he shouted 'No *baylo* leads prayer here [in Medina Diallobé]!'. He asked his son 'How did you let this happen?' – although his son replied, 'He knows more Qur'an than you'!

The result was that Ahmed stopped pushing the issue and, as Hamidou explained, "he prays behind people now [does not lead prayer] because it's not good in the religion to create these tensions, and there are risks of curses [sorcery]".

These stories have implications for wider debates about decolonising education and how education scholars might identify and support such struggles. There is already a large social movement which challenges descent-based hierarchies in the Futa Tooro region, namely *Endam Bilaali* which fights for the religious, political and economic rights of the descendants of slaves (*gallunkooɓe*) (Thioub, N'Gaïde and Seck, 2014). The movement benefits from access to considerable economic and political capital, usually from members of the diaspora, and as a result it is quite exceptional. In contrast, the behaviour of individual men such as Kalidou and Ahmed in Medina Diallobé reflect what political scientist Asef Bayat (2010) has described as 'life as politics'. This involves quiet encroachment into public spaces and enactment of alternatives with the acceptance or at least tolerance of many inhabitants. Such small alternatives gently widen the range of possibilities and, although less visible to the external observer than large-scale social movements, can have accumulated effects. Such apparently minor incidents can, over time, prove equally powerful in bringing about social change.

Resistance and rejection: Contestation in The Big Mosque

In contrast, El Hajji, Demba and Youssouf went even further than Kalidou and Ahmed by challenging clerical authority associated with The Big Mosque itself. A *toorodo* friend of El Hajji's son, 40-year-old Habib, explained how their actions were opposed by members of the *seereembe* elite, including the imam of The Big Mosque and the cleric of one of the bigger Qur'anic schools:

> In the early 2000s, whenever someone died, at the cemetery they [El Hajji, Demba and Youssouf] would use the occasion to talk about the religion. Or before the imam arrived for Friday prayer [at The Big Mosque], they would take the microphone and start talking about religious issues. . . . I attended the burial of one old man, and Demba started talking into the microphone about God and the Prophet. The imam [of The Big Mosque] got up and took away the microphone! Forbade him from speaking.

The same thing happened to El Hajji when he tried to take the microphone in The Big Mosque before Friday prayer. Habib recounted that for El Hajji the situation was then made even worse:

> Afterwards, he was at the bus station one day, and an old man hit him with a stick! So El Hajji punched him, floored him! It was a big deal in the village.

People familiar with this group of men explained that they were all Tijani Sufis but that, to use Thayer-Bacon's (2017) terminology, their onto-epistemological nets contained reformist threads. They were critical of excessive veneration of – and obedience to – the Sufi *shaykhs* of the Futa Tooro region who, they argued, sometimes promoted 'local customs' which deviated from 'correct' Islamic practice. Instead, they promoted a return to the founding texts of the religion for guidance. As Habib explained:

> El Hajji always wanted to wed Futa traditions and modernity. But if there was a contradiction, he wanted to base it on textual references – not on the whims of a certain *marabout* [Muslim cleric] who manages to convince any old twit!

As a consequence, El Hajji and his friends were frequently accused of being extremists or '*ibadou*' which is a label often used in Senegal to refer to proponents of Salafism.[2] Habib explained:

> The old men in the village said 'They're against the religion, they're bringing Islamism. . . . They called El Hajji '*ibadou*', 'Wahhabi', 'Islamist', you know. But he wasn't a Wahhabi, he was always Tijani [Sufi] – he was never an extremist.

My friend Yaya gave a similar opinion: "The moment he was no longer with them [the *seerembe* elite], they labelled him *ibadou*". Indeed, El Hajji's nephew Moussa stressed how the resistance of the clerical elite was linked to *who* the members of the group were, as much as *what* they were saying:

> *La grande mosquée* [The Big Mosque] has radical power, and non-democratic. And if you're not a member of one of the big *seerembe* families, it's very hard to be known as an erudite or to talk [with authority] about religious matters. . . . The people El Hajji fought with were often affiliated to Shaykh Ousmane [cleric of one of the large Qur'anic schools]. . . . And Youssouf wasn't considered to be of good family, he was a *maccudo* [derogatory term for a slave]. "Now he's studied, he wants to prove he's someone", that's how people judged him.

As a result of such opposition from the *toorodo* elite, both physical and discursive, the group was effectively silenced. Interestingly, the responses to these men's actions were similar to the four forms of 'in-group policing' that Cédric Jourde (2017, p. 143) observed among the Haalpulaar'en in southern Mauritania when they also criticised the Tijaniyya Umariyya. The four reactions Jourde identified were: (a) accusations of betrayal; (b) accusations of heresy; (c) shunning and banishing; and (d) mystical attacks.

Conclusion

First, this chapter has shown that individuals positioned lower in the racialised, descent-based hierarchy in the Futa Tooro region have used access to the knowledge, skills and spaces offered by state schools to advance their social positions since the colonial period (Newman, 2021). Yet, such opportunities could not fully compensate for their exclusion from Qur'anic education as they could not challenge the essentialised logics of honour/shame which underpinned their inferiority, bound up as they were with local Islamic onto-epistemologies (Schmitz, 2009). Education and development studies scholars often fail to appreciate such racialised hierarchies embedded in other-than-secular ontologies, and this failure can be seen as another example of secular erasure. The secular bias in educational research renders invisible these significant local barriers to the exercise of the human right to education as well as people's struggles to overcome them. In addition, recent work on race within the field of EID has yet to theorise race in a way that can encompass forms of racialised inequality whose origins lie outside of Euro-North American classification schemes and worldviews. This is where wider definitions of race based on descent (Baber, 2022; Modood and Sealy, 2022) and the concept of race-religion constellation (Topolski, 2018) prove analytically useful.

Far from being parochial concerns, the stories of these men have significant implications for debates around the decolonisation of education in West Africa and the Sahel. As explained in Chapter 4, EFA is ostensibly about ensuring that everyone has access to a life-long education that they consider valuable and that enables their full participation in society. Yet, as demonstrated in Chapters 1, 2 and 4, access to Islamic schooling and faith-based education generally are given little attention within international debates which assume that only secular schooling bears emancipatory promise. Alternatively, faith-based education is only mentioned if instrumentalised to meet secular agendas. However, in the Futa Tooro region specifically – and in Islamic West Africa more widely (Einarsdóttir and Boiro, 2016) – individuals from lower social strata can pursue an Islamic education because of its emancipatory potential. They do this even though exclusive access to Qur'anic schools and control of religious discourse have been co-opted by the clerical elite to impose racialised distinction across the region for centuries.

The actions of the five men in Medina Diallobé tell us several things about the relationships between Islamic education and contestations over the dominant race-religion constellation (Topolski, 2018) in the Futa Tooro region today. First, their onto-epistemological positions differed significantly. Kalidou followed more Salafi-oriented interpretations of Islam and rejected Sufism, while the others were all Tijani Sufis but were nonetheless critical of the discourses and practices of many of the clerics affiliated to the Tijaniyya Umariyya. They hailed from different status groups and ranks (*gallunke,* warrior, blacksmith, *toorodo*). Despite these differences, it was through their shared political objectives that they found common cause. They all desired to advance a more inclusive race-religion constellation grounded in onto-epistemological nets (Thayer-Bacon, 2017) which they argued were based more on the texts of the Qur'an and *hadith* than cultural norms. In their different ways, their views supported democratic access to Islamic education and the exercise of religious authority on the basis of knowledge rather than lineage and inherited *baraka*. Second, these individual struggles need to be understood as part of an ongoing process of contestation over Islamic onto-epistemologies and race-religion constellations in the Futa Tooro region which reach back over 300 years. They are also reflective of contemporary trends which are only a few decades old, such as increased religious diversity and greater access to alternative forms of Islamic education beyond the Qur'anic school.

However, descent-based hierarchies were not the only barriers that prevented Medina Diallobé's inhabitants from accessing Islamic knowledge. The next chapter considers the women who struggled to overcome their own exclusion from classical Qur'anic schools, this time on grounds of gender.

Notes

1 The Fula are part of the same broad Pulaar-speaking group as the Haalpulaar'en but live in southern Senegal, The Gambia, Guinea Bissau and Guinea.

2 The word '*ibadou*' or '*ibado*' is a Wolof term derived from one of the first Senegalese reformist associations, the *Jama'at 'Ibad ar-Rahman*, which emerged in the 1970s (Loimeier, 2000).

References

Baber, Z. (2010) 'Racism without races: Reflections on racialization and racial projects', *Sociology Compass*, 4(4), pp. 241–248.

Baber, Z. (2022) '"Race might be a unicorn, but its horn could draw blood": Racialisation, class and racism in a non-Western context', *Critical Sociology*, 48(1), pp. 151–169.

Bayart, J.-F. (2010) 'Les très fâché(e)s des études postcoloniales', *Sociétés Politiques Comparées*, 23, pp. 1–12.

Bayat, A. (2010) *Life as Politics: How Ordinary People Change the Middle-East.* Stanford, CA: Stanford University Press.

Bonilla-Silva, E. (1997) 'Rethinking racism: Toward a structural interpretation', *American Sociological Review*, pp. 465–480.

Cantone, C. (2012) *Making and Remaking Mosques in Senegal.* Leiden: Brill.

Conrad, D.C. and Frank, B.E. (1995) 'Nyamakalaya: Contradiction and ambiguity in Mande society', in D.C. Conrad and B.E. Frank (eds) *Status and Identity in West Africa: Nyamakalaw of Mande.* Indianapolis, IN: Indiana University Press, pp. 1–26.

Coulon, C. (1975) 'Pouvoir oligarchique et mutations sociales et politiques au Fouta-Toro', in J.-L. Balans, C. Coulon and J.-M. Gastellu (eds) *Autonomie locale et intégration nationale au Sénégal.* Paris: Pedone, pp. 23–80.

Dilley, R.M. (2000) 'The question of caste in West Africa with special reference to Tukulor craftsmen', *Anthropos*, 95(May), pp. 149–165.

Dilley, R.M. (2004) *Islamic and Caste Knowledge Practices Among Haalpulaar'en in Senegal: Between Mosque and Termite Mound.* Edinburgh: Edinburgh University Press.

Einarsdóttir, J. and Boiro, H. (2016) 'Becoming somebody: Bissau-Guinean talibés in Senegal', *The International Journal of Human Rights*, 20(7), pp. 857–874.

Hahonou, E.K. and Strandsbjerg, C. (2011) *Yesterday's Slaves: Democracy and Ethnicity in Benin.* www.youtube.com/watch?v=vW3Zr0e3pU0.

Hall, B.S. (2011) *A History of Race in Muslim West Africa, 1600–1960.* Cambridge: Cambridge University Press.

Hall, S. (1980) 'Race, articulation and societies structured in dominance', in D. Morley (ed) *Essential Essays, Volume 1: Foundations of Cultural Studies.* New York: Duke University Press, pp. 172–221. https://doi.org/10.1515/9781478002413-011.

Human Rights Watch (2001) *Caste Discrimination: A Global Concern*. Durban, South Africa: Human Rights Watch.

Huméry, M.-È. (2012) 'Lire et écrire en pulaar au Sénégal: le "mouvement pulaar", lieu de toutes les résistances', in D. Gary-Tounkara and D. Nativel (eds) *L'Afrique des savoirs au sud du Sahara (XVIe–XXIe siècle): acteurs, supports, pratiques*. Paris: Karthala, pp. 287–312.

Janson, M. (2014) *Islam, Youth and Modernity in the Gambia: The Tablighi Jama'at*. Cambridge: Cambridge University Press.

Jourde, C. (2012) 'Groupes de jeunes, configuration ethnique et affiliation confrérique en milieu haalpulaar (Mauritanie et Sénégal)', in M. Gomez-Perez and M.N. Leblanc (eds) *L'Afrique des générations: Entre tensions et négociations*. Paris: Karthala, pp. 37–72.

Jourde, C. (2017) 'Betrayal, heresy, exile and mystical attacks: The cost of changing Islamic affiliation in an ethnicized society (Mauritania and Senegal)', *Mediterranean Politics*, 22(1), pp. 135–154.

Kane, M.M. (1997) 'La vie et l'oeuvre d'Al-Hajj Mahmoud Ba Diowol (1905–1978) Du pâtre au patron de la "Revolution Al-Falah"', in D. Robinson and J.-L. Triaud (eds) *Le temps des marabouts: Itinéraires et stratégies islamiques en Afrique occidentale française v. 1880–1960*. Paris: Karthala, pp. 431–466.

Klein, M. (1998) *Slavery and Colonial Rule in French West Africa*. Cambridge: Cambridge University Press.

Klein, M. (2005) 'The concept of honour and the persistence of servility in the Western Soudan', *Cahiers d'études africaines*, 179/180, pp. 831–852.

Launay, R. and Soares, B.F. (1999) 'The formation of an "Islamic sphere" in French colonial West Africa', *Economy and Society*, 28(4), pp. 497–519.

Lentin, A. (2022) *Race as a Technology, Alanalentin.net*. Available at: www.alanalentin.net/2022/05/02/race-as-a-technology/ (Accessed: 14 July 2023).

Loimeier, R. (2000) 'L'Islam ne se vend plus: The Islamic reform movement and the state in Senegal', *Journal of Religion in Africa*, 30(2), pp. 168–190.

Masquelier, A. (2001) *Prayer Has Spoiled Everything: Possession, Power, and Identity in an Islamic Town of Niger*. Durham, NC: Duke University Press.

Mbow, P. (2000) 'Démocratie, droits humains et castes au Sénégal', *Journal des africanistes*, 70(1), pp. 71–91.

Modood, T. and Sealy, T. (2022) 'Beyond Euro-Americancentric forms of racism and anti-racism', *The Political Quarterly*, 93(3), pp. 433–441.

Mosse, D. (2018) 'Caste and development: Contemporary perspectives on a structure of discrimination and advantage', *World Development*, 110, pp. 422–436.

Newman, A. (2019) 'The influence of migration on the educational aspirations of young men in northern Senegal: Implications for policy', *International Journal of Educational Development*, 65(3), pp. 216–226.

Newman, A. (2020) 'Honour, respectability and "noble" work: Descent and gender-based obstacles to the education and employment of young Haalpulaar women in northern Senegal', *Children's Geographies*, 18(6), pp. 654–666.

Newman, A. (2021) 'How descent-based hierarchies and youth culture shape secondary school engagement in Senegal', *Anthropology & Education Quarterly*, 52(4), pp. 412–429.

N'Gaïde, A. (2003) 'Stéréotypes et imaginaires en milieu sociaux haalpulaar: classer, stigmatiser et toiser', *Cahiers d'études africaines*, 172, pp. 707–738.

Ould Ahmed Salem, Z. (2009) 'Barefoot activists: Transformations in the Haratine movement in Mauritania', in S. Ellis and I. van Kessel (eds) *Movers and Shakers: Social Movements in Africa*. Leiden and Boston, MA: Brill, pp. 156–177.

Pelckmans, L. (2011) *Travelling Hierarchies: Moving in and Out of Slave Status in a Central Malian Fulbe Network*. Leiden: Africa Studies Centre (ASC).

Pelckmans, L. (2012) '"Having a road": Social and spatial mobility of persons of slave and mixed descent in post-independence centram Mali', *Journal of African History*, 53, pp. 235–255.

Pelckmans, L. (2015) 'Stereotypes of past-slavery and "stereo-styles" in post-slavery: A multidimensional, interactionist perspective on contemporary hierarchies', *International Journal of African Historical Studies*, 48(2), pp. 281–301.

Pelckmans, L. and Hahonou, E.K. (2011) 'West African slavery movements: Citizenship struggles and the legacies of slavery in West Africa', *Vienna Journal of African Studies*, 20, pp. 141–162.

Pelckmans, L. and Hardung, C. (2015) 'La question de l'esclavage en Afrique: politicisation et mobilisations', *Politique africaine*, 4(140), pp. 5–22.

Regnier, D. (2020) *Slavery and Essentialism in Highland Madagascar: Ethnography, History, Cognition*. London: Routledge.

Rodet, M. (2014) *The Diambourou: Slavery and Emancipation in Kayes – Mali*. SOAS University of London.

Rodet, M. and Maximin, C. (2020) *Bouillagui: A Free Village*. SOAS University of London.

Rossi, B. (2016) *Reconfiguring Slavery: West African Trajectories*. Edited by B. Rossi. Liverpool: Liverpool University Press.

Rudolph, S., Sriprakash, A. and Gerrard, J. (2018) 'Knowledge and racial violence: The shine and shadow of "powerful knowledge"', *Ethics and Education*, 13(1), pp. 22–38.

Schmitz, J. (2009) 'Islamic patronage and "republican" emancipation: The slaves of the Almaami in the Senegal River Valley', in B. Rossi (ed) *Reconfiguring Slavery: West African Trajectories*. Liverpool: Liverpool University Press, pp. 85–115.

Séhou, A. (2019) 'Esclavage, émancipation et citoyenneté dans les lamidats de l'Adamaoua (Nord-Cameroun)', *Esclavages & post~esclavages/Slaveries & Post~Slaveries*, 1, pp. 1–18.

Sheth, F.A. (2009) *Towards a Political Philosophy of Race*. Albany, NY: Suny Press.

Sriprakash, A., Tikly, L. and Walker, S. (2020) 'The erasures of racism in education and international development: Re-reading the "global learning crisis"', *Compare: A Journal of Comparative and International Education*, 50(5), pp. 676–692.

Tamari, T. (1991) 'The development of caste systems in West Africa', *The Journal of African History*, 32(2), pp. 221–250.

Thayer-Bacon, B.J. (2017) *Relational Ontologies*. New York: Peter Lang Incorporated, International Academic Publishers.

Thioub, I., N'Gaïde, A. and Seck, I. (2014) *Endam Bilaali: renégocier les identités en situation post-esclavagiste*. Senegal: Centre Africain de Recherches sur les Traite et les Esclavages en Afrique (CARTE).

Tlostanova, M. (2015) 'Can the post-Soviet think? On coloniality of knowledge, external imperial and double colonial difference', *Intersections*, 1(2), pp. 38–58.

Topolski, A. (2018) 'The race-religion constellation: A European contribution to the critical philosophy of race', *Critical Philosophy of Race*, 6(1), pp. 58–81.

UNESCO (2010) *EFA Global Monitoring Report 2010. Reaching the Marginalised*. Paris: United Nations Educational, Scientific and Cultural Organization (UNESCO).

UNESCO (2020) *Global Education Monitoring Report 2020. Inclusion and Education*. Paris: United Nations Educational, Scientific and Cultural Organization (UNESCO).

Wane, Y. (1974) 'Ceerno Muhamadu Sayid Baa ou le soufisme intégral de Madiina Gunaas (Sénégal)', *Cahiers d'études africaines*, 14(56), pp. 671–698.

Ware, R.T. (2014) *The Walking Qur'an: Islamic Education, Embodied Knowledge, and History in West Africa*. Chapel Hill, NC: The University of North Carolina Press.

Weheliye, A.G. (2014) *Habeas Viscus: Racializing Assemblages, Biopolitics, and Black Feminist Theories of the Human*. Durham, NC: Duke University Press.

Willis, J.R. (1978) 'The torodbe clerisy: A social view', *The Journal of African History*, 19(2), pp. 195–212.

7 Islamic knowledge and women's agency

One of the international development conundrums that first inspired my doctoral research was the promise of girls' education, so once in Senegal I started to compare the views of practitioners, parents and young people on the value of schooling for girls. On the one hand, I found that development actors in Dakar universally considered state schooling to be empowering for girls. In line with Senegalese policy frameworks like the *Cadre de Coordination des Interventions sur l'Education des Filles* (Coordinating Framework for Interventions on Girls' Schooling) (CCIEF, 2011), they argued that girls' schooling would promote gender equality, enhance their participation in decision-making, encourage their economic independence and have positive knock-on effects like reducing fertility. Secular state schools were perceived to have the potential to overcome barriers to girls' empowerment stemming from patriarchal Islamic or cultural values. Again, grey literature like *Les Sénégalaises en chiffres* (Senegalese Women in Numbers) (Sow et al., 2000) supported the idea that gender roles based on both pre-Islamic customs and local interpretations of Islam limited girls' achievement in state schools. In contrast, the secular state school system was presented as the "key to breaking the cycle of [gendered] disadvantage" (Griffiths, 2011, p. 204). These ideas were – and arguably still are – widespread throughout policy and academic literature in international education and development (EID) (Tomalin, 2007, p. 1; Khoja-Moolji, 2015, 2018).

On the other hand, the situation I found in Medina Diallobé totally contradicted the predictions of development actors. As explained in Chapter 5, Islam had reached the Futa Tooro region in the tenth century and was firmly entrenched by the eighteenth and nineteenth centuries. Medina Diallobé was a hub of religious scholarship, and both Islamic norms and the authority of Muslim clerics provided the foundation for community life. Based on the previous stereotypes circulating in policy and academic discourses, I therefore assumed that contemporary female state school enrolment in Medina Diallobé would be low, as Muslim parents would either not send their daughters to school at all or would prefer to educate them in Islamic schools. Indeed, many Sahelian countries do show higher rates of secular school enrolment among boys and parental preference for Islamic schools for girls (Hima, 2020,

DOI: 10.4324/9781003172475-9

p. 465). I was therefore surprised to discover that in 2011 the majority of girls in Medina Diallobé completed primary and then enrolled in lower secondary (*collège*). Many also attended upper secondary (*lycée*), and some were even at university in Dakar – including the daughter of the commune's most renowned *shaykh*. As we saw in Chapter 5, it was boys and young men who were less likely to attend state schools, preferring to memorise the Qur'an in Qur'anic schools or *daaras*. Hence, I decided to make unpacking this supposed paradox a central focus of my research.

Over time, however, I made two more interesting observations. First, despite girls' outnumbering boys in state schools at primary level and early *collège*, their drop-out during secondary was steep as they tended to get married from age 13 onwards. Even those who did manage to complete *collège* or *lycée* struggled to convert their education into decision-making authority. As I have analysed in-depth elsewhere (Newman, 2020), the pressure to conform to dominant socio-religious norms from peers, parents, fiancés, husbands and in-laws meant that adolescent girls and young women struggled to finish school, marry men of their choosing at a time that suited them, or work outside the home. The link between state schooling and 'girls' empowerment', as measured through decision-making authority or economic independence, was weak indeed (see also Griffiths, 2011; Khoja-Moolji, 2015).

Second, despite widespread assertions by Medina Diallobé's inhabitants that "women don't learn the Qur'an", the reality turned out to be more complex. This hit home for me after six months of living in Medina Diallobé, during the hot dry season (*ceedu*). *Ceedu* begins in March and lasts until the first welcome rains in June. After the balmy cool season where temperatures hovered between 15–25°C, from March temperatures soared to 35–42°C. The sun's white rays pounded us relentlessly, and our flip-flops melted on the boiling tarmac. We moved our mattresses and mosquito nets outside to the compound's high-walled courtyard, soaking ourselves in a wet sheet in order to fall asleep, only to wake at dawn already sweaty with a fine layer of red Harmattan dust coating our eyelashes. It was during this time that the occasional whirling dust devil zig-zagged a chaotic trail through the village, and a ferocious sandstorm or *yiiwonde* from the deep Sahara barrelled through the region – tearing at everything in its path – and for several hours reduced visibility to a dark red, orange and then milky yellow haze.

My host family made it clear that those who did not have to leave the house should avoid venturing outside between 8am and 6pm – to do so ran the risk of dehydration and sunstroke or, at best, severe exhaustion. Yet, it was during this time of confinement in the shutter-darkened house that an unexpected stillness took hold. Moments of spare time sprouted like green shoots as women took out their Qur'ans for the first time all year and began to study and recite. Only from then onwards did I appreciate the extent to which, despite their exclusion from formal Islamic education, many women harboured a deep desire to learn their religion. From then on, I also noticed that they frequently used this hard-won knowledge for personal fulfilment and to deal with everyday struggles.

My observations during the *ceedu* in Medina Diallobé force us to ask, what if access to Islamic knowledge were just as necessary as a secular education for enabling Muslim women to realise their desired presents and futures and negotiate the local power dynamics that constrained them? What implications would this have for education policy in Senegal and, equally, other contexts with large Muslim populations which have inherited secular education systems from the colonial period? In answer to these questions, this chapter unpacks the reasons why, despite relatively high levels of state school attendance, women in Medina Diallobé went to great lengths to pursue Islamic knowledge informally and the uses to which they put it.

I embed this discussion within theoretical debates on the relationships between education and women's agency. I have reviewed these debates at length elsewhere (Newman, 2020) where I follow definitions of agency as the socioculturally mediated capacity to act (Ahearn, 2001, p. 112). In general, it is rare that qualitative comparative/international education scholarship on education and agency embeds these discussions within people's onto-epistemologies. Indeed, none of the extensive scholarship that I reviewed addressed this issue – which is arguably another form of secular erasure. Meanwhile, economic analyses on Islamic contexts tend to reflect assumptions that Islam is automatically constraining of female agency (c.f. Bano, 2018).

Meanwhile, informed by postcolonial scholarship (e.g. Dunne et al., 2017), more sensitive literature on Muslim women's agency in comparative/international education often references Saba Mahmood's seminal book *The Politics of Piety: The Islamic Revival and the Feminist Subject* (2005). Based on women participating in the mosque movement in Cairo, Mahmood made the important argument that Western observers must avoid imposing on women their own Euro-North American value judgements regarding how – and to what ends – agency ought to be exercised. While this point is essential to acknowledge, I sensed that Mahmood's insights could not capture the extent of women's actions in Medina Diallobé, and in this chapter I set out an intersectional theoretical framework tailored specifically to *African Muslim women's* aspirations and agency. For this task, the work of Mahmood – and others theorising from the perspective of the Middle East or North Africa – is not necessarily sufficient. In what follows, I unpack the strengths and weaknesses of four bodies of academic scholarship that I turned to in order to make sense of the relationships among knowledge, education and women's agency in African Islamic contexts. I then present a brief history of women's access to Islamic education in Senegal, before unpacking how women in Medina Diallobé pursued and deployed Islamic knowledge in their everyday lives. The chapter closes with a discussion of the implications of these insights for research and policy-making in education and development.

Coloniality in discussions about African Muslim women's agency

Compared to research on women's engagement with Islamic education in other parts of the Muslim world, scholarship on women's religious knowledge-seeking practices in Sub-Saharan Africa is relatively limited (c.f. Alidou, 2005, pp. 5–6; Edwin, 2011). To understand the dynamics within Medina Diallobé, I consulted literature in four fields: development discourses including those relating to EFA; Euro-North American sociology and anthropology of religion; African feminisms/womanisms; and Islamic feminisms. While they all made useful points, I found that each alone was limited in its capacity to appreciate the intersectional experiences of *African Muslim women*. Various forms of coloniality, including coloniality of secularity, racism and Orientalism, can be found in these bodies of scholarship which need drawing out and/or challenging if we are to appreciate female agency in Islamic Sub-Saharan African contexts. Below I consider, in turn, each of the four fields.

The gendering of Education for All and development discourses

First, we must consider how mainstream development discourses, including those related to EFA, frame the relationship between state schooling and the agency or empowerment of Muslim girls. It is precisely these discourses which gave rise to the flawed predictions about probable gender dynamics in Medina Diallobé mentioned earlier. The one EFA GEM Report which focused on gender, namely *Gender and Education For All: The Leap to Equality*, includes a lengthy discussion on faith-based schooling and gender equality. In covers several debates and includes a great deal of nuance (UNESCO, 2003, pp. 141–157). For instance, it acknowledges that increases in school enrolment in many Islamic contexts have been due to a preference for faith-based schooling (ibid., p. 141). Even access to 'conservative' forms of education, as in Iran or Saudi Arabia, can increase women's status by delaying marriage and providing economic opportunities (ibid., p. 142). It recognises that religious norms can and do change in response to social, economic and political change (ibid., p. 267) and, because religion is subject to textual (re)interpretation, religious schools can address gender inequality (ibid., p. 143). However, the overall thrust of the report, which argues that religious schools have increased gender parity but not gender equality, is supported by frequent assertions such as "most religious schools tend to reinforce stereotypes of women as submissive and dependent, rather than undermine them" (ibid., p. 141) or "religious schools are more likely to uphold gender differences than eradicate them" (ibid., p. 142). Implicit throughout the report is the assumption that secular schools and NGOs are, on balance, better placed to empower girls and women than their religious equivalents.

Later reports lack the nuance of *Gender and Education For All*. For instance, *Reaching the Marginalized* (UNESCO, 2010) includes a text box on education for Hausa girls in northern Nigeria. It presents evidence that girls' enrolment is very low and parents prefer Islamic schools over secular schools because of poverty, the poor quality of government schools, and fears that girls might experience sexual assault *en route*. However, despite the evidence provided on such structural factors, the section concludes by asserting that "in northern Nigeria the most tenacious barriers to girls' education are often embedded in parental and community attitudes and gender practices" (ibid., p. 167). Meanwhile, the recent *Non-state Actors* report (UNESCO, 2021) includes a text box on faith-based schools which features a number of negative stereotypes, including associations with sexual abuse or resistance to sexuality education, all of which can be associated equally with secular schools (ibid., p. 85).

These tropes that religion, especially Islam, is a barrier to female education are a general trend within development discourse. Education scholar Shenila Khoja-Moolji, in her book *Forging the Ideal Educated Girl: The Production of Desirable Subjects in Muslim South Asia* (2018), explains how EID policy discourse – and to an extent academic debates – reflect a 'suturing together' of three mutually allusive discourses about girls' empowerment, the emancipatory promise of schooling and colonialist stereotypes about Islam. First, girl-centric development, which rose to prominence in the 1980s and 90s, framed adolescent girls in the global South as particularly vulnerable to oppressive patriarchal forces rooted within their families and cultures but also uniquely capable of overcoming these constraints through individualistic and neoliberal forms of agency grounded in Euro-North American values and cultural norms.

Second, these homogenising constructions of 'the girl child' became tied to the education imperative in development – namely the belief that schooling, using a Western secular model as per the liberal humanist tradition in philosophy of education, is the panacea for achieving economic growth and social development. Within this framing, formal schooling is presented as the primary avenue for girls' empowerment. This discourse excludes other structural or political explanations for gender inequality in the global South, appreciation of the failures of Western schooling and its colonial history, and possibilities of non-Western or Indigenous educational alternatives.

Third, these afore-mentioned discourses are sutured together with older Orientalist stereotypes that Islam is inherently oppressive and violent towards women. This discourse assumes that Muslims will prevent girls from accessing 'empowering' secular forms of education and/or orient them instead towards Islamic education which supposedly indoctrinates them into submission to patriarchal authority. Movements like the Taliban and Boko Haram are frequently mobilised in public and policy discourses to legitimise these logics, as if these cases reflect Islam and Muslims everywhere. This ignores, for instance, recent quantitative findings by the Pew Research Center that, worldwide, the education of Muslim girls and women is limited more by a country's economic conditions than religion (Hackett and Fahmy, 2018). Despite the many flaws in this discourse, it exerts as Khoja-Moolji argues "immense epistemic influence" within policy-making as well as academic circles (2015, p. 88).

Khoja-Moolji's work proved useful for unpacking the flawed assumptions about secular education and Muslim girls' empowerment that I encountered in development and EFA discourses. However, to find theories of female agency that do justice to the experiences of girls and women in Medina Diallobé, I had to turn elsewhere.

Euro-North American sociology and anthropology of religion

Women's agency is an important focus of interest within Euro-North American sociology and anthropology of religion. From at least the 1970s, Euro-North American second-wave feminist scholarship framed institutionalised religion as an oppressive patriarchal tradition. It proposed that women who subscribed to conservative religious norms must therefore be oppressed or operating within false consciousness. In turn, female agency could only take the form of non-compliance or subversion of religious norms (Tomalin, 2007). This trope has exerted such powerful influence that sociology ever since has treated women's involvement in conservative religions as a conundrum to be explained (Edwin, 2016, p. 37). Meanwhile, sociologist Orit Avishai has explained that, in response to the prevailing argument that religious women are "doormats" (2008, p. 410), other sociologists of religion have proposed a third explanation for their behaviour, namely 'strategic compliance'. This theory argues that "religious women strategize and appropriate religion to further extra-religious ends such as economic opportunities, domestic relations, political ideologies, and cultural affiliation" (ibid., p. 411).

Although Avishai argues that "the strategic compliance frame extends the analysis of agency beyond the dichotomization of subordination versus subversion", she also says that it rests on problematic assumptions (2008, p. 412). First, religious subjects rarely explain their behaviour as being primarily motivated by the strategic pursuit of extra-religious ends. Rather, they are often motivated by *religious* ends – which is something I also saw in Medina Diallobé. Avishai explains that women tend to describe their actions in terms of religious 'observance' which reflects choice, rather than 'compliance' which presumes coercion. I argue, therefore, that to frame their acts as 'strategic compliance' does not do justice to women's own intentions and motivations and represents yet another form of secular erasure whereby religious behaviour is interpreted through the lenses of secular values and worldviews. It also reflects assumptions among researchers that the *outcome* of a religious action constituted its actor's primary *motivation* – when the outcome could instead reflect an unintended consequence of action or "a boon not a motivator" which obscures a deeper, underlying motivation (ibid., p. 422).

In contrast to the strategic compliance argument, Avishai proposes the concept of 'doing religion' which focuses on performativity in a similar way to Judith Butler's 'doing gender' (1993). Avishai's framing embraces the idea that "subjects operate, perform, and become within power relations and normative expectations" and that "doing religion is a mode of conduct and being, a performance of identity – not only a purposeful or strategic action" (2008, p. 413). A complementary observation has been articulated by Masooda Bano (2012) whose work was described in depth in Chapter 5. She argues that religious behaviour, including preference for Islamic education, is based on both religious and extra-religious motivations. Yet, religious behaviour is more likely to occur when these two forms of reward are mutually reinforcing. Hence, it is common to see both motivations occurring simultaneously, as opposed to one being present and the other totally absent, as the concept of 'strategic compliance' assumes. This kind of nuanced thinking is evident in other qualitative studies of African Muslim women's religious behaviour (Alidou, 2005; Sieveking, 2022).

African feminisms/womanisms

While recent Euro-North American sociology of religion has nuanced our understanding of women's agency in religious contexts, some of the feminist paradigms that originally informed its scholarship have been critiqued by African feminists/womanists. African feminism/womanism is an intellectual movement which dates from the 1980s. It is a counter-discourse by women on the African continent and in the diaspora which seeks to both challenge Euro-North American stereotypes about the oppression and victimhood of African women and propose forms of feminism rooted in African women's experiences and contexts (Amadiume, 1987). Key concepts from this movement include 'womanism' defined by Chikwenye Ogunyemi (1996) which rejects White and African-American feminisms for being too combative and instead proposes a form of feminism that is conciliatory and collaborative. Meanwhile, 'nego-feminism', developed by Obioma Nnaemeka (2004) is a feminism of negotiation, accommodation and compromise. These terms definitely resonated with my observations of women's everyday agency in Medina Diallobé.

However, despite the apparent compatibility between Sub-Saharan African Muslim women's religious activities and African feminist/womanist thought, Shirin Edwin (a scholar of Islamic African postcolonial literature) has identified a disappointingly Orientalist current within the work of many of the latter's scholars (2016, pp. 18, 38–52). This tendency stems from the thinking of Afrocentric scholars which gained particular currency in the 1970s which I unpacked in depth in Chapter 1. The architects of Afrocentric thinking appropriated Euro-North American racial categories. Their logic, which I describe as Afrocentric race-religion constellations, employs an essentialised and empirically inaccurate distinction between 'Black Africans' adhering to 'pagan' traditional religions who are supposedly 'Indigenous' to Sub-Saharan Africa, versus 'Muslims' supposedly native to North Africa or Arabia. As Edwin explains, scholars adhering to these logics dismiss Islam as a monolithic institution of patriarchal oppression, while many go even further to frame Islam as a 'foreign' force, not authentically 'African' and akin to European colonisation in its displacement of supposedly gender-equal Indigenous institutions (ibid., p. 18).

It is very disappointing that the stereotype that Islam is 'foreign' to Africa – and that female agency is impossible within its ontology – has been accepted by many renowned African feminists/womanists. As Edwin argues, despite taking pains to distinguish their agenda from that of Western feminism and warning against ethnocentrism, "these same theorists reveal tones that can be termed as ethnocentric and even racist vis-à-vis African Muslim women" (2016, p. 52). I use several of the concepts coined by African feminists/ womanists, particularly womanism (Ogunyemi, 1996) and nego-feminism (Nnaemeka, 2004), to make sense of women's behaviour in Medina Diallobé. However, when doing so, I acknowledge Islam as an equal part of Africa's rich ontological and cultural diversity and Muslim women's agency as potentially different from – but not inferior to – that of their counterparts who adhere to Christianity, African Traditional Religions or secular worldviews.

Islamic feminisms

Finally, I looked towards the Islamic feminist movements to understand the educational activities of Muslim women in Medina Diallobé. Religious studies scholar Leila Ahmed argued in her influential book *Women and Gender in Islam: Historical Roots of a Modern Debate* (1992) that, from its origins, there has existed within Islam a tension between the Qur'an's statements on spiritual equality between men and women, on the one hand, and the patriarchal institutions that the religion implanted and maintains, on the other. How women have dealt with this contradiction has varied significantly and has included the development of movements that are today called 'Islamic feminisms' (Khalaf-Elledge, 2021, pp. 18–19).

Contemporary Islamic feminist thought is both a project of reform directed at Islamic societies as well as a counter-discourse against Orientalist stereotypes entrenched within Euro-North American academic and policy discourses (Edwin, 2016, pp. 55–56). A hallmark of much Islamic feminist thought is the criticism that feminist goals which aim to make men and women more similar reflect an imposition of Western secular values. In a review of Islamic feminist thought, Emma Tomalin explains that these theorists mainly consider that Islam frames women as different than men and that they play complementary roles but should nonetheless be treated equally (2007, pp. 21–22).

Shirin Edwin offers a different perspective when she argues that, despite their critique of Western framings, contemporary Islamic feminists often reproduce value judgements about gendered agency which align with assumptions embedded in Euro-North American second-wave feminism (2016, p. 56). They often write from the perspective of countries in the Middle East or North Africa which tend to be Islamic nation-states where Islam constitutes a totalising spiritual, legal, and political system. Hence, the Islamic feminisms that have emerged from these contexts are a reaction to laws based on interpretations of religious texts that are patriarchal, literalist and restrictive. As such these feminisms reflect a critical public, political, legal and activist engagement with Islam which is articulated through the grammar of struggle, gender equality and legal and social justice inspired by Euro-North American feminism (ibid., pp. 55–62). They focus on laws (*sharia*), the interpretation and implementation of law (Islamic jurisprudence or *fiqh*), and feminist (re-)interpretation of Islamic texts such as the Qur'an (*tafsir*) that gave rise to the laws in the first place (ibid., pp. 7–8). The Qur'an is, therefore, framed as a legal resource above all else.

Whilst such activism is understandable in these contexts, the problem is that most academic scholarship on Islamic feminisms has come to define such activities as the ideal to which Muslim women everywhere should aspire (Edwin, 2016, p. 9). However, this idealisation is a problem because most Muslim women in Sub-Saharan Africa live less in Islamic states and more in secular democracies where only a small part of the legal system is based on *sharia* law, usually relating to family law, and adherence to it is often optional. As a result, in such societies feminist legal debate is less prevalent and Muslim women's feminism is oriented towards quite different ends and means (ibid., pp. 9–10).

In practice, the kinds of strategies described in Middle Eastern Islamic feminist literature were not practiced by women in Medina Diallobé. Rather, many of their actions reflected what anthropologists and other social scientists have documented in African contexts, namely agency which is often exercised in the domestic sphere or in the context of close relationships. This agency is oriented towards pursuit of spiritual transformation and personal fulfilment (Edwin, 2016; Sieveking, 2022), the manipulation of esoteric knowledge (Gemmeke, 2009) and a subtle negotiation of gender relations whilst observing dominant norms (Alidou, 2005; Hill, 2010, 2017, 2023). This type of agency is much closer to Ogunyemi's womanism (1996) and Nnaemeka's nego-feminism (2004).

With these insights in mind, I briefly describe the evolution of female Islamic education in the Futa Tooro region in order to frame the later discussion on the forms of female negotiation and agency in Medina Diallobé.

Situating female Islamic education in northern Senegal

Over the last century, and since the 1970s in particular, more formal Islamic educational opportunities have become available to women throughout the Muslim world. This is through a combination of previously male-dominated institutions opening up to women or women organising to demand and create spaces catering to their needs (Bano, 2017). Access to Islamic education historically had been restricted along gender lines. While norms have varied, even where women have had access to an Islamic education, they have often been excluded from the most powerful forms of knowledge (Kalmbach, 2012).

These patterns are equally applicable to West African contexts, including Senegal. Qur'anic schools teaching memorisation of the Qur'an, textual interpretation, and jurisprudence were historically the preserve of boys and men. Girls' Islamic education was largely informal and received within the home. It often involved learning Qur'anic verses for daily prayers, combined with socialisation into norms of feminine piety, modesty and submission to the authority of men and elders (Alidou, 2005, p. 36; Ware, 2014, p. 172). However, given the expertise of their male kin, women from clerical families were sometimes offered an advanced informal education at home, including in esoteric knowledge (Gemmeke, 2009; Edwin, 2011; Sieveking, 2022). During the era of Sufi *jihads* of the eighteenth and nineteenth centuries, a stronger emphasis on girls' education within clerical families emerged, as in Mauritania (Lydon, 2004), southern Senegambia (Robinson, 2000) and northern Nigeria (Mack and Boyd, 2000). It was during this period that notable West African women became respected scholars, teachers or jurists in their own right (Mack and Boyd, 2000; Hill, 2023).

The colonial period further expanded girls' access to formal Islamic education. Leaders of the Sufi orders in Western Senegal opened up Qur'anic schools to girls, allowing them to attend as day students. Consequently, by the 1940s, attendance of girls was far higher in Islamic schools than in the secular schools provided by the French administration (Ware, 2014, pp. 174–175). However, from the 1970s, the influence of Muslim reformists of Salafi orientation was felt in the Senegalese landscape. Their onto-epistemological nets (Thayer-Bacon, 2017) included new gender norms inspired by Middle Eastern cultural influences. They encouraged a lower rather than higher participation of women in economic activities and stricter norms of gender segregation and veiling than was customarily the case in West Africa, and yet they gave expanded roles to women as Islamic teachers and preachers (Augis, 2013). Islamic esoteric knowledges and training within Sufi orders have also become more accessible to women in recent decades (Gemmeke, 2009; Hill, 2010).

Despite these examples, the Futa Tooro region represents an anomaly in Senegal as far as women are concerned since, until extremely recently, they have had few opportunities for obtaining a formal Islamic education. There were no examples of renowned female Haalpulaar scholars during the *jihads* of the eighteenth and nineteenth centuries (Robinson, 2000, p. 143). In 2011, the Qur'anic schools in Medina Diallobé represented an almost exclusively male environment. Girls were taught basic verses in their homes by male kin or older Qur'anic school students (*sandas*) or in small *daaras* dedicated to young children. There was only a tradition within one *seerembe* or clerical *toorodo* family in the village of men providing Islamic education for women within the home. The family considered their great-grandmother to be a Sufi saint, and her son had travelled widely in the Islamic world as well as to the US and Europe. He had made sure that his daughters and grand-daughters studied the Qur'an and basic *sharia* at home.

The influence of those Islamic schools which were open to girls only started to permeate into the Futa Tooro region in the early 2010s. In 2009, a 23-year-old *toorodo* named Aissata started teaching girls and women basic religious practice and Qur'anic verses from her home in Medina Diallobé. She told me that, at age ten, two of her female cousins in Dakar had started Qur'anic boarding schools there:

> I really, really wanted to go, as I preferred to learn the Qur'an [than go to state school]. I cried until my parents sent me.

Aissata completed memorisation of the Qur'an when she was 15, and at 16 she started studying Arabic and French at a private Franco-Arab school, reaching the equivalent of the second year of lower secondary (*collège*). At the age of 18, Aissata married and returned to Medina Diallobé to live with her husband and in-laws. She told me that she had stopped studying formally, "but the Qur'an says that if you have knowledge you should teach it". Hence, she followed a pattern common among reformist-educated Muslim women who establish schools in their own communities (Kalmbach, 2012). Aissata's practice had no precedent in Medina Diallobé because, prior to 2009, girls tended to be taught by male clerics or *sandas.*

Although Aissata's initiative in 2009 created a new non-formal religious educational opportunity for girls and women, her teaching of local girls fell far short of a full-time formal Islamic school catering to them. Nevertheless, Aissata's actions at both the personal and the professional level illustrate the sorts of educational actions which resist complete male control over female learning. In the following section I consider other such examples of females seeking Islamic knowledge informally and the uses to which they put it.

Women mobilising Islamic knowledge in Medina Diallobé

Here I consider three examples of females from Medina Diallobé who had attended state schools to at least primary level and after that sought to supplement their education with non-formal or informal study of Islamic knowledge. This pattern reflects a growing trend in West Africa in the last 20 years (Hima, 2020, p. 502; Sieveking, 2022). The different uses I describe to which women such as Fatimata, Maimouna and Souadou put their knowledge included: spiritual development for personal ends; manipulation of esoteric knowledge for extra-religious ends; and knowledge of women's rights in Islam in order to 'negotiate within tradition'. I present these uses in the order of their relative prevalence in the village, at least following the testimonies of the women that I spoke to in depth. I present these strategies separately for clarity and analytical purposes but, in reality, women's narratives showed that they were often intertwined in practice.

Fatimata: Spiritual transformation for religious ends

My first example is that of 16-year-old Fatimata, a *toorodo* who was in the final year of upper secondary (*lycée*). In conversation she revealed that she complemented her state schooling with informal religious study whenever she could. She invited me to spend the afternoon with her family where she showed me a battered copy of *Al Akhdari.* It is a short primer on prayer for beginners according to the Maliki school of law and possibly the most widespread didactic text used across the Sahel from Mauritania to northern Nigeria in the nineteenth century (Hall and Stewart, 2011, p. 134). This was the most common book on Islamic practice that I saw families possess, usually as a French translation accompanying the Arabic original, although I did see one version in Pulaar written in Roman/Latin script. Several young *toorobe* mentioned this book when explaining how they had learned to pray. Fatimata also explained that she attended public conferences given by Muslim clerics and sometimes took written notes alongside:

> I write it all down in a notebook and learn it. Like what is good, what is bad. I learn at conferences when clerics talk, on the TV, people telling stories. . . . For instance, a cleric here was saying *qul huwallahu*[1] is such an important *surah* [chapter of the Qur'an], you can recite it three times for protection or healing.

One day, I bumped into Fatimata and her cousin on their way to Aissata's home, when they explained that they tried to attend her school several times a month during the summer holidays.

Fatimata's pursuit of Islamic knowledge was primarily oriented towards reinforcing her Islamic ritual proficiency for her own spiritual benefit, as well as learning esoteric knowledge of the secret meanings of Qur'anic verses which, when recited, have protective power and confer good fortune. Fatimata's focus dovetails with the findings of a number of empirical studies suggesting that African Muslim women's mobilisation of Islamic knowledges often takes place in private spaces and is articulated towards personal spiritual transformation predicated on building a strong relationship with God (Edwin, 2011, 2016). Extra-religious benefits include personal fulfilment, positive relationships with family members and psychological dispositions to deal with life's challenges. For instance, anthropologist Nadine Sieveking (2022, p. 791) quotes one state school-educated Senegalese woman who told her that reading the Qur'an after work "makes me more and more zen-zen [relaxed]!" (my translation from French). In such examples, therefore, the Qur'an constitutes a personal and spiritual, rather than legal, resource.

Interestingly, I observed significant differences and ongoing shifts in the onto-epistemological nets (Thayer-Bacon, 2017) of women like Fatimata, Muslim clerics and other men in Medina Diallobé when it came to the value of women's Islamic education. When I asked middle-aged male villagers why women in the Futa Tooro did not receive a formal Islamic education, they invariably stressed 'natural' biological and social differences between men and women. They argued frequently that, for example: women could not touch the Qur'an when menstruating; they had no time to study due to domestic work; they could not work afterwards as imams or clerics so there was no point that they study the religion; they could obtain blessing or *baraka* from God by obeying their husbands rather than memorising the Qur'an; and that if women learned esoteric secrets they would share them widely, so teaching them this knowledge was ill-advised. However, during my fieldwork, I noticed a growing trend whereby clerics throughout the Futa Tooro region had started preaching in favour of women's Islamic education, largely to temper the influence of Western norms and values. This likely reflected the parallel influence of both reformist discourse and increased female state school enrolment.

However, Aissata gave another explanation for why women did not traditionally learn in the Futa Tooro region which referred directly to gender hierarchies: "It's because people here in the Futa only teach the girls how to pray, but God says that both men and women are equal in terms of education". She explained that girls and women like Fatimata mainly came to her to learn principles of Islamic ritual practice for their own personal spiritual benefit:

> Even older women here don't know how to pray. They come to ask me, they're ashamed to ask the clerics about that. Like how to do their ablutions [ritual washing before prayer] and how to pray, as no one ever taught them exactly.

She added "Often women have regrets that they didn't learn more when they were younger. *Ina yurminii* [it's a shame]". This difference between men and women's perceptions of the value of women's Islamic education is significant and has been documented elsewhere. For example, Bradley and Saigol found that in Pakistan, men justified women's Islamic education for upholding the patriarchal social order, while women argued for its empowering value for their personal and spiritual development (2012, pp. 679–683).

Maimouna: Esoteric knowledge for extra-religious ends

My second example is 30-year-old Maimouna who had left state school after completing primary at the age of 18 when she married. She was one of the women whom I observed studying the Qur'an for the first time during the hot *ceedu* season. She had been ill for some time and was stressed, anxious and had trouble sleeping because of nightmares. Her cousin, who worked using the Islamic esoteric sciences (*dabotoodo*), diagnosed her illness as '*rafi baleejo*', a 'black illness' caused by spirits (*jinn*). It could only be cured using the Qur'an, unlike '*rafi daneejo*' or 'white illness' which could be treated using biomedicine. As part of her healing strategy, Maimouna kept a notebook of invocations and Qur'anic verses that she would recite to herself. I was with her when she asked two of her brothers, one of whom had memorised the entire Qur'an at a *daara*, if they could teach her the chapter Ya-Sin (36:1) which is considered to have powerful protective and healing properties. Her brothers made excuses saying that they were too busy, and one asked "Why don't you ask Aissata?" Maimouna shook her head, as Aissata's onto-epistemological net was woven with Salafi threads, and she might not have approved of learning the Qur'an for esoteric purposes. Besides, Maimouna would not have wanted to share personal details of her illness with a woman with whom she had no personal relationship.

The way Maimouna sought esoteric secrets – and used them to address her everyday challenges – was very common among men and women alike in Medina Diallobé and is widely documented in Senegal generally (Gemmeke, 2009; Hill, 2023). It is important to stress such agency rooted in esoteric knowledges because it is often absent from scholarship on the agency of religious subjects and even in Islamic feminist literature focused on the Middle East. The exclusion or dismissal of esoteric knowledges – and side-lining of Sub-Saharan African perspectives – from debates about Muslim women's agency reflects modernist binaries. It privileges the literal rather than hidden meanings of the Qur'an and side-lines practices often rejected as superstitious or immoral within Euro-North American modernist framings or Salafi interpretations of Islam.

Souadou: Negotiating within tradition

The third example I encountered was 35-year-old Souadou who had learned basic *sharia* from her father at home. She had obtained a state primary education, but it was Islamic knowledge that she used in order to negotiate a divorce from her husband. Souadou and Hassan were related, and their marriage was initially amicable. However, they struggled financially and Souadou had turned to petty trade to provide for their children. Hassan opposed this out of shame and started beating her. Souadou asked her father for support, but he stressed that she should be patient and endure the situation because a divorce would cause family conflict. It was only once her father died that Souadou left her husband. She told me that she knew that:

> In Islam, I'm allowed to work for money and all my earnings are mine to keep. The Qur'an says that! And I'm only doing it to feed my children. And I am correct [in my behaviour with men] my husband can't reproach me. He's not allowed to beat me for this, it's not right.

Souadou's family first tried to persuade her to return her husband, but once they realised how stubborn she was, they agreed that it was better that they divorce as their separated status was shameful. Eventually, Hassan reluctantly agreed to divorce her. For Souadou's family, her rights in Islam came second to the social imperative to maintain family cohesion. Yet, the fact that Souadou knew her rights as a Muslim gave her the courage to be steadfast in this situation knowing that her behaviour was morally correct.

Souadou's use of her Islamic knowledge echoes similar instances that have been observed by anthropologists in Islamic Africa that I refer to as *negotiating within tradition*. The performativity involved in doing religion involves not only upholding stasis (as Mahmood (2005) suggests) or contesting it (as the Islamic feminists propose). Rather, as Joseph Hill shows through ethnography with Sufi women in Senegal, this performativity instead involves "satisfying immediate needs and challenges which involves subtle negotiation" (Hill, 2023, p. 12). With this orientation, women observe dominant Islamic norms including the principle of hierarchical complementarity between men and women – even if it constrains (to an extent) women's authority – in order to "subtly reconfigure established norms to accommodate changing social realities" (ibid., p. 1). Hill argues that to understand Muslim women's agency we have to look "less at official doctrines and rather at how people reconfigure and renegotiate norms and teachings" (ibid., p. 3). Such dynamics have been observed elsewhere, for instance in Ousseina Alidou's analysis of Nigerien women who used patriarchal Islamic discourses to argue for girls' education and women's economic participation (2005, pp. 38–42).

For decades, many external observers had taken women's acceptance of patriarchal authority to mean that their empowerment was impossible within Senegalese Sufi structures. However, anthropologists have argued that Sufi women's exercise of agency is covert; the problem is, rather, that academics have not recognised it (Gemmeke, 2009, p. 133). These dynamics are also not restricted to Sub-Saharan Africa. Studies of women's agency throughout the Muslim world (Bano and Kalmbach, 2012; Bano, 2017) have found that, when women do master Islamic texts, they overwhelmingly "respect sharia and Sunni scholarship but push *ulama* (the male clerical elite) to find optimal answers to questions of modern life" (Bano, 2017, p. xi). However, my findings in Medina Diallobé contrast with such analyses which tend to focus on women with advanced Islamic education and Arabic literacy (e.g. Alidou, 2005). Evidence from my study suggests that female negotiation within the Islamic tradition does not require sophisticated mastery of Islamic texts.

From another point of view, the prevalence of Muslim women negotiating within tradition in Sub-Saharan Africa poses a challenge to Islamic feminist scholarship which privileges the act of re-interpretation of the Qur'an and the use of legal texts as a basis for combative political activism. The latter are presented as ideal forms of agency that Muslim women can engage in. Meanwhile, Mahmood (2005) even suggested that Egyptian women's private cultivation of pious dispositions had no connection to broader political dynamics (Edwin, 2016, p. 62). Yet, Africanist scholars have shown that women's negotiation of tradition exercised in the 'private' or domestic spheres does have political implications because, at scale, it has significant impacts on social life, community affairs and economic dynamics (Hill, 2010; Edwin, 2016, p. 58). Such observations suggest that Islamic feminisms grounded in the Middle Eastern experience unconsciously reproduce assumptions grounded in Western feminist thought which assumes that political influence – and personal and economic autonomy – are contingent on visibility and presence in the 'public' sphere. In contrast, the insights I gained from Senegalese Islamic contexts reveal diverse routes to these ends.

The activities of Fatimata, Maimouna and Souadou showed that spiritual and extra-religious motivations were intimately combined within their pursuit and use of Islamic knowledge. Yet, what are the implications of their trajectories for discussions about women's agency and education in comparative/international education? It is to this question that I now turn.

Islamic education and women's empowerment: Implications for policy

Policy and academic scholarship continue to rest, it seems, upon assumptions about the 'empowering' potential of secular as opposed to Islamic education which are not supported by robust evidence (Bano, 2018). The implications of Khoja-Moolji's argument (2018) for comparative/international education is that there remains an urgent need for empirical study to investigate exactly how limiting constructions of gender are shaped by worldviews, whether 'secular' or 'religious', as well as by other contributory factors like poverty (Bano, 2018). Likewise, the relationships between onto-epistemologies, knowledges and norms as well as girls' and women's decision-making authority and agency and their access to education and employment must be investigated rather than assumed (Tomalin, 2007, p. 27). Yet, to this day, there exists very little qualitative empirical research on the relationships among religion, gender and development (Istratii, 2021; Khalaf-Elledge, 2021).

From different research studies, it would appear that access to education for Muslim girls and women is shaped more by their country's overall economic level than by religion per se (Hackett and Fahmy, 2018). For example, in a comparative quantitative study of Muslim girls' aspirations in Pakistan and northern Nigeria, Bano found that both girls in secular schools and Islamic *madrasas* had high levels of religiosity and aspired to professional careers. It was noticeable that those in secular schools had more liberal interpretations of Islam that could support their realisation of such aspirations. Rather than jump to the conclusion that their secular education was the explanation for their 'progressive' attitudes, Bano found that socio-economic explanations – father's income, mother's education, time spent watching television and urban location – were better predictors. She concluded that the socio-economic status of the girls' families was the explanation for both their parents' preferences for secular education and girls' high aspirations, rather than girls' personal religiosity or Islamic education (Bano, 2018).

Meanwhile, on a return visit to Senegal in 2018 and through more recent phone conversations, I have seen that much has changed in Medina Diallobé over the decade since I undertook my doctoral fieldwork. Average age of marriage among girls has risen by a few years, and more women are working outside the home after leaving school – especially in vocational employment as seamstresses, hairdressers or beauticians – particularly if they have re-located to Dakar. This shift seems mostly related to steeply rising costs of living and the influence of norms and lifestyles in Dakar. This situation should remind us that religious and social norms are not always as deterministic as EID and gender and development actors often assume and instead evolve, often rapidly, in tandem with wider socio-economic trends. Bano suggests that, in such contexts, development programmes aimed at increasing female empowerment should focus on these structural factors rather than on changing community-level religious and social norms (2018).

That said, I found that women in Medina Diallobé still struggled to exercise agency, particularly in the context of marriage, as a result of constraining socio-religious norms. Their relatively high levels of state schooling did not necessarily provide them with the knowledge, skills or authority to challenge these norms, and instead they tended to negotiate within tradition by appealing to rights enshrined within Islamic or customary frameworks (Newman, 2023). While full-time formal or even non-formal Islamic education options are available today to middle-class women in Dakar (Sieveking, 2022), they are neither affordable nor accessible for most women in rural Senegal. My findings – that religious education can be as, if not more, empowering for women than secular state education in contexts where Islamic ontology and norms prevail – are corroborated in many other Islamic contexts. Muslim women's own educational trajectories reflect these realities, grounded as they are in pursuit of Islamic knowledge for both religious and extra-religious ends. These goals range from relaxation, self-esteem, psychological well-being, and greater choice of marriage partners and hence routes for social mobility. Women also aim for social support networks, performance of 'intellectual' or middle-class status, respect and authority in their families and communities and potential income as religious teachers or preachers (Alidou, 2005; Bano, 2012; Kalmbach, 2012; Rao, 2012; Borker, 2020; Hima, 2020; Sieveking, 2022).

Evidence from Medina Diallobé – and elsewhere in Islamic Sub-Saharan Africa – also shows that one of the primary forms of agency employed by women is both to observe dominant religious norms within an ontological framework that positions men and women within a relation of hierarchical complementarity – which can appear oppressive to outsiders – and to negotiate subtly within this tradition (Alidou, 2005). It is through these means that Senegalese women have undertaken significant economic, educational, political and development-related activities which expand their own opportunities as well as those of others in their communities (Sieveking, 2007; Hill, 2010, 2017; Latha, 2010; Edwin, 2016). Interestingly, women's Islamic NGOs in Senegal have also started applying this approach to legal reform after more combative 'Islamic feminist' strategies failed. This approach has been described by gender studies scholar Rizwana Latha as 'African-Islamic Womanism' (Sieveking, 2007; Hill, 2010, 2017; Latha, 2010; Edwin, 2016), interestingly because it resembles womanism described by African feminist/womanist Chikwenye Ogunyemi (1996). It is, therefore, high time that policy-makers and proponents of EFA acknowledge to a greater extent the empowering potential of Islamic education for Muslim women in Islamic contexts.

Finally, if we agree that Islamic education promotes Muslim women's spiritual and personal well-being and supports their everyday struggles, what knowledge exactly is most used by women and could inform education provision? Evidence from Medina Diallobé – and other contexts in West Africa – shows that women often value the Qur'anic text as a spiritual and esoteric resource and use basic knowledge of classical interpretations of *sharia* to demand their rights in Islam.

These findings are significant because current scholarship on Islamic feminism, focused on examples from the Middle East, privileges activism grounded in legal re-interpretation and mobilisation of this knowledge for political ends in the public sphere, which relies on advanced Islamic education. Meanwhile, some Senegalese women certainly seek out mastery of Arabic language and Qur'anic exegesis for personal and social ends (Sieveking, 2022). Yet, even with just proficiency in Islamic rituals, quite basic understanding of *sharia* and often limited knowledge of the Qur'anic text, Muslim women can negotiate within tradition by grounding their demands for changes in gendered norms from within their concrete everyday experiences and traditional roles (Sieveking, 2007; Latha, 2010). The most pragmatic route to expanding women's agency in Islamic contexts, like Senegal, could therefore be as simple as embedding a basic religious education into the existing secular school system or providing it through accessible non-formal means (see Sieveking, 2022) and trusting women to use the knowledge acquired to their advantage.

Conclusion

This chapter focused on the pursuit and use of Islamic knowledge among women in the Futa Tooro region given their exclusion from classical Qur'anic schools. Contrary to development and EFA discourses, secular state schools showed limited emancipatory potential in terms of increasing young women's agency through economic opportunities or decision-making autonomy. Importantly, hierarchical gendered norms continued to be upheld through religious discourses and by Muslim clerics. In order to capture and understand how the women in Medina Diallobé seek out and use Islamic knowledge – and to capture religious agency – I suggest that we need to overcome both the Middle Eastern-centrism of scholarship on Islamic feminisms and Orientalist biases in literature on African feminisms/womanisms. In line with other fine-grained qualitative studies of Islamic West Africa, I have shown how women used their knowledges for personal spiritual benefits, for its esoteric potential and to negotiate within tradition to improve their personal circumstances including in relationships with men. Any lack of attention that EID scholars and policy-makers pay to Muslim women's unmet demand for Islamic knowledges and, moreover, their deployment of these knowledges in their struggles for gender equality, is a form of secular erasure.

The following chapter circles back, building on this and the two previous chapters to consider young people's struggles to combine knowledges from different onto-epistemological paradigms. It investigates how they strove to acquire knowledge and skills from both the Islamic and state school systems against the backdrop of a national education system embedded in an ontological regime complex still steeped in coloniality of secularity.

Note

1 *Qul huwallahu* are the first two words of *Al Ikhlas,* the 112th chapter in the Qur'an and the shortest at only four verses. It is often taught to young children after they memorise the opening verse *Al-fatihah.* According to Islamic tradition, it is equal in value to a third part of the whole Qur'an. It is held in particular veneration by Muslims and recited or worn in amulets for protective purposes.

References

Ahearn, L.M. (2001) 'Language and agency', *Annual Review of Anthropology*, 30, pp. 109–137.

Ahmed, L. (1992) *Women and Gender in Islam: Historical Roots of a Modern Debate.* New Haven, CT: Yale University Press.

Alidou, O. (2005) *Engaging Modernity: Muslim Women and the Politics of Agency in Postcolonial Niger.* Madison, WI: University of Wisconsin Press.

Amadiume, I. (1987) *Male Daughters, Female Husbands: Gender and Sex in an African Society.* London: Zed Press.

Augis, E. (2013) 'Dakar's sunnite women: The dialectic of submission and defiance in a globalizing city', in M. Diouf (ed) *Tolerance, Democracy and Sufis in Senegal.* New York: Columbia University Press, pp. 73–93.

Avishai, O. (2008) '"Doing religion" in a secular world: Women in conservative religions and the question of agency', *Gender & Society*, 22(4), pp. 409–433.

Bano, M. (2012) *The Rational Believer: Choices and Decisions in the Madrasas of Pakistan.* Ithaca, NY and London: Cornell University Press.

Bano, M. (2017) *Female Islamic Education Movements: The Re-Democratisation of Islamic Knowledge.* Cambridge: Cambridge University Press.

Bano, M. (2018) 'Religion and female empowerment: Evidence from Pakistan and northern Nigeria', *Canadian Journal of Development Studies/Revue canadienne d'études du développement*, 40(2), pp. 163–181.

Bano, M. and Kalmbach, H. (eds) (2012) *Women, Leadership, and Mosques: Changes in Contemporary Islamic Authority.* Leiden and Boston, MA: Brill.

Borker, H. (2020) 'Talim, Dindari aur Shaadi (education, religiosity and marriage): Choosing Madrasa education for girls', *Social Change*, 50(2), pp. 236–253.

Bradley, T. and Saigol, R. (2012) 'Religious values and beliefs and education for women in Pakistan', *Development in Practice*, 22(5–6), pp. 675–688.

Butler, J. (1993) *Bodies that Matter: On the Discursive Limits of 'Sex'.* London: Routledge.

CCIEF (2011) *Education des filles au Sénégal: Document de référence.* Dakar: Cadre de coordination des interventions sur l'éducation des filles (CCIEF) du Ministère de l'éducation nationale (MEN).

Dunne, M., et al. (2017) *Troubling Muslim Youth Identities: Nation, Religion, Gender.* London: Palgrave Macmillan.

Edwin, S. (2011) 'Shaping futures and feminisms: Qur'anic schools in West African francophone fiction', *Gender and Education*, 23(7), pp. 873–888.

Edwin, S. (2016) *Privately Empowered: Expressing Feminism in Islam in Northern Nigerian Fiction.* Evanston, IL: Northwestern University Press.

Gemmeke, A.B. (2009) 'Marabout women in Dakar: Creating authority in religious knowledge', *Africa: Journal of the International African Institute*, 79(1), pp. 128–147.

Griffiths, C.H. (2011) *Globalising the Postcolony: Contesting Discourses of Gender and Development in Francophone Africa.* Plymouth: Lexington Books.

Hackett, C. and Fahmy, D. (2018) *Education of Muslim Women Is Limited by Economic Conditions, Not Religion, Pew Research Center.* Available at: www.pewresearch.org/short-reads/2018/06/12/education-of-muslim-women-is-limited-by-economic-conditions-not-religion/ (Accessed: 3 October 2023).

Hall, B.S. and Stewart, C.S. (2011) 'The historic "core curriculum" and the book market in Islamic West Africa', in G. Krätli and G. Lydon (eds) *The Trans-Saharan Book Trade: Manuscript Culture, Arabic Literacy and Intellectual History in Muslim Africa*. Leiden: Brill, pp. 109–174.

Hill, J. (2010) '"All women are guides": Sufi leadership and womanhood among taalibe baay in Senegal', *Journal of Religion in Africa*, 40(4), pp. 375–412.

Hill, J. (2017) 'Charismatic discipleship: A Sufi woman and the divine mission of development in Senegal', *Africa: Journal of the International African Institute*, 87(4), pp. 832–852.

Hill, J. (2023) 'Muslim women's interpretive authority reconsidered: Everyday interpretation among female Islamic leaders in Senegal', in unpublished keynote paper delivered during the workshop *'Global and Local Political Debates Over Women's Rights and Everyday Life in Muslim Africa', Africa Studies Centre, University of Leiden, 21–22 September 2023.*

Hima, H. (2020) '"Francophone" education and intersectionalities: Gender, language, and religion', in J.M. Abidogun and T. Falola (eds) *The Palgrave Handbook of African Education and Indigenous Knowledge*. Cham, Switzerland: Palgrave Macmillan, pp. 463–525.

Istratii, R. (2021) *Adapting Gender and Development to Local Religious Contexts: A Decolonial Approach to Domestic Violence in Ethiopia*. London: Routledge.

Kalmbach, H. (2012) 'Introduction: Islamic authority and the study of female religious leaders', in M. Bano and H. Kalmbach (eds) *Women, Leadership, and Mosques: Changes in Contemporary Islamic Authority*. Leiden and Boston, MA: Brill, pp. 1–27.

Khalaf-Elledge, N. (2021) *The Religion–Gender Nexus in Development: Policy and Practice Considerations*. London: Routledge.

Khoja-Moolji, S. (2015) 'Suturing together girls and education: An investigation into the social (re)production of girls' education as a hegemonic ideology', *Diaspora, Indigenous, and Minority Education*, 9(2), pp. 87–107.

Khoja-Moolji, S. (2018) *Forging the Ideal Educated Girl: The Production of Desirable Subjects in Muslim South Asia*. Oakland, CA: University of California Press.

Latha, R.H. (2010) 'A re-shaping of gender activism in a Muslim context – Senegal', *Agenda: Empowering Women for Gender Equity*, 83, pp. 55–67.

Lydon, G. (2004) 'Inkwells of the Sahara: Reflections on the production of Islamic knowledge in Bilad Shinqit', in S.S. Reese (ed) *The Transmission of Learning in Islamic Africaearning in Islamic Africa*. Leiden and Boston, MA: Brill, pp. 39–71.

Mack, B.B. and Boyd, J. (2000) *One Woman's Jihad: Nana Asma'u, Scholar and Scribe*. Bloomington, IN: University of Indiana Press.

Mahmood, S. (2005) *Politics of Piety: The Islamic Revival and the Feminist Subject*. Princeton, NJ and Oxford: Princeton University Press.

Newman, A. (2020) '"Getting the best of both worlds": Aspirations and agency in relation to marriage and schooling among Haalpulaar women in northern Senegal', *Compare – A Journal of Comparative and International Education*, 51(8), pp. 1157–1173.

Newman, A. (2023) 'Decolonising women's rights discourse in African Islamic contexts: Theoretical and practical insights from Senegal', in unpublished paper delivered during the workshop *'Global and Local Political Debates Over Women's Rights and Everyday Life in Islamic Africa', Africa Studies Centre, University of Leiden, 21–22 September 2023.*

Nnaemeka, O. (2004) '"Nego-feminism": Theorizing, practicing, and pruning Africa's way', *Signs: A Journal of Women and Culture in Society*, 29(2), pp. 357–385.

Ogunyemi, C.O. (1996) *Africa Wo/Man Palava: The Nigerian Novel by Women*. Chicago, IL: University of Chicago Press.

Rao, N. (2012) 'Breadwinners and homemakers: Migration and changing conjugal expectations in rural Bangladesh', *Journal Of Development Studies*, 48(1), pp. 26–40.

Robinson, D. (2000) 'Revolutions in the Western Sahara', in N. Levtzion and R.L. Pouwels (eds) *The History of Islam in Africa.* Oxford: James Currey, pp. 131–152.
Sieveking, N. (2007) '"We don't want equality; we want to be given our rights": Muslim women negotiating global development concepts in Senegal', *Africa Spectrum*, 42(1), pp. 29–48.
Sieveking, N. (2022) '"Madame est au niveau 2, et moi…?" Gendered dynamics of Qur'an reading courses in dakarois francophone educated middle-class milieus', *Cahiers d'études africaines*, 4(248), pp. 771–796.
Sow, F., et al. (2000) *Les Sénégalaises en chiffres.* Dakar: United Nations Development Programme (UNDP).
Thayer-Bacon, B.J. (2017) *Relational Ontologies.* New York: Peter Lang Incorporated, International Academic Publishers.
Tomalin, E. (2007) *Gender Studies Approaches to the Relationships Between Religion and Development.* Religion and Development Research Programme: Working Paper 8. Birmingham: International Development Department, University of Birmingham.
UNESCO (2003) *EFA Global Monitoring Report 2003/4. Gender and Education for All: The Leap to Equality.* Paris: United Nations Educational, Scientific and Cultural Organization (UNESCO).
UNESCO (2010) *EFA Global Monitoring Report 2010. Reaching the Marginalised.* Paris: United Nations Educational, Scientific and Cultural Organization (UNESCO).
UNESCO (2021) *Global Education Monitoring Report 2021/2022. Non-State Actors in Education: Who Chooses? Who Loses?* Paris: United Nations Educational, Scientific and Cultural Organization (UNESCO).
Ware, R.T. (2014) *The Walking Qur'an: Islamic Education, Embodied Knowledge, and History in West Africa.* Chapel Hill, NC: The University of North Carolina Press.

8 Pursuing Islamic and state school knowledges: 'You need both'

According to the logic of dominant development discourses, 15-year-old Mohamed was doing well for a youth from a lower-middle-income African country in 2012: he was in the penultimate year of *collège* and was on track to obtain a lower secondary diploma by the age of 16. However, halfway through the academic year he dropped out to attend a full-time *daara* instead. The determining factor was that Mohamed was passionate about memorising the Qur'an and perceived the state school to be a barrier to this project. He had tried to juggle both types of schooling but ultimately found this frustrating and exhausting:

> I've wanted to quit [state] school for ages, because it's hard to do both at once. The hours overlap, I can't study the Qur'an 8–10am *and* then go to lessons at 10am, and I can't study in the evenings because I'm tired.

From a development perspective, Mohamed might be classified as 'out-of-school' or a 'drop-out'. In EFA GEM Reports he might be alluded to in statements like "fifty-seven million children are still failing to learn, simply because they are not in school" (UNESCO, 2014, p. i) or explicitly labelled as "marginalized" as a result of being "enrolled in a Koranic school" (UNESCO, 2006, p. 68). A more accurate assessment is that it was Mohamed's passion for learning that had led him to deepen his religious education which he could not do in the state system. Ignoring why people value such non-accredited non-Western educational options is a form of colonialist bias and secular erasure.

Compared to the previous chapters which focused solely on the pursuit of Islamic knowledge, this chapter considers how the parents and young people I interviewed in Medina Diallobé valued the cultural capital associated with both Qur'anic and state schools. Seeking knowledges associated with both types of school was an integral part of Mohamed's and his peers' learning strategies. In this chapter therefore I draw attention to the 'mixed trajectories' through which youth combined the knowledges and skills associated with different schools and, crucially, the challenges they faced in achieving their objectives.

DOI: 10.4324/9781003172475-10

There were two important aspects of young people's trajectories which were evident in Mohamed's narrative but are largely absent from comparative/international education literature on educational decision-making in Islamic contexts. The first was the practice of studying in different schools at the same time. Some Africanist anthropologists have noted the importance of this phenomenon (e.g. Hoechner, 2018, p. 83) as well as its scholarly neglect. Noah Butler argues that "simultaneously studying in dual systems" is "under-explored historically and ethnographically" and "calls for increased analytical attention" (2016, p. 286). The second trend was the importance of informal or non-formal study as a complement to full-time formal schooling. On the basis of Hausa women's educational practices in Nigeria, Shirin Edwin argued that informal learning is highly significant in people's life projects yet under-valued within Western education debates (2016, pp. 71–72). This finding dovetails with the experiences of Senegalese women presented in Chapter 7. Such dynamics are significant because studies of school preference in Islamic contexts have tended to look at people's preferences for a specific school at a particular point in time and have used it to infer their decision-making logics. However, the trajectories of young people in Medina Diallobé demonstrate that we cannot understand the influence of Islamic worldviews on school preference without considering patterns of educational engagement in multiple school systems over their life course and encompassing in our understanding the pursuit of knowledge outside of institutional contexts.

Finally, young people's engagement with multiple educational options reflected the fact that Senegal exhibits a plural educational landscape. However, a plural educational landscape is not the same as an "educationally pluralistic system", which Anthony D'Agostino and Ignazi Callizo (2022, p. 366) define as:

> One that embraces a diversity of forms of educational provision beyond the exclusive role of state-provided schooling and that embraces and allows for distinctive philosophical, cultural, and religious perspectives in alignment with parental choices.

They defend educational pluralism by arguing that it "is a foundational dimension of the right to education as recognized in foundational international human rights instruments" (ibid., p. 383). Yet, educational pluralism is often criticised within international education discourse on the basis of the flawed stereotype that it is only within secular schools that children can develop tolerance and critical thinking skills (ibid., p. 367). Moreover, the GEM Report on *Non-state Actors in Education* (UNESCO, 2021) recognises that although "faith-based schools account for a significant share of enrolment in many countries" (ibid., p. 68) it focuses its discussion on the challenges that such schools pose to the goals of regulation and alignment with national curricula (ibid., p. 83), particularly given contestation over the relative amount of religious instruction and language of instruction (ibid., p. 84). The issue with the report is that it fails to acknowledge that national systems in post-colonial contexts reflect coloniality of knowledge. It takes for granted the perspectives of policy-makers frustrated that faith-based schools refuse to 'conform' to state standards, rather than the education providers or parents obliged to accommodate to such injunctions in ontological regime complexes characterised by coloniality.

In contrast, D'Agostino and Callizo go on to explain the factors that are needed in order to achieve educational pluralism (ibid., p. 367; my italics):

> Educational pluralism flourishes to the degree that the role of non-state actors is *embraced* and *supported* alongside state educational provision and to the degree that nonstate providers are given an adequate *degree of independence* to allow for their *philosophical distinctiveness.*

While D'Agostino and Callizo's position is, in my opinion, a valuable contribution to debates on non-Western education and faith-based schooling which can support decolonial projects in education and development, it is very abstract. It fails to provide insights into *how* to achieve this 'embrace', 'support', 'independence' and 'philosophical distinctiveness' in specific contexts especially if learners, like Mohamed mentioned earlier, wish to benefit from multiple types of education. Their paper also fails to expose how educational pluralism might be impeded given the influence of coloniality of power, knowledge and secularity in the fields of comparative/international education and in the definition of educational agendas and policies under EFA as Chapters 1, 2 and 4 demonstrated.

As we shall see, young people in Medina Diallobé were motivated by similar preoccupations: they were inspired by the desire to be good Muslims and wished to acquire knowledges and skills for their intrinsic value and/or for their social and economic benefits. They wanted to achieve these goals before the demands of adulthood became too acute which meant reproductive labour for women and earning a livelihood for men. Yet, the abilities of youth to combine different knowledges were heavily constrained by social and economic inequalities. However, the dynamics of *how* youth like Mohamed tried to benefit from diverse offers in Senegal can shed valuable light on the challenges of achieving educational pluralism (D'Agostino and Callizo, 2022). Such struggles, as I argue later, can be considered a form of decolonial border-thinking or, indeed, "border praxis" (Walsh and Mignolo, 2018, p. 7) where people selectively appropriate educational options from the vantage point of non-Western worldviews.

I start by trying to make sense of three themes that recurred throughout young people's attempts at combining knowledges, namely: the impact of socioeconomic inequalities on youth trajectories; the role of onto-epistemologies in shaping educational engagement; and the influence of attitudes regarding time and educational sequentialism, otherwise referred to as temporalities. I then present the three most common solutions people found to combine knowledges which were: (a) attending private Islamic or 'hybrid' schools; (b) studying across – or alternating between – different institutionalised education options; and (c) studying informally alongside full-time formal schooling. These diverse trajectories merit our attention as my interviewees in Dakar (whether Senegalese professionals or ex-pats) tended only to mention one way of 'doing both'. This was the option common among the urban middle-class and documented since the colonial period (Ware, 2014, p. 193) whereby preschool-aged children attend the *daara* as day students to learn basic Qur'anic verses before dropping out before or within the first few years of primary school. While this trajectory was followed by many children in Medina Diallobé, the range of additional strategies that inhabitants pursued was far more diverse. Mohamed's action is an example of this trend, although dropping out of state school to attend a *daara* has, to my knowledge, received very little attention (c.f. Newman, 2017; Hoechner, 2018, p. 84).

I conclude the chapter by unpacking how young people's creative trajectories exposed the coloniality of secularity in Senegal's national education policy and its consequent role in entrenching social inequalities.

Social inequalities, onto-epistemologies and temporalities in young people's trajectories

To make sense of young people's agency in negotiating social inequalities, I draw on sociologist Michel De Certeau's distinction between 'strategies' and 'tactics' (1984). Strategies align with the hidden means through which powerful institutions structure social space while tactics are acts of everyday creative resistance in the midst of constraining structures. Hence, a tactic "must play on and with a terrain imposed on it and organised by the law of a foreign power". In short, "a tactic is the art of the weak" (ibid., p. 37). Here I use 'strategies' to refer to trajectories that met the stated needs of parents and youth, namely those which involved learning a combination of knowledges which conferred economic and symbolic capital within a reasonable time-frame and in an optimal learning environment. In contrast, 'tactics' refers to trajectories that were perceived as unsatisfactory somehow, reflecting attempts to 'make do' in the face of constraints. As we shall see, coloniality in the state's educational offer – and secular Eurocentric biases in its accreditation of Islamic schools – proved one of the defining constraints that youth had to negotiate.

Meanwhile, socioeconomic status also proved central to the difference between those youth who could engage in 'strategies' versus 'tactics'. By unpacking these distinctions, I speak to recent debates about the influence of social class on Muslim subjectivities in West Africa. Fabienne Samson and Marie LeBlanc (2022) propose that we can understand "social class" not just in terms of economic wealth but also as cultural markers associated with group identity (ibid., p. 680). They argue that "religiosity", which is defined as the ways in which individuals live their religion in everyday terms (ibid., p. 679), shapes – and is shaped by – social class. This is because people's environments shape the range of activities (including 'religious' activities) that they can engage in. As a consequence, certain expressions of religiosity come to be associated with certain social classes and are hence pursued or performed as markers of class distinction (ibid., p. 285). While I find this approach interesting, it reflects a common flaw in Euro-North American social scientific studies of religion described in Chapter 2 which is the tendency to emphasise the observable and material manifestations of religion rather than people's affective experiences or subjective onto-epistemologies. This tendency can, in my view, lead to overly deterministic conclusions about the links between class and religiosity which fail to do justice to the experiences and thinking of people of faith. Hence, in this chapter I attempt to illustrate how evolving relationships between Islam, education and social class were supported by onto-epistemological shifts and affective states beyond the pursuit of class distinction.

The second overarching theme in this chapter is the role of Islamic onto-epistemologies in informing youth educational trajectories. Paying attention to these dynamics is necessary to challenge the tendency among comparative/international education scholars to only study the influence of worldviews on educational engagement in cases of preference for faith-based schools and not when the education in question is 'secular'. This is a manifestation of the secular/religious binary identified in Chapter 1. Indeed, as we shall see, 'being a good Muslim' was just as important for individuals who attended 'secular' state schools, evidenced by the considerable lengths they went to compensate for these schools' lack of religious content.

To make sense of the influence of onto-epistemologies on youth educational engagement, I am inspired by Joseph Hill's ethnography of Senegalese Sufi women's engagement in development activities (2017). He found that they had appropriated many aspects of neoliberal development discourse like the notion of entrepreneurship and institutional practices. However, they used development to serve religious projects, thereby understanding and embedding their activities within an overarching Sufi Islamic worldview and "locally relevant notions of progress and change" (ibid., p. 834). Development, therefore, became an extension of their religious mission and was guided by Islamic ethical principles like not asking for interest on loans (ibid., pp. 838–846). Importantly, for the purposes of this chapter, Hill observed that individuals easily navigated "multiple regimes with contrasting approaches to personhood, agency, knowledge, and moral order" (ibid., p. 834). Ultimately, Hill forces us to ask "how do subjects continually resignify neoliberal power to serve non-neoliberal ends?" (ibid., p. 834). I propose that we can use similar logics to ask "to what extent did Muslim youth in Medina Diallobé resignify development agendas, and educational formats from contrasting onto-epistemological paradigms, to realise ends grounded in their own onto-epistemological frameworks?" To capture these processes, I describe youth as ***ontologically creative subjects***.

The third theme which reoccurred within youth trajectories were attitudes towards time and temporalities. This is because "all forms of education involve sequence" and youth trajectories reflected "processes of accumulation" (Butler, 2016, p. 294) by combining different knowledges over time. However, such projects presented an inevitable challenge: combining knowledges entailed 'doing more' within a similar amount of time and hence a necessary compromise of 'doing less' of something else. As we shall see, there were significant differences among policy-makers, parents and youth regarding how much time should be dedicated to a given learning activity, at what stage of the life-course and in what sequence. Ultimately, these different attitudes towards temporality – which reflected diverse worldviews and socio-economic positions – proved significant in structuring Senegalese Muslims' struggles to navigate different school types within an ontological regime complex characterised by Euro-North American centric coloniality.

All of these issues lead me to the solutions that youth found to combine knowledges, such as by attending full-time private schools, alternating between different institutionalised education options or studying informally alongside one main type of schooling. By unpacking each in turn, I explore the themes of inequalities, onto-epistemologies and temporalities as they emerge within youth's trajectories.

'Hierarchical complementarity': Islamic and state school knowledges

All young people whom I spoke to in Medina Diallobé argued that both Islamic and state school knowledges were useful and 'complementary' in the sense of providing something that the other did not (Butler, 2016, p. 299). Many of the older full-time Qur'anic school students (*sandas*) agreed that French literacy was needed to find work afterwards. The following statement, for example, recounted by 28-year-old *toorodo* Lamine, revealed a common trope among Medina Diallobé's inhabitants of the economic pitfalls of only memorising the Qur'an but not learning French:

> You need French, it's good as you can read and write, and get by talking to people. And with a bit of Arabic too you can read the Qur'an. That's why the Franco-Arab school is good, you can do both. But here, it's either one or the other – it's hard to do both. . . . But if you have a bit of French you can get by, if you go to Cameroon, or Gabon. If you learn a bit of both, it's good.

Meanwhile, parents and teachers often stated that basic knowledge of the Qur'an helped children succeed in state school. Hammadi, a *toorodo* primary school teacher, observed that "children who learn both are the best students, they are good at memorisation but also have a good analytical capacity". This view has been documented across a range of Islamic contexts from Senegal to Morocco, Nigeria and Yemen (Boyle, 2006, p. 495; Ware, 2014, p. 193). Similarly, all students attending secondary schools that I spoke to insisted that every child needed some Islamic education first. For example, Aliou, an 18-year-old *toorodo collège* student, said "You can have the Qur'an but not French school – but the other way around isn't possible, to just have French school!" Such opinions were not restricted to *toorobe* as Zakaria, a 26-year-old man of slave descent (*gallunke*), said:

> When you learn the Qur'an, you have to learn it for life, it's not permitted to forget any of it. In French school, you learn something for the exam and then you move on.

Therefore, youth considered the relationship between state and Islamic school knowledges to be one of 'hierarchical complementarity'. Islamic knowledge was considered the necessary foundation for the acquisition of other knowledges. As I explained in Chapter 3, this idea is central to classical Islamic onto-epistemology (Boyle, 2006; Ogunnaike, 2020).

However, despite the desires of youth to acquire Islamic education as well as state school knowledges, especially French language and literacy, achieving this objective was far from straightforward because "the different educational options are not puzzle pieces" (Butler, 2016, pp. 299–300) that fitted neatly together. Following reforms in the 2000s, six hours a week of religious education and Arabic language had been added to the primary school curriculum. However, at the time of my study, the *collège* and *lycée* syllabi had not been altered and, while students learned some Islamic history and Arabic as a foreign language, they were not taught religious studies (Villalón and Bodian, 2012). Therefore, many secondary school students perceived the schools to be insufficient for learning their religion to advanced level. Kalidou, a 24-year-old of the warrior status group (*ceddo*) in the final year of *lycée* shook his head, saying:

> My history teacher knows nothing of Islamic history. It's embarrassing – I know more, and I go to books and better teachers elsewhere to find out more.

This trend, whereby "youth in formal francophone education increasingly value *advanced* Islamic studies, not instead of but in addition to francophone education", has also been documented by Halimatou Hima (2020, p. 465) in Niger.

As explained in Chapters 3 and 4, other kinds of Islamic schools have been developed in Senegal by non-state actors over the last century to address popular demand to 'do both', whether by Sufis, Salafi-inspired reformists or collaborations between the two. Private fee-charging schools without state recognition include: boarding *daaras* (*internat*) dedicated to intensive memorisation of the Qur'an within a few years; Arabo-Islamic institutes teaching Arabic literacy and advanced religious subjects alongside the Qur'an; and Franco-Arab schools teaching French, Arabic and additional subjects alongside religion (D'Aoust, 2013). However, there is variation *within* these types and they should be thought of more as "a spectrum than as a definitive classificatory typology" (Butler, 2016, p. 294). All of these schools are open to girls as well as boys and apparently exhibit no barriers to access based on status group. Yet, none of these models was present in or near Medina Diallobé at the time of my fieldwork, so students had to travel to the cities of Saint-Louis or Dakar to find the equivalent.

From the early 2000s, the state also created public Franco-Arab primary schools and some *collèges* which split teaching equally between the state-school curriculum taught in French and Islamic subjects taught in Arabic. Existing Franco-Arab schools could also gain accreditation by delivering the state-approved curriculum. The state also created *daaras moderne* (modern *daaras*) which taught some memorisation of the Qur'an as well as French literacy and vocational subjects (D'Aoust, 2013; Binaté and Hugon, 2019). However, such schools were located several hundreds of kilometres away from Medina Diallobé in the regions of Kaolack, Diourbel and Louga. They had had no impact on school trajectories of youth in Medina Diallobé; no one I spoke to appeared aware of their existence.

Mixed trajectories: Common concerns, diverse strategies

Given the lack of hybrid options available in Medina Diallobé, local youth used diverse strategies and tactics (De Certeau, 1984) to acquire the knowledges associated with different types of schools.

Full-time study in boarding daaras

Private Islamic schools in Saint-Louis and Dakar appealed to many parents and youth. The most frequented type was the boarding *daara* or *internat* which taught memorisation of the Qur'an with board, lodging and tuition paid through monthly fees of 25,000–30,000CFA (equivalent to £32–40 a month). These schools offered intensive memorisation of the Qur'an within four or five years but did not teach French or Arabic. In comparison to *daaras* in the Futa Tooro region, where the average length of time needed to memorise the Qur'an is ten years, 33% of talibés in the Dakar region memorise the Qur'an fully within only three years (MEN, 2010, p. 53).

The first reason people gave for preferring the *internat* over the classical rural *daara* was because students completed memorisation in a shorter period and therefore had more time to acquire other knowledge afterwards. As I described in Chapter 5, the implantation of colonial schools led to "changing perceptions of time and labour regimes" (Butler, 2016, p. 298) as long-term study alongside work for a cleric increasingly conflicted with young men's aspirations to earn a living quickly. Such concerns were also evident in the case of Binta, a 45-year-old *toorodo* who sent her sons to boarding *daaras* in Dakar. She explained how she preferred them for the speed at which boys were taught and learned the Qur'an:

> Seydina [age 26] went to a private *internat*, he is abroad now. But he finished the Qur'an in 2003 and his cousin Abderahmane who is the same age [and studied in a *daara* in the Futa Tooro region] finished in 2010.

Fifteen-year-old Mohamed, cited at the beginning of this chapter, also told me why he would be able to study faster at an *internat:*

> There [in the boarding *daara*] you can forget everything about your life here because you don't go out at all, only Fridays for prayers, and you only see your family on religious holidays. If I stay here [in a classical *daara* in the Futa Tooro region] I won't learn well. At the *internat* you only learn, you don't have to work for the cleric. So what you learn in one year there could take you four years here. There aren't many schools like that in the Futa.

The second reason given by parents for preferring the *internat* was safety. For instance, 35-year-old *toorodo* Diara was very concerned that her 12-year-old son Racine was not well supervised in the *daara* in the Medina Diallobé. He had been found wandering in the highlands (*jeeri*) with friends when a dangerous Harmattan sandstorm swept through the village. She did research to find a boarding *daara* in Dakar which was run by a distant relative who she felt sure would take better care of Racine. When she told other women in her extended family, they also expressed concern and Diara spent several weeks reassuring them that Racine would be safe.

The affluent *toorodo* families in Medina Diallobé were most likely to have at least one son who had attended a boarding *daara*. However, the overall number of boys who frequented them was fairly low given the high tuition fees. In effect, the lack of affordable Islamic school options in or near Medina Diallobé was leading to stratified access to valued knowledge. As Chapter 3 indicated, in the colonial period, only urban middle-class families could afford to get the best of both forms of education by paying tuition fees for their children to attend the *daara* as day students, while simultaneously sending them to state schools. Poorer families valuing Qur'anic education were obliged to enrol their sons as live-in students in the rural *daaras* and were excluded from the privileges that the state school conferred (Ware, 2014, p. 193). The colonial period therefore established inequalities between those who could (not) afford to do both, which has not changed substantially for all the state's education reforms. Even today, only middle-class families in Medina Diallobé, who are usually *toorobe* and have converted their families' inherited wealth into migration opportunities or successful careers in trade, can afford the *internat*. These enable students to pursue trajectories that allow them to gain access to both forms of knowledge within a reasonable timeframe in establishments which align more with 'international' norms of child protection where students did not beg outdoors and are instead confined to the school premises.

The perceived benefits of the *internat* model – and its association with more affluent social classes – appears to be leading to subtle changes in the onto-epistemological nets (Thayer-Bacon, 2017) of people in Medina Diallobé. The *internat* affected their perceptions of the pedagogies central to the classical *daara* including working for the cleric and the hardship experienced by children. To clarify, as Chapter 5 showed, the view was still widespread in Medina Diallobé that memorising the Qur'an was worthwhile as it conferred considerable quantities of *baraka* or blessing. However, debates between *sandas* suggested that differences were emerging in people's perceptions of how best to acquire *baraka*. One 22-year-old *sanda*, Hammadi, was extremely diligent in practicing recitation of the Qur'an according to a strict personal schedule, in order to complete memorisation as quickly as possible so he could start working. The other *sandas* agreed that he was making good progress. However, Alfa, another *sanda* who spent less time reciting as he regularly worked his cleric's fields, remarked behind his back, "but Hammadi never works for his cleric, and that's not good [for *baraka*]". Therefore, while young peoples' worldviews continue to share threads on the importance of *baraka,* they differ as to whether it should be best acquired through working for the cleric or solely memorising the Qur'an. Indeed, many of Medina Diallobé's inhabitants I spoke to argued that paying tuition fees at a boarding *daara,* in order to memorise the Qur'an within five years, was preferable to long-term study in a rural *daara* for twice or three times as long. Such shifts in preference represent a transition away from an education embedded in long-term relationships of reciprocity and gift exchange with Muslims clerics towards one-off transactions in a cash economy. Similar shifts have also been documented in northern Nigeria (Hoechner, 2018, p. 199) and Niger (Butler, 2006).

Meanwhile, anxieties over the safety of children in classical rural *daaras* tended to be voiced by (lower) middle-class parents who could (just about) afford the *internat* alternative. Hence, aspirations for a learning environment more aligned with 'international' norms of child protection were a luxury available to more affluent parents. In contrast, Hoechner explains that, in northern Nigeria, caregivers living in unpredictable and precarious circumstances can perceive itinerant Qur'anic schools as a better prospect for children than their staying 'at home' (Hoechner, 2018, pp. 93–121). This challenges the stereotypes in the development world, which I unpacked in Chapter 5, that parents who opt for itinerant *daaras* do not care about their children. Rather, I found that, irrespective of socio-economic status, parents' levels of affection for their children were similar, as were their levels of religiosity. It was their unequal social circumstances that contributed to their divergent preferences for different types of Qur'anic education. In other words, in Medina Diallobé, the ability to afford a 'safer' option was potentially becoming a marker of social class distinction. However, no parents I knew articulated their preference in such terms and, in contrast to Hoechner's findings (2018, p. 122), I heard no negative judgements of parents who continued to send their children away to classical residential Qur'anic schools.

Alternating between schools to learn Arabic and French

As well as urban *internat*, some Medina Diallobé inhabitants also sought out private Arabo-Islamic or Franco-Arab schools which taught Arabic, Islamic knowledges additional to memorisation of the Qur'an and sometimes French. These schools were, however, less popular than the boarding *daaras*. I only knew a handful of youth attending such schools, such as the Al-Falah schools of reformist orientation located in Dakar (described in Chapter 6). One reason was that monthly fees were often higher than the *internat*, at around 40,000CFA (approximately £52 a month). However, other testimonies revealed that learning Arabic was not considered particularly useful. One 35-year-old *toorodo* man, Samba, explained why Franco-Arab schools were less attractive:

> They're just secular schools with a bit of Arabic thrown in, invented by people who brought back knowledge of Arabic culture, etc., from the Arab world. But knowing Arabic isn't the same as knowing Islam.

Attending Arabo-Islamic or Franco-Arab schools to learn Arabic and/or French reflected the principle of 'hierarchical complementarity' as it took place *after* memorisation of the Qur'an. I knew of no youth who had only attended Arabo-Islamic or Franco-Arab schools without having memorised a large proportion, if not all, of the Qur'an first. The following quote from 21-year-old *toorodo* woman Juulde captures this sentiment:

> My little [8-year-old] brother is at a [boarding] *daara* in Dakar. My mother wants him to learn fast, because he's young he can, and he can finish in a few years. Then, when he's 11 or 12, he can go to a Franco-Arab school. Some teach Arabic with a bit of the Qur'an, others less Qur'an or not at all. But the Qur'an is the most mportant – it's the religion. The Franco-Arab school is like French school with something added, i.e. Arabic. But Arabic is just a language, not the Qur'an. . . . It's important to put it in perspective – the Qur'an *is* the religion.

Significantly, the Franco-Arab or Arabo-Islamic schools whose teaching reflected Salafi onto-epistemologies appeal to parents and youth who adhere to both Sufi and Salafi-reformist orientations. However, youth cited different incentives and benefits which appeared to reflect their social positioning. For instance, Kalidou, from the lower middle-class *ceddo* family I described in Chapter 6, valued his Salafi-inspired Arabo-Islamic school in Saint-Louis because he considered that Arabic literacy and Qur'anic exegesis were more worthwhile than memorising the Qur'an without understanding its literal meaning. Like many Salafis, Kalidou framed his knowledge as more legitimate than that of Sufi clerics:

> People here are ignorant, and follow *marabouts* rather than the Qur'an and *sunna*. I see clerics here and I'm ashamed of their behaviour. Yet people go to see these charlatans, with their divinations and so on.

This knowledge enabled Kalidou to challenge the exclusionary race-religion constellation (Topolski, 2018) in the Futa Tooro that excluded people from his status group or caste from Qur'anic schools and religious authority.

In contrast, the son of one of Medina Diallobé's most respected clerics and a proud member of the Tijaniyya Umariyya Sufi order, 16-year-old son Amara, also attended an Al-Falah school in Dakar. However, he had a very different view of its advantages since he hoped to use his education to obtain a scholarship to study in the Middle East and hence access more job opportunities. This reflected a broader trend whereby, from the 1950s, the leaders of the Senegalese Sufi orders had been sending their sons to Arabic-speaking countries for higher education after they had attended classical *daaras* and/or regional Sufi-affiliated Arabic institutes (Kane, 2016, p. 4). They did this to invigorate their own practice and guide the reform movement away from anti-Sufi critiques (Ware, 2014, p. 227).

In showing themselves to be 'ontologically creative subjects', parents and youth in Medina Diallobé easily took advantage of knowledges and pedagogies offered by schools to meet their own agendas, even if they disagreed with the various schools' overall onto-epistemological orientation (for similar observations in Nigeria, see Hoechner, 2018, pp. 192–193).

It was also noticeable that, overall, young people saw more economic utility in learning French than Arabic: "There's not much you can do with [Arabo-Islamic] schooling, just go to an Arabic country or teach in Senegal", said 21-year-old *toorodo* Juulde. Similarly, Malik, a 24-year-old *toorodo sharia* student, commented:

> Here *arabisants* [Arabic-speakers] have nothing, there are lots of well-educated people – but it doesn't pay. You can teach in a private Arabic school and only earn 50,000CFA (approximately £65) a month, that's nothing. French is privileged.

This perception reflects a longstanding debate in Senegal whereby Arabic speakers are perceived to be economically disadvantaged compared to French speakers (Sieveking, 2022, p. 775).

In addition, by learning French and/or Arabic in different schools, the kinds of professions that young *toorodo* men hoped to secure through "multiskilling" (Froerer and Portisch, 2012, p. 339) reveals the associations made between Sufi onto-epistemologies and economic opportunities. *Toorodo* men from Medina Diallobé who combined memorisation of the Qur'an with French and/or Arabic literacy appeared not to be interested in becoming Arabic teachers in Senegal. Instead, they usually hoped to use their language skills to pursue livelihoods in the transnational economy of esoteric services in the Middle

East, Africa, Europe or the US. It was this option that inspired 15-year-old Mohamed, whom we met earlier, to drop out of the penultimate year of *collège* to attend a boarding *daara*. Being a *toorodo* of *sharif* descent, he explained how, seeing as he already had the skill of French literacy, a *collège* or *lycée* diploma was less economically useful than memorising the Qur'an:

> If I did the Qur'an to the end, I would go to America and do *dabaade* [work using the esoteric sciences]. My uncle does that in the Congo. Especially if you say you're a *sharif*, people will give you *addiya* [large gifts]. Or you can be the imam of a mosque, they pay you each month. My uncle, he's an imam at a mosque in America. Even my father did that, getting *addiya* in America. If I finished French school I could still go to the US – but what job could I do?!

Mohamed's uncle Omar was another example of a *toorodo* man with an educational trajectory combining state and Islamic education who had used his knowledge repertoire to reinvent the customary profession of *dabotoodo* [provider of esoteric services]. Forty-eight-year-old Omar was fluent in French and Arabic having been raised in Mauritania where he obtained the baccalaureate.[1] He had also memorised one-tenth of the Qur'an from *sandas* who tutored him at home. At age 18, he started to learn *dabaade* from his father in Medina Diallobé. After completing his studies, he trained as a teacher, worked as a school director and moonlighted as a *dabotoodo* during the school holidays:

> *Mystique*, healing, divination is my job, alongside teaching. People come from five, ten, even fifteen kilometres away in Mauritania to consult me. I have travelled a lot, to Morocco over 100 times, to Tunisia, Saudi Arabia. I hope to go to Jordan during the holidays, to earn a bit of money, and invest it back in some business projects. With my job and some contacts I have in the government, I could get a visa to go to France. I think it would work, there is a lot of demand there.

This kind of trajectory whereby West African Sufi elites have appropriated the benefits, not only of reformist Islamic schools but also French language of instruction education to reinforce their *baraka* and religious professions, has a long history. For an early example, Peter Clarke (1988) described the case of Muhammad Jumat Imam, a charismatic Sufi leader from Ijebuland in south-western Nigeria, who claimed in 1941 to be the Mahdi or renewer of the age. At the time, the position of Chief Imam at the mosque in the capital of Ijebuland was contested. Jumat Imam successfully argued that the other candidates were not qualified as they lacked knowledge of Arabic *and English*. Clarke stated "That such a view was met with the support of many is an indication of how both the expansion of Western education and the improvements in Islamic education . . . were altering the traditional criteria for leadership" (1988, pp. 159–160).

These educational trajectories and associated evaluations of knowledge push us to question the applicability to Senegal of conclusions made by, for example, anthropologists like Brenner (2000, p. 16) in Mali or Hoechner (2018, pp. 190–193, 211) in northern Nigeria. These scholars found that the influence of reformist Islamic schools had led to greater symbolic capital being accorded to Arabic literacy and knowledge of *hadith* (traditions of the Prophet) than memorisation of the Qur'an in classical Qur'anic schools. In contrast, however, the Medina Diallobé inhabitants I met revealed that memorisation of the Qur'an was still accorded the highest value among the types of religious knowledge available, for spiritual benefits, *baraka* and esoteric properties. Similar evaluations have been documented in other parts of Senegal including Dakar, Medina Gounass and the Mouride heartland of Djourbel (see Smith, 2008, pp. 58, 88).

In contrast to Mali and Nigeria, the continued dominance of classical Islamic onto-epistemologies in Senegal is largely connected to the Sufi orders' political, economic and cultural influence. Moreover, as Chapter 5 showed, the *toorodo* aristocracy of the Futa Tooro region had translated their customary symbolic capital (derived through memorisation of the Qur'an and inherited *baraka*), political power and economic capital into contemporary opportunities. Their customary occupations of religious professions, esoteric sciences and trade, combined with recent mobility capital to migrate internationally, are more lucrative and prestigious than the jobs available to graduates of reformist Islamic schools. As a result, aspirational middle-class male *toorodo* youth in Medina Diallobé appeared to want to use their privileges to harness the opportunities presented by globalisation, re-inventing the religious profession of *dabotoodo* which is grounded in classical Islamic onto-epistemologies and esoteric sciences.

These findings challenge another bias within academic literature on Muslim societies which finds that middle-class religiosity tends to involve piety movements or rationalist interpretations of Islam which denounce mysticism (Marsden and Retsikas, 2013, p. 13). This narrative echoes the secularisation thesis. The cultural dynamics in Senegal demand that more attention be paid to the empirical – and ultimately theoretical – implications of the growing phenomenon that is "a reinvigorated, deeply reflective, and highly literate and globalised Sufism" (ibid., p. 22). Such implications must include questioning the dominant definitions of – and judgements about – 'quality' Islamic education within education and development agendas that are grounded in rationalist rather than spiritual onto-epistemologies (see Chapter 4).

Informal part-time study alongside formal school

Finally, many of the young people I interviewed considered the *daara* insufficient for learning French and the state school inadequate for teaching religion. However, they lacked the means to attend private schools which combined both. Instead, they studied part-time informally alongside full-time attendance in, for example, the *daara* or state school. If we consider attending fee-charging schools as a 'strategy' of the affluent, informal learning was, by contrast, an example of 'tactical' agency (De Certeau, 1984) for those without this privilege.

One group of youth who engaged in informal study were *sandas* who attended *daaras* full-time and tried to learn French alongside. "My brother memorised the Qur'an just, in the Futa. But he also spoke French", explained 20-year-old *toorodo* Aliou. "He learned it off the students he shared a room with, he would take a notebook and ask them questions". Another 25-year-old *sanda* told me:

> I'm learning the Qur'an and *sharia*, but I also have a French teacher, and an English teacher [pointing to his two friends]. Wolof too. You need to know a bit of everything.

The first thing most *sandas* asked me when we met was whether I could teach them French. Openness to learning French was considered 'modern'. *Sandas* who studied it, along with activities like listening to rap music or playing football, referred to each other jokingly as '*sandas modernes*' (modern *sandas*). Such ontological creativity was valued by youth, although not necessarily by older *toorobe* who subscribed to more customary markers of Islamic piety. The 'modern' label conferred symbolic capital and a degree of distinction among *sandas* and their peers. Indeed, Hoechner has noted a similar openness among Qur'anic-schooled youth in northern Nigeria to pursue multiple forms of knowledge associated with different school types which sometimes went against the preferences of their parents or clerics (2018, pp. 192–193).

However, learning French informally while at the *daara* was extremely burdensome. Instead, many *sandas* hoped to take private lessons after completing memorisation of the Qur'an. For instance, 26-year-old Abderahmane had dropped out of the final year of primary at age 12 and then memorised the Qur'an to completion in a rural *daara* by 24. He asked me for advice on where he could learn English and French in Dakar for around 35,000CFA a month (approximately £46). He hoped to do three months of intensive study to get up to speed and fund himself by tutoring in Arabic. However, after spending two months in Dakar, Abderahmane found finding employment much harder than expected and his plans to learn French fell through. He returned home disappointed and unsure of what to try next, and his parents grumbled at him for not working. Likewise, 28-year-old Lamine ridiculed his cousin for not learning French, revealing how *daara* students were blamed by others for lacking this particular foundational skill when, in reality, acquiring it was far from straightforward. Lamine pointed out:

> Without French it's seriously bad. My cousin studied the Qur'an at a *daara* in the Futa and finished when he was 30. He went to France and couldn't do anything, he couldn't speak the language at all. He said to people "Give me French lessons!" before he went – but by then, it was

> too late. If you study the Qur'an it's possible to get French lessons on Thursdays and Fridays, the days you have off. But if you learn nothing, you have no chance. . . . Now he's back in Dakar trying to find work.

The second group I found were the young *toorodo* men who sought to complement state schooling with informal memorisation of the Qur'an. Some had followed the common sequential model of attending the *daara* when they were young and then continued informally once they began state school. A handful of boys had managed to continue memorising even while at *collège*. I was particularly interested to hear how Bachir, a 28-year-old *toorodo* and law student at university in Dakar, had memorised the entire Qur'an while attending state school. He explained how it was important for his identity as a *toorodo* of a clerical lineage:

> I finished memorising the Qur'an about four years ago. Because my father is a cleric, it was obligatory! When we went to school, he would make us wake up at 6:30am, we could study the Qur'an for half an hour. We would also do half an hour before going back to school at 4pm. During the summer holidays too, my father would let us rest for one week doing nothing, then we would learn the Qur'an! We were allowed half-an-hour a day of football and so on, but we had to learn the Qur'an too. All my brothers did the Qur'an and French school this way. If I finish my degree and do a Masters', I'd like to spend a year just learning *sharia* somewhere, it's a hobby of mine.

Bachir's experience echoes that of Harvard Professor of Islamic studies Ousmane Kane, grandson of one of Senegal's most renowned Sufi leaders. Kane (2016) described his education in the 1960s which involved an intense schedule of *daara* exclusively when very young, followed by state school full-time complemented with informal Qur'anic study before school, during lunch-breaks, in the evening, on weekends and school holidays: "When did I rest? Only at night! There was no other time to rest" (ibid., p. 3).

Memorising the Qur'an informally alongside the state school was difficult and took great self-discipline which is why some, like Mohamed described earlier, preferred to drop out to attend a *daara* full-time instead. Boubacar, a *toorodo* in the penultimate year of *lycée* who diligently recited the Qur'an with the *sandas* resident in his compound when not attending school, remarked, "It's hard to blend the two, it takes a lot of time". Indeed, even Boubacar's ability to invest time studying the Qur'an reflected his privilege: he was exempt from housework because a *gallunke* youth (the status group of slave descent) did most of the chores in his household. In contrast, most *toorodo* boys at state school were reluctantly obliged to abandon their informal religious study as the demands of the former became too onerous. Similarly, Hoechner (2018) found in Nigeria that poorer Qur'anic school students could not afford the opportunity costs of such intensive study regimes (ibid., pp. 196, 200).

The third group who studied religion informally alongside state school were women and men from non-*toorodo* status groups. They studied Islam by attending non-formal classes or took up informal study through books or audio-visual media. In regard to the non-formal classes, as described in Chapter 7, 23-year-old *toorodo* and reformist Aissata taught girls in her own home Qur'anic verses, the five pillars of Islam and how to perform ablution and prayer. Most of her younger students attended on weekdays after school, on weekends or during the school holidays. Similar to engagement with Al-Falah schools, parents did not necessarily agree with the Salafi onto-epistemology underpinning Aissata's teaching, but they valued her school for knowledges not taught in the *daara*. Oumoul was a 32-year-old *toorodo*, who sent her 8-year-old daughter Zara to Aissata and explained "it's a very good education. They don't just learn verses but for instance invocations, like what to say when you enter the toilet and so on".

However, Oumoul admitted to being wary of Aissata's reformist tendencies and monitored Zara's behaviour lest she pick up such influences. For instance, girls in the Futa Tooro region customarily would not wear head-coverings until after puberty, and then they would wear headwraps. In contrast, Aissata wore a tight Middle Eastern-style *hijab* that covered her neck, which is more characteristic of Muslim women of reformist orientation, and encouraged such dress among adolescent girls and even children who attended her school. I once saw Oumoul tell Zara off when she started imitating Aissata's practice of wearing a tight *hijab* around the house which was indicative of her encouraging Zara's acquisition of Islamic knowledge but not a worldview or norms associated with reformism.

In addition, several youth studied informally by attending Islamic conferences delivered by clerics in the Futa Tooro region. This was evident among members of the blacksmith status group who compensated for their exclusion from the local *daaras* (see Chapter 6) by travelling to a village called Bélinaybé Mbayla (sometimes spelled Belnaïbe Mbaïla). It was one of the rare villages in the Futa Tooro region inhabited solely by a group of artisan/musicians (in this case blacksmiths, many of whom had abandoned their customary profession to become Muslim clerics). One in particular, Ceerno Abdoulaye Paate Mbow, was well known throughout the region for his erudition and esoteric skills (Kyburz, 1994, p. 152). As a 40-year-old *baylo* (blacksmith), Hamidou, explained to me:

> My uncles and grandparents live in a village called Bélinaybé Mbayla. They are all *wayluɓe* [blacksmiths], but they are also big *marabouts*, all have learnt the Qur'an to the end but are smiths too. . . . The youth [from Medina Diallobé] go to Bélinaybé Mbayla for a *ziara* [event in celebration of a Muslim saint] which takes place after *korité* [Eid Al-Fitr]. That way, they celebrate religious learning and their caste.

Young people also learned religion informally through books – usually written in French – and audio-visual media. Twenty-eight-year-old *baylo* and *lycée* teacher Ismaila told me that:

> I try to learn from time to time, I have a Qur'an translated into French that I bought in Dakar. That way I understand what God says. And I go to my friends, the *sandas* who live nearby, and ask them for clarifications.

In addition to copies of the Qur'an, whether the original or versions translated into French, young and old owned a variety of other works reflecting a range of Sufi and Salafi-reformist onto-epistemologies. In a similar way to attendance at Islamic schools, the religious books people read were not necessarily indicative of their personal Islamic philosophy. For instance, the consumption of Salafi literature for information on *sharia* did not preclude affiliation to the Tijaniyya Sufi order. However, while informal learning from religious books enabled those excluded from *daaras* to study Islam, in general, such materials were a luxury. A trader sold Islamic books and pamphlets at the weekly market in Medina Diallobé, but most books were purchased in towns further away or even during visits to Mecca (on the sale of Islamic books in Senegal see Cohen and Timéra, 2022). Households commonly did not have any books, and the people cited earlier came from affluent *toorodo* families and/or had rare salaried jobs. Hence, access to book knowledge reflected socioeconomic hierarchies.

In addition to books, people learned from audio-visual media. Most households consumed religious programming on televisions or radios which is widespread throughout Senegal (Sieveking, 2022, p. 791). Some youth showed me videos on their phones, but this was also rare, as I did my fieldwork before smartphones became widespread. Nowadays, consumption of videos is far more prevalent, whether locally recorded or consumed through social media platforms (Hima, 2020, p. 502). These examples corroborate a trend documented in Muslim societies around the globe, namely how increased availability of print and electronic media has facilitated alternatives to face-to-face, individualised knowledge transmission. In West Africa, this has enabled more people to study outside of formal Islamic schools, thus challenging the exclusive patterns of access to knowledge and religious authority upheld by local clerical classes (Sounaye, 2014; Hoechner, 2018, p. 191). These practices in Medina Diallobé also reveal that French literacy was an important factor which enabled those educated in state schools to access informal and non-formal Islamic education. This trend has been well documented in Senegal from the 2000s (Sieveking, 2022, p. 772). It is another example of 'creative ontological subjects' putting 'secular' state school knowledges to use for 'religious' objectives.

Barriers to educational pluralism in Senegal

Despite their creativity, youth trajectories exposed several limitations of Senegal's education reforms targeting Islamic education. In Chapter 4, I reviewed these policies, arguing that they reflected coloniality of secularity because the kinds of Islamic knowledges prioritised tended to reflect Euro-North

American centric cultural norms and secularist onto-epistemologies. However, this chapter's close-up investigation of youth attempts at combining knowledges reveals even more limitations of the current policies. In particular, their trajectories expose how Euro-North American centric temporalities and assumptions about 'educational sequentialism' (Butler, 2016, p. 289) create obstacles for students hoping to transition between schools.

To clarify, the state school system (including public Franco-Arab schools and 'modern' *daaras*) exhibit fundamentally different sequential logics regarding *when* and *how* the Qur'an is best learned – if at all – compared to classical Qur'anic schools. In short, *daaras* are based on a '*task-based logic*' where each student is expected to achieve the same result (memorisation of the Qur'an). Differences in students' abilities are managed by varying the time they take to complete. Meanwhile, Western-style schools are based on '*timed performance logic*'. Time allocated to each task is fixed through a system of age-grades, and variation in students' performance is managed through ranking and, in extreme cases, failing (Kane, 2016, p. 17). Secondly, *daara* pedagogy is based on the sequential principle of '*specialisation-before-differentiation*', following centuries of observation that it is easiest to fully memorise the Qur'an at a young age without the competing demands of other subjects. In contrast, the state school is based on a sequential model of '*differentiation-before-specialisation*' where multiple subjects are learned simultaneously at first and specialisation takes place much later (Boyle, 2002). Teaching is based on groups of common age rather than shared ability, although there is no evidence that this is always necessary for effective learning (Serpell, 1999, p. 115).

These assumptions about pedagogy and temporal sequentialism are embedded in the very framework of the EFA agenda. Every GEM Report (e.g. UNESCO, 2021, p. 479) includes an annex or glossary classifying different types of schools. The definition of 'primary' or 'elementary' schooling is as follows:

> Primary education (ISCED level 1). Programmes normally designed on a unit or project basis to give pupils a sound basic education in reading, writing and mathematics and an elementary understanding of subjects such as history, geography, natural sciences, social sciences, art and music. Religious instruction may also be featured. These subjects serve to develop pupils' ability to obtain and use information they need about their home, community, country, etc. Sometimes called elementary education.

The definition of 'secondary' education is as follows (ibid., p. 479):

> Secondary education. Programmes at ISCED levels 2 and 3. Lower secondary education (ISCED 2) is generally designed to continue the basic programmes of the primary level but the teaching is typically more subject-focused, requiring more specialized teachers for each subject area. The end of this level often coincides with the end of compulsory

> education. In upper secondary education (ISCED 3), the final stage of secondary education in most countries, instruction is often organized even more along subject lines and teachers typically need a higher or more subject-specific qualification than at ISCED level 2.

According to these definitions, which are not neutral but have emerged specifically in the Euro-North American cultural context, classical Qur'anic schools can never conform to the label of 'primary education' unless they adopt a more diversified curriculum, which raises challenges when policy-makers try to integrate them alongside secular or hybrid Islamic schools within a common national framework.

Indeed, recent discussions within donor organisations like UNICEF have stressed the importance of accrediting all schools in West Africa in order to facilitate *passerelles* or transitions between different school models (Roy and Humeau, 2018; Binaté and Hugon, 2019). However, as part of this process, development agencies often try to impose on classical Qur'anic schools the norms of the Western-style school (which devalue memorisation of the Qur'an and reflect pedagogical norms of timed performance and diversity-before-specialisation). In Senegal, these logics were reflected in a proposed curriculum that would award *daaras* government accreditation and hence potential subsidies. Not surprisingly, a Ministry of Education report in 2010 found that clerics in Senegal were unhappy about the proposed curriculum because it demanded the incorporation of other subjects, including French, into their *daaras.* Of clerics surveyed in Dakar, Louga, Saint Louis and Matam regions, 33% refused integration of state school subjects into their *daaras* before Qur'anic memorisation was complete. Of this group, 67% accepted but only on the condition that French teaching took place on *talibés'* days off (Thursdays and Fridays) and did not interfere with the existing timetable of 30–40 weekly hours of Qur'anic study (MEN, 2010, p. 67). Many clerics therefore opposed the newly promoted curriculum, accusing the state of unconstitutionally trying to control religious education. They argued that the *daaras* were being treated like Catholic private schools which followed European models, rather than as independent system with their own logics grounded in a different onto-epistemology (Abdourahman, 2015; Lo, 2015).

In terms of educational decision-making strategies, this variation in attitudes towards educational sequentialism and pedagogy (grounded in different onto-epistemologies) means that the primary state school timetable is incompatible with many people's priorities of fully memorising the Qur'an and then transitioning into primary school. This is because the official age of starting primary is seven, and children enrolling later are considered for statistical purposes as 'over-age' and hence perceived by state and development actors as a 'problem' because curricula are not adapted for multi-grade classes (Lewin, 2008). Faced with this challenge, a widespread tactic documented throughout Senegal since the colonial period is when parents send their children to *daaras* and then arrange for their birth certificate to be forged so that they can enrol them in primary afterwards at the 'correct' official age, when they are in fact around 12 years old (Ware, 2004, p. 86). A common reason why people in Medina Diallobé preferred the sequence of *daara*-then-private-Franco-Arab-school was because the latter are designed by Senegalese educators and adapted to popular temporalities by teaching state primary school-level content to older children or adolescents. Moreover, students have internalised this negative construction of their being 'behind' which can be considered a form of symbolic violence. For example, Kalidou told me that he was taking his *baccalaureate* at age 24 because he spent his childhood in *daaras* and Islamic schools. He stated, gloomily, "I'm behind. But being behind is programmed into being African". Far from being 'intrinsic' to being African, this 'behindness' is a product of education policies grounded in Euro-North American norms and coloniality of secularity.

Finally, education policies overwhelmingly address formal education at the primary level and hence cater to today's children but then neglect the needs of adolescents or adults. Many adolescent boys and men have studied in classical Qur'anic schools while working for their cleric but lack the funds or time to study the Qur'an quickly in a boarding *daara* or supplement their foundational skills in Franco-Arab schools or through private French lessons. Those who did not learn this additional useful knowledge felt frustrated and stressed about their prospects and were sometimes shamed by others for not having 'tried harder'. The neglect of the needs of this cohort is due to the education reforms being elaborated under pressure to meet donor requirements for universal primary education (UPE) under the MDGs rather than addressing the life-long educational needs of the whole population.

To return to the principle of educational pluralism presented at the start of this chapter, D'Agostino and Callizo (2022) provide a number of criteria for its realisation, the first being *access,* as they explain in this quotation (ibid., p. 379, emphasis in the original):

> The freedom of education is rooted in the prior right of parents to choose the form of education of their children, which implies both an adequate supply of non-state and philosophically distinctive options as well as the accessibility of that supply, which – in turn, is associated with the degree to which public funding enables access to non-state schools. We label this as degree of **access.**

In addition to access, the second criterion required for educational pluralism is *autonomy* (ibid., p. 379, emphasis in the original):

> The second key factor is the degree to which schools are able to be distinctive in their educational philosophy and reflection of moral, religious, and cultural beliefs and values. This is significantly contingent upon the degree of **autonomy** of non-state actors to provide education without intrusive regulatory or governance interference. This entails

> their freedom to open, operate, and control key aspects of schools' mission and educational provision, while nonetheless respecting minimum standards. We can conceptualize these two dimensions on two axes, and see a spectrum from low to high pluralism when considering these concepts together.

In relation to autonomy, the extremely poor conditions and cases of child endangerment in a very small number of Qur'anic schools remains a cause for concern (see Chapter 4) and should, in my view, be one of the 'minimum standards' required for state support. However *daaras* more generally are not considered deserving of public funds because international donors and state elites still appear to resist entertaining the possibility that a focus on full memorisation of the Qur'an (as provided by classical residential *daaras* in rural areas or boarding *internat daaras* in urban areas) could constitute a 'basic education' of value. This then has a negative impact on safeguarding and access. Therefore, coloniality of secularity and Eurocentric biases built into international agendas continue to pose a barrier to genuine educational pluralism in many West African contexts.

Conclusion

This chapter illuminated the methods employed by parents and youth in Medina Diallobé to enable the latter to combine knowledges associated with Islamic and state schools. These trajectories break down the notion that a choice in favour of a particular school at a given time can be held to reflect an absolute pattern of preference, as combining knowledges was the norm. Meanwhile, these varied pathways reflect similar preoccupations – namely the desire to become good Muslims and acquire knowledges which confer spiritual benefits and economic and symbolic capital in the shortest time and most optimal conditions possible. However, the abilities of young people to realise these aspirations diverge significantly, grounded as they are in socioeconomic differences, gendered or descent-based hierarchies and changes to the educational landscape wrought during and after colonisation. These inequalities result in 'strategies' of the privileged versus 'tactics' of the disadvantaged (De Certeau, 1984).

Youth trajectories also reveal the complex influence of onto-epistemologies on educational engagement. Medina Diallobé's inhabitants all experience the world through the lenses of Islamic onto-epistemologies. The majority are closer to holding a classical or Sufi worldview while only a minority are more Salafi-inspired, characterised by the rejection of Sufi clerics' authority and esoteric practices. Nonetheless, Senegalese youth in my study revealed themselves to be 'ontologically creative subjects' who consumed knowledges and engaged with schools with diverse onto-epistemological foundations, in order to realise their individual projects. Consequently, in practice, the strong distinction between 'secular' and 'religious' fields and knowledges, characteristic of the secular/religious binary, fall apart. Knowledges typically labelled as 'secular', like French proficiency, are put to 'religious' ends like consuming Islamic books or audio-visual media and working in the transnational prayer economy. And 'religious' knowledge is put to 'secular' ends like challenging gender and racialised descent-based hierarchies.

However, closer inspection reveals how people's onto-epistemological positions have evolved in tandem with structural changes including increased socio-economic inequalities. This is especially evident in growing contestation over pedagogies central to the classical Qur'anic schools. This is illustrated in youth opinions that suggest that working for a cleric long term is no longer necessary for acquiring *baraka* or parents' criticisms that children are safer and better supervised in boarding *daaras*. While I prefer to avoid linear and deterministic correlations, particular onto-epistemological perspectives nonetheless appear to thrive when reinforced by positive affective experiences and economic and social returns. In turn, more privileged individuals are better placed to access the forms of religiosity reflective of dominant onto-epistemologies and can shame others for not conforming. Current anthropological research on the co-constitution of social class and Islamic identities in West Africa (e.g. Samson and LeBlanc, 2022) tends to emphasise how religious practices are deployed as markers of social class distinction. Based on my findings, I believe that such extra-religious motivations or returns should not eclipse a focus on the more hidden aspects of Islamic subjectivities such as affective experiences or the value accorded to other-than-secular onto-epistemologies as valued cognitive or moral frameworks.

The trajectories of Medina Diallobé's youth have important implications for debates about educational pluralism. This project is, I suggest, compatible with a decolonial commitment to onto-epistemological pluriversity (Walsh and Mignolo, 2018, pp. 2–3) in comparative/international education. While Senegal's education system can be considered plural, it is not pluralistic. Despite reforms from the early 2000s to integrate more religious content into the state system, development actors overall display coloniality of secularity by failing to support popular demand for classical Qur'anic education. The result is a stratified system in which only the privileged can combine this form of education with other knowledges perceived as useful in the contemporary context.

In the following final chapter, I conclude by offering some practical suggestions on how decolonial and postsecular principles might inform theory and praxis in comparative/international education and in relation to the development-education-religion (DER) nexus specifically. I also propose more inclusive approaches to policy-making and programming in relation to Qur'anic schools in West Africa.

Note

1 Senegal and Mauritania were both part of the French colony *Afrique Occidentale Française*. However, after they gained independence their trajectories diverged: Senegal is a secular democracy while Mauritania is an Islamic Republic. Contrary to Senegal's largely secular school system taught in French, Mauritania's system teaches

in both French and Arabic. At the secondary level, Mauritania offers an Arabic and Islamic stream to baccalaureate level in addition to the secular streams of humanities and languages, natural sciences and mathematics.

References

Abdourahman, S.B. (2015) *Projet de loi portant statut du daara: Les sources d'une polémique, Seneweb.com.* Available at: www.seneweb.com/news/Contribution/projet-de-loi-portant-statut-du-daara-le_n_144110.html (Accessed: 20 March 2015).

Binaté, I. and Hugon, C. (2019) 'Les réformes de l'éducation arabo-islamique en Côte d'Ivoire et au Sénégal: dynamiques, acteurs et stratégies', *Education Comparée*, 21, pp. 55–75.

Boyle, H.N. (2002) 'The growth of Qur'anic schooling and the marginalization of Islamic pedagogy: The case of Morocco', in *Paper Presented at the Annual Meeting of the Comparative and International Education Society, March 6–9, 2002.* Orlando, FL.

Boyle, H.N. (2006) 'Memorization and learning in Islamic schools', *Comparative Education Review*, 50(3), pp. 478–495.

Brenner, L. (2000) *Controlling Knowledge: Religion, Power and Schooling in a West African Muslim Society.* Bloomington, IN and Indianapolis, IN: University of Indiana Press.

Butler, N. (2006) 'Costs of knowledge: Some economic underpinnings of spiritual relations in Islam in Niger', in N. Dannhaeuser and C. Werner (eds) *Markets and Market Liberalization: Ethnographic Reflections. Research in Economic Anthropology, Volume 24.* Oxford: Elsevier Ltd, pp. 309–328.

Butler, N. (2016) 'Collapsed pluralities: Islamic education, learning, and creativity Niger', in R. Launay (ed) *Islamic Education in Africa: Writing Boards and Blackboards.* Indianapolis, IN: Indiana University Press, pp. 285–306.

Clarke, P. (1988) 'Charismatic authority and the creation of a new order: The case of the mahdiyyat movement in South-Western Nigeria', in *Charisma and Brotherhood in African Islam.* Oxford: Oxford University Press, pp. 135–156.

Cohen, A. and Timéra, M. (2022) 'Tentations d'islam et écrits d'élites europhones au Sénégal. Quelle production de nouvelles normativités islamiques?', *Cahiers d'études africaines*, 248(4), pp. 829–857.

D'Agostino, A. and Callizo, I.G.I. (2022) 'Toward understanding the global landscape of educational pluralism', *Journal of School Choice*, 16(3), pp. 365–387.

D'Aoust, S. (2013) 'Écoles franco-arabes publiques et daaras modernes au Sénégal: hybridation des ordres normatifs concernant l'éducation', *Cahiers de la recherche sur l'éducation et les savoirs*, 12, pp. 313–338.

De Certeau, M. (1984) *The Practice of Everyday Life.* Berkeley, CA: University of California Press.

Edwin, S. (2016) *Privately Empowered: Expressing Feminism in Islam in Northern Nigerian Fiction.* Evanston, IL: Northwestern University Press.

Froerer, P. and Portisch, A. (2012) 'Introduction to the special issue: Learning, livelihoods, and social mobility', *Anthropology & Education Quarterly*, 43(4), pp. 332–343.

Hill, J. (2017) 'Charismatic discipleship: A Sufi woman and the divine mission of development in Senegal', *Africa: Journal of the International African Institute*, 87(4), pp. 832–852.

Hima, H. (2020) '"Francophone" education and intersectionalities: Gender, language, and religion', in J.M. Abidogun and T. Falola (eds) *The Palgrave Handbook of African Education and Indigenous Knowledge.* Cham, Switzerland: Palgrave Macmillan, pp. 463–525.

Hoechner, H. (2018) *Quranic Schools in Northern Nigeria: Everyday Experiences of Youth, Faith, and Poverty*. Cambridge: Cambridge University Press.

Kane, O.O. (2016) *Beyond Timbuktu: An Intellectual History of Muslim West Africa*. Harvard University Press.

Kyburz, O. (1994) *Les hiérarchies sociales et leurs fondements idéologiques chez les Haalpulaar'en (Sénégal)*. PhD thesis, Université Paris X-Nanterre.

Lewin, K.M. (2008) *Access, Age and Grade. CREATE Policy Brief 2. 2*. Falmer: Consortium for Research on Educational Access, Transitions and Equity (CREATE): University of Sussex.

Lo, M. (2015) *Projet de loi portant statut des "daaras", Le Quotidien*. www.lequotidien.sn/new/index.php/opinions-debats/projet-de-loi-portant-statut-des-daaras (Accessed: 20 March 2015).

Marsden, M. and Retsikas, K. (2013) 'Introduction', in M. Marsden and K. Retsikas (eds) *Articulating Islam: Anthropological Approaches to Muslim Worlds*. Dordrecht, Heidelberg, New York and London: Springer, pp. 1–31.

MEN (2010) *Étude de la situation de référence des structures d'accueil, des structures de formation, des daaras, des enfants de la rue, des talibés, des associations de maîtres coraniques et d'autres acteurs pour les régions de Dakar, Louga, Saint-Louis et Matam*. Dakar: Ministère de l'Education Nationale (MEN) Sénégal et Emergence Consulting.

Newman, A. (2017) 'Passive victims or actively seeking a religious education? Qur'anic school students in Senegal', in A. Strhan, S. Ridgley and S. Parker (eds) *The Bloomsbury Reader in Religion and Childhood*. London and New York: Bloomsbury Publishing, pp. 173–180.

Ogunnaike, O. (2020) 'Islamic philosophies of education in Africa', in J.M. Abidogun and T. Falola (eds) *The Palgrave Handbook of African Education and Indigenous Knowledge*. Cham, Switzerland: Palgrave Macmillan, pp. 421–450.

Roy, É. and Humeau, P. (2018) *Etat des lieux sur l'offre et les mécanismes institutionnels relatifs à l'éducation coranique et à l'enseignement islamique dans les pays de l'Afrique de l'Ouest et du Centre*. Dakar: UNICEF and Qualé.

Samson, F. and LeBlanc, M.N. (2022) 'Repenser les religiosités islamiques en Afrique: classes sociales et manières de se montrer musulman.e', *Cahiers d'études africaines*, 4(248), pp. 679–695.

Serpell, R. (1999) 'Local accountability to rural communities: A challenge for educational planning in Africa', in F. Leach and A.W. Little (eds) *Education, Cultures and Economics*. New York and London: Falmer, pp. 111–142.

Sieveking, N. (2022) '"Madame est au niveau 2, et moi...?" Gendered dynamics of Qur'an reading courses in dakarois francophone educated middle-class milieus', *Cahiers d'études africaines*, 4(248), pp. 771–796.

Smith, G.G. (2008) *Medina Gounass: Challenges to Village Sufism in Senegal*. Copenhagen: University of Copenhagen.

Sounaye, A. (2014) 'Mobile Sunna: Islam, small media and community in Niger', *Social Compass*, 61(1), pp. 21–29.

Thayer-Bacon, B.J. (2017) *Relational Ontologies*. New York: Peter Lang Incorporated, International Academic Publishers.

Topolski, A. (2018) 'The race-religion constellation: A European contribution to the critical philosophy of race', *Critical Philosophy of Race*, 6(1), pp. 58–81.

UNESCO (2006) *EFA Global Monitoring Report 2007. Strong Foundations: Early Childhood Care and Education*. Paris: United Nations Educational, Scientific and Cultural Organization (UNESCO).

UNESCO (2014) *EFA Global Monitoring Report 2013/2014. Teaching and Learning: Achieving Equality for All*. Paris: United Nations Educational, Scientific and Cultural Organization (UNESCO).

UNESCO (2021) *Global Education Monitoring Report 2021/2022. Non-State Actors in Education: Who Chooses? Who Loses?* Paris: United Nations Educational, Scientific and Cultural Organization (UNESCO).

Villalón, L.A. and Bodian, M. (2012) *Religion, demande sociale, et réformes éducatives au Sénégal.* Miami, Niamey and London: University of Florida, Laboratoire d'Etudes et de Recherches sur les Dynamiques Sociales et le Développement Local, Overseas Development Institute.

Walsh, C.E. and Mignolo, W.D. (2018) 'Introduction', in W.D. Mignolo and C.E. Walsh (eds) *On Decoloniality: Concepts, Analytics, Praxis.* Durham, NC and London: Duke University Press, pp. 1–12.

Ware, R.T. (2004) *Knowledge, Faith and Power: A History of Qur'anic Schooling in 20th Century Senegal.* PhD thesis. Department of History, University of Pennsylvania.

Ware, R.T. (2014) *The Walking Qur'an: Islamic Education, Embodied Knowledge, and History in West Africa.* Chapel Hill, NC: The University of North Carolina Press.

Part III

Decolonising education in Islamic West Africa: From research to policy

9 Embracing African Islamic knowledge traditions: From critique to 'border praxis'

I first presented my doctoral fieldwork data to an audience of comparative/international educationalists at a research-in-progress seminar in 2013. I explained why many Senegalese Muslims preferred Qur'anic schools over state schools despite development critiques of the latter's 'poor quality' whose roots lie in colonial stereotypes. I felt frustrated when the first question I received from a professor in the audience was "OK, but what about the *talibés* [Qur'anic school students who beg]?" This would not be the last time that I was asked the same question. I was disappointed that Islamic schooling in West Africa had become synonymous with the sensationalised narratives of begging *talibés* within academic education debates (see Chapter 4) and which had eclipsed the myriad other aspects of the region's rich intellectual traditions (Chapter 3). A decade later, unfortunately, colonialist assumptions about Islamic education are still alive and well in the fields of Comparative and International Education (CIE) and Education and International Development (EID).

In 2018 I was contacted by an NGO which works on children's well-being in Senegal. They sought my advice on their future projects in the Djourbel region which has a high density of Qur'anic schools but some of the lowest rates of state school enrolment in the country. A European and a Senegalese representative explained that they wanted to alleviate the 'problem' that children lacked access to a French-medium 'secular' education. They proposed to do this by creating a 'modern' Qur'anic school combining Qur'anic memorisation with French literacy and vocational skills. I asked them whether they had asked the local population if they also perceived this situation to be a 'problem'. It transpired that the NGO representatives were unaware that the *daaras*' hidden curriculum reinforced support networks, agricultural skills, *Ajami* literacy, esoteric literacy and currency-based numeracy which aided Qur'anic students' insertion into informal economies (c.f. Chapters 4 and 5). In their defence, the NGO officials listened attentively and were interested to learn about the advantages conferred by Qur'anic schools *in their current form*. However, I had to wonder why their initiatives had not been informed by a scoping study of local needs or why they had preferred to contact me, a White researcher based in the global North, rather than one of the many Senegalese experts of Islamic education.

DOI: 10.4324/9781003172475-12

Finally, in 2012, Shaykh Amadou, one of the clerics of one of Medina Dialobé's larger Qur'anic schools, asked me for help in supporting changes to his school. He explained that, for the past five years, a small European NGO had brought around twenty students to the village for two weeks each year. They had donated to the *daaras* rice, oil and shoes as the child students often went barefoot. Amadou told me that, while he appreciated this gesture, he was looking for larger and more sustainable ways to improve conditions for his students. He showed me a funding proposal that he had submitted to a regional state development agency (*l'Agence regionale de développement*) in 2006, requesting 7.5 million CFA (£9,644) to improve the irrigation of his fields. He was unsuccessful but explained that he was always on the lookout for other funding sources and asked whether I could suggest any (unfortunately I could not). He also wanted to collaborate with the imam's nephew, a respected teacher of Arabic and *sharia,* to set up a boarding school in the village teaching Arabic and French given local demand for this kind of offer. Once again, they struggled to find the capital for such a project. This situation made me wonder why there is apparently so much money available for the state or INGOs to build ambitious *daara modernes* (modern *daaras*) or operate costly 'rescue-repatriation-reintegration' missions to send *talibés* home (Chapter 4) yet a dearth of funding for projects run by and for Muslim clerics, parents and youth which might be small-scale but tailored to local realities.

It is such examples – and many more like them – that inspired this book. I have advanced the argument that theory and praxis relating to the development-education-religion (DER) nexus, including policies developed under the EFA agenda, are characterised by coloniality of knowledge (Mignolo, 2002, 2007; Grosfoguel, 2007), secularity (Vizcaíno, 2021), being (Maldonado-Torres, 2007) and gender (Lugones, 2007). These power hierarchies define who is able to produce knowledge, how and for what ends in the fields of CIE and EID. Ultimately, these processes side-line the perspectives of people who participate within Islamic knowledge traditions, especially if they are people of colour, women and youth and based in global South contexts.

It is now time that scholars of CIE/EID engage in the rigorous process of decolonising the canons of these fields and address the uneven power relations in knowledge production. For 40 years, postcolonial theorists have criticised the ways in which the discipline of CIE celebrates the intellectual traditions of different regional comparative education societies but the prestigious debates remain dominated by anglophone scholarship produced in North America, Canada, the UK, Australia, New Zealand and Western European countries (Takayama, Sriprakash and Connell, 2017, pp. 5–6). The subsequent racial biases in CIE/EID have recently been exposed (Sriprakash, Tikly and Walker, 2020), but its Orientalist tendencies and coloniality of secularity continue to be overlooked.

This situation reveals the urgent need for epistemic decolonisation (Mignolo, 2002, p. 80) and a postsecular approach (Crockett, 2018) which would involve, for example: *critiquing* manifestations of colonialist hierarchies in elite knowledge production spaces; ***dismantling*** the structures and processes that support these inequalities; and ***re-building*** a more just world grounded in a plurality of perspectives rather than Western universals. I am convinced that such projects are only possible through genuine inclusion of border thinking/border praxis (Mignolo, 2002, p. 71; Walsh and Mignolo, 2018) by people who are embedded in intellectual traditions de-linked from Western modernity (Mignolo, 2007, p. 459) and who theorise from the standpoints of other-than-secular worldviews and positions of colonial difference (Maldonado-Torres, 2007, p. 262).

In this chapter I conclude by outlining what is now needed for such a postsecular critique of scholarship on educational engagement in post-colonial contexts. Second, I show how the decolonial potential of border thinking/border praxis might be enabled in CIE/EID through inclusive applied research and development programming. In doing so, I realise that I have developed these arguments as a White Muslim by conversion in an academic setting that privileges a secular perspective on a continent where Muslims are a minority and Islamophobia is rife. Therefore, my epistemic standpoint is semi-peripheral (Blagojević, 2009) in the sense that I am Muslim and married to a Senegalese man but on the privileged side of most colonial hierarchies because of my White race, 'secular passing' appearance, global North citizenship, middle-class upbringing and prestigious education. This means that my privileged positioning has enabled me to gain a certain degree of legitimacy in academic sites which wield significant epistemic power. As a result, despite my attempts at reflexivity, I will likely commit some 'decolonial woes' (Ortega, 2017, p. 504) which is when scholars using decolonial theory fall into colonialist tropes when critiquing other forms of coloniality.

Overcoming coloniality in education and development scholarship

Critical scholars of CIE/EID like Raewyn Connell (2014) have long argued that we need to understand the "discontinuities and asymmetries in knowledge" generated by coloniality (2014, p. 212) including through practices like (ibid., p. 218):

> Critical unpacking of mainstream literature in a field of practice – textbooks, established paradigms and bibliographies – revealing northern dominance of the discourse, and extraversion in the global south.

Moreover, Lewis Gordon (2014) has coined the term 'disciplinary decadence' to capture how the norms of an academic discipline narrowly determine the questions that scholars ask and the theories and methods they use. In CIE, this can entail comparison at all costs – which often involves Northern actors defining the topics of comparison, questions of interest and methodologies. In contrast, the 'decolonial option' requires advancing the causes of people rather than the priorities of academic disciplines (Walsh and Mignolo, 2018). In CIE, this could involve what Madina Tlostanova (2012, p. 131) has called an 'imparative' rather than a comparative approach:

> What is needed for a real dialogue is a true intersectionality; not a comparative, but . . . an "imparative" – from the Latin *imparare* (to learn in the atmosphere of plurality) – approach. Instead of comparing everything and everyone with the western ideal used as a model for the whole of humanity, we can turn to an imparative mutual learning process based on a pluritopic hermeneutics.

An imparative approach requires uncovering and celebrating local specificities despite the challenges this poses for comparison because, as Shailaja Fennell and Madeleine Arnot (2008, p. 534) argue:

> The promise [of decentring hegemonic power] can only become a reality if serious consideration is given to how to ensure that local and national specificities are brought into the centre of . . . education research.

In what follows, I suggest how CIE/EID scholarship and praxis can start working on such local specificities in Islamic West Africa and Senegal specifically.

Coloniality in scholarship on Islamic West Africa

Throughout this book, I have put epistemic decolonial principles into practice mainly by exposing coloniality of secularity (Vizcaíno, 2021) as the process whereby a secular worldview has been imposed throughout the world in scientific discourse and development praxis as a result of European colonisation and imperialism. As I have shown, this is closely related to coloniality of knowledge (Mignolo, 2002, 2007; Grosfoguel, 2007) which captures how Euro-North American centric modernist/colonialist binaries continue to shape the organisation of academic disciplines, scientific theory and international policy discourses (c.f. Chapter 1). The field of CIE/EID needs to engage with its own secular worldview and its use of the modernist dichotomy of the 'secular/religious binary' (Wilson, 2017, pp. 1079–1080; Chapter 2). Throughout the preceding chapters, I have unpacked how six interlinked assumptions of this binary have created obstacles to the elaboration of theory and practice which embrace the worldviews and educational demands of Muslims in Islamic West Africa (Wilson, 2017, pp. 1079–1080):

1) 'religion' can be clearly distinguished from the 'secular';
2) 'religion' should be separated from other areas of human activity grouped under the 'secular' label;
3) a 'religious' worldview is subjective and irrational while a 'secular' perspective is neutral and universal;

4) 'religion' is a fundamental cause of violence and intolerance;
5) 'religion' should be kept out of the 'public' sphere and confined to the 'private' in order to maintain social order; and
6) even if 'religion' can positively contribute to social life, it is subordinate to the 'secular' such that 'religious' interventions should be regulated by 'secular' institutions.

Related to the first assumption, that the 'secular' can be clearly distinguished from 'religion', this can be overcome, as I have shown, through advancing a "cognitive turn" in the study of worldviews (see Chapter 2). I have argued that all worldviews entail ontologies (theories of being) and epistemologies (theories of knowledge) which are lenses for perceiving and being in the world. Through these concepts, it has been possible to show how "religion is no longer an exotic 'other' to the secular; both are ontological positions including both immanent and transcendent sources" (Pool, 2020, p. 1043). To visualise these abstract notions, my strategy has been to use Barbara Thayer-Bacon's analogy of an Ocean representing the human experience of the infinite universe. Fishing nets woven with ontologies as warp threads and epistemologies as weft (2017, pp. 16–19) are the tools that we use to make sense of this experience.

Thayer-Bacon's metaphor is valuable because it captures what I observed in Senegal and have experienced myself. People in a given community share elements of their onto-epistemological nets which can endure over time. However, our worldviews are ultimately unique and we constantly (re-)weave them in an ongoing and dynamic process in the face of new influences, challenges and experiences. The concept of onto-epistemological nets overcomes tendencies among some social scientists, including decolonial theorists, to imagine onto-epistemologies as homogenous blocs or resort to clunky metaphors like 'hybridity' when describing their fluid boundaries. Thayer-Bacon's metaphor also inspired my concept of 'ontologically creative subjects' which I used to describe how Senegalese youth resourcefully drew on knowledges and educational spaces from diverse onto-epistemological paradigms in their everyday practice (see Chapter 8).

The second assumption of the secular/religious binary is that 'religious' phenomena should be clearly separated from other areas of human activity such as politics, economics, law or education which are grouped under the secular label. One consequence of these logics is the negation within CIE/EID scholarship of the influence of religion, which results in what I have termed secular erasure. This results in the general scholarly neglect within CIE/EID of the influence of religious or spiritual worldviews on educational engagement (see Chapters 1 and 2). Secular erasure also manifests in the tendency for education literature and policy discourse to render invisible the nuanced ways that other-than-secular knowledges and education systems can operate in an oppressive manner but equally their liberatory potential as resources in people's struggles against inequalities derived from coloniality as well as local hierarchies such as gender (see Chapter 7) or descent/race/caste (see Chapter 6).

The third assumption is that 'religious' perspectives are subjective while a 'secular' one is neutral and objective. This has encouraged the notion that social scientific knowledge on 'religions' – understood as bounded, monolithic entities – is best produced by 'outsiders' with a secular worldview rather than 'insiders' to these communities who appreciate their onto-epistemological nuances. Due to coloniality of knowledge (Mignolo, 2002, 2007; Grosfoguel, 2007), outsiders tend to judge 'religions' against secular and Euro-North American centric values and modernist binaries. Hence, interest in Islam and Islamic education is proportional to policy interest, which is triggered only where there is a 'problem' defined from the perspective of development actors. Examples include when populations show large-scale preference for 'strong' faith-based schools assumed to be a barrier to 'quality education' or in contexts marred by violent religious extremism.

Furthermore, modernist and Orientalist biases undermine other bodies of academic scholarship that are relevant to our understanding of the relationships between Islamic worldviews and educational engagement. In Chapter 3, I unpacked how French colonial administrators categorised people on the basis of both race and religion – a dynamic that Anya Topolski calls a race-religion constellation (2018). The 'natural' religion of Arabs was supposedly Islam while Black Africans were assumed to be 'pagan'. If the latter claimed to be Muslim, the French assumed that they practiced *islam noir* or 'Black Islam' – a supposedly recent, syncretic and unorthodox version of the religion tainted by African cultural elements like esoteric practices and support for charismatic Sufi leaders.

While empirically flawed, the logics of *islam noir* continue to permeate Euro-North American academic literature. For example, Islamic studies neglects Sub-Saharan Africa in its study of the Muslim world, as well as esoteric practices on the basis that they are 'unorthodox' or 'irrational' and constitute 'magic', 'superstition' or 'syncretic' practice. CIE/EID scholarship, on the whole, has tended to repeat the trope that Islam in Africa is syncretic and unorthodox. Meanwhile, some African theorists frame Islam as 'foreign' to Sub-Saharan Africa and assume that it is inherently oppressive compared to African Traditional Religions or secular perspectives. Such tropes, which I call Afrocentric race-religion constellations, are found in the work of African feminists/womanists (see Chapter 7) as well as scholarship which applies an African Indigenous Knowledges (AIK) framework to debates about 'decolonising' education (cf. Chapter 1).

The fourth and fifth assumptions of the secular/religious binary which I have discussed in the book are that religions are largely violent, oppressive and an obstacle to development. Such biases have led to the widespread assumptions, found in CIE/EID, that strong faith-based schools cultivate intolerance. In relation to Islamic West Africa, colonialist biases amongst scholars and practitioners have added stereotypes that Qur'anic schools are an obstacle to development because they are of 'poor quality'. Supposedly they harm children, fail to teach literacy and numeracy or confer economic skills, and are oppressive to girls and women. I have shown that these flawed stereotypes date from the early colonial period and are surprisingly resistant to empirical evidence to the contrary (c.f. Chapters 3 and 4). We can add to this scenario the failure among policy-makers to give due importance to the rights of people to choose the education they have reason to value in their specific social and economic context (c.f. Chapters 5–8).

Finally, the sixth assumption of the secular/religious binary is that religion can be divided into 'good' and 'bad' forms and that secular institutions should judge and regulate religion on this basis (Wilson, 2017, p. 1080). This we see in relation to the 'turn to religion' from the 1990s onwards whereby development agencies have shifted towards engagement with faith-based schools as a way of meeting the EFA agenda. Yet, they usually fail to appreciate these schools' intellectual traditions on their own terms and instead judge them against secular and Euro-North American centric norms and objectives (see Chapter 1). In West Africa, Islamic schools which are closer to international definitions of 'quality education' are instrumentalised to meet development objectives. Meanwhile, Qur'anic schools operating according to different logics are disregarded or pressured to 'reform' to meet these standards. Policy-makers focus on 'coaxing' parents and youth towards options that meet their own logics of 'quality' rather than attempting to appreciate and cater to existing patterns of preference (see Chapters 4 and 8). As a result, national education policies fail to meet the demands of the population who value Qur'anic schools in their existing form (see Chapter 5). Hence, parents and youth struggle to acquire all the knowledges that they find useful in the contemporary Senegalese context. Their uneven access to combinations of knowledges associated with different schools and intellectual traditions are leading to further entrenchment of socioeconomic inequalities, a process which began during the colonial period and which represents a barrier to educational pluralism (D'Agostino and Callizo, 2022) (see Chapter 8).

A postsecular theoretical perspective on educational engagement in post-colonial contexts

Bearing in mind the previously mentioned limitations of the secular/religious binary, a decolonial postsecular perspective requires not just dismantling the binary but also re-building knowledge production structures in Euro-North American academia and development policy-making. The goal is to embrace a greater diversity of forms of intellectual expression and promote a pluriversity of viewpoints – which is still a minority practice within CIE/EID. In line with this project, I have been inspired by the work of Jamie Barnes (2020) who has proposed that ontologies are informed by affective, embodied experiences that are difficult to articulate through discourse. Hence, people of faith often find that metaphors or stories can be more appropriate for communicating our perspectives, although these are also inevitably approximations as we can only make the hidden apparent to a certain extent. I have used several metaphors throughout this book – oasis gardens, sweet mangoes, fishing nets – to allude to my own Sufi understandings of knowledge.

Using a grounded theory approach, I have also proposed some concepts that I hope go further than current frameworks in describing the priorities, experiences and struggles of my Senegalese research participants. For example, I coined the concept of an ontological regime complex (Chapter 3) which captures how education supply and engagement in post-colonial settings, as well as representations of these phenomena in policy and academic discourse, are shaped by a plurality of worldviews but where colonialist perspectives are dominant.

In Chapter 5, I also present the secular limitations of the theoretical frameworks that are widely used to understand educational decision-making in CIE/EID. Using my empirical data from Medina Diallobé, I suggest here some ways that Pierre Bourdieu's (1986) framework of field, capital and habitus could be re-imagined from a postsecular perspective which expands it to accommodate educational engagement from an emic perspective of other-than-secular worldviews. To clarify, Bourdieu conceptualised the 'field' to capture 'spaces' of social interaction as well as 'structures' (Esquerre, 2016). Sociologist of religion Bradford Verter (2003) critiqued Bourdieu for implying that fields were relatively self-contained and argued instead that religion "intersects a number of distinct fields at different levels" (ibid., p. 164). Verter then proposed the concept of 'spiritual capital' which, he argued, circulates in the religious field and behaves like cultural capital (ibid., p. 152). It is *embodied* in knowledge, skills, dispositions and personal piety; *objectified* in sacred or ritual objects; and *institutionalised* in religious organisations, training programmes and qualifications (ibid., pp. 159–160).

While Verter's framework enables a more subtle sociological analysis of religious behaviour than Bourdieu's original works, especially by revealing the agency of lay-people (Verter, 2003, p. 152), it exhibits two problems for our understanding of the subtleties of educational engagement. First, from a postsecular perspective, there is no 'religious field' that exists separate from 'secular' social phenomena, and to suggest so again reflects the first assumption of the secular/religious binary.[1] Moreover, Bourdieu and Verter's fields only refer to the material realm and secular temporality. Crucially, from an Islamic onto-epistemological perspective, the universe consists of many additional beyond-material realms, including those which extend before and after our current lifetime. As I showed in Chapter 5, the educational strategies of people in Medina Diallobé were often oriented towards these spaces. Muslims in West Africa usually refer to them using the terms 'here' or 'now' and the 'hereafter'. While most sociologists and anthropologists of Islamic education in West Africa have noticed this discursive framing in their research participants' accounts (Gérard, 1997; Chehami, 2016), few have attempted to theoretically reconcile their use of Bourdieu's secular framework with the empirical reality of temporalities and realms derived from other-than-secular ontologies.

Bourdieu's concept of social capital can also be re-imagined from a postsecular stance. In Bourdieu's framing (1986, p. 21), social capital refers to:

> Actual or potential resources which are linked to possession of a durable network of more or less institutionalized relationships of mutual acquaintance and recognition – or in other words, to membership in a group.

What is implicit from this definition is that the 'social' refers to humans, nothing more. People's relationships to their peer group – and their peers' perceptions of them – thus become paramount in sociological explanations for behaviour. However, within Islamic onto-epistemologies, the range of possible relationships one can experience, cultivate and eventually benefit from in one's pursuit of capitals include those with other-than-human entities including God, angels, deceased ancestors, saints and spirits or *jinn*. As we saw in Medina Diallobé, such relationships constituted important motivations and explanations for knowledge-seeking behaviour. In particular, people's individual relationships with God were often as important to them as the perceptions of their human peers, to the extent that they might pursue goals that they felt God wanted of them even it meant social sanction or economic sacrifice. Yet, such other-than-secular relationships and their social significance are under-emphasised in sociological and anthropological literature on Islamic education and almost entirely absent from CIE/EID scholarship.

The concept of *baraka* [blessing] also poses a challenge to those using a Bourdieusian framework as anthropologists have tended to reduce it to its capital-resembling characteristics (Hoechner, 2018, p. 99; Wright, 2018, p. 24). From observations in Medina Diallobé as well as my own experiences, I would argue that *baraka* cannot be shoe-horned so easily into a single category – or indeed a secular framework – more generally. For instance, a 'classical' sociological or anthropological analysis might suggest that *baraka* could be considered a form of spiritual capital (Verter, 2003) which can be converted into other valued forms of capital, including cultural capital (e.g. moral behaviour, pious habitus) and economic capital. *Baraka* circulates through networks of social capital (although to really understand this process we would have to expand social capital's definition to encompass network members who are other-than-secular beings) and its possession confers symbolic capital or status. While such an analysis captures some of the characteristics of *baraka*, it does not tell the whole story as *baraka* cannot be reduced to the calculated logics of capital accumulation or Bourdieu's assumptions about the primarily 'social' (read: human) formation of the habitus. In reality, many of my research participants sought to acquire *baraka* because they had sensed or experienced it, describing its force in terms of metaphors like magnetism. This experiential dimension of *baraka* was an important factor which underpinned people's Sufi onto-epistemologies – and, in turn, knowledge-seeking behaviour – but is absent from the anthropological literature.

Finally, to Bourdieu's four capitals we could also add the category of 'motility' or 'mobility as capital' which geographers define as the potential to be mobile, travel or migrate, given the close links between spatial and social mobility (Kaufmann, Bergman and Joye, 2004). The application of this concept to Qur'anic school preference needs to acknowledge how EFA and its associated regimes are infused with narrow 'spatial imaginaries'. These are assumptions about space and mobility among policy-makers which reduce complexity and focus on some things to the exclusion of others when defining problems and solutions (Bürkner and Scott, 2018). International development mandates subscribe to spatial imaginaries that reflect the values of the Euro-North American centric global knowledge economy which is embedded in the global system of racialised capitalism (Rudolph, Sriprakash and Gerrard, 2018). National education policies, such as those of the successive Senegalese governments, tend either to reflect territorial nationalism (assuming that students and graduates will stay in their country of birth) or promote the regular migration of adult students and 'skilled' labour, particularly to countries of the global North (Newman, Hoechner and Sancho, 2019). These policy frameworks therefore ignore, devalue or oppose migration flows which do not align with these values and interests but which often reflect longer histories and larger numbers of people (Newman, 2022).

In Senegal, migration flows which fall outside of the officially endorsed spatial imaginaries include internal and international migration of children to Senegal's Qur'anic schools (which are problematically made synonymous in development discourse with child trafficking as explained in Chapter 4) as well as South-South migration within the African continent or to the Middle East and undocumented migration to the global North. The unquestioned privileging of the logics of Euro-North American centric spatial imaginaries is another reason why EID practitioners and scholars alike are unlikely to appreciate the value of Qur'anic schools in West Africa. From a postsecular perspective, we need to recognise that these schools are embedded within undocumented or South-South migration flows that represent important sources of survival and opportunity for people disadvantaged by global colonialist hierarchies (see also Newman, 2022).

These criticisms of current scholarship about Islamic education notwithstanding, a postsecular approach to the study of faith-based schools in West Africa does not absolve one of needing to offer a critical analysis of different school types. In Chapters 6 and 7, I demonstrated how educational engagement in Senegal is shaped not only by coloniality but also hierarchies which pre-date Euro-North American imperialisms. In their drive to defend Senegal's Qur'anic schools from colonialist critique, some prominent scholars of Islamic education have, in my view, tended to emphasise the liberatory potential of Islam in West Africa while under-playing these communities' own internal hierarchies. Accounts of the movements spearheaded by Muslim intellectuals against Transatlantic slavery and colonisation must be counter-balanced by nuanced analyses of the more oppressive and imperialistic tendencies of Muslim elites. Throughout this book I have illustrated how any analysis of coloniality, including coloniality of secularity, must also study the interactions between coloniality *and other local inequalities* like gender and descent-based hierarchies, whose logics pre-date and interact with Euro-North American frameworks.

On that note, no postsecular approach would be sustainable without reference to issues of race and racialisation in the African context. Earlier I argued that European racial classification frameworks underpinned the French colonial response to the presence of Islam in West Africa as the administration's concept of *islam noir* reflected a unique race-religion constellation (Topolski, 2018) which combined Orientalist and anti-Black stereotypes. Yet, in Chapter 1, I explained that educational dynamics in Islamic West Africa cannot be understood without appreciating two earlier forms of racialisation: that emanating from the Middle Eastern or Arabian Islamic intellectual traditions whereby 'White' superiority referred to Arabs rather than Europeans (Hall, 2011) and descent-based hierarchies found in West Africa and the Sahel from at least the twelfth century (Tamari, 1991).

To understand these dynamics, in Chapter 6, I deployed a theoretical framework developed by British and non-Western sociologists of race who have criticised frameworks emanating from North American Critical Race Theory (CRT) which shapes debates on race and development and EID. I fully agree with CRT's position that anti-Black racism stemming from European colonial classification schemes merits focused attention because it is integral to Euro-North American modernist logics and is globally hegemonic, including within development theory and praxis. However, I employ a definition of racialisation as consisting of any essentialised constructions based on 'descent' defined in biological and cultural terms. According to this logic, Euro-North American categories are but one form of racialisation. This framing of race-as-descent overcomes the 'Eurocentric myopia' (Modood and Sealy, 2022, p. 438) of much postcolonial and decolonial thought which has focused on the racial legacies of European empires, while ignoring other forms of racialisation and imperialisms in non-White populations outside of the West. In Chapters 1, 3 and 6 I have also found it valuable to use Anya Topolski's (2018) concept of race-religion constellation to unpack the imbrication of religious categories and worldviews in the construction of racial hierarchies within European, Islamic and West African traditions. I call out the neglect of religion in discussions of race and development as a form of secular erasure.

Finally, although I have used a postsecular critique of the six assumptions of the secular/religious binary which are often to be found in CIE/EID research as the guiding thread throughout this book, overcoming coloniality of secularity also requires a methodological approach that appreciates how secular bias intersects with other colonialist hierarchies. It is to the topic of methodologies that can contribute to decolonial projects in CIE/EID that I now turn.

Decolonial research methodologies in comparative education

I had not heard of a decolonial approach when I developed my doctoral project, so it did not involve power-sharing or collaboration with my research participants in design or analysis. That said, my anthropological ethnography in Medina Diallobé did have some advantages over the approaches typically used in CIE/EID when it came to identifying the influence of coloniality on educational engagement. CIE/EID research has tended to be dominated by statistical correlations based on large-scale survey data or by the use of mixed methods where the qualitative component includes interviews, focus groups or classroom observations to back up quantitative data. Yet, it was only through ethnography that I was able to discern the influence of not only coloniality but also local inequalities on educational engagement in Medina Diallobé. In particular, this involved participant observation of people's everyday knowledge-seeking practices beyond formal schools in the context of long-term relationships of trust. My ethnography revealed that the worldviews and education systems in Senegal had both liberatory and oppressive potentials, and throughout this book I have attempted to show how these competing forces are intertwined in the current moment.

Some of the questions that informed my ethnographic study were how pre-colonial and colonial histories shaped social inequalities linked to social class, gender and descent and how they, in turn, influenced education provision, aspirations and choices. Africanist scholars have long documented how descent-based inequalities restrict people's everyday lives and opportunities – with transgressions from dominant social norms met with verbal and physical harassment, physical violence or ostracisation. Yet, because it is taboo to speak about these hierarchies explicitly, they are neither noticed by outsiders unfamiliar with the cultural context nor frequently discussed by academics or policy-makers hailing from these societies (Chapter 6). In contrast, by living in Medina Diallobé over a long period, I was able to unravel how these hierarchies played out in practice. Clerics in the Futa Tooro region excluded men not of Muslim clerical lineages from classical Qur'anic schools who nevertheless sought out Islamic knowledges to challenge this form of descent-based discrimination (Chapter 6). Similarly, women were excluded from Qur'anic schools but informally pursued Islamic knowledge, including ritual proficiency and esoteric knowledge, to serve spiritual and extra-religious ends (Chapter 7).

An important part of my analysis involved focusing not only on the oppression of these groups but also on the forms of negotiation and resistance that they pursued when faced with these challenges. In order to overcome gendered and descent-based hierarchies, people in Medina Diallobé mainly engaged in small-scale instances of resistance, rather than large-scale movements for change (Chapters 6 and 7). These observations have significant implications for education scholars and practitioners in terms of how local projects to advance social justice are studied and supported. Within decolonial circles, the current emphasis is on social movements as agents of change. However, focusing on such collective, public initiatives obscures the influence of more subtle, individual, everyday practices which Asef Bayat calls life as politics (2010) (Chapter 6) and I describe as negotiating within tradition (Chapter 7). The advantage of ethnography is that it reveals these everyday struggles for social justice, which can then be factored into debates about decolonising education.

Moreover, my ethnographic method was able to reveal how Qur'anic school graduates in Senegal often work in the prayer economy using the esoteric sciences (Chapter 5). The prevalence of these practices across the Islamic world has been overlooked in Islamic studies, Africanist scholarship, development studies and CIE/EID. It is likely that my non-judgemental interest in these practices, conversion to Islam and affiliation with a Sufi order helped me develop relationships wherein people shared their knowledge of these phenomena (Chapter 5).

These efforts notwithstanding, my ethnography of educational engagement in Medina Diallobé was impeded by my ignorance of another possible advantage of Qur'anic school education – namely, *Ajami* literacy or writing African languages using Arabic script (Chapter 4). As noted in Chapter 5, I only learned about this phenomenon after fieldwork and might have missed evidence of its prevalence in the Futa Tooro. Indeed, as Friederike Lüpke and Sokhna Bao-Diop explained, their research participants in Cameroon only admitted to proficiency in *Ajami* when a local Muslim researcher was present (2014, p. 97). These examples show that classical anthropological ethnography has its limits when clouded by the biases of researchers studying cultural contexts and education systems that are not their own.

The possibility that I might miss – or misrepresent – aspects of Senegalese people's realities reveals a need for more opportunities for local scholars – and those versed in non-Western knowledge traditions – to lead research projects in EID. This is urgently needed because "what is not officially recognised doesn't inform any policies; what doesn't inform educational policies is not taken into consideration" (Lüpke, 2004, p. 98). Such scholars can engage in border thinking (Mignolo, 2007) which brings these under-appreciated bodies of intellectual production to a Euro-North American audience. Hence, decolonising knowledge production also requires decolonising research methodologies in ways that involve power-sharing and linking theory and analysis to future praxis (Walsh and Mignolo, 2018).

Drawing inspiration from education scholars Bagele Chilisa and Gabo Ntseane (2010, p. 620), I propose the following questions that could guide future research on education provision and engagement in post-colonial contexts when informed by decolonial and postsecular principles:

Research design: Is the project solely focused on education systems inherited from colonisation, or does it also pay adequate attention to pre-colonial or Indigenous educational practices? Does the research project draw upon non-Western and other-than-secular knowledges and literatures in its conceptualisation? Are these knowledges communicated by people participating within those knowledge traditions to enable an insider understanding of their educational systems and experiences?

Methodologies: Does the research demonstrate a genuine search for methodologies that respect other-than-secular worlds and promote an investigation into the learning and interdependence across diverse ontologies, knowledge systems and political standpoints? According to the people who experience the world through other-than-secular onto-epistemologies, do these methodologies enable the communication of spiritual or affective experiences which can be difficult to translate into discourse? Are members of the communities concerned involved in the analysis of data as well as processes of data collection?

Values and relationality: Is this research grounded in the values of plurality and power-sharing in its conception and implementation? Is the research undertaken by and for the participants of non-Western knowledge traditions on the basis of their standpoints, priorities, values and struggles? Are relationship-building, local values of accountability, reciprocity and ethics of care integrated into the research process? Have concrete steps been taken to minimise the potential for power inequalities to influence the research?

Transformation: Is the research action-oriented? Does it have the potential to translate description and analysis into structural change and practical solutions which dismantle the structures that underpin coloniality or propose pluriversal alternatives? Are change-oriented methodologies being employed, ideally grounded in non-Western onto-epistemologies? Are the practical objectives defined by and implemented with the most marginalised people in this context?

Dissemination: Have equitable dialogues about research communication been integrated into research design? Have efforts been taken to enable the communication of experiences from non-Western and other-than-secular standpoints, in ways that might not conform to the norms of traditional scientific outputs? What measures will be taken to ensure that more marginalised perspectives are centred in outputs and dissemination activities?

Beyond the design of research projects and their methodological approach, other practical steps can also be taken to promote border thinking. The onus is on academics in CIE/EID today to reflect deeply on the extent of their appreciation for the non-Western education systems in the contexts in which they work. This could involve refraining from reviewing publications or research proposals if not sufficiently familiar with insider scholarship on the knowledge tradition in question. Academics might wish to 'step up' by 'stepping back' and ceding space for thinkers embedded within those traditions.

This need for epistemic humility applies equally to scholars from the global South. In West Africa, many wealthy urban families (who often work for the state or development organisations) never send their children to *daaras* because they are Christians, or have not for generations. They have sometimes internalised colonialist biases about Qur'anic schools and can be poorly positioned to comment on their contemporary benefits particularly for less-affluent Muslim families (Ware, 2014, p. 238). In short, anyone can commit decolonial woes by falling prey to colonialist logics, including scholars using decolonial theory (Ortega, 2017) while nativist decolonisation involves assuming that scholarship is inherently flawed or superior simply because it was produced in the North or South respectively (Moosavi, 2020, p. 347). Rather, we must always remain vigilant to the possibility that we unwittingly reproduce essentialisms and hierarchies and constantly strive to cultivate relationships and spaces that enable critical feedback and pluralistic dialogue.

Towards pluralistic education policy and programming

In recent decades we have seen an increase in research on Qur'anic schools in the descriptive disciplines of African, religious and Islamic studies which is inspired by decolonial principles and produces knowledge *with* and *for* the people who participate in these intellectual traditions. At the crossroads between African studies and critical development studies, Hannah Hoechner's (2018) ethnography and participatory documentary with Qur'anic school students in northern Nigeria represents a gold standard in this regard (as explained in Chapter 5). However, there still remains a lack of more applied research in traditionally prescriptive disciplines which both appreciates the schools' onto-epistemologies and is oriented towards finding solutions to the practical problems that the clerics and *talibés* face. In West Africa, such challenges include the poor conditions experienced by a minority of *talibés* (see Chapter 4) or the unmet demand for education which combines both 'secular' and 'religious' elements according to local people's realities and priorities (see Chapter 8).

Many existing methodologies are available which could be adapted to such questions. In the book I highlighted the potential of, for example, New Literacy Studies (NLS) which recognises that literacies are multiple and situated in specific contexts and communities of practice and tailored to particular needs. This approach offers an excellent opportunity to understand how different onto-epistemologies are historically linked to different literacy practices which continue to be useful in contemporary settings. Literacy learned in state schools is only one form of literacy, although it tends to be dominant and eclipses other 'vernacular' or 'Indigenous' literacies. However, NLS is not just about celebrating "small-scale literacies of resistance". It moves from a position of critique to intervention by "empirically examining . . . how the mainstream education system can draw on the insights provided by various community literacy practices" (Abdelhay, Asfaha and Juffermans, 2014, p. 21).

Applied ethnographies on community literacies and numeracies – which share power with local research partners, teachers and learners – are an approach particularly well suited to decolonial praxis in relation to Islamic education. Alemayehu Gebre et al.'s study, *Everyday Literacies in Africa: Ethnographic studies of literacy and numeracy practices in Ethiopia* is an inspirational example. It provided recommendations for developing ethnographic research to inform the planning of literacy programmes (2009, pp. 18–19) which, the authors argued, are more successful if they draw on people's existing motivations and practices (ibid., p. 125). The authors' approach involved *collecting* information on local practices, *reflecting* and discussing the gaps in what people wanted or needed to know, then *building* or developing worksheets that connected the two together (Collect, Reflect, Build) (ibid., p. 141).

They emphasise the importance of horizontal collaboration among researchers, classroom facilitators and learners in order to harness these tacit funds of knowledge (ibid., pp. 133–135).

Such insights could be applied to both research and policy development on Islamic education in West Africa. Education policy-makers urgently need to be provided with evidence on what foundational skills Qur'anic schools actually teach and how – such as *Ajami* literacy and currency-derived numeracies – and work to support these activities rather than dismiss the schools on the basis of colonialist stereotypes. This requires looking at the hidden curriculum and how schools operate and confer advantages embedded in their respective contexts. For instance, Friederike Lüpke and Sokhna Bao-Diop (2014) argue that we need to address the widespread ignorance of West African writing practices among language planners, researchers, governments and development institutions (ibid., p. 88). Their proposition is to identify the steps that language planners can consider in order to integrate *Ajami* into literacy programmes. These are: (a) an unbiased assessment of literacy traditions; (b) recognition of the observer's paradox in research on *Ajami*; (c) better communication between language planners and scholars of different disciplines; and (d) the political will to embed learning programmes in their cultural and social environments rather than just imposing Western constructions of literacy on populations framed as deficient (ibid., p. 110).

To add to this, I have suggested that young people's creative strategies and tactics to acquire knowledges associated with state and Islamic schools also needs to be harnessed if better 'second chance' or 'transitional' programmes are to be developed. For example, as I observed in Chapter 8, there is a significant unmet need for French language and literacy skills among boys and men in Senegal who have attended classical rural *daaras*. Transitioning between *daaras* and state primary schools is made difficult for children because of the state schools' rigid age-grade structure and French as the language of instruction. Meanwhile, there are few low-cost non-formal French classes available for adults. This problem reflects the observations made in the GEM Report *Literacy for Life* (UNESCO, 2005) that "the use of mother tongues is pedagogically sound but must offer a smooth transition to learning opportunities in regional and official languages" (ibid., p. 17). It adds that "further research is needed . . . to ensure a smooth transition to literacy in other languages" (ibid., p. 205).

Harnessing *talibés'* (extensive but under-appreciated) knowledge of *Ajami* literacy would speed up the teaching of French, if the latter were taught first in *Ajami* and then in Roman/Latin script. Such a transitional pedagogy could be used to facilitate students' *passerelles* or transitions between *daaras* and state schools or non-formal classes. Embracing the skills that Qur'anic schools already confer would, therefore, inform the development of policies and programmes that bring West African education systems one step closer to the model of educational pluralism as put forward by Anthony D'Agostino and Ignazi Callizo (2022) which embraces and supports popular preference for non-Western knowledge traditions.

Second, we have seen that the 'rescue-repatriation-reintegration' programmes designed by international development organisations – which are meant to address the excessive hardship that some *talibés* in urban centres experience – fail to address the underlying causes of this problem and conflict with cultural dynamics and religious values. Kae Amo's ethnographic research adds insight into grassroots solutions to this challenge through her documentation of many examples of Senegalese Muslim clerics who were independently organising to improve *talibé* well-being. Some have collaborated with the (under-acknowledged) women of their communities, who act as stand-in mothers to the children, providing them once a week with a hot meal, shower, clean clothes, psychological support and affection (2014, pp. 11–12). Such practices build on and reinforce norms of community solidarity, the breakdown of which has exacerbated the plight of *talibés* in Dakar (ibid., pp. 23–24).

A different approach to this challenge is to engage families directly at the source in communities which send high numbers of children to accompany local clerics to itinerant *daaras* in Dakar which depend on the begging of *talibés*. In 2012, I interviewed Amadou Bamba Diaw, the coordinator of an NGO called *Partenariat pour la retrait et reinsertion des enfants de la rue* (Partnership for the Removal and Reinsertion of Street Children). In the *talibé*-sending region of Kolda, PARRER conducted culturally sensitive awareness-raising of the harms *talibés* experience and facilitated dialogues with parents and clerics about Islamic and cultural norms of child protection. As a result of this process, parents and clerics consensually agreed to stop this practice and instead raised money through livestock rearing to fund local *daaras*. The new status quo was sustained through collective customary social norms mechanisms which promoted social cohesion rather than confrontation and division.[2]

Finally, policy-makers need to acknowledge the social networks and transferable and technical/vocational skills that Qur'anic schools already confer, which enable students' insertion into informal economies both urban and rural. As Chapter 4 showed, GEM Reports already promote the reinforcement of: 'traditional' apprenticeships tailored to African informal economies (UNESCO, 2012, p. 271); 'farmer field schools' where farmers without state schooling learn sustainable agricultural techniques (ibid., p. 288); agricultural extension programmes that are bottom-up, participatory, teach in local languages and incorporate local knowledges (UNESCO, 2016, p. 45); and the development of curricula in collaboration with community elders to support Indigenous livelihoods and the transmission of traditional knowledge (ibid., p. 160). In line with these recommendations, education policies in West Africa ought to be elaborated in alignment with rural development policies which include Muslim clerics and Qur'anic students as partners. Bottom-up development of programmes can reinforce the schools' existing activities in imparting foundational, technical and vocational skills and support them to integrate additional knowledge, on their own terms, to promote both sustainable agriculture and lifelong learning tailored to local economic realities.

These kinds of projects are worlds apart from the top-down, aggressive, carceral, zero-tolerance approaches currently applied by international human rights NGOs to child begging or the costly implantation of ambitious modern *daaras* operated by organisations external to local communities which risk side-lining Muslim clerics. Instead, the projects reviewed involve catalysing change through community-led mobilisation, equitable dialogue, consensus-building, and harnessing cherished onto-epistemological traditions and values. Such initiatives and change methodologies which centre community agency and cultural and religious assets could inform the development of programmes informed by decolonial and postsecular principles. They have the potential to combine classical Islamic onto-epistemologies, values and locally valued knowledges with international norms of child protection.

In conclusion, West African Sufis have long contributed to what they describe as the *jihad* or struggle of the pen which involves defending Islam against its detractors through scholarship. I hope that this book lives up to this definition and that my postsecular approach can support the decolonial border thinking of my brothers and sisters in Africa and beyond whose knowledge and experience of Islamic intellectual traditions far surpasses my own. I look forward to a day when scholars and practitioners in CIE/EID genuinely embrace the knowledges, research and theorising of Muslim intellectuals in Africa and its diasporas. Their insights are not only relevant for informing more pluralistic school systems in post-colonial contexts. They are also essential if we are to deepen Euro-North American appreciation of relational onto-epistemologies, educational dynamics and decolonial struggles in order to build a more just, peaceful and sustainable world.

Notes

1 To take one example, the prayer economy and market for esoteric sciences in West Africa touch on all other aspects of social life as these services are sought out for ventures from business to politics, travel, education, love and fertility.

2 Another NGO, The Grandmother Project-Change Through Culture, will start a similar initiative in the same region in 2024 with funding from The Talibé Trust (Judi Aubel and Melanie Horstead, personal communication).

References

Abdelhay, A., Asfaha, Y.M. and Juffermans, K. (2014) 'African literacies, ideologies, scripts, education', in K. Juffermans, Y.M. Asfaha and A. Abdelhay (eds) *African Literacies: Ideologies, Scripts, Education*. Newcastle: Cambridge Scholars Publishing, pp. 1–62.

Amo, K. (2014) 'Note de recherche: L'anthropologue à l'écolé coranique: Faire face à la "bonne souffrance" des taalibés (Sénégal)', *AnthropoChildren*, 4, pp. 1–30.

Barnes, J. (2020) *Stories, Senses and the Charismatic Relation: A Reflexive Ethnography of Christian Experience*. London: Routledge.

Bayat, A. (2010) *Life as Politics: How Ordinary People Change the Middle-East*. Stanford, CA: Stanford University Press.

Blagojević, M. (2009) *Knowledge Production at the Semiperiphery: A Gender Perspective.* Belgrade: Institut za kriminološka i sociološka istraživanja.

Bourdieu, P. (1986) 'The forms of capital', in J. Richardson (ed) *Handbook of Theory and Research for the Sociology of Education.* New York: Greenwood Press, pp. 241–258.

Bürkner, H.-J. and Scott, J.W. (2018) 'Spatial imaginaries and selective in/visibility: Mediterranean neighbourhood and the European Union's engagement with civil society after the "Arab Spring"', *European Urban and Regional Studies*, 26(1), pp. 22–36.

Chehami, J. (2016) 'Les familles et le daara au Sénégal: Entre facteurs macrosociaux, stratégies collectives et choix individuels', *Afrique Contemporaine*, 257(1), pp. 77–89.

Chilisa, B. and Ntseane, G. (2010) 'Resisting dominant discourses: Implications of indigenous, African feminist theory and methods for gender and education research', *Gender and Education*, 22(6), pp. 617–632.

Connell, R. (2014) 'Using southern theory: Decolonizing social thought in theory, research and application', *Planning Theory*, 13(2), pp. 210–223.

Crockett, C. (2018) 'What is postsecularism?', *American Book Review*, 39(5), pp. 6–14.

D'Agostino, A. and Callizo, I.G.I. (2022) 'Toward understanding the global landscape of educational pluralism', *Journal of School Choice*, 16(3), pp. 365–387.

Esquerre, A. (2016) *Compte rendu. Pierre Bourdieu, Sociologie générale. Volume 1. Cours au Collège de France 1981–1983.* Paris: Le Seuil.

Fennell, S. and Arnot, M. (2008) 'Decentring hegemonic gender theory: The implications for educational research', *Compare – A Journal of Comparative and International Education*, 38(5), pp. 525–538.

Gebre, A.H., et al. (2009) *Everyday Literacies in Africa: Ethnographic Studies of Literacy and Numeracy Practices in Ethiopia.* Kampala: Fountain Publishers Limited.

Gérard, E. (1997) *La tentation du savoir en Afrique: Politiques, mythes et stratégies d'éducation au Mali.* Paris: Karthala.

Gordon, L.R. (2014) 'Disciplinary decadence and the decolonisation of knowledge', *Africa Development*, XXXIX(1), pp. 81–92.

Grosfoguel, R. (2007) 'The epistemic decolonial turn', *Cultural Studies*, 21(2–3), pp. 211–223.

Hall, B.S. (2011) *A History of Race in Muslim West Africa, 1600–1960.* Cambridge: Cambridge University Press.

Hoechner, H. (2018) *Quranic Schools in Northern Nigeria: Everyday Experiences of Youth, Faith, and Poverty.* Cambridge: Cambridge University Press.

Kaufmann, V., Bergman, M.M. and Joye, D. (2004) 'Motility: Mobility as capital', *International Journal of Urban and Regional Research*, 28(4), pp. 745–756.

Lugones, M. (2007) 'Heterosexualism and the colonial/modern gender system', *Hypatia*, 22(1), pp. 186–209.

Lüpke, F. (2004) 'Language planning in West Africa: Who writes the script?', *Language Documentation and Description*, 2, pp. 90–107.

Lüpke, F. and Bao-Diop, S. (2014) 'Beneath the surface? Contemporary ajami writing', in K. Juffermans, Y.M. Asfaha and A. Abdelhay (eds) *African Literacies: Ideologies, Scripts, Education.* Newcastle: Cambridge Scholars Publishing, pp. 88–117.

Maldonado-Torres, N. (2007) 'On the coloniality of being', *Cultural Studies*, 21(2–3), pp. 240–270.

Mignolo, W.D. (2002) 'The geopolitics of knowledge and the colonial difference', *South Atlantic Quarterly*, 101(1), pp. 57–96.

Mignolo, W.D. (2007) 'Delinking: The rhetoric of modernity, the logic of coloniality and the grammar of de-coloniality', *Cultural Studies*, 21(2–3), pp. 449–514.

Modood, T. and Sealy, T. (2022) 'Beyond Euro-Americancentric forms of racism and anti-racism', *The Political Quarterly*, 93(3), pp. 433–441.

Moosavi, L. (2020) 'The decolonial bandwagon and the dangers of intellectual decolonisation', *International Review of Sociology*, 30(2), pp. 332–354.

Newman, A. (2022) 'Revisiting "eduscape" through a postcolonial lens: The influence of globalisation and migration on educational offer and demand in Senegal', in A. North and E. Chase (eds) *Education, Migration and Development: Critical Perspectives in a Moving World*. London: Bloomsbury Press, pp. 111–128.

Newman, A., Hoechner, H. and Sancho, D. (2019) 'Constructions of the "educated person" in the context of mobility, migration and globalisation', *Globalisation, Societies and Education*, 18(3), pp. 233–249.

Ortega, M. (2017) 'Decolonial woes and practices of un-knowing', *Journal of Speculative Philosophy*, 31(3), pp. 504–516.

Pool, F.W. (2020) 'Development within a religious ontology? The argument from Islamic Dharma', *European Journal of Development Research*, 32, pp. 1038–1056.

Rudolph, S., Sriprakash, A. and Gerrard, J. (2018) 'Knowledge and racial violence: The shine and shadow of "powerful knowledge"', *Ethics and Education*, 13(1), pp. 22–38.

Sriprakash, A., Tikly, L. and Walker, S. (2020) 'The erasures of racism in education and international development: Re-reading the "global learning crisis"', *Compare: A Journal of Comparative and International Education*, 50(5), pp. 676–692.

Takayama, K., Sriprakash, A. and Connell, R. (2017) 'Toward a postcolonial comparative and international education', *Comparative Education Review*, 61(S1), pp. S1–S24.

Tamari, T. (1991) 'The development of caste systems in West Africa', *The Journal of African History*, 32(2), pp. 221–250.

Thayer-Bacon, B.J. (2017) *Relational Ontologies*. New York: Peter Lang Incorporated, International Academic Publishers.

Tlostanova, M. (2012) 'Postsocialist ≠ postcolonial? On post-Soviet imaginary and global coloniality', *Journal of Postcolonial Writing*, 48(2), pp. 130–142.

Topolski, A. (2018) 'The race-religion constellation: A European contribution to the critical philosophy of race', *Critical Philosophy of Race*, 6(1), pp. 58–81.

UNESCO (2005) *EFA Global Monitoring Report 2006. Literacy for Life*. Paris: United Nations Educational, Scientific and Cultural Organization (UNESCO).

UNESCO (2012) *EFA Global Monitoring Report 2012. Youth and Skills: Putting Education to Work*. Paris: United Nations Educational, Scientific and Cultural Organization (UNESCO).

UNESCO (2016) *Global Education Monitoring Report 2016. Education for People and Planet: Creating Sustainable Futures for All*. Paris: United Nations Educational, Scientific and Cultural Organization (UNESCO).

Verter, B. (2003) 'Spiritual capital: Theorizing religion with Bourdieu against Bourdieu', *Sociological Theory*, 21(2), pp. 150–174.

Vizcaíno, R. (2021) 'Secular decolonial woes', *The Journal of Speculative Philosophy*, 35(1), pp. 71–92.

Walsh, C.E. and Mignolo, W.D. (2018) 'Introduction', in W.D. Mignolo and C.E. Walsh (eds) *On Decoloniality: Concepts, Analytics, Praxis*. Durham, NC and London: Duke University Press, pp. 1–12.

Ware, R.T. (2014) *The Walking Qur'an: Islamic Education, Embodied Knowledge, and History in West Africa*. Chapel Hill, NC: The University of North Carolina Press.

Wilson, E.K. (2017) '"Power differences" and "the power of difference": The dominance of secularism as ontological injustice', *Globalizations*, 14(7), pp. 1076–1093.

Wright, Z.V. (2018) *Living Knowledge in West African Islam*. New York and Accra: Fayda Books.

Note on orthography

All direct quotes from secondary sources reproduce the author(s)' terms exactly even when their spelling is different from the conventions used throughout the rest of this book.

All foreign words except proper nouns are italicised. The orthography (conventional spelling) of place names in Senegal is complex as they vary according to author, historical period in which they were recorded and linguistic variation in spelling conventions used (French, English or recent standardised systems for Pulaar). I have tried to use the most common forms of spelling to avoid confusion. Similarly, names of persons can be transcribed in diverse ways. My research participants generally spelled their own names according to French orthography which has become widespread due to state procedures such as birth certificates and identity cards. While all research participants' names are rendered using pseudonyms unless otherwise indicated, I use the French orthography for Senegalese names as it is these versions that my interlocutors would be most familiar with.

To transcribe Arabic words, names and honorific titles, many of which have been loaned into Pulaar and French, I have followed a simplified system omitting diacritical marks with the exception of the *ayn* (') and *hamza* ('). I have employed the most common and simplified transcriptions for places and people's names used in English language publications and standard bibliographic reference texts. I have used the common anglicised construction of plurals using an 's', for instance *jihads* (meaning struggles) as opposed to the correct Arabic but less familiar *jihaduri*.

The first formal attempt to designate a standardised writing system for Pulaar in the Roman/Latin alphabet took place at a UNESCO conference in Bamako in 1966. The norms adopted in this book follow the conventions of the Bamako system including representations of the implosive consonants specific to Pulaar as *ɓ* and *ɗ* and the nasal 'ny' sound as *ñ*. Short vowels are transcribed as single vowels and long vowels are transcribed by a doubling of the letter. With the exception of the letter 'c' pronounced as in 'church', consonants are pronounced as in English.

Glossary

adab **(Arabic)**	religious disposition or comportment
addiya **(Arabic)**	gift, especially given to Qur'an teachers, clerics and Sufi *shaykhs*
Ajami **(Arabic)**	African languages written in Arabic script
alluwal **(Pulaar)**	wooden boards for Qur'an learning, from the Arabic *alwah*
Almamy **(French)**	leader or guide; from the Pulaar *almaami*, from the Arabic al-imam
almuuɗo **(pl.** ***almuuɓe*****) (Pulaar)**	Qur'anic school student
al-zahir **(Arabic)**	hidden, unseen
ʿamal **(Arabic)**	morally righteous actions
arabisant **(French)**	Arabophone
ʿaql **(Arabic)**	faculties of reason, power of the intellect
assimilé (French)	Black African person during the colonial period who assimilated to French culture
baraka **(Arabic)**	blessing, grace, benediction, divine force
bayda **(Pulaar)**	beginner Qur'anic school student
baylo **pl.** ***wayluɓe*** **(Pulaar)**	member of the Haalpulaar blacksmith status group
batin **(Pulaar)**	hidden or concealed; from the Arabic *al-batin*
bidʿah **(Arabic)**	innovation considered unlawful within Islamic jurisprudence
ceɗɗo **pl.** ***seɓɓe*** **(Pulaar)**	member of the Haalpulaar warrior status group
ceedu **(Pulaar)**	hot dry season in the Futa Tooro
ceerno **pl.** ***seeremɓe*** **(Pulaar)**	Qur'an teacher, cleric; plural denotes a clerical lineage
collège **(French)**	lower secondary school
cuballo **pl.** ***subalɓe*** **(Pulaar)**	member of the Haalpulaar fisherman status group
daara **(Wolof)**	Qur'anic school; from the Arabic *dar al-Qur'an* meaning house of the Qur'an
dabaade **(Pulaar)**	to practice the esoteric sciences
dabotooɗo **pl.** ***dabotooɓe*** **(Pulaar)**	practitioner of the esoteric sciences
duʿa **(Arabic)**	supplication, invocation, call to God
duɗal **pl.** ***duɗe*** **(Pulaar)**	hearth, Quranic school; referring to study around a fire
fahm **(Arabic)**	faculties of understanding
fiqh **(Arabic)**	Islamic law as a discipline in the curriculum of Islamic study

***gallunke* pl. *gallunkooɓe* (Pulaar)**	member of the Haalpulaar slave rank; from the French legal term denoting a freedman or emancipated slave
***hadith* (Arabic)**	collection of traditions containing sayings of the Prophet Mohammed
***hafiz* (Arabic)**	keeper or guardian; someone who has memorised the Qur'an
***hajj* (Arabic)**	pilgrimage to Mecca; fifth pillar of the Islamic faith
***halal* (Arabic)**	moral, licit
***haram* (Arabic)**	immoral, forbidden
***hijab* (Arabic)**	veil, head-covering
***ibadou* (Wolof)**	Salafi-inspired Muslim; from the Senegalese association *Jama'at 'Ibad ar-Rahman*
***'ilm* (Arabic)**	knowledge
***indigène* (French)**	Black African person during the colonial period who did not adopt French culture
***inshallah* (Arabic)**	God willing
***internat* (French)**	boarding school, especially a Qur'anic/Islamic boarding school
***ijaza* (Arabic)**	authorisation to teach within Islam
***jeeri* (Pulaar)**	less-fertile land beyond the floodplain of the Senegal River basin
***jihad* (Arabic)**	struggle, holy war
***jinn* (Arabic)**	intelligent non-human spirit in Islamic cosmology
***korité* (Pulaar)**	celebration of *Eid al-Fitr* at the end of the fast of Ramadan
***laïcité* (French)**	French form of secularism
***lasarar* (Pulaar)**	esoteric knowledge; from the Arabic *al-asrar* meaning secret
***lycée* (French)**	upper secondary school
***maccuɗo* pl. *maccuɓe* (Pulaar)**	bondsman, male member of the Haalpulaar slave rank; carries derogatory connotations
***marabout* (French)**	Muslim religious leader or notable; from the Arabic *murabit*
***mashallah* (Arabic)**	God has willed it; used to express appreciation
***médersa* (French)**	French colonial Islamic school; from the Arabic *madrasa*
***mbaaral* (Pulaar)**	public event to celebrate completion of Qur'anic memorisation
***métis* (French)**	colonial category of mixed-race individuals with French citizenship
***mystique* (French)**	esoteric sciences
***ñeeño* pl. *ñeeñɓe* (Pulaar)**	member of the Haalpulaar artisan/musician rank
***passerelle* (French)**	transition; referring to transition between school types
***pullo* pl. *fulɓe* (Pulaar)**	member of the Haalpulaar cattle-herding status group
***qalb* (Arabic)**	heart
***sadaqa* (Arabic)**	voluntary or expiatory alms; especially given to Qur'anic students

salaf **(Arabic)**	predecessors; used to refer to the first three generations of Muslims
sanda **(Pulaar)**	adolescent or adult student of the Qur'an or Islamic sciences
sharia **(Arabic)**	Islamic canonical law based on the Qur'an, *hadith* and *sunna*
sharif **(Pulaar)**	descendant of the Prophet or his Companions
shaykh **(Arabic)**	honorific title for a male leader, elder or noble
shirk **(Arabic)**	sin in Islamic law of practicing idolatry or polytheism
sunna **(Arabic)**	normative example, especially of the Prophet
surah **(Arabic)**	chapter of the Qur'an
surah al-fatiha **(Arabic)**	opening chapter of the Qur'an
talibé **(Wolof)**	Qur'an student, disciple of a religious leader; from the Arabic *taalib*
tafsir **(Arabic)**	Qur'anic exegesis or interpretation
ta'lim **(Arabic)**	teaching through discursive means
taqlid **(Arabic)**	teaching through imitation
tarbiya **(Arabic)**	teaching through socialisation
tawhid **(Arabic)**	God's oneness and the unity of His creation
toorodo **pl.** ***toorobe*** **(Pulaar)**	member of the Haalpulaar Muslim clerical status group
turabu **(Wolof)**	Qur'anic verses written on paper, amulet
waalo **(Pulaar)**	floodplain in the middle valley of the Senegal River basin
waliou **(Wolof)**	saint, spiritual guide; from the Arabic *wali*
yiiwonde **(Pulaar)**	storm
zakat **(Arabic)**	alms-giving; third pillar of the Islamic faith
ziara **(Pulaar)**	event in celebration of a Muslim saint living or dead

Index